Havana

DOMINICAN
REPUBLIC
HAITI
PUERTO
RICO
VIRGIN
ISL.

Barranquilla
Maracaibo
Caracas
TRINIDAD
Cartagena
Orinoco R.
VENEZUELA
Georgetown
Medellín
Paramaribo
Bogotá
GUIANAS
Cayenne
COLOMBIA

PAGOS
IS.

Quito
Guayaquil
ECUADOR
Amazon
Manaus
River
Belém
Natal
Jurúa R.
R.
Recife
P
Purús
R.
B R A Z I L
E
Madeira R.
Tapajós R.
Xingu R.
Tocantins R.
R
Callao
U
Salvador
Lima
São Francisco R.
La Paz
Brasília
Arequipa
BOLIVIA
Belo Horizonte
Vitório
Arica
Sucre
Paraguay R.
Paraná R.
Antofagasta
PARAGUAY
São Paulo
Rio de Janeiro
SAN
AMBROSIO I.
Asunción
Santos
SAN FELIX
I.
R.
R.
Paraná
JUAN
FERNANDEZ
IS.
Valparaíso
Córdoba
Uruguay R.
Pôrto Alegre
Santiago
Mendoza
URU-
GUAY
Concepción
Buenos
Aires
Montevideo
A R G E N T I N A
C H I L E
Bahía Blanca

SOUTH
AMERICA

SCALE IN MILES
0   200   400   600   800   1000

FALKLAND IS.

Strait of
Magellan
TIERRA DEL FUEGO

SOUTH
GEORGIA

Cape Horn

LATIN AMERICA

BY WILLIAM LYTLE SCHURZ

BRAZIL: THE INFINITE COUNTRY

THIS NEW WORLD: THE CIVILIZATION OF LATIN AMERICA

LATIN AMERICA: A DESCRIPTIVE SURVEY

LATIN AMERICA

A Descriptive Survey

BY

WILLIAM LYTLE SCHURZ

COMPLETELY REVISED AND BROUGHT UP-TO-DATE

1963
NEW YORK: E. P. DUTTON & CO., INC.

Library of Congress Catalog Card Number: 62-14714

Preface

In any discussion of the lands to the south of us, nomenclature presents an initial problem. The Latin Americans are only Latin in so far as the speech of their ruling classes, their official language, is derived from the tongue of ancient Rome. The mass of Mexicans and Bolivians and Paraguayans are not a Latinized people in the sense that the Spaniards and the Portuguese, or the Argentines and the Uruguayans and the Paulistas, are. They, and the populations of several other republics, are predominantly Indian. Though Spain and Portugal occupy the lands of the ancient Roman province of Hispania, the term "Hispanic America" meets the same objections as "Latin America" when it is applied to the countries of overwhelmingly Indian blood. The Latin Americans call themselves "Americans," in which they include ourselves and the Canadians, that is all the occupants of the American continent or of the Americas. To them we are "North Americans," but so are Mexicans and Canadians. We are certainly not that horrific thing which the Pan American Union has called *Estadunienses* or "Unitedstatesers." While our State Department, in its reluctance to offend the sensibilities of the Latin American, refers to us, rather verbosely, as "the people of the United States," it has failed to provide us with a suitable adjective and persists in calling its outposts in Latin America "the American Consulate" and "the American Embassy." At least, the familiar shield over the door still bears that legend. To Europeans—and to ourselves—we are Americans. Otherwise we should be an anonymous people. After all, each of the Latin-American nations has a perfectly satisfactory name of its own. Its people are Cubans or Peruvians or Nicaraguans. If we use the name "Americans" for ourselves, it is because we have no other name, and no slight to the other peoples of the continent is implied in its use.

In this book I have endeavored to consider Latin America as a unit. I have not ignored the factors of differentiation, which often are very great, but yet not sufficient to break the essential unity that causes a Colombian and a Uruguayan to meet the same situation in much the same way. To have treated the twenty republics in any other way would only have created in the reader's mind the confusion that comes from an effort to follow the separate fortunes of the Saxon kingdoms of early England or of the city-states of medieval Italy.

Where I have appeared critical of the customs and institutions of Latin America, it has been with no more animus or intent of disparagement than if I were pointing out the defects in our own very fallible way of life. Neither have I stressed the ephemeral elements of Latin-American culture, but have emphasized those things which, like the Andes and the Amazon, the example of Bolívar and the inspiration of Martí, have been and will continue to be, long after the various "menaces" and the local dictatorships of the moment are forgotten. For, in the evolution of a people the contemporary scene, like today's weather, shifts too rapidly to have more than a passing significance in the long-range sweep of history.

Those to whom I am indebted for whatever knowledge or understanding I may have of the Latin-American peoples are too many to include in any routine list of acknowledgments. To them all, many of whose names, but not their courtesies and their helpfulness, are forgotten, I freely give my thanks and beg their forbearance for the unintentional errors and limitations of this book.

Contents

CONTENTS

LATIN AMERICA

Part I

THE LAND

ᘰᘰ

ONLY one of the twenty Latin-American republics—Uruguay—lies within the temperate zone. Fourteen of them are wholly of the hot middle belt of the earth. One of them is even named for the Equator. The remaining five overlap either Cancer in the north or Capricorn in the south. The bulk of the land mass of Latin America is in the tropics. In South America, it includes all of the continent north of Antofagasta in Chile and São Paulo in Brazil, that is, its widest part. In North America, though Mexico broadens out above the line of the tropic, over half of the country is in the torrid zone, as are also the republics of the Antilles and of Central America. But for the circumstance that altitude compensates for latitude over much of its area, the common physiographic pattern of most of Latin America would be the tropical lowlands of the Amazon valley and the physical setting would be correspondingly unfavorable to the development of a high civilization. It is the vast extent of highlands which determines the environmental conditions of Latin America south to the edge of the Argentine plains. The primary modifying factor is the unexampled mountain system of the Andes and its northern prolongation into Cen-

3

tral America and Mexico. Only secondary in extent and importance is
the Brazilian plateau. Though still undeveloped, the isolated highlands
of southern Venezuela are of considerable potential value as a future
area of settlement. In tropical Latin America, population is concentrated on the two great temperate plateaus. The single exception is
the small Republic of Panama. Nowhere is this tendency better illustrated than in Venezuela, whose population has been largely confined
to the narrow strip of upland country that branches off northeastward
from the body of the Andes and reaches the sea near Caracas. It is
significant that half the capitals of Latin America are highland cities.
In order of their altitude, they are as follows: La Paz (Bolivia), 11,910
feet; Quito (Ecuador), 9,350 feet; Bogotá (Colombia), 8,560 feet;
Mexico City (Mexico), 7,870 feet; Guatemala (Guatemala), 4,877 feet;
San José (Costa Rica), 3,870 feet; Tegucigalpa (Honduras), 3,200 feet;
Caracas (Venezuela), 3,040 feet; San Salvador (El Salvador), 2,155
feet; Santiago (Chile), 1,710 feet. São Paulo, first city of Brazil, is
located at 2,500 feet above sea level, and Belo Horizonte, capital of the
important State of Minas Gerais, lies at an altitude of about 3,000 feet.

As the Spanish word implies, the cordillera which extends southward from the Sierra Madres of northern Mexico until it falls into
the Antarctic at Cape Horn is a mighty *cord*, an orographic link,
that binds all Latin America together. Its aspect changes greatly
from one section to another, but in spite of the low gaps, as in
southern Nicaragua, at Culebra Hill in Panama, and the Atrato divide
in Colombia, its continuity is never entirely broken. Sometimes it is a
chaotic tangle of mountains; sometimes, as in Bolivia, it is an orderly
array of gigantic ranges, between which lie the floors of lofty tablelands. The average height of the Andean mountain mass is over 10,000
feet. For long distances it is much higher, and there are cities, like
Potosí, at nearly 14,000 feet above sea level.

Not only is the cordillera a major conditioning element in the
climate of Latin America, by creating a wide and horizontal temperate
zone within the tropics. It divides Latin America into two unequal
parts, for it constitutes a formidable barrier to east and west movement. Ever since Pizarro conquered Peru from Panama, the isthmus
has remained the gateway to the west coast of South America, and
more than ever so since the opening of the Panama Canal. After four

centuries there is still only one practicable through land route across the southern continent. Due to the greater narrowness of the land area, the building of transcontinental railroads has not met such barriers in Central America, but those republics look out to the Pacific almost as truly as does Chile, walled in by a mountain rampart to the east. On the other hand, though Mexico fronts on both oceans, its central plateau has always maintained closer connection with its Atlantic than with its Pacific coast.

The circumstance that the cordillera is highly mineralized has been an important factor in the economic history of Latin America. It early gave direction to the currents of Spanish conquest and settlement, and has ever since determined the course of the industrial life of large areas.

Also, since the Andes and their northern extensions are geologically young mountains, they represent one of the world's great areas of seismic and volcanic disturbances. Of the hundreds of volcanic peaks from Colima in Mexico to Corcovado in southern Chile, many are active or have been in violent eruption during the past century. Closely associated with volcanic activity have been the frequent earthquakes which have stricken the zone of the cordillera. Many cities have been destroyed and most other cities within the mountain belt have been devastated at one time or another. No city has suffered more than the capital of Guatemala. In 1541 the original city of Santiago de los Cabelleros was destroyed, and among those who perished in the ruins was the *Gobernadora*, Doña Beatriz, widow of the *Conquistador*, Pedro de Alvarado, and one of the few women who have ever headed a government in Latin America. A second capital of the same name was built on a different site, and before it was destroyed in 1773 it had survived four eruptions of the near-by volcano of Fuego and fourteen severe earthquakes, one of which razed over 3,000 buildings. After the catastrophe of 1773 most of the inhabitants abandoned the ruins of the ill-fated city that is now known as Antigua, or "the ancient." The third capital, the present Guatemala City, which was officially inaugurated on New Year's Day, 1776, was shaken down by a series of violent shocks during six weeks of the winter of 1917–18.

Before its destruction in 1746, Lima had experienced many devastating earthquakes.[1] At the same time almost the entire population of Callao, the port of Lima, was wiped out by high seas which swept over the city. Arica and other port towns of northern Chile have also been destroyed by great waves which followed seaquakes off the coast. Other cities which have been wrecked by earthquakes have been Santiago, Chile (1647), Cuzco, Peru (1650), Quito and Riobamba, Ecuador (1797), Caracas, Venezuela (1812), Concepción, Chile (1835),[2] and Mendoza, Argentina (1861). Cities which have been heavily damaged by earthquakes within the present century have been Valparaiso, Chile (1906), Cartago, Costa Rica (destroyed in 1723, 1841, and 1910), Managua, Nicaragua (1931), and Chillán and Cauquenes, Chile (1938). During May and June, 1960, ten provinces of southern Chile were stricken by a combination of earthquakes, avalanches, volcanic eruptions, and tidal waves that killed nearly 10,000 persons and destroyed almost $500,000,000 worth of property. Earlier in the same year much of the oasis city of Arequipa in southern Peru was shaken down by an earthquake. Twice in twenty years part of the Callejón de Huaylas, a large valley in the Peruvian Andes, has been devastated by avalanches or glaciers that were released by earthquakes or melting snow. The losses in life and property from these many disasters have been very great and at certain periods have represented a major blow to the normal economic progress of the stricken nations. The psychological effects on the population of the recurrent or prolonged terrors of these earthquakes, while intangible, have frequently been serious disturbing factors in the public mind.

In Bolivia, there are three quite clearly definable ranges of the Andes. On the side toward the Pacific is the Cordillera Occidental, whose greatest heights lie over the border in Chile. The main range of the Bolivian Andes is the Cordillera Real, which culminates in a series of Himalaya-like peaks in the Department of La Paz. As the traveler approaches the capital from the railroad junction at Viacha, he sees before him a mighty wall of snow-capped mountains. Loftiest

---

[1] Jorge Juan and Antonio de Ulloa, *A Voyage to South America*, tr. from the Spanish (London, 1806), Vol. II, Ch. VII, "Inconveniences, Distempers, and Evils, to which the City of Lima is subject; particularly Earthquakes."

[2] Charles Darwin, the famous English scientist, was in Chile at the time of this earthquake and describes the effects which he saw at Concepción and Valdivia. *Voyage of the Beagle* (Everyman edition, New York, 1906), pp. 289-99.

of these peaks are Illampu, or Sorata, to the northeast, and Illimani, which towers above La Paz, both over 21,000 feet high, while between them several other peaks rise to heights of more than 20,000 feet. Near the point where the three Departments of La Paz, Oruro, and Cochabamba meet, another chain of the Andes, known as the Cordillera Oriental, or eastern cordillera, branches off to the east and finally descends by the rugged foothills beyond the valley of Cochabamba into the plains of Santa Cruz. Between the western and "Royal" ranges of the Andes lies the *altiplano* or *meseta*, the bleak and desolate tableland, that is the home of the Aymará race and the center of modern Bolivia's national life. The plateau floor is about 450 miles long, with an average width of about 80 miles. Its average height above the sea is about 12,500 feet, ranking it with the Tibetan plateau as the highest inhabited region of the globe. Its cities and towns, like Oruro and Uyuni, are cheerless and silent places, with nights of penetrating cold. Only the warmth and brightness of the sun relieve the forbidding chill and grayness of these inhospitable heights, as they recall by some distant atavism the peculiar appeal of the solar worship of the Incas. Yet, a few thousand feet below the general level of the plateau to the east, as at Cochabamba and Sucre, is a climate of perpetual spring and a habitat highly favorable to human existence. Over the high divide of the Cordillera Real above La Paz the descent is rapid into the semi-tropical zone of the *Yungas*. This is a region of deep valleys among mountains that fall away toward the lowlands of the Beni. Due to the warm climate and heavy summer rains, these mountains are covered with vegetation, and wherever there is a relatively level shelf of land it is intensively cultivated. The similar zones in Peru and Ecuador are known as the *montaña*. In contrast to the *Yungas* and *montaña* districts on the eastern side of the Andes, the western slopes and outridges are barren wastes, since the humid winds which blow from the east across the continent precipitate their moisture on the eastern watershed.

The western Cordillera of the Andes continues southward as the boundary between Chile and Argentina. In its northern reaches its heights are known as the *puna* of Atacama, which is a barren waste as desolate as the nitrate desert that parallels it on the west. Unlike the more northerly Andes, where the tablelands between the ranges and valleys like that of the Urubamba are seats of a considerable population, the cordillera in Chile is virtually uninhabited. The only economic development which it harbors is in the few mining camps like Chuquicamata and El Teniente, which are located in its western out-ridges. In the peak of Aconcagua, which is visible on the way between Santiago and Mendoza, the cordillera attains a height of about 23,000 feet, the loftiest spot in the western hemisphere, and a half dozen other peaks are almost as high. To the south of the latitude of Concepción the Andes are lower. Several valleys afford access into Argentina, and in the region near Puerto Montt a combination of glacial lakes like Llan-quihue and Todos los Santos and of symmetrical peaks like Osorno provides a district of rare beauty, which is one of the favorite tourist resorts of South America. Still farther to the south, to the rear of the labyrinthine rain belt of the archipelagoes, the mountains form an impassable barrier between Chile and Argentina. As in northern British Columbia and southern Alaska, deep fiords here penetrate inland to the edge of great glaciers. Prevailing gales and sleet or cold, wind-driven rains, icy summits, a tangled growth of hardy forest on the water-logged slopes, and steep approaches, like the Murallón, or "great wall," on the Argentine side, all contribute to make this one of the most forbidding and little-known quarters of the earth. The small groups of half-naked Indian nomads who exist among the recesses of its outer edge are among the world's most wretched inhabitants.

The central system of the Bolivian Andes straggles down into Argentina and accounts for the mountainous character of the north-western part of that country, while much of the high Atacama plateau in the western cordillera lies on the Argentine side of the range. In the valleys of this rugged region of sparse rainfall there is considerable irrigated farming and a long-established cattle industry. Some of the cities, like Salta and Tucumán, have been important centers of popula-tion and trade since early colonial times. Along the lower edge of this zone there are large salt plains, like the Salinas Grandes, and wide de-pressions in the land which are flooded during the rainy season. Still farther to the south the Córdoba hills reach out from the mountain mass on the west deep into the northern edge of the great pampa. Beyond the region of the pampa the low wind-swept tableland of Patagonia stretches away to the Straits of Magellan, seamed by a few river valleys with precipitous rims.

Beyond Lake Titicaca on the border between Bolivia and Peru the two great ranges of the Bolivian Andes meet in the so-called knot of Vilcañota. The two ranges then resume their separate and roughly parallel courses in a general northwesterly direction, to clash again in the knot of Cerro de Pasco, before continuing on into Ecuador. Rivers like the Marañón, the Apurimac, and the Mantaro flow through the deep troughs between the gigantic Andean ridges. In spite of all the modern developments which have taken place in the coastal region, this high sierra country remains the heart of Peru, as it was in Incaic times. About seventy percent of the population of the republic cling to the land of the mountain valleys and *pampas* which their ancestors have farmed since the Middle Ages. In few parts of the world has there been such a close spiritual and physical adjustment between a people and its environment. To an extraordinary degree these Peruvian Indians are of a piece with their part of the earth.

The Ecuadorean Andes are distinguished from those of Peru and Bolivia by the greater narrowness of the mountain zone and by the presence of a remarkable series of volcanic peaks. This "avenue" of more than twenty volcanoes, some active like Tungurahua and Sangay, some extinct or quiescent, like Chimborazo and Cayambe, give a special character to the landscape of Ecuador. The inter-mountain plateau, which is divided into the three basins of Quito, Ambato, and Cuenca, plays the same part in the life of the nation as the Peruvian and Bolivian highlands play in the national life of those countries.

Similarly, in Colombia population and economic activity are largely concentrated on the temperate plateau, and cities like Barranquilla and Cartagena only have importance as gateways into the high interior tableland. North of the knot of Pasto the Andes break up into three great ranges, which are divided from each other by the deep valleys of the Cauca and the Magdalena. Bogotá lies on a high *sabana* or plain in the eastern cordillera, while Medellín, the important agricultural and commercial center, is located in the central range. The eastern range branches off in two directions in the region of Bucaramanga. One spur leads down to the Caribbean at Santa Marta as the Sierra de Perijá and at the very coast rises to a height of over 17,000 feet in the *nevado* or snow-capped peak of Santa Marta; the other branch crosses into Venezuela as the Cordillera de Mérida and continues, with a low break in the vicinity of Barcelona, until it disappears in the peninsula of Paria opposite the island of Trinidad.

The Andes are linked with the mountain system of Central

America by means of the low and heavily forested Cordillera of Baudo, which is a continuation of the Colombian coast range and connects with the *serranía* of Darién in Panama. The surface of all the six Central American republics is prevailingly mountainous. The mountain back-bone of Central America runs close to the Pacific coast and it is in this highland region that most of the population lives. Where the land mass widens out to the north of Costa Rica the mountain area spreads eastward toward the Caribbean in a great number of irregular ridges. Communications between the settlements in these rugged districts are very difficult, except for the extensive road network of the Guate-malan highlands and the better highways of El Salvador. Veritable nests of volcanoes are encountered at intervals along the mountain divide of Central America. There are several in Costa Rica and in the lake region of Nicaragua. The active Salvadorean volcano of Izalco, which rose to a height of several thousand feet in a few weeks of 1770, is known locally as "the lighthouse of the Pacific." Nearly thirty volcanic peaks tower above the beautiful upland country of Guate-mala, many of them in the vicinity of the lapis-blue lake of Atitlán. In 1902, the volcano of Santa María erupted violently and did consider-able damage to the near-by city of Quetzaltenango.

Entering the Mexican State of Chiapas, the main Central Ameri-can range continues parallel to the Pacific coast at a short distance from the sea. At the Isthmus of Tehuantepec it breaks down into a tangled maze of hills. This pleasant and fertile land is the habitat of the superior Tehuanas, a branch of the Zapotec race, whose temperament reflects the favored environment of their traditional home.[3] North of the isth-mus the basic Mexican range bifurcates, the Sierra Madre Occidental following the west coast and the Sierra Madre Oriental, the east, or Gulf, coast. The two enclose the great plateau that comprises most of the area of Mexico. The southern rim of the true plateau is formed by a transversal range which leads eastward from the region of Colima across Michoacán and northern Morelos into Puebla. This range con-tains the highest peaks in the country, including Orizaba and the two

[3] "In contrast to the highlands, where people seldom laugh, there is much laughter in Tehuantepec. This is not the realm of the sad Indian." H. A. Franck and H. C. Lanks, *The Pan American Highway* (New York: Appleton-Century, 1940), p. 100. See Miguel Covarrubias, *Mexico South: the Isthmus of Tehuantepec* (New York: Alfred A. Knopf, 1946).

famous extinct volcanoes which overlook the valley of Mexico. The traveler who enters Mexico by the railroad from Vera Cruz to the capital climbs onto the plateau at the junction of this cross range with the eastern Sierra Madre. In a few hours he ascends from the *tierra caliente* of the lowlands through the *tierra templada* of the middle altitudes to the *tierra fria* of the high divide which the train crosses to reach the floor of the valley. Those who enter the country by the highway from Laredo plunge into the eastern Sierra Madre at Tamazunchale, about 220 miles from Mexico City. Except for a few wide valleys like that of Jalisco and such depressions as the Bolsón de Mapimi in Chihuahua, and the basin of Mexico, the surface of the plateau is everywhere broken by irregular chains of low mountains and hills.

While the great Brazilian plateau nowhere reaches altitudes comparable to those of the Andean cordilleras, its general level of between 1,500 and 4,000 feet is sufficiently high to exert a decisive influence on the climate of what would otherwise be a true tropical region. Over so large an area, climatic conditions naturally vary considerably in detail. As in most of South America, the year is divided into well-defined dry and rainy seasons, the former of which generally corresponds to the southern winter. This seasonal inequality of precipitation often works serious hardships on agriculture, particularly in the *sertão* region of the northwest. Though the total annual rainfall may exceed the apparently safe level of 30 inches, the existence of several months without rain has the effect of browning all pastures and other vegetation and of drying up surface sources of water. The dry atmosphere of the *caatinga* lands furthers this process by the rapid evaporation of moisture over that area. In the belt of the trade winds along the coast, the fall is plentiful over the year, but the rains decrease as one goes inland, and are lowest in the vicinity of Joazeiro in the interior of Bahia. Variations of temperature are also marked in the highland country of Brazil. On the relatively high plateau of São Paulo and Paraná frosts are common in certain localities in the winter and snow occasionally falls in the latter state. The climate of that region is generally comfortable and invigorating, as it also is over most of the Minas highlands. Farther to the north the sun is hot under the cloudless skies, but due to the low humidity the heat is not depressing and the climate is notably healthful.

This elevated land mass of nearly 1,000,000 square miles is the major physical factor in the life of the republic and affords a setting

for its highest economic development. The two key States of Minas
Gerais and São Paulo contain 35 percent of the population of the
Brazilian Union and account for a far larger proportion of its wealth.
Though these states are geographically typical of the plateau country,
the highlands extend over a much wider area on both sides. They reach
far to the northeast across Bahia into the hinterland of the smaller states
in the region of "the bulge," and northwest and west into the vast
States of Goiás and Mato Grosso. The Serra dos Parecís, in the upper
basin of the Roosevelt and the Juruena, is a distant outwork of the
central plateau system. The long valley of the Rio São Francisco is
confined between the lines of ridges known, on the eastern side, as the
Serra do Espinhaço and Chapada Diamantina and, on the western rim,
as Serra Geral de Goiás and Serra da Tabatinga.

In the interior of the northeastern part of the upland region there
is a wide semi-arid belt. The characteristic natural vegetation of this region is the thornbush growth known as *caatinga*. The native horsemen
of these dry lands of the *sertão* go dressed in leather from head to foot
as protection against the sharp spines of the low *caatinga* forest, which
include cactus and a variety of other xerophytic trees and shrubs. In
fact, the sun-browned inhabitants of this region have a leathery and
gnarled appearance that seems to fit into the natural scheme of the
long dry season. Around to the west across Goiás and Mato Grosso,
following the line of the watershed between the Amazon tributaries
and the upper basin of the Paraná, extends the highlands zone of the
chapada or *chapadão*. The steppe-like lands of this region are locally
known as *campos cerrados*, or "closed country," and are largely covered with a sparse scrub vegetation. The margin of the *chapada* on the
west and south is indicated by a well-defined line of bluffs, below
which lie the *campos limpos*, or "clean country," that is the center
of an important cattle-raising industry.

The Mineiro and Paulista highlands, and their southern continuation into the temperate States of Paraná and Santa Catarina, have certain characteristics which set them apart from the rest of the Brazilian
plateau. One distinguishing feature is their greater height, which
reaches over 9,000 feet in Mt. Itatiaia and the Pico da Bandeira. Another
is the superior fertility of their soil, which accounts for the notable
agricultural development of Minas Gerais and of the "red earth" lands
of São Paulo. Finally, the drainage system of this region is very un-

usual. From a short distance above Rio de Janeiro south to the border of Rio Grande do Sul, the Serra do Mar, or coast range, rises abruptly from a narrow fringe of lowland to heights of 3,000 to 4,000 feet. The railroads which climb to the floor of the plateau from Rio de Janeiro, Santos, and Paranaguá faced difficult engineering problems in mounting the face of this steep escarpment. Practically all the rivers of this part of the plateau flow westward into the Paraná, so that their waters eventually reach the Atlantic by the River Plate, even though they may rise within a few miles of the ocean and over a thousand miles from Buenos Aires. This circumstance has been utilized in connection with one of the most remarkable hydroelectric installations in the world. A series of streams which rise in the heavy rainfall belt at the crest of the Serra do Mar between São Paulo and Santos were dammed to form a lake, whose waters were then diverted in the opposite direction, to plunge into the turbines of the power plant at the foot of the mountain. An exception to this general rule is the Rio Paraíba, which after flowing for a long way parallel to the coast through a deep trough between the Serra da Mantiqueira and the Serra do Mar, breaks through to the low country near Campos in the State of Rio de Janeiro.

The third highland area in Latin America is the so-called Guiana plateau, which also covers a considerable area in southeastern Venezuela and a narrow zone of the Brazilian Guiana. This region is almost entirely undeveloped, much of it is heavily forested, and large parts of it are little known.

The surface of the three West Indian republics is predominantly rough. That of Haiti and the Dominican Republic is particularly so. Except for the famous *vega* in the heart of the latter country, there are very few sizable expanses of level land in either end of the island. On the other hand, much of their area is quite mountainous and unfitted for use. Although there are ranges of hills in all the six provinces of Cuba, in those of Havana, Matanzas, and Camaguey the elevations are generally low. In Oriente, in the eastern part of the island, much of the topography is very rugged and even attains the proportions of mountains, with altitudes up to 8,400 feet. Also, there are heights of nearly 4,000 feet in the Sierra de Trinidad, in southern Santa Clara, and the Sierra del Rosario, in Pinar del Rio, is almost 2,000 feet high. However, a very large part of Cuba consists of fertile plains and valleys, with rolling country between.

The Amazon valley is the largest lowland area in Latin America. It includes most of Brazil above the 15th parallel, that is, the greater part of that gigantic country, and parts of Venezuela, Colombia, Ecuador, Peru, and Bolivia. The basin of the Amazon and that of the Orinoco merge imperceptibly into one another where the Negro or Guainia and the Atabapo approach within a short distance of each other, and the two river systems are actually connected by the natural canal of the Cassiquiare. To the south, the plains of the Amazon join those of the River Plate system in that distant corner of Mato Grosso where the Guaporé-Itenes branch of the Madeira, the Juruena, one of the confluents of the Tapajós, and an arm of the Paraguay all rise in the same vicinity. Though of greatly varying width, this belt of lowlands thus bisects South America from north to south, and forms a single area of low altitude. At a certain season of the year, it would be possible to travel by water from the mouth of the Orinoco to that of the Plate, without entering the Atlantic at any intermediate point and with only a short portage at the divide between the Amazon and Paraguay systems. In fact, this feat was accomplished in 1958 by two Americans. The vast forested plain of Amazonia, as it spreads out westward between the line of the Negro and that of the Madeira, continues with very little rise until it reaches the last outworks of the Andes. Where the Marañón-Amazon suddenly breaks out through the narrow canyon of the Pongo de Manseriche into the Amazonian plain, the lowlands approach to within less than 300 miles of the Pacific. The lower basin of the Amazon is confined on the north by the edge of the Guiana plateau, where the watershed follows the jagged line of the Serra Pacaraima, the Mountains of the Moon, and the Tumac Humac Mountains. To the south of the main river, outcroppings of the great Brazilian plateau reach far up between the Tapajós, the Xingu, and the Araguaia. In ascending the Xingu, for example, the first hills come into view in the neighborhood of Altamira, immediately above the *Volta Grande* or "great bend."

Contrary to a common impression, the Amazon valley is not an immense swamp. At its worst, few areas of the earth are less suited to human habitation than the tidal forest of the Amazon delta. Yet people live in this periodically drowned jungle, which is the true "green hell" of the Brazilian writer, Rangel. Probably even more inhospitable is the belt of the Mondongos in the large island of Marajó. The flood plain of the Amazon is wide over most of its length and during the period of the annual rise conditions on the broad flats among the labyrinth of channels are highly unfavorable to anything but an amphibian existence. The same is true of the large alluvial tributaries of the State of Amazonas, like the Purús and the Juruá. For much of the year these rivers meander toward the Amazon in a series of great oxbows, but at the time of the annual floods their channels spread out over the intervening lowlands, and their courses temporarily lose their characteristic pattern. Throughout the Amazonia one finds little groups of people living in huts that are set on piles above the normal flood level; they move about in canoes through the waterlogged forest until the rivers subside into their regular channels.

However, most of the Amazon country is *terra firme* and well above the level of the yearly inundations. Going up the river from Pará to Manaus, this fact soon becomes apparent after leaving the Straits of Breves. Ranges of hills several hundred feet in height begin to appear to the north. At Monte Alegre the hills come down almost to the water's edge and behind the first rise of ground there is a wide expanse of open *campos* lands with more ridges along their northern edge. These natural *campos* are an interesting feature of the Amazonian landscape and occur in many places. The largest of them, the *campos gerais* of the Rio Branco, are several thousand square miles in extent. Their soil is hardpan and except along the watercourses they are covered with a sparse growth of low grass, which provides scant pasturage for scattered herds of cattle. Farther up the Amazon, one encounters high ground at Santarém, at the mouth of the Tapajós, which is one of the finest natural sites in the Amazon valley, and again at the pleasant town of Óbidos, where the river, constricted between hills on both sides, flows through a single channel at the only place in its length.[4] Similarly, the long line of bluffs along the river bank be-

---

[4] At the narrows at Óbidos, the Amazon is about a mile and a quarter wide. In the middle of the channel the depth is over 270 feet and in places reaches a depth of more than 430 feet. The current is so strong at this point that steamers ascending the river generally keep close to the north bank. For a comparison in widths—the Negro, largest northern tributary of the Amazon, is over 18 miles wide in the Boioçu section above Manaus.

low Manaus are typical of this important topographical feature of Amazonia. Not only along streams like the Tapajós, whose shores rise abruptly to a waterless plateau, and among the beautiful channels of the Maués, but along the typical alluvial rivers, one frequently passes high bluffs that are a part of the main land mass of the valley. It is on these elevated shelves of land that most of the towns of the Amazon valley, like Iquitos on the Marañón, Tefé on the Solimões, Humaitá on the Madeira, and Riberalta on the Beni, are located.

There is a great difference between the characteristic vegetation of the *terra firme* and of the so-called *varzea* lands along the flooded margins of the rivers. The former is the habitat of the hardwoods that are typical of the higher tropical jungle. Large areas of this forest are quite open and without undergrowth, so that it is often possible to move freely through it for long distances. On the other hand, the jungle of the floodplain is a tangled mass of softwood trees, lianas, and impenetrable undergrowth. An interesting feature of this zone is the islands which are built up by the deposits of sediment during the floods, some of which are of considerable extent. As the waters recede, trees, usually Cecropias, and an exuberant growth of other plant life, spring up. By the time of the next annual rise of the river, this luxuriant vegetation may have reached a height of several feet, only to be swept away with the island itself in the course of a single day. It is these antediluvian aspects of an unfinished world which led Paul Le Cointe, the Frenchman who knew the Amazon country with a more complete and precise knowledge than any other man, to remark: "Geologically speaking, the Amazonia is in full process of formation; to bring it to completion, Nature needs many centuries more. Man has arrived too soon—'he is only an impertinent intruder,' as Euclydes da Cunha has said—and many are the obstacles which he must overcome to satisfy his impatience and establish there his domain."

First of these obstacles is the relentless fecundity and savagery of the jungle, against which man must struggle ceaselessly. Even the trees war with each other for a place in the soil and the sun, and often literally strangle one another to death. The jungle threatens eternally to reclaim the little parcels of land which man clears so laboriously with ax or machete on the flats of the *várzea*. The voracious *saúva* ants may destroy his diminutive plantings in a day, and districts have been abandoned because of the ravages of these insects. The very water is full of terrors—alligators, the saw-toothed piranha fish, and the tiny but equally rapacious candiru,[5] the electric eel, the sting-ray, and the more forbidding than dangerous *sucuri* or anaconda. Among the pullulating insect life that torments the existence of men in the jungle are mosquitoes and the greatest variety of ants in the world. The ants, who are the real lords of the jungle, include the well-named *formigas de fogo*, or "fire ants," the equally burning *taxi*, the big aggressive *tocandira*, and the destructive *carregadeiras*. Though there are several varieties of poisonous serpents, including the various species of *Lachesis* known in the Tupi *língua geral* as *surucucu*, the violet-gray *jararaca*, and the tiny coral snake, due to the caution of the jungle dwellers, the loss of life from their bites is much less than is generally supposed. While the boa constrictor is common, he is relatively harmless and is sometimes kept in the huts of the natives as a ratter. The Amazon jungle is singularly poor in large mammals, and none of them, not even the big *onça* or jaguar, is aggressive. Some of the Amazonian fauna is decidedly primeval in its state of evolution. These prehistoric animals include the tapir (a hoofed quadruped whose nearest relatives are the horse and rhinoceros), the anteater, the slow-moving sloth, known as *preguiça*, or laziness, by the natives, and the ungainly *cigana* or hoatzin, a bird with reptilian characteristics that appears to have straggled out of some antediluvian swamp.

The environment of the jungle induces melancholy and taciturnity in man. The dark green walls of the rain forest press closely on him and he lives in a world of deep shadows, into which the sunlight trickles all too sparingly. The heavy, steaming atmosphere; the sense of futility and inadequacy that comes from the struggle with inexorable forces—floods, the daily inundation of the tide, the drenching rains, the matted vegetation—which dwarf him at every turn; the debilitating effects of malaria and hookworm; the inhospitality of the forest that offers him only such food as he can kill; the discomforts of a half-aquatic existence—all these provide a physical setting for human life, in which nearly all the odds are against him who is so bold—or so

[5] Of another habit of this fish, Le Cointe writes as follows: "Très petit, mais uniquement préoccupé à mal faire . . . il pénètre parfois dans les cavités anales ou vaginales des baigneurs ou des baigneuses et là, hérissant ses terribles éperons qui s'opposent à tout recul, peut causer de graves désordres s'il n'est pas extrait aussitôt avec les précautions nécessaires."

hopeless—as to challenge its handicaps. People do not sing or laugh in this diabolical world.

Such are the conditions of the habitat of the tropical rain forest within the flood plain of the great rivers. On the higher lands of the *terra firme* the contest between man and nature is much less unequal. Though the rainfall is heavy—from 75 to 100 inches—the land is not perennially waterlogged, as it is in the tidal region of the lower Amazon. During the months of the dry season, the weather is generally clear and refreshing and the nights are pleasantly cool. People look healthier and more vital than in the lowlands. The very forest is friendlier and less depressive on the human spirit. The natural forces in the environment are capable of some restraint and control by man and of being utilized for his purposes. Though the conditions for its clearing and development are hard, this region constitutes an enormous reserve of land for eventual settlement.

The outstanding physical features of the basin of the Platine fluvial system differ markedly from those of the Amazon valley. In the first place, due to its higher latitude, its vegetation is generally less luxuriant. Thus, the sparse plant life of the bush country of the *cha-pada*, which extends across Mato Grosso in the region of the head-waters of the Paraguay, is in contrast to the heavy growth that covers the Amazonian belt beyond the low divide. To the south of the shelf of the *chapada* lies the grazing zone of the *campos de vacaria*, the broken, rolling prairies which reach down into the cattle ranges of northern Paraguay, interspersed with forested areas in which *yerba maté* is worked. Along the upper course of the Paraguay the river spreads out in the rainy season over a wide flood plain. This *pantanal* region consists of open grasslands and when the river retires into its channel it affords excellent pasturage for large herds of cattle.

On the right bank of the river there begins in this latitude the characteristic topography and vegetation of the Chaco, which reaches its most typical form farther south in the Gran Chaco of Paraguay. Nowhere in the world does a river separate two regions of such diverse character. On the east side of the river is the true Paraguay, a rolling land of varied features—upland, tropical forest, open farming country of good soil, areas of marshland, ranges of hills and low mountains, and clear, swift-flowing streams. To the west is a flat plain with no perceptible tilt toward the main river, its impermeable surface covered with a layer of water from local rains during the wet season, sluggish and brackish streams, open savannahs dotted with carandai palms and broken by large islands of dense jungle in which the red quebracho tree occurs widely. The one region is highly favorable to human settlement; the other is shunned by men in search of homes, in spite of all the blood which has been shed for its possession. Southward below the Pilcomayo, on one side, and the bend of the Paraná, on the other, the main features of differentiation continue for a distance, though gradually modified by other physiographic factors, into the Argentine Chaco and the Province of Corrientes. From these intermediate zones the transition is rapid into the great agricultural regions of Argentina—the rich and highly developed Province of Sante Fé on the right bank and the Mesopotamian Province of Entre Rios on the left bank. Eastward beyond the latter and across the line of the Uruguay the Entre Rios lands merge easily into the rolling country of the Banda Oriental of Uruguay and the Brazilian State of Rio Grande do Sul.

The Argentine pampa is the culmination of the great belt of lowlands which extends north and south through the interior of the continent. In economic importance it corresponds to the Mississippi Valley in the United States, though of much smaller extent. In many respects it differs from its North American counterpart. It faces directly on the sea, which gives it an important advantage in the export of its products to foreign markets. Except for the Paraná, which skirts its edge and affords a navigable way into some of its richest territories, its river system is very deficient. As the bed of the ancient pampean sea, its uniformly level surface retards its natural drainage and prevents the development of large streams with well-defined beds and networks of tributaries. Its outstanding resources, which make it the seat of the most advanced agricultural industry in Latin America, are the unexcelled richness of its deep alluvial soil and its moderate climate, combined with a rainfall which is adequate for the needs of its crops and herds.

Returning to the north of the continent, the Orinoco basin, though covering a vast area between the Venezuelan Andes and the Guyana plateau, is considerably smaller in extent than either of the two other lowland regions. It is, also, even more backward in its economic development than is the Amazon valley. Its principal physical features distinguish it from either the Amazonia or the Platine basin. While its forest lands are of considerable size, particularly in its eastern part and in the maze of the Orinoco's delta, its distinguishing characteristic is the wide zone of *llanos* or tropical savannahs, with scattered trees breaking the monotony of the low grasslands. In spite of the alternate floods and droughts which scourge these plains, they have great possibilities for the raising of cattle. The Venezuelan government has recently made extensive surveys of their economic potentialities, particularly of the region known as the Gran Sabana, in order to determine the best means of bringing them under fuller development. The skilled horsemen of the *llanos*, though excellent material for irregular cavalry, as they demonstrated on both sides during the wars of independence, have persistently remained outside the influence of whatever currents of progress have affected the life of the republic.

The only other considerable area of lowlands in Latin America is found on the east side of the northern continent, where the land mass widens out between the Isthmus of Tehuantepec and the narrows of southern Central America. The coastal plain along the Gulf of Mexico, within the States of Tamaulipas and Vera Cruz, expands eastward along the Gulf of Campeche across Yucatán, and down into Belize and the Petén district of Guatemala. The Yucatán peninsula is a unique physiographic area, and largely consists of a limestone shelf projecting out between the Gulf and the Caribbean. A thin layer of soil supports crops of short-rooted plants, like corn and henequen, and a dense growth of low jungle. There are no surface streams, but the rainfall permeates through the surface layer of limestone to form an interesting series of underground rivers.

On the eastern side of the bulge of Central America there is another, and fairly broad, coastal plain within the borders of Honduras and Nicaragua. The governments of the two republics have given little attention to the development of this region, but the American fruit companies have established extensive banana plantations in clearings made for the purpose, particularly in Honduras.

The narrow belt along the West Coast of South America, lying between the Andes and the Pacific, presents a wide diversity of physiographic and climatic conditions. A dense growth of forest covers the western slopes of the Colombian plateau. In this zone of extraordinarily high rainfall, which reaches a maximum of 28 feet, there is virtually no economic development. This rain belt, which is accounted for by the warm, south-flowing ocean current known as *El Niño*, extends down into the wider coastal plain of Ecuador, where it is the seat of important cacao and banana industries. Below Tumbéz, near the border between Ecuador and Peru, the aspect of the land changes radically. The warm current is diverted away from the coast and the influence of the cool north-flowing Humboldt Current takes its place. Thence south along the Peruvian and Chilean coasts to the neighborhood of Coquimbo there continues one of the most remarkable desert regions in the world. This section of coast is practically rainless, though the heavy mist which hangs over the land for much of the year provides a minimum of moisture. The only break in the monotonous dryness comes at irregular and widely separated intervals, when a momentary deviation of the prevailing ocean current from its usual path brings torrential—and devastating—rains. The only continuous vegetation is found in the narrow valleys of the streams which flow down from the Andes and where the volume of water is sufficient it provides the basis for an intensive development of irrigated agriculture. Between the thin green ribbons of the river margins the country is barren and desolate. Below Arica no stream flows into the Pacific until the vale of La Serena is reached in the bay of Coquimbo. This is the region of the absolute desert, and in the *pampa* or depression between the coast range and the Andes there is located the famous nitrate region of Chile. South of Coquimbo, the rainfall, combined with a network of streams from the high valleys of the Andes, makes possible a flourishing development of agriculture, particularly in the famous Central Valley. In many respects, the physical pattern of Chile closely parallels, though in reverse order, that of part of the Pacific coast of North America. The dry peninsula of Lower California corresponds to the desert zone of northern Chile and the interior valley of California to the rich longitudinal depression of central Chile, while the rain belt of southern Chile is similar to the Pacific Northwest, extending from the Puget Sound country to the Alaska "panhandle."

The islands off the coast of Latin America are of singularly little importance. The only islands which have ever had any economic value in themselves are the Venezuelan island of Margarita, once famous for its pearl fisheries, and the barren guano islands off Peru, which formerly yielded a fabulous revenue to the Peruvian government. Many of them are uninhabited, either because their natural conditions are unattractive to settlers or due to lack of interest of the owning country in their development. Some, like Mexico's Tres Marias and Brazil's Fernando de' Noronha, have only been utilized as prison colonies. Others, like Roatan and other islands off the Caribbean coast of Central America, have been abandoned to West Indian fishermen. Cocos Island, famous for its buried treasure, has been only lightly held by Costa Rica and has no permanent population. While Chile owns Juan Fernández, reputed to be the scene of Robinson Crusoe's adventures, and distant Easter Island, an isolated outpost of the Polynesian archipelagoes, little has been done to develop whatever resources they have, beyond a British-operated sheep-raising enterprise on Easter. The Galápagos group, which belongs to Ecuador, has been best known for its extraordinary natural features, and only perfunctory efforts have been made to exploit the islands or even to assert Ecuadorean sovereignty over them. The islands are geological curiosities, and the strange differentiation of related animal forms among the various and highly dissimilar islands of the group confirmed Darwin in his famous hypothesis of the origin and evolution of species.

A number of islands, like Cozumel, off the coast of Yucatán, Caviana and Mexiana, to the north of the Amazon's mouth, Marajó, lying across the outer edge of the Amazon delta, Tierra del Fuego, and the myriad Chilean islands to the south of Puerto Montt, are detached pieces of the continental land mass, separated from the mainland by arms of the sea.

The Falklands, which lie at some distance from the Patagonian coast, are claimed by Argentina, which knows them as the Maluinas. The Argentine government has never recognized the British right to them and has made persistent representations for their return. In spite of the fact that they have one of the world's most inclement climates and that they lost some of their importance as a port of call for ships when the Panama Canal was built, they are of considerable value as the seat of a sheep-raising industry, which is in the hands of Scotch breeders.

Part II

HISTORY

꧅꧅꧅

Pre-Colonial

WHEN the Spaniards and Portuguese arrived in the New World they everywhere found the land occupied by native races. Because of the illusion of Columbus that he had discovered the Eastern, or true, Indies, they have ever since been known by the name which he applied to them. These aboriginal peoples evidently had a common ethnic origin in Asia and had crossed to the American continent from Siberia by way of Bering Strait. In the course of a southward migration extending over many centuries—or even millennia—differentiation of cultures had taken place on a wide scale. Variations from the original physical type had developed marked characteristics under the influence of the natural environment and as a result of more artificial factors of breeding. Definite lingual stocks had grown up that seemed to bear no relation to a common tongue. At the time of the coming of Europeans some relatively high civilizations had already vanished completely, like that which centered about the colossal ruins of Tiahuanaco, in Bolivia. Others, like the Maya, in Middle America, and the Chimú, in coastal Peru, had proceeded so far in their decline that the contemporaries of the Spanish conquerors had no memory of the great ages of their people's history, and could not explain the existence of the dead cities about them, like Chichén and Chan-Chan.

Our knowledge of the past of these Indian peoples is derived from a number of sources. Some of the native civilizations were in full flower at the time of the *Conquista*, and though most of the *conquistadores* were unlettered men who looked with undiscriminating eyes on what they saw, some, like Cortés, left intelligent descriptions of a way of life which they were to destroy or at least radically to alter. A few of the priests who accompanied the conquerors made valuable contributions in this respect, in spite of their contempt for the native religions and their overemphasis on the missionary aspects of the Spanish occupation. Among them, Bishop Landa, of Yucatán, partially atoned for his destruction of irreplaceable Mayan manuscripts by his account of Mayan traditions and cultural survivals. As it was, a few precious codices in the Mayan glyphs and the Aztec pictographs escaped the intolerant vandalism of the conquerors, eventually to add to a store of knowledge painfully built up by the resources of paleography and archaeology. Until recently, archaeological research did comparatively little to illuminate the dark shadows of Latin America's pre-Columbian era. The governments were not interested in the Indian past of their countries. From the days of the *Conquista* the ruins of ancient cities had served as convenient stone quarries for builders of lesser stature. Tombs had been ransacked for precious art works which had been scattered to the ends of the earth, instead of being preserved in national museums of antiquities. However, some of the republics, notably Mexico and Peru, have become conscious of the significance of their Indian heritage and have made efforts to conserve the material remains of early civilizations. Mexican anthropologists, like Manuel Gamio, and archaeologists, like Alfonso Caso, who excavated the rich Monte Albán field in Oaxaca, have done much to reconstruct the aboriginal cultures of their country. Meanwhile, organized research, carried on by such institutions as the Carnegie Institution and the Museum of the American Indian, has opened up vast fields of historical evidences and artistic treasures in Yucatán and other regions. The airplane has been the means of discovering many cities buried by the lush jungle of Middle America. Finally, the survival of pre-colonial customs in such places as the Imbabura valley in Ecuador has enabled archaeologists to bridge the gap of centuries and to observe the living remnants of an ancient culture which has successfully resisted the alien forces of change.

The Indian population of the New World south of the Rio Grande, as the Spaniards and Portuguese saw it in the early years of the sixteenth century, was divided among a number of widespread racial stocks occupying fairly well-defined areas. Some were sedentary peoples, leading a settled existence that was based on a highly developed agriculture. Others were still in a nomadic or village state of evolution, and were dependent on hunting and fishing, supplemented by a more elementary system of agriculture. Of such was the great Tupi family, which ranged the immense territory between the Amazon and the River Plate, and whose most famous branch was the Guarani tribe in the lands of the present Paraguayan republic. The gentle Arawaks, whom Columbus found in the Antilles and who were virtually exterminated by the Spaniards in the first years of the *Conquista*, were in a similar stage of development, as were the warlike and intractable Araucanians of Chile and Yaquis of northern Mexico. Some of the peoples were aggressive and predatory, like the fierce Caribs of the Spanish Main, who were given to raiding the settlements of the more peaceful Arawaks in the islands of the sea that was named for them. Certain peoples, at the coming of the Europeans, had reached a high state of culture, which as yet showed no signs of decline. Of such were the Aztecs and the Incas. Others, as the Maya, had degenerated to a point where the original greatness of the race was only a memory. On the other hand, the Chibchas of the Colombian plateau were just emerging into a relatively high state of civilization. Still other peoples, like the tribes of the Gran Chaco wilderness, the miserable Seris of northwestern Mexico, and the prototypes of Shakespeare's Caliban, whom Magellan encountered on the bleak shores of Patagonia, were examples of the flotsam and jetsam of the secular migrations, which had been pushed into the less desirable recesses of the continent, there to vegetate in a hopeless barbarism. One of the most numerous and important groups of peoples was that which inhabited the lands from the Mexican plateau down into the highlands of Central America, and including the low limestone shelf that constitutes the peninsula of Yucatán. The chronology of these peoples, the details of their migrations, their ethnic relationships, and the interactions of their cultures, are still obscure in many respects. However, as their descendants still comprise the main body of the Mexican nation, their past is of unusual interest as a stage of an historical process that has been diverted from its original channels, but remains unbroken in many of its essential circumstances.

Six or seven separate and major groups of these related peoples are recognized, though sometimes dimly—the so-called Olmecs, the ruins of whose civilization have lately been found in the northern part of the isthmus; the mysterious Toltecs; the Mixtecs; the attractive Zapotecs, who still occupy most of the Tehuantepec country; the half-savage Chichimecs, to the north, who caused the Spaniards so much trouble after the initial conquest of Mexico; the Aztecs; and the Mayas. Some of these peoples were only a memory when the Spaniards arrived. In the course of centuries of tribal comings and goings on the plateau and in the low country to the south, they left such long-dead cities as Tula and Teotihuacán and Monte Albán as relics of their struggles for domination and racial expression.

The rise of the Aztecs to dominance on the Mexican plateau bears a remarkable parallel to the circumstances that made the early Romans masters of Italy.[1] They were an aggressive folk with a marked talent for war and organization, who established themselves in the strategical heart of the country and from there built up a great league of dependent or tributary states that extended from one sea to the other. On an island in the lacustrine Valley of Mexico they had constructed a city, Tenochtitlán, whose buildings and other manifestations of an advanced culture immensely impressed the Spanish conquerors. Many of the arts were developed with a high degree of skill and esthetic sense. A state-craft that had in it more than terror of Aztec power and cruelty held in awed subjection a congeries of widely separated peoples. Though stained by the human sacrifices that were made to the war-god, a highly developed system of religion permeated the common life of the nation, and with the ceremonials and observances of a rich folklore reached everywhere into the daily existence of the population, to give color and meaning to its ordinary actions. An elaborate system of pictograph devices was used to record events and transmit ideas.

As the Maya civilization was in an advanced state of decay at

[1] See George C. Vaillant, *Aztecs of Mexico* (Garden City: Doubleday, Doran & Co., 1941).

the time of the Spanish Conquest, contemporary evidence is lacking on conditions which prevailed during its prime. However, from oral traditions set down by the early Spanish chroniclers and from the later revelations of archaeology, we are able to reconstruct the principal features of this extraordinary culture. Like the Spaniards themselves, the Mayas were great city builders, and the ruins of many of these centers of Mayan life have been brought to light in our time. The Mayas also recorded outstanding events of their history in hieroglyphic form, as bas-reliefs on the walls of their buildings and monuments. The key has not yet been found to these sculptured writings, but the Mayan calendar has been deciphered and adjusted to our own, so that it is possible to place accurately in time many of the important events in the annals of the Mayan people, which have been represented pictorially in stone.

Over a long period of time, whose beginnings antedated the Christian era, the Mayan power flourished successively in the Yucatán peninsula and in the northern part of Central America. The exact course of the migrations is obscure, as are the circumstances attending the political vicissitudes of the race. The seat of the Mayan hegemony shifted several times, according to the changing fortunes of war and other circumstances, and long periods of decline intervened between the periods when the Mayan civilization attained its highest development, as between the so-called Old and New Empires. The reasons for the collapse of the Mayan world are one of the great riddles of aboriginal America. Among the theories advanced to account for the destruction of a civilization that held such brilliant promise are devastating wars between the city-states of the peninsula, a widespread pestilence, a change of climate that radically altered the natural conditions of the Mayan habitat, and a growth of population in excess of the available food supply that could be derived from the thin soil of Yucatán.

As with the Aztecs and the Incas, religion was an ever-present force in the life of the Mayan people. Buildings that were clearly places of worship and religious ceremonial dominate their cities, some of which were veritable ecclesiastical centers, like the Toltec Cholula. The Mayas had a deep knowledge of astronomy and the most accurate calendar in use anywhere in the world before the revision of the Gregorian calendar of western Christendom. Their system of mathe-

matics was practical and advanced, and was based on a vigesimal principle of numbers. They showed remarkable skill in the handicrafts,
though, like most of the Indian races, they were deficient in a knowledge of mechanics. Their traders ventured far along the shores of the
Gulf and the Caribbean and into the neighboring lands.

The foremost native race in South America was that known from
its ruling class as the Incas. At the time the Inca power was overthrown
by the Pizarros, it extended from the mountain knot of southern
Colombia, among whose valleys lived the war-like tribe of the Cañaris,
south to the Desert of Atacama, beyond which lay the lands of the
redoubtable Mapochos of the Araucanian race. Place names and survivals in the speech of the local population in northwestern Argentina
bear testimony to the fact that Inca influence once reached down from
the high Andes into that region. The far-flung empire extended on the
east into the Amazon jungle, where some of the forest peoples still
speak an archaic form of Quechua. On the west the Inca world was
bounded by the Pacific Ocean, on whose shores dwelt the decadent
survivors of the once-mighty Chimú nation, now vassals of the Inca. A
scattered population of subject peoples, who inhabited mountain valleys, irrigated oases and river margins in the coastal desert, and expanses of lofty plateau country, was held together by a remarkable
system of administration and control. This system was, in turn, made
possible by the existence of excellent roads throughout the empire
and by the use of swift couriers and signaling methods whereby messages could be transmitted over a thousand miles in a few hours. Power
over this closely knit and firmly held world was concentrated in Cuzco,
the mountain capital of the Incas. Nowhere else in Latin America is
one so vividly aware of the pre-Spanish past of the New World as in
this ancient city and in the upper valley of the Urubamba, through
which the railroad follows the old Inca road from Lake Titicaca and
the bleak Aymará lands beyond the lake.

The Inca state held in its hands absolute power—political, economic, and religious—over the peoples under its sway. At the awesome apex of the hierarchical structure of skillfully pyramided authority was the Inca himself. By reason of the accumulated prestige
of a dynasty of great rulers, of the pomp which surrounded his
life, and of his accepted kinship to the Andean pantheon, his position
was something more than imperial. The numerous members of the

Incaic clan constituted an aristocracy which held the high places in the public service of the state. Below this ruling caste were the warrior class, whose duty was to extend the bounds of the empire and to prevent the rebellion of the conquered peoples, and a numerous priesthood, who conducted the elaborate religious rites associated with the advanced polytheism of the Andes. At the base of the political and social pyramid were the masses, mostly Quechuan in race and speech.

Under a remarkable system of state socialism, unknown elsewhere in the world, the Peruvian peoples gave abject obedience to the Inca and to his agents and emissaries; in return for the surrender of all individual initiative, they received a guarantee of their collective security against the normal hazards of life. By wise regulation of agriculture and utilization of soil resources, that included irrigation, the terracing of hillsides, and the use of guano as fertilizer; the distribution of lands in accordance with the needs of the family; and the provident storage of surplus crops against the chance of scarcity, everyone was assured an adequate food supply. Materials for housing were everywhere at hand, and the llama supplied wool for clothing as well as meat for a better-balanced diet than was possible among the Aztecs and the Mayas. At the approach of old age men were relieved of the obligations of physical labor and provision was made for their support for the remainder of their lives.

This people displayed a high degree of skill as artificers of the metals, though they never learned the secret of smelting iron, and of other materials. As weavers of woolen cloth they have probably never been equaled. Their pottery bore evidence not only of great deftness in the molding of clay vessels and figures, but of a real feeling for the beautiful. With copper tools and without the most elementary mechanical devices, they built cyclopean structures of stone, like the fortress of Sacsahuaman, above Cuzco, and the mysterious refuge-city of Machu Pichu, situated on a mountain crag two thousand feet above the Urubamba, that have excited the wonder and admiration of all observers. To change the course of streams, they dug tunnels through mountains, sometimes working from both sides to meet in the middle, so carefully made were their calculations. They even trepanned skulls to treat diseases of the brain and sutured the edges of the opening without resultant infection.

Yet this ingenious and diligent people, disciplined in the service of an all-embracing state and of the common welfare of its subjects, never developed a means of recording ideas. They had no system of writing, but perfected a satisfactory method of counting and were able to transmit numerical computations from place to place and as permanent records of the government, by means of knotted cords known as quipus.

Spain

The entrance of Spain into the New World of the Americas coincided with the end of an epoch in the history of that nation. Throughout the Middle Ages Spain was a congeries of shifting states, over which two of them, Castile and Aragon, gradually gained the ascendency. Meanwhile, Christian Spain had for centuries slowly been pushing back the Moslem into the south of the peninsula. The final achievement of these two secular processes was contemporaneous. The marriage in 1469 of Ferdinand of Aragon and Isabella of Castile brought about the unification of the Spanish peoples under one government, while these able rulers reduced the feudal nobility and the military orders into subjection to the authority of the crown. Also, the last obstacle to the complete political consolidation of Spain was removed by the subjugation of the Moorish kingdom of Granada and the expulsion of its Mohammedan inhabitants from Europe.

It is significant that the completion of the reconquest of Spain from the power of Islam occurred in the year of the discovery of America by Columbus. Full racial and religious unification was achieved the same year by the banishment of the Jews from the country. The new order assured by the triumph of unity and orthodoxy, Spain was ready for other ventures afield that might utilize the force of the momentum suddenly released by the cessation of centuries of war at home. The land was full of arrogant and restless men, accustomed to the pursuit of arms and possessed of prodigious vitality and of limitless faith in their own prowess. It was these supreme individualists who explored and conquered another world for Spain and her kings, even though at times their very individualism was to sow the dragon's teeth of discord among the conquerors. Under the first Hapsburgs, Charles V and

Philip II, the continuance of an all-powerful monarchy gave a strong direction to the imperial plan of the *Conquista*, of which this superb soldiery was the instrument. In spite of the vast outpouring of energies in the overseas enterprises, enough remained to make Spain the dominant power in continental Europe during the hundred years that was to be known as "the Spanish century."

Discovery and Exploration

The four voyages of Columbus span the twelve years 1492-1504. Before the ignominious end of his career of discovery others had broken into the area of the Caribbean, which was to become a secondary nucleus for subsequent explorations and conquests. Hispaniola, and later Cuba, were the local bases for these further advances toward the mainland, but the results of the first enterprises among the islands and along the coasts of the Caribbean disappointed the cupidity of the gold-hungry adventurers. It was only when they secured footholds on the continent, from which they could penetrate inland to the scenes of the great Indian cultures, that the Conquest received a decisive impetus. On the coasts of Yucatán and Tabasco roving Spanish navigators saw evidences of a richer and more advanced civilization than had been encountered in the Antilles, and on the isthmus Vasco Nuñez de Balboa not only found appreciable quantities of gold among the Indians, but evidently heard of greater riches to the southward.

It was with the epic conquest of Mexico by Cortés (1518–21) and of Peru by Pizarro (1531–36) that the colonial empire of Spain was definitely established. From Mexico lieutenants of Cortés pushed down into Central America, where they met other bands of Spaniards moving northward from the increasingly important base at Panama. From the heart of the old Inca dominions in Peru other Spanish forces spread out north and south over the Andean plateau and far down into the Araucanian lands of Chile. Still other groups of resolute men crossed the mountain barrier from the Central Valley of Chile into the western Argentine. Meanwhile, an expedition under Gonzalo Jiménez de Quesada climbed up from the Caribbean coast and out onto the highlands of Colombia, where it overthrew the power of the Chibchas and closed the gap between the Spanish Main and the conquered regions of Ecuador and Peru. By the middle of the sixteenth century Spaniards had explored the west coast of the Americas from 40 degrees north latitude to 40 degrees south. Within that coastal area and the mountain lands behind they founded dozens of settlements that were to grow into important cities and laid the foundations of a colonial empire that was to endure for three centuries with little curtailment at the hands of their enemies.

On the other side of the continent Spanish ships had early sailed along the low shores from the mouth of the Orinoco to well below that of the Amazon. Several years before Magellan passed that way to the southward the well-publicized Italian adventurer, Amerigo Vespucci, explored the south Atlantic coast as far as the River Plate, to be followed by the better-substantiated voyage of Juan Díaz de Solís to the same region. The first establishment of a settlement on the site of Buenos Aires in 1535 proved abortive, but the present Argentine metropolis was refounded 45 years later by colonists who came down river from Asunción in Paraguay.

Between the settlements on the Spanish Main and those in the River Plate basin lay a vast expanse of territory which was early preempted by Portugal. Occupied with the exploitation of their rich empire in the East, the Portuguese were slow to develop their huge but prosaic holdings in the New World. Even before Pedro Alvares Cabral, outbound for India, accidentally discovered the Brazilian coast in 1500, the Pope, by virtue of his famous line of demarcation, had reserved that quarter of the continent for Portugal. Desultory attempts at exploring the long coast were made from Lisbon, but it was not until 1530 that Martim Affonso de Souza was sent out to make a serious effort at colonization. During the next twenty years other colonists settled a number of towns along the upper coast, including Pernambuco and Bahia, but in spite of occasional penetrations into the interior, Brazil remained for several decades a coastal colony, clinging to the seaboard and the ocean lanes that bound its lonely settlers to their motherland.

The exploration of the South American hinterland proceeded slowly, and until the eighteenth century made little permanent impress on the great *terra incognita* that lay beyond the coast settlements and the Inca lands of the Andean plateau. Search for the mythical El Dorado led to several expeditions into the wilderness of the northwestern corner of the continent, but the jungle closed quickly behind these deluded wanderers. In 1539 one of the Pizarros crossed the divide from Quito in quest of the Land of Cinnamon, a counterpart of El Dorado, but returned with only a remnant of his force. However, one of his officers, Francisco de Orellana, continued on down the Amazon to its mouth in an epoch-making river voyage. There is good reason to believe that at least two small parties of men crossed from the south-eastern part of the continent to the borders of the Inca empire in the Andes before the middle of the century. In 1542, Alvar Nuñez Cabeza de Vaca, the famous explorer of our southwest, led a party overland from the lower Brazilian coast to the new colony in Paraguay, of which he was to assume the governorship. In 1573, Spaniards from the Bolivian highlands founded the town of Córdoba near the edge of the Argentine pampa, and shortly afterwards came into touch with the current of settlement in the basin of the Paraná.

For a century and a half after the Portuguese gained a foothold on the uplands of São Paulo, bold frontiersmen continued to push farther out across the wide expanse of Brazil. In search of slaves, which they sometimes obtained by raiding the Jesuit mission which had preceded them, or of gold and diamonds, which they found in Minas Gerais, Goiás, and Mato Grosso, they performed a valuable work in opening up the interior and making good the claims of Portugal to that enormous territory. Some of these indomitable *bandeirantes*, as they were known, penetrated beyond the low divide into the basin of the north-flowing Madeira. One of them, Antonio Raposo, even crossed Peru to the Pacific coast, returning after many years to São Paulo by way of the Amazon and the settlements along the Atlantic coast.

Colonial

Long before the original military phase of the *Conquista* had ended, the government of Spain took steps to set up the framework of civil authority in the conquered lands. Antonio de Mendoza was sent out to Mexico as Viceroy of New Spain in 1535, and Viceroy Blasco Nuñez Vela arrived in Peru in 1544, while civil war was still raging among the conquerors. In the one case, the prestige of the crown was so great that Cortés relinquished his position of supremacy to the king's agent without a struggle; in the other, the viceroy came prematurely into a field of loosened passions and ambitions and was killed; but his successors, culminating in the able Francisco de Toledo, early established the royal power on a solid foundation.

In its efforts to rule so far-flung a colonial empire, the home government faced serious problems of administration. First of these was the lack of experience in governing peoples beyond the peninsula, for the Aragonese ventures in southern Italy scarcely furnished a precedent which might be applied to the overseas dominions in the Americas. The great distances separating the court from the centers of government in the colonies, with the slowness and infrequency of communications, inevitably weakened the power of the central authority to control its representatives. For example, messages from Madrid to Buenos Aires went by the roundabout way of Panama, Lima, and Tucumán. The task of ruling large native populations, among which the numbers of the conquering races represented only an insignificant minority, was one which tried the ingenuity and wisdom of the imperial government. Finally, the defense of an empire which was the envy of every other maritime state was a major responsibility of the viceroys and their subordinates. Yet, in spite of all the designs of her enemies and the elements of weakness which developed in Spain in the seventeenth century, the Spanish colonial empire was actually larger in extent in 1800 than it had been two centuries earlier. Many attacks by English and French and Dutch had been beaten off, and such permanent inroads as had been made into the Spanish possessions were mostly among the islands of the Caribbean area.

Similarly, footholds which the Dutch and the French gained on the Brazilian coast at the expense of Portugal were only temporary, though the Dutch occupation of much of the north country endured for a relatively long time. After the conquest of Portugal by the Duke of Alba in 1580, Brazil remained a part of the Spanish Empire until 1640. Brazil thereupon became legitimate prey for the seafaring patriots of the Low Countries, who founded the Dutch West India Company with the object of taking Brazil from Spain. In 1623 a Dutch fleet seized the key city of Bahia, and seven years later another took Pernambuco. The Dutch, under Maurice of Nassau as their first governor, made serious efforts to develop the occupied territory, which they held until driven out by a creole uprising in 1661. French Huguenots established themselves on an island in Rio Bay for over ten years in the middle of the sixteenth century. Another French settlement on the Maranhão coast in the far north lasted from 1612 to 1615.

It was a centralized system of government which Spain imposed on her great colonial empire. The king was the source of all power, and under the meticulous Philip II (1556–98) the supremacy of the royal prerogative was a reality; under his successors, until the "benevolent despotism" of the Bourbon Charles III (1759–88), the royal absolutism was largely a grandiose fiction. However, by then the position of the monarchy was secure enough to dispense with strong kings. As might be expected, the king's ministers exercised the real authority in his name, and even affixed the *"Yo el Rey"* with a metal stamp to royal decrees. In practice, the supreme administrative body in the Spanish colonial system was the Council of the Indies, on which sat men with wide experience in colonial affairs. After the Spanish occupation, Portuguese colonial affairs were administered by a *Conselho de Ultramar*, whose position was similar to that of the Spanish *Consejo de las Indias*.

Whatever wisdom was displayed in Spain's rule of her empire was largely due to the influence of the Council. In spite of the calumnies of Spain's rivals, this wisdom was very considerable. The "laws of the Indies," in which the basic legislation of the empire was codified, generally reflect a high degree of humanity, and, except in economic matters, much sound administrative sense. In an age when all colonial legislation was liable to be illiberal and restrictive, that of Spain compared very favorably with the colonial systems of other nations. The serious abuses which crept into the administration of the colonies were due to the inability of the central authority in Spain to control the actions of its agents, who were so far removed from its immediate oversight. Even the rigors of the *residencia*, the investigation which was held at the termination of a viceroy's or governor-general's term of office, or the chance of a *visita* by an extraordinary royal inspector, were sometimes insufficient to restrain the cupidity of colonial officials.

The colonial empire in the Americas was early divided into the two viceroyalties of New Spain and Peru, whose respective jurisdictions roughly corresponded to the two continents. The seat of the northern viceroyalty was Mexico City; of the southern, Lima. In the eighteenth century, parts of the Viceroyalty of Peru were broken off to form the Viceroyalty of New Granada, with its capital at Bogotá, and that of La Plata, with the viceregal headquarters at Buenos Aires. Brazil was also governed by a viceroy, whose seat of government was first located at Bahia, and later at Rio de Janeiro.

The outlying regions of the viceroyalties, such as Chile and Guatemala, were early set up as provinces under a captain-general, whose authority tended at times to be virtually independent of the viceroy. Some of the more settled districts were governed by the bodies known as *audiencias*, though this semi-administrative, semi-judicial court also existed in the capitals of the viceroyalties and captaincies-general, where it served as a check on too arbitrary or independent actions by the king's representatives. In Brazil, the country was early divided into about twelve *capitanias*. A strip of coast was granted to a *donatário*, on condition that he undertake its colonization. The grant extended west between parallels of latitude to the "line of demarcation." Within these great feudal territories the *donatários* exercised most of the attributes of sovereignty, but as the royal government increasingly asserted its authority in the colony, the powers of the *donatários* declined accordingly.

Throughout the colonial regime the high posts in the service were held by natives of the peninsula. There were few exceptions to this rule, which barred offices in their government to the creoles, or Spaniards or Portuguese born in the colonies. The only road to political experience open to the colonials was in the government of their cities. Even in this restricted field their authority was generally limited by a royal agent in the person of the *corregidor* or by the encroachment of the viceroy or captain-general on the prerogative of the municipal councils. Under such auspices the colonial system of Spain proved an inadequate school for the responsibilities of self-government which followed the attainment of independence in the last century.

The dominant institution in colonial life, and frequently the co-equal and rival of the lay power, was the Church. The conquest and occupation of the New World coincided with a period of militant religious zeal in Spain. The feeling was intensified by the recent triumph of Catholic Spain over the Moors of Granada, which had taken on the character of a crusade. Also, Spain remained steadily orthodox in the face of the Protestant revolt against Rome and became, in fact, more intolerant of heresy than ever. Priests accompanied the first explorers and conquerors and mass conversions of the natives quickly followed their subjugation by the sword. Missionary work in the colonies was early organized on a systematic scale by the orders, which sometimes indulged in bitter rivalries with one another for control of the more tempting missionary fields. Some proselyting groups, particularly the Jesuits, carried their activities far afield into the wilderness. They not only increased the geographical knowledge of the interior of both continents, but served as instruments for the dissemination of Spanish civilization among the more backward native peoples. In the famous mission establishments of Paraguay, the Jesuits founded a society on a theocratic model until their expulsion from the Spanish dominions in the latter part of the eighteenth century. In many places, intrepid missionaries, like the famous Bartolomé de las Casas, Vasco de Quiroga, Bishop of Michoacán, and Fathers Vieira and Anchieta, in Brazil, protected the Indians against the attempts of lay Europeans to enslave or exploit them. Until their expulsion in 1760, the Jesuits were particularly influential in Brazil, where they also held a virtual monopoly of whatever educational facilities were available.

As the vigor of the colonial administration declined in the seventeenth century, the power and wealth of the Church increased. In spite of the royal *patronato*, or patronage, whereby the king confirmed the appointments of all prelates in the colonial hierarchy, bishops and archbishops frequently defied the mandates of viceroys and governors and undermined their authority in the eyes of their pious subjects. The large property holdings which the Church accumulated by the bequests of the faithful and the business acumen of its leaders not only made it a major economic factor to be reckoned with, but were to leave a heritage of problems for anti-clerical republican governments in the nineteenth century.

The Inquisition, or Holy Office, early established its operations in such important colonial centers as Cartagena and Lima. Though its primary function was the suppression of heresy, as guardians of conformity in general the agents of this powerful institution exercised a great—and restraining—influence over colonial thought. Extreme recourse to the auto-da-fé, or burning of heretics, was rare, but the air of mystery in which the Inquisition worked and its power to ruin an individual by confiscation of property or by casting doubts on his orthodoxy gave it a sinister prestige among the colonists. However, on the naïve theory that the Indian was not a "reasonable" being and therefore incapable of heretical ideas, the native peoples were exempt from the attentions of the Holy Office. In fact, the Church as a whole was generally satisfied with the Indians' outward observance of its rites and wisely refused to inquire too closely into whatever vestiges of pagan faiths may have persisted in his mind. The Inquisition was not introduced into Brazil until almost the end of the sixteenth century. Though it was never as active in the pursuit of heretics as in the Spanish colonies, its control over the written expression of ideas was probably complete. Whereas the first printing press was set up in Mexico in 1532 and the first book printed five years later, there was no printing press in Rio de Janeiro until 1747. In spite of occasional orders from Lisbon, even the Inquisition was lax in the suppression of heresy and the easy-going creoles freely tolerated the entry of individual Jews and Protestants into the country.

The Spaniards were great city builders, and it was natural that the typical expression of Spanish culture in the New World should be urban. Some of these cities, like Havana and Cartagena and Panama, owed their importance to their position on the major trade routes between Spain and the American colonies. Some, like Potosí, long the largest city in the New World, were mining centers. Others, like Mexico City and Lima and Santiago de Chile, were primarily political and ecclesiastical capitals, to which much of the wealth of their tributary regions inevitably gravitated. Still others, like Concepción, Chuquisaca (now Sucre), and Mendoza, were essentially frontier outposts. In Brazil, Bahia and Pernambuco in the north and Rio de Janeiro in the south long remained the only important centers of population.

The physical pattern of most Spanish colonial cities was as uniform as the topography of their sites would permit. The model prescribed by law provided for a checkerboard street plan that was very different from the aimless meanderings so characteristic of city streets in the peninsula. The heart of the city was always the central plaza around which were grouped the principal public buildings, such as the palace of government and the cathedral. Here the citizens promenaded daily, as they still do in most Spanish-American cities, exchanging news and small talk and exhibiting their charms and their finery. Except for the churches of the later period, the architecture was heavy and substantial, with little effort at exterior ornamentation. The houses of the well-to-do, good examples of which may still be seen in a few places like Cuzco, had a fortress-like appearance. Massive doors opened through thick walls into patios or gardens, around which the life of the house revolved, as it had in the half-Moorish cities of Andalusia. Not only did this style of building serve to guard the privacy of the family, which Spaniards have always cherished, but it was a protection in times of disorder, and in the more tropical cities, like Cartagena, it moderated the excessive midday heat.

At the top of colonial society was the small class of royal officials and their families, which served as the retinue of the viceroy or governor-general. As peninsula-born Spaniards or Portuguese, they were proud and exclusive, conservative in their social customs and rigidly orthodox in all matters of religion. The real tone of social life in the cities was generally set by the creole, or colonial-born, families. There was liable to be much wealth in this large and important group, gained from mining or trade or from the landed properties of its members. The creoles were much given to display and a lavish way of life, so that there were frequent ups and downs in their fortunes. Social customs among them tended to be freer than among the more solemn arrivals from the homeland, who looked down upon them as provincials.

Between these members of the ruling race and the mass of Indians there grew up everywhere a large class of mestizos or mixed breeds. With leanings toward the dominant white minority, whose superior status they envied, this intermediate element in the population often gained a position of considerable influence in the community. Many of the skilled trades and small businesses were in their hands and they frequently held positions of responsibility in the service of the local aristocracy.

At the bottom of the social order were the descendants of the conquered races. The Indians furnished a cheap and docile supply of unskilled labor, which performed the multitude of menial tasks necessary for the support of an aristocratic social system. Their subordinate place in colonial society was unchangeable, except as the far-away crown might occasionally decree better treatment for them or an exceptional master display more humane consideration for the lot of his dependents. In the hot countries Negro slaves might take the places ordinarily held by the aborigines, or Negroes and Indians might exist side by side as virtual equals in the same community. In either case, special social problems arose as a result of the miscegenation which always occurred wherever the three races lived at close quarters with each other. The mulattoes and zambos, as the mixture of Indian and Negro were called, proved to be a more assertive and unmanageable element in the population than were the less mercurial mestizos, and tended to threaten the social peace on which the security of the colonial regime rested. In Brazil, the Indians were at first mercilessly hunted as slaves. Many committed suicide rather than submit to forced labor for the Portuguese colonists and the Indians generally proved to be an unsatisfactory labor force. The introduction of Negro slaves from the Portuguese colonies in Africa began very early, and the blacks soon became the very base of the plantation economy which prevailed in Brazil. By 1700, they already outnumbered the whites two to one in the colonial population and the position of the Portuguese overlords was several times threatened by local uprisings of the Negro slaves.

The original *conquistadores* had subsisted by raiding the larders of the subjugated peoples, but it was early found necessary to establish some more regular system of agriculture on which the growing Spanish settlements could depend for their food supply. As pacification proceeded, the Indians brought provisions into the towns from the surrounding country and sold them in the public markets that were always to remain a prominent feature of urban life in Latin America. Dependence for certain staples came to be placed on the larger farming operations carried on in connection with the landed estates of the conquerors.

The best farming lands were usually parceled out among the Spanish overlords under the system known as the *encomienda*, whereby the native occupants of the land remained on the soil in a situation bordering on serfdom, moderated in time to the slightly freer status of peonage. As a settled economy succeeded the more openly predatory conditions of the *Conquista*, some of the Spaniards settled on these large estates and personally oversaw their operation. Others left the management of the property to a major-domo, who was frequently a mestizo, and paid only occasional visits to their country places from the city. Thus, a pattern of landholding and agricultural development was set which has endured to the present in most Latin-American countries. Until the rise of the mining industry in the eighteenth century, Brazil was essentially a land of great plantations, devoted primarily to the cultivation of sugar cane, tobacco, cacao, rice, and cotton, and the raising of cattle, sheep, and hogs.

Almost from the beginning every colonizing expedition which left the peninsula carried with it seeds of the crops to which Spaniards and Portuguese were accustomed at home, and breeding stock of all the familiar domestic animals. This was a condition of most licenses granted by the crown for the exploration and colonization of the New World, and the requirement was early incorporated into the laws of the Indies. Europeans found in the Americas corn, potatoes, yams, manioc or yuca, cacao and tobacco, yerba maté or Paraguayan tea; they brought with them wheat, rice, sugar cane, and several varieties of beans. However, beans, an especially important item of diet among Brazilians and Mexicans, were grown by the Indians before the discovery of America by Europeans. Very late, coffee was introduced by way of French Guiana. Of fruits, the Spaniards and Portuguese introduced oranges, bananas, grapes, mangoes, coconuts, and a wide variety of other fruits native to Europe or the Orient. They found growing in the western hemisphere the pineapple, the papaya or Brazilian *mamão*, the nutritious avocado, and a number of other fruits whose cultivation is still largely restricted to Latin America. Previous to their conquest by Europeans, the inhabitants of the American continent had no domesticated animals which they killed for food. Their only meat supply was derived from game and from a few birds, like turkey, which they had learned to domesticate, but fish was an important item of diet in many regions. The only beast of burden, except for human beings, was the llama of the Andean lands. Though the llama had serious limitations as a cargo animal, it was too valuable for transport purposes and for its wool to be slaughtered regularly for its meat. Spaniards and Portuguese made no greater contribution to the original economy of the Americas than in the domestic animals which they introduced. These included the incalculable boon of horses, cattle, hogs, sheep, and poultry. It would be difficult to imagine Latin America without the donkey and the mule, whose arrival in the New World was almost contemporaneous with that of the first Spanish conquerors.

It is well known that gold and silver mining was the foundation of the industrial system established by Spain in the New World. The

Antilles yielded little of the precious metals, but the golden loot of the Aztec and Inca empires exceeded the wildest expectations of the Spanish conquerors. Gold continued to be produced by the Spaniards, and later by the Portuguese, but in the Spanish colonies silver early superseded gold in the value of its output. Potosí, in the high Andes, was probably the greatest mining center in all history, and its famous peak is said to have yielded over a billion dollars' worth of silver in the two centuries that followed the first "strike" in 1545. The rich silver mines of Zacatecas, Guanajuato, and Pachuca, in Mexico, were only second in importance to the South American bonanza. Though the existence of iron, copper, zinc, tin, and lead was known, the exploitation of these baser metals was neglected under the exaggerated spell which gold and silver cast over the Spaniards and their ever-needy rulers.

Silver held such an important place in the economy of the Spanish empire that the rich convoys which carried on trade between the ports of the Americas and Spain were known to foreigners as "plate fleets." One such fleet left Vera Cruz yearly with the proceeds of the Mexican mines and with other products of the northern viceroyalty. Another cleared from Cartagena on the Spanish Main at approximately the same time, laden with the year's shipments of Peruvian silver and any gold or South American merchandise consigned to the royal treasury or to private interests in the peninsula. The two fleets made a junction in the heavily guarded harbor of Havana, from where they departed with an escort of armed galleons for the port of Cadiz or of Seville.

Most of the cargo for the Cartagena fleet had been transported up the west coast of South America to Panama, from where it was portaged across the isthmus by mule trains to the point of transshipment at Portobello. It had originally proceeded from posts as far south as Valparaiso in Chile, and was made up of additional shipments loaded at other ports between Coquimbo and Guayaquil. Other ships brought to the rendezvous before the great fortifications of Cartagena lading from ports along the Spanish Main as far as Cumaná. In line with the prevailing commercial principles of the time and in order to safeguard the very substantial interests of the crown, the operation of this trade was regulated in minute detail. Individual trading voyages were discouraged as offering an opening for smugglers and threatening the strict government control which was made possible by the system of trading fleets. Isolated ships also offered too serious a temptation to piratical attacks, and for the greater safety of ships and cargoes the government imposed the arrangement of armed convoys. This plan remained in effect until more orderly times in the eighteenth century made the seas safer for trading ships. For much of the colonial period the Portuguese also resorted to a system of convoyed fleets in the conduct of their trade with Brazil. Government regulation of the trade was even more rigorous at its Spanish end. Here the *Casa de Contratación*, or House of Trade, took charge of the receipt and distribution of cargo, the levying of duties, and the manifold activities connected with the preparation of the fleet for its return voyage.

Exports to the colonies by way of the trading fleets consisted largely of manufactures, such as textiles, hardware, military supplies for the royal account, leather goods, equipment for the churches, olive oil, flour, and wines. Some of these were produced in the peninsula; others were of Flemish or Italian origin. Manufacturing was never developed to meet the needs of the colonial population, and Spanish policy used this dependence as a means of assuring its hold on its overseas empire. Whatever competition there was with goods imported through Cadiz and Seville came from Chinese and other Oriental products brought into Mexico by the Manila galleons and transshipped thence throughout the two viceroyalties. Intermittent smuggling operations, usually carried on by English or French traders with the connivance of the creoles, became an increasingly important factor in the trade of the colonies. The liberalizing of the commercial system in the later eighteenth century, which resulted in the opening of direct trading connections between Spain and a number of colonial ports hitherto supplied through Vera Cruz or Cartagena, was in part an answer to the problem created by these widespread smuggling activities. Probably the most illiberal feature of the old commercial regime had been the requirement that trade between Buenos Aires and Spain should be carried on by the long and roundabout land and sea route via Peru and Panama.

Concessions made by Spain to her colonies came too late and were too insubstantial to forestall the inevitable movement for independence. A number of forces were working toward separation from the mother country at the end of the eighteenth century. The creole class had become increasingly restive under the discriminations that were still in force against it in the colonial service. Meanwhile, the American-born families of Spanish blood had long since firmly established a dominant position in the economic life of the colonies. Some of their members had traveled in Europe, where they absorbed enough of the liberal thought then in vogue to make them question much of the traditional order at home. Now that the Inquisition had lost its dominion over the colonial mind, the books of the French philosophers found their way into creole circles, where they were eagerly read and started new currents of thought dangerous to the *status quo*. The successful revolt of the North American colonies of England provided a concrete example for those bold souls who had dreamed of independence. The French Revolution which followed it served to strengthen the convictions of the liberals in the colonies.

On the side of Spain were the habits and traditions of centuries, the inertia of the masses and the active support of the hierarchy of the Church, the entrenched power of colonial officialdom and its supporting garrisons, and the physical obstacles to a concerted revolt offered by the vast distances between the colonies. It was some comfort to the Spanish-American patriots that the leaders of the new North American republic gave their blessing to the separatist movement against Spain; England, which expected to profit from the opening of Spanish-American ports to world commerce, encouraged the colonial cause. When the absolutist powers of Europe, united in the Holy Alliance, were ready to come to the aid of Spain in recovering her rebellious colonies, it was too late. For the Monroe Doctrine, made effective by the tacit support of English seapower, prevented their active intervention in the affairs of the New World.

The first local conspiracies and outbreaks against the Spanish government were ruthlessly suppressed by the royal authorities. However, events in the peninsula following on the occupation of Spain by the armies of Napoleon offered a more favorable opportunity to the better-organized movements which followed these abortive attempts. Paradoxically, by some quixotic survival of loyalty to the crown, some of these movements were undertaken in the name of Ferdinand VII, most reactionary of the Bourbon kings, who was then a prisoner of the French emperor. On his restoration to the throne, the benighted king moved to put down the too independent manifestation of his overseas subjects and thereby clarified in their minds the issue of independence.

The *Independencia* was not a unified struggle, undertaken simultaneously and with a common understanding by the widely separated colonies. There was no general pattern of revolt and no coordination of action by the various groups of revolutionaries. Geographically, there were four major phases of the revolt, to be merged ultimately in three distinct fields of operation. One was the country along the Spanish Main, comprising Venezuela and the vice-kingdom of New Granada, now Colombia. Another was the west coast of South America, whose provinces had been politically subject to the viceregal government in Peru. A third was the River Plate lands centering on Buenos Aires. Finally, Mexico and the satellite regions of Central America constituted an isolated field of rebellion. As the larger movement progressed, the west coast lost its separate identity, and the northern portion, including Peru and the Quito country, was brought within the sphere of Bolívar's activities, which were based on New Granada and Venezuela. At the same time the old captaincy-general of Chile was linked to the Argentine provinces in a common effort under the leadership of San Martín.

In most parts of Spanish America the wars of independence lasted many years, during which the patriots suffered frequent reverses and setbacks before the final attainment of their aims. Miranda's ill-fated rising in Venezuela took place in 1806. Miguel Hidalgo, parish priest of the town of Dolores, raised the standard of revolt in Mexico four years later. The same year, a group of Argentine creoles under the leadership of Manuel Belgrano overthrew the viceregal government in Buenos Aires, though independence from Spain was not formally proclaimed until 1816. Mexico did not gain its independence until 1821, and the last serious resistance of the royalist forces in Peru was not broken until late in 1824, while the Spanish garrison of Callao, the port of Lima, held out until January, 1826.

Whatever unity there was in the long struggles for independence was provided by the masterly leadership of Simón Bolívar. Though this extraordinary figure was directly responsible for the liberation of only five of the ten original Spanish-American republics—Venezuela, Colombia, Ecuador, Peru, and Bolivia—his example exerted a great influence over the movement from Mexico to Chile. His virtual apotheosis by later generations of Spanish Americans is recognition of the supreme importance of his services in the creation of a new political order in the other Americas.

Bolívar was a young Venezuelan aristocrat who threw in his fortunes with the movement which had been initiated by the older Miranda. For fifteen years he waged a relentless war against the Spaniards, undaunted by reverses that repeatedly destroyed or scattered his armies. By 1819 his position was sufficiently strong to undertake a decisive campaign for the liberation of Colombia. With a nucleus of hardened veterans of many battles and the addition of a large body of English and Irish soldiers of fortune, he crossed the Andes from Venezuela by one of the boldest strokes in military history and completely defeated the royalist forces on the field of Boyacá. Two years later he recrossed the mountains and repeated his success at the Battle of Carabobo, which sealed the deliverance of his homeland from Spain. Made head of a new state composed of Venezuela and Colombia, he then turned his attention to the liberation of the old viceroyalty of Peru, which was still a stronghold of Spanish power. His able lieutenant, José Antonio de Sucre, one of the noblest characters in the history of Latin America, cleared Ecuador of the royalists with the aid of Argentine troops sent from Peru by San Martín.

It was at this juncture of his career that the two main currents of the *Independencia* met. José de San Martín was an Argentine creole who had gained considerable reputation in the military service of Spain when he assumed the leadership of the patriot cause in the River Plate provinces. A man of great dignity and serenity of character, without the dramatic qualities of Bolívar, he had a genius for organization. He recognized that the independence of Argentina could only be assured if the Spaniards were driven out of Chile and Peru, and to that end he trained and disciplined an international army in the western part of the country. When his preparations had been completed, he moved his army over the high passes of the Andes and overwhelmed the royalists at the Battle of Chacabuco near Santiago. Bernardo O'Higgins, a Chilean patriot who had collaborated in the joint enterprise, was proclaimed head of the new Republic of Chile.

After further military operations had secured the independence of Chile, San Martín laid his plans for the invasion of Peru. On a fleet commanded by the Scotchman, Alexander Cochrane, he transported his army to the Peruvian coast in the neighborhood of Lima. Though he occupied the viceregal capital, the royalist position in the rest of the country proved too strong for him to overcome. From Peru he participated in the liberation of Ecuador, where he met Bolívar in a famous conference at Guayaquil. Shortly afterwards, San Martín withdrew to his native Argentina, leaving to the great Venezuelan the task of freeing Peru from the Spaniards.

A crisis had come in Bolívar's career as a soldier. For the royal forces outnumbered his own and were composed of seasoned and disciplined troops, and the loyalty of the population was everywhere doubtful. In August, 1824, he won a great, but inconclusive, cavalry battle on the high plain of Junín. A few months later the fate of Peru, and of South America, was determined by Sucre's decisive victory on the field of Ayacucho, fought over two miles above the sea. Significant of the end of an epoch—among the prisoners taken was La Serna, last of the viceroys. All that remained to complete Bolívar's triumph was to clear the Spanish forces from the lands beyond Lake Titicaca known as Upper Peru. This was shortly accomplished by the devoted Sucre, who became the first president of the republic that was named for his great chieftain.

In Lima Bolívar enjoyed a brief respite of glory. The long struggle for the liberation of South America was over. Ahead of Bolívar and of the young nations whom he and other patriot leaders had freed lay another task, as difficult as that which was now ended. A political order had to be erected to take the place of the regime under which Spanish America had lived for three centuries. To meet this gigantic problem, there was, on one side, a slate wiped clean by the thoroughness of the patriot victories, a great fund of idealism and militant patriotism, the momentarily dominant personality of Bolívar, and the good will of the United States and England; on the other was an almost total absence of political experience, the lack of a literate and independent electorate schooled in self-government, who might give stability to the new republics during the period of adjustment, an aristocratic economic system, widespread habits of disorder and violence engendered by the long wars, a welter of local interests jealous of all unifying authority, and the personal ambitions now released after long repression in the common effort for independence. The odds against a peaceful and orderly transition to a settled republican order were overwhelming.

It was against these conditions that Bolívar broke the remnants of his mighty strength, to write in his final despair, "All who have served the Revolution have ploughed the sea," and to die, worn out and disillusioned, at forty-seven. In the five years that were left to him after the triumphs of his Peruvian campaign he had labored to construct a political system adapted to the peculiar genius and traditions of the peoples whom he had liberated. The prestige of his name did not avail against the forces of dissolution that gathered increasing strength around him. Some of his ablest lieutenants, like Santander and Córdova and Paez, chieftain of the Venezuelan plainsmen, rose against him. Sucre, harassed by revolution, resigned his office in Bolivia, to be murdered a few years later. The Quito country seceded from his Republic of Gran Colombia, to set up the independent state of Ecuador, and the Peruvians drove his government from Lima. Meanwhile, far away to the south San Martín had retired to France from the dissensions of the new republic by the River Plate and the ingratitude of the people he had served so unselfishly. On the other side of the Andes, O'Higgins, first president of Chile, had been driven from power and taken refuge in Peru. In Mexico, an officer of the royal army, Agustín de Iturbide, who had freed the country from Spain by forming a combination with the patriot forces, had had himself proclaimed emperor, only to end his opportunist career in exile and to make place for the fantastic adventures of Antonio López de Santa Anna. The political stage of Spanish America was set for the familiar cycle of revolution and anarchy and dictatorship.

In the latter part of the eighteenth century, whatever active sentiment there was among Brazilians for independence from Portugal was confined to a small group of creoles who were in touch with liberal political philosophies and movements in France and the United States. A plot headed by a versatile dentist and engineer, Joaquim José da Silva Xavier, known to the Brazilians as Tiradentes, or "the tooth puller," was revealed to the royal authorities and its leader executed in 1792.

When Brazilian independence came, it was by peaceful methods and as the result of a chain of circumstances connected with the fortunes of the ruling dynasty in Portugal. In 1807, a French army under Marshal Junot occupied Lisbon and seized the country for Napoleon. The Portuguese royal family fled to Brazil, where it set up the seat of the monarchy. When the King, João VI, returned to Portugal in 1821, he left as Regent his 21-year-old son, Dom Pedro. The issue of independence was precipitated shortly afterwards, when the young Regent refused to obey an order from the court at Lisbon to return to Portugal. The rather grandiloquent cry of "Independence or death!" which Dom Pedro uttered on the banks of the Ypiranga near São Paulo was really the announcement of an accomplished fact. The date, September 7, 1822, is still celebrated by Brazilians as the anniversary of their independence. The following month the defiant young Regent, secure in the support of creole opinion, was proclaimed Constitutional Emperor of Brazil as Pedro I.

Part III

THE PEOPLE

25252525252525252525252525252525252525252525252525252525252525252525252525

I N VERY round numbers, the population of Latin America in mid-
1962 was probably 200,000,000, or about ten percent larger than
that of the United States. Most of the twenty figures which make up
this total are "official estimates" and therefore of doubtful credibility.
Such estimates are arrived at by a progressive annual addition to the
base figure, taking into consideration the balance of births and deaths
and of immigration and emigration. After a long period without a
census to serve as a new index base, these estimates sometimes get out
of hand and are then pared down for a fresh start, as happened with
the official Brazilian estimates a few years ago. Though more faith
can be placed in the occasional censuses of population, such as were
held in 1960, even the results of these enumerations may leave much
to be desired in the way of accuracy. In the Indian countries, for example, a large part of the population generally live in places that are
not easily accessible, and, moreover, are liable to consider any counting
of heads by the government as preliminary to the levying of taxes or
the forced recruiting of soldiers. In these respects, population figures
from Argentina are much more dependable than those of Bolivia or

Ecuador. In some countries, the last census was taken so long ago and was of such questionable reliability that it no longer has any validity as a point from which to calculate subsequent estimates of the population. Two or three countries have never taken a real census of their population. Due to the infrequency and irregularity of censuses, a sound base is generally lacking for charting population trends.[1]

In spite of the present inadequacy of statistical data, considerable progress has been made in recent years in setting up statistical departments with more exacting standards of certitude. In international conferences of government statisticians steps have been taken toward agreement on greater uniformity in the basic terms and concepts. For example, there has been so much diversity in the classification of populations according to color or race that, not only are the usual figures on the relative numbers of whites, Indians, and mixed-breeds unreliable, but there exists no common denominator on which comparisons or totals embracing more than one country might be based. The various countries disagree widely on the definition of "white" and "Negro" and "Indian," and of "mestizo" and "mulatto." The tendency is to consider as white anyone whose skin is light and whose features are European. In most localities a quadroon would be classified as white, and in all countries an octoroon would certainly be placed in that category. The same liberal interpretation is generally followed in the case of mixtures of white and Indian. Also, in drawing the line between Negro and mulatto, and between Indian and mestizo, any benefit of the doubt is to the advantage of mixed blood. While the official statistics of most Latin-American countries, as they pertain to population and economic matters, still lack exactness and completeness, as reasonable approximations they adequately serve the purpose of giving a very general picture of conditions.

---

[1] As a rule, Latin Americans lack a sense of numerical precision, with the result that the national statistical services are likely to suffer from a general disregard of accuracy. The frequency with which Latin Americans qualify a statement of numerable fact with the phrase *mas o menos*—"more or less"—is indicative of a certain looseness of thought wherever figures are involved. Anyone who has traveled in the interior of Latin America and has inquired of a native the distance to the next town will recall the "near" or "far" he received for answer, and how, if he insisted on greater exactness, the distance was almost uniformly "two leagues." For two leagues is a short ride, and the tired stranger is liable to push on and annoy one no further with demands for mathematical details.

Of the estimated total population of 200,000,000, South America accounts for approximately 70 percent, Mexico and Central America for approximately 24 percent, and the three West Indian republics for about 6 percent. Brazil, as fecund as she is colossal, has within her borders approximately half the population of the South American continent. Of European nations only Russia has more people. Only seven countries in the world exceed it in population. Mexico has 35,000,000 people, or more than Spain. Argentina, with a population of about 21,000,000, has more inhabitants than Canada. Colombia has about the combined population of Denmark, Norway, and Sweden, and Peru has about as many people as Australia. Cuba, Venezuela, and Chile are in the 7–8,000,000 category. Panama and Costa Rica, least populous of the republics, rank with Libya and Togo.

The rate of population increase in Latin America is probably the highest of any major area of the world—higher even than in eastern Asia. The over-all growth rate is about half again as high as in the United States. However, there is little uniformity in the national rates, which vary from 1.2 percent in Haiti to 4 percent in Costa Rica. Of the three largest countries, Argentina has an annual net increase of about 1.9 percent, only a little higher than that of the United States. Brazil's increase rate is 2.4 percent and Mexico's 2.9.

The factors involved in these calculations—the spread between crude birth and death rates—may occasionally have a considerable margin of error that is liable to occur in the field of vital statistics, with the result that many births and deaths are not registered at all. The basic elements are abnormal fecundity, unrestrained by concerted programs of "birth control," the conditions of marriage, or economic realities; infant mortality rates, which in Chile are five times those of the United States, and in Brazil, seven times; and, generally, low life expectancy. The variables are important, and, for example, life expectancy rates may be almost as high as in the United States—or little more than half as high. Another resultant of a genetic process which is out of hand is the circumstance that in most of Latin America the majority of the population in under 19 years of age. Typical of this age grouping are Brazil, Mexico, and Venezuela, where the population of children and "teen-agers" is about forty percent higher than in the United States. The economic, political, and social consequences of this ill-balanced ratio of age composition are very great. Among other effects, the heavy burden of providing for so large and growing an unproductive segment of the population may tend to nullify the gains of whatever economic progress is made from year to year. Yet with the exception of some of the smaller republics, Latin America is still greatly under-populated. The heaviest concentration of population is in Haiti and in El Salvador. The largest grouping of people is in certain well-defined and limited areas. In Brazil, it is a comparatively narrow coastal belt which extends from the State of Maranhão, with a break of low popula-tion in southern Bahia and northern Espirito Santo, to the southern limits of the republic. In the south the area expands westward up on-to the highlands of Minas Gerais and São Paulo, to narrow again on the plateau of Paraná. The center of Brazil's population lies to the south-east of Belo Horizonte in the State of Minas Gerais. In Argentina, the heaviest distribution of inhabitants is in the northern Province of Tucumán and in the rich agricultural region of the pampa. This rela-tively well-peopled area reaches well up the west side of the Paraná into the Province of Sante Fé and across into the Argentine Mesopo-tamia, lying between the two great confluents of the River Plate, and thence eastward into the Banda Oriental of Uruguay.

On the west coast of South America, Chile's densest population is in the favored Central Valley, with minor concentrations around a few southerly cities. In Bolivia, Peru, and Ecuador, the bulk of the inhabitants dwell in the old Inca lands of the high Sierra country, where protected valleys and the plateau floor between the Andean ranges offer sites for an intensive agriculture or for the grazing of flocks. In Peru, there are secondary concentrations of considerable population in the oasis of Arequipa, the irrigated district about Trujillo, and the valley of the Rimac in the neighborhood of Lima. Colombia's heaviest density of population is found in isolated regions of the central plateau of Cundinamarca, such as the *Sabana* of Bogotá, the valley of the Cauca, and the lands tributary to the important city of Medellín. In Venezuela, the most thickly settled area is in the highland zone that extends from the vicinity of Caracas west of Valencia and thence in a southwesterly direction toward the main chain of the northern Andes.

In Central America, over ninety percent of the population is settled in the upland belt of the interior and among the foothills on the Pacific side. Except in localities where the large-scale cultivation of bananas is carried on, the population of the low jungle-covered plain along the Caribbean is negligible in quantity. Panama is the exception to the rule among the other Central American countries in that most of its inhabitants are found along the two coasts or in close proximity to them. While there are many widely separated localities of relatively high population density throughout most of Mexico, as in the fine valley of Jalisco about Guadalajara, the largest of such areas is in the heart of the central plateau and surrounding the federal capital.

In extent the thinly populated parts of Latin America exceed by many times the districts where there is a reasonably heavy population. Except where it spreads out over the wide Argentine plain, population tends to cling to the coasts or to the inland valleys and tablelands among the mountains. With few exceptions, the frontiers between the republics run through a wilderness and the centers of national population are usually remote from one another. The whole interior of South America east of the Andes and north of the Tropic of Capricorn probably has fewer inhabitants than the island of Puerto Rico, though the difference in size is nearly a thousand-fold. This enormous hinterland of millions of square miles includes the tropical forest of Amazonia as far as the vicinity of Belém, the valley of the Orinoco, and the upper basin of the Paraguay. Patagonia, behind the narrow belt of coast settlement, and including the southern Andes below the region of the Chilean lakes and the islands below Puerto Montt, is another very large area of thinly diffused population.

Latin America has ten cities of over a million inhabitants, or twice as many as the United States. Four of them—Rio de Janeiro, São Paulo, Mexico City, and Buenos Aires—have a population of over 3,000,000 each, and comprise one-sixth of the world's largest cities. The six other cities with more than a million people are Havana, Santiago, Bogotá, Lima, Caracas, and Montevideo—all national capitals. There are eight cities of between 500,000 and 1,000,000. Considering the circumstances that the Latin-American countries are essentially producers of raw materials, the prevailing ratio of urban to rural population is unhealthily large in many of the republics. In nearly every country, the rate of growth of the cities has greatly exceeded that of the country as a whole. During the past decade this trend has been so accentuated that acute shortages of housing, water, electricity, and food have developed in several cities. Due to the weakness of the Spaniards for city life and their failure to make country life more attractive, urbanization has proceeded faster than would be justified by the state of economic development, even in regions where there is a substantial growth of manufacturing. As a consequence, most of the republics carry an excessive overhead in their cities. Since the cities live indirectly from the product of the soil or the subsoil, the inordinate drain on the resources of the country districts not only depresses the net return from agriculture and mining, but tends to make more precarious the livelihood of the urban population. However, the disparity in terms of relative standards of living as between city and country is even greater than is indicated by comparative figures of urban and rural population.

In Uruguay, which is largely a pastoral country, Montevideo has over one-third of the inhabitants of the republic. The population of Buenos Aires, a city of some 6,000,000 people, is out of all sound proportion to the total population of Argentina, but the wide disparity between its wealth and living standards and those of the interior of the republic is an even unhealthier condition. The ratio of city population to the population of the country is much lower in Brazil, where the nation's cities of over 100,000 have only about 14 percent of the total. The State of Minas Gerais, with about 7,000,000 people, has only one city—Belo Horizonte—of over 100,000. With a high ratio of rural population of over 70 percent, Brazil in fact lacks enough cities to provide the needed centers for her economic and cultural life. Sixty percent of all Chileans and half of all Cubans are classified as "urban."

According to the predominant racial element in the population, the twenty Latin-American republics may be grouped in five distinct ethnic patterns. However, the degree to which any particular element predominates is neither uniform as between countries nor fixed in any one of them. For miscegenation, immigration, and other factors, such as relative birth and death rates, may appreciably alter the ethnic grouping within a few decades. Thus, the Indian countries tend to become progressively mesticized as cross-breeding continues, and wherever the Negro is an important factor in the population the development of a mulatto group, lighter skinned and more numerous with each generation, proceeds apace.

Three countries, Argentina, Uruguay, and Costa Rica, can be classified as "white." The first two are overwhelmingly so, and their percentage of white population is considerably higher than in the United States. Five countries are predominantly Indian in their racial composition. In descending order of the ratio of Indian blood to the total population, they probably rank as follows: Guatemala, Bolivia, Ecuador, Peru, Mexico. All have a large number of mixed breeds, in which the Indian prevails. The Indian population of Guatemala may be conservatively estimated at from 60 to 70 percent of the total. Of the three Andean countries, nearly 60 percent of the population of Bolivia is Indian, and at least 30 percent consists of *cholos* or mixed breeds. While the ratio of full-blood Indians in Ecuador is lower—between 30 and 40 percent—the percentage of mestizos is over half the population. In Peru, the respective proportion of Indians and mixed breeds is around 50 and 35 percent, and in Mexico it is approximately in the reverse order of that of Peru. The Haitian masses are Negroes, but the ruling class largely consists of a minority of mulattoes.

The countries in which the mestizos, or mixture of whites and Indians, comprise the majority of the population are Honduras, Nicaragua, El Salvador, Colombia, Venezuela, Chile, and Paraguay. In Chile, there is a numerically large and important minority of pure whites, and the prevailing blood strain of the lower classes, who are a product of very remote cross-breeding, is white. In Honduras and Paraguay, the mass of the population consists of well-mixed cross-breeds.

In Panama, Negro blood is widespread. The mixture of white and black in Cuba has also proceeded so far since the early introduction of Negro slavery into the island that, however light their complexion, many of the old families could not pass a test of *puro sangre*. However, the large immigration of north Spaniards during the past fifty years has done much to strengthen the relative numerical position of the white element in the Cuban population.

Around the low shores of the Caribbean mixtures of Indian and Negro, generally known as zambos, are common. The so-called Mosquito region of Honduras and Nicaragua is peopled with this hybrid race, members of which are also frequently encountered in Panama. In the Colombian and Venezuelan littoral, along the Spanish Main, are many descendants of the early interbreeding of Carib Indians and renegade Negro slaves. There is, in fact, much Negro blood throughout the coastal zone of the Caribbean. In Central America it has been introduced largely by latecomers from the British West Indies; elsewhere the African element in the population dates from the colonial period. Negroes and mulattoes are also found in considerable numbers along the hot Ecuadorean coast and in the irrigated sugar and cotton districts of Peru.

By its very size Brazil represents a variety of ethnic groups that defy uniform cataloguing of the national population. An estimate made in 1922 by the National Museum classified the Brazilian population as follows: white, 51 percent; Negro, 14 percent; mulatto, 22 percent; mestizo, 11 percent; and Indian, 2 percent. This grouping clearly followed the accepted Brazilian formula of giving wide latitude to the category of whites. A narrower interpretation of terms would probably give the relative proportions as approximately 40 percent white, 15 percent Negro, 35 percent mulatto, 9 percent mestizo, and 1 percent Indian. One authority estimates the proportion of the various racial elements in the blood of the Brazilian population as follows: white, 45 percent; Negro, 30 percent; Indian, 24 percent; Japanese, 1 percent. The four southernmost States of Rio Grande do Sul, Santa Catarina, Paraná, and São Paulo are overwhelmingly white. This circumstance was originally due to the temperate climate of the highlands that extend south of Capricorn, and which precluded the growing of sugar cane, that traditional base of slavery in Latin America. While Negro slavery existed on the Paulista plateau, it never formed the foundation of the local economy, as it did on the hot lowlands of the upper coast. Some of the liberated slaves moved down to the more congenial climate of the narrow coastal plain below the Serra do Mar, where they joined others of their race who had been settled there long before. As farther south into the littoral of Santa Catarina, miscegenation has produced a noticeable admixture of mulattoes. The crossbreeding of the early Portuguese settlers with the Indians, which formed the famous *mameluco* stock in the uplands of São Paulo and which went on widely during the colonial period, has long since resulted in the complete assimilation of the aboriginal element, so that evidences of Indian blood are rare below the tenth parallel. Heavy European immigration into southern Brazil under the republic has speeded up the process of breeding the characteristic features of the colored races out of the population.

A similar process has gone on in the city of Rio de Janeiro, in which the blacks were numerous during the empire. Through widespread miscegenation the descendants of the Carioca slaves have appreciably lightened in color, and mulattoes are very common among the laboring class of Rio. As during the colonial period, the Portuguese have little color prejudice, and immigrants from the mother country often form households with colored women. There is little public sentiment anywhere in Brazil against the mixture of the races, though white blood is a distinct social asset in the aristocracy. Many mulattoes have held high places in the government of the republic and in the army, though not in the navy. In their desire to avoid a race question the Brazilians follow a thoroughgoing policy of assimilation of all the various ethnic elements that make up the population of the country.

While a large part of the inhabitants of the populous and important State of Minas Gerais are of fairly unmixed Portuguese ancestry, the colored element is very much in evidence in the rural districts. In the coastal States of Rio de Janeiro and Espírito Santo the mulatto admixture is especially prominent, as it is in the lower belt of states along the northeastern bulge of the country, which include Pernambuco, Alagoas, and Sergipe. This zone of maritime states was the original seat of the Brazilian sugar industry, whose labor force was largely recruited in the Portuguese colonies in Africa. The introduction of African slaves into Brazil continued for over three centuries, until the gradual suppression of the trade after 1850. Miscegenation proceeded actively throughout the period, with the result that the population of the coastal states within the tropical zone of Brazil became predominantly mulatto. More than the rest, the States of Bahia and Rio de Janeiro have retained their Negro character. The ratio of black blood to white in the city of Salvador is probably the highest of any large city in the world. Salvador differs from the city of Pernambuco, or Recife, and from Rio de Janeiro in that Negroes are a common sight on its streets and have maintained their identity as a distinct social group in the local population. Since the abolition of slavery the north coast states have drawn only a very small part of the European immigration into Brazil. However, the assimilation of the Negro continues rapidly in those states.

Above the latitude of Recife Negroes and mulattoes comprise a considerable part of the population, but the original Indian element becomes increasingly important, especially in the States of Ceará and Piauí. In these states Indian features are common among the people, who also have certain characteristics of temperament which differentiate them from the predominantly mulatto population to the southward. In the two enormous, but thinly populated, States of Pará and Amazonas the Indian element is very prominent, either in its pure condition among the tribal Indians or in the various degree of mixture with whites and blacks. To a somewhat lesser extent, this is also true of the huge interior States of Goiás and Mato Grosso. In Amazonas and the remote Acre Territory, a considerable immigration of the hardy Cearenses, or mestizos from the drought-ridden State of Ceará, has given a special quality to the ethnic make-up of the population.

In view of all this diversity, it is too early to expect the appearance of a definite Brazilian racial type. The process of miscegenation, which is the decisive force working toward the eventual creation of such a type, is still very incomplete. The various trends in the ethnic evolution of Brazil have also operated unevenly, so that relative stability of the population elements is much nearer in some regions of the country than in others. Due to differences of climate and other circumstances, an absolutely uniform racial pattern is no more likely to evolve in Brazil than in the United States. However, the development of a population with certain well-recognized and common physical and mental characteristics is clearly under way. The core of the national type is white—the original Portuguese, conditioned by long residence in its New World environment and subjected to the special influences of other European stocks who have migrated to Brazil. Due to its superior absorptive power, it may safely be assumed that the white element will prevail in the determination of the color and basic qualities of the final resultant of the assimilative processes now at work. Brazilians recognize this principle, which they call *branqueamento*, or "bleaching"—and sometimes "Aryanization"— as the crux of the trend toward complete ethnic unity. Of the minor ethnic strains, the Negro represents the most important problem in molding the racial amalgam of the Brazilian people. His blood already pervades the collective body of the nation, and he has contributed much to shape the national character in the present stage of its evolution. He appears destined to disappear altogether as a separate racial factor in the country and eventually to merge his identity, through progressive cross-breeding, with the nuclear white element in the population. The Indians are a less numerous and relatively passive element in the intermingling of races in Brazil. Wherever their absorption has continued over a long period, they have generally left few recognizable traces in the mixture, unless their original numbers approximated those of the whites, as in parts of the northeastern *sertão* country.

An interesting phase of population movement in Latin America is the migrations from one country to another. While the total volume of this intra-American migration is not heavy, it is sufficiently large to constitute a significant trend in the relations between the various republics. Sometimes there is a reciprocal movement across a particular frontier, but it is generally a one-way current of population, promoted by superior opportunities which exist on one side of a border. Thus, Argentines from the Province of Corrientes are common in southern Paraguay, as Paraguayan *vaqueros* are on the cattle ranches of Mato Grosso in western Brazil. Many Uruguayans cross into the Brazilian State of Rio Grande do Sul and the Argentine Province of Entre Rios, and there is always a certain amount of movement in the opposite direction. Chileans, who are probably the most restless of South American peoples, have long been in the habit of crossing the low passes of the Andes in search of work in southern Argentina. Though the movement has largely ceased with the decline of the Brazilian rubber industry, hardy Peruvian *caucheros*, or hunters of the *Hevea brasiliensis* tree, opened up much of the Brazilian jungle by their far-flung wanderings. On the other hand, many Brazilians left the Acre Territory to settle in the neighboring Bolivian Territory of Colonias. It was these same bold pioneers who, by a process of infiltration similar to that by which the Americans acquired Texas from Mexico, originally won the Acre country from Bolivia. In North America there has been a certain amount of migration between Mexico and Guatemala and from Nicaragua into the Guanacaste region of Costa Rica. In the Antilles, while the Haitians who were formerly brought into Cuba for the cane-cutting season were required to be repatriated at the end of the *zafra*, considerable numbers of them managed to remain in the eastern Province of Oriente. Also, many Haitians have moved from their own over-crowded country into the Dominican Republic, where a few years ago they were reported to have been subjected to mistreatment by the Dominican authorities.

Much more than in the United States, the Indian is an ethnic and social factor to be reckoned with in most of Latin America. His relative numbers are greater and his racial traditions generally more deep-rooted and persistent. He constitutes an actual majority of the population in several of the republics, and through extensive miscegenation with the whites, he has often exercised a profound influence in forming a national type.

For a long time the republican governments had no fixed Indian policy. Many of the abuses of the colonial regime continued after independence, but without the restraining hand of the crown, which ever since the era of Las Casas and "the New Laws" had at least moderated the worst features of Indian exploitation. The Catholic mission system, which had protected the natives in many localities by bringing them under the direct tutelage of the Church, had been disrupted by the expulsion of the Jesuits from the Spanish dominions in 1767 and by the disorders of the wars of independence. Peonage, often bordering on a condition of slavery, was the frequent lot of the Indian during most of the nineteenth century.

The survivors of the aboriginal peoples of Latin America can be conveniently grouped in two quite distinct categories: the sedentary Indians of the Andean countries, and of Mexico and Guatemala; and the tribal Indians of the tropical forest and the remote south of the continent. The former are more numerous. They live in settled communities and are the heirs of comparatively advanced indigenous civilizations of pre-Columbian times. They belong to a few great lingual stocks, with certain well-defined ethnic affinities among the members of each of these families. The extent of their dispersal within historic times is often indicated by the occurrence of widely scattered place names.

In Mexico, a large number of separate idioms and dialects have been classified by anthropologists in a very few lingual groups. Most of the Indian peoples of the central plateau are branches of the Nahua race, whose most important representative is the Aztec nation. In a wide belt to the north of the Anahuac highlands, that are the home of the Nahuatl stock, dwell the Otomis, who never developed as high a social organization as the Indians to the south. In the warmer lands of Oaxaca and beyond, where the plateau falls down towards the Isthmus of Tehuantepec, are the Zapotecs, one of the most attractive, physically and culturally, of all Indian peoples. Outstanding product of this remarkable race was Benito Juárez, president of the Mexican Republic. In the Yucatán peninsula, and extending into the neighboring

States of Campeche, Tabasco, and Chiapas, and thence down into Guatemala, are the descendants of the famous Mayan race. Among other less numerous groups in Mexico are the Tarascans of Michoacán, found in their most typical and highest form about Lake Patzcuaro.

In South America, the two principal linguistic families are the Quechua and the Aymará, which occupy the old Inca lands of the Andean plateau region. Quechua is spoken by millions of Indians in Ecuador, the Peruvian *Sierra* country, and over much of Bolivia, and Aymará is the speech of large numbers of Indians who inhabit the country about Lake Titicaca and the Bolivian *planalto* to well beyond La Paz. The Chibchas, whom the Spanish conquerors found on the plateau of Colombia, have been largely assimilated into the body of the Colombian people. Whereas the Araucanian people formerly occupied most of central Chile, the remnants of the race are now confined to the country south of the Bio-Bio River, which empties into the Pacific near Concepción.

Between Sonora and Tierra del Fuego there are several hundred groups of the second category of Indians. In many cases their ethnic and linguistic relationships have not been established, while others, as in Brazil, are recognized as members of such widely dispersed stocks as the Tupi-Guarani. When the Portuguese reached South America, this speech prevailed as a *lingua franca* among the Indians who inhabited the coast lands from a little above the mouth of the River Plate to that of the Amazon. In the interior of Brazil, beyond a wide belt of Tapuya stock, are large islands of Tupi-Guarani peoples, one of which reaches down into Paraguay, where Guarani is still the speech of the mestizo population, and across the Paraná into the Argentine Province of Corrientes. Familiar Tupi words and place names are encountered throughout this vast territory. Among them are *paraná* (river), *i* (water), and the common suffixes, *guaçu* (large) and *mirim* (small). In northern South America, and reaching well under the Equator in places, are widely scattered groups of peoples who have a lingual connection with either the Carib or Arawak families of the Spanish Main and the islands to the north of the Caribbean Coast. The diminishing tribes who inhabit southern Patagonia and Chile have a common lingual bond, even though with wide variations, in the Tehuelche language.

The many tribes of "savage" Indians differ widely in habitat, numbers, physical appearance, and degree of cultural advancement. The typical Indian of this category lives deep in the tropical forest. Among tribes living under these conditions are the Chamulas, of Mexico, the Xavantes, of Brazil, the Motilones, of northern Colombia, and the interesting Jíbaros, of Ecuador. However, the miserable Seris exist on the barren island of Tiburón in the Gulf of California, and the tribes of inner Patagonia live on the bleak moors that rise to the foothills of the cold southern range of the Andes. The wretched Indians of the remote archipelago in the south of Chile pass their existence in exposure to one of the most inhospitable environments on earth. Many tribes are dwindling in numbers. This may be due to a declining supply of game, to pestilences contracted from contact with the whites, or to inter-tribal wars. Though the birth rate is generally high among the forest Indians, a correspondingly high infant mortality may threaten the very survival of the group if to it is added one of the three factors listed above.

Whereas a few of the wild tribes have taken the first steps out of a state of "barbarism," most of them have shown little inclination or capacity for change. They are by nature socially conservative and cling tenaciously to their traditional folkways. The customary working of their minds and all their normal sensory reactions have been fixed by long adaptation to the peculiar milieu of the jungle. It sets the pattern of all their beliefs and attitudes so firmly that they are seldom willing to make more than very superficial concessions to the civilization of the white man when it encroaches on their habitat. While some groups live in settled communities and practice a rudimentary agriculture sufficient for their needs, others lead a nomadic existence, sometimes lower than that of the Stone Age, and move restlessly from place to place in search of game or fishing grounds. In spite of travelers' stories, there is very little cannibalism or even wanton killing on any considerable scale. Indian society is essentially static and, except for a few aggressive and predatory groups, the principal concern of its leaders is to conserve the tribe intact against the forces, tangible or unseen, that menace its precarious existence. If it strikes blindly and with apparent cruelty at times, as in its infrequent raids on white settlements, it is usually out of a desperate fear for the preservation of its own corner of the jungle and of the primitive way of life that is so intimately associated with its dark recesses.

In the present century the governments of Latin America have shown an increasing interest in the welfare of their Indian peoples. Legislation has been passed for their protection, and sometimes, as in Mexico, special departments have been set up for the purpose of guarding the Indians against the abuses to which they are peculiarly subject. Sometimes these measures are dictated by considerations of pure humanitarianism or by a sentimental feeling for the Indian as a symbol of the country's more heroic past; at other times they have been prompted by more worldly arguments, such as a desire to perpetuate the civilized Indians as a necessary labor force or gradually to prepare the forest aborigines for a place in the national economy.

The movement to improve the condition of the Indians received considerable impetus from the exposure of the famous Putumayo "atrocities" in the early years of this century. The Huitoto Indians, who dwelt in the forests along the Putumayo River, were impressed into the service of a British-owned rubber company, whose operations were under Peruvian management. When stories reached the outside world of the cruelties inflicted on the enslaved Indians, the British government sent Roger Casement, then consul-general at Rio de Janeiro, to investigate the charges. Casement's revelations of conditions on the Putumayo and the findings of the subsequent official hearings caused widespread indignation and tended to arouse the conscience of Latin-American governments to the situation of their Indian wards. Similar conditions, though on a smaller scale and not so widely publicized, had existed in other parts of the Amazon valley during the rubber boom that followed the introduction of the automobile. There was much oppression of the Indians in the Beni country of Bolivia, along the Javari between Peru and Brazil, in the valley of the Purús in Brazil, and in the Venezuelan Amazonas under the local dictatorship of the notorious Tomás Funes. Meanwhile, the development of rubber plantations in the middle East and the consequent decline of the Amazonian wild rubber industry removed the incentive for the forced labor of the Indians, just as the production of synthetic indigo and the artificial cultivation of the cinchona tree in Asia and the American ban on the use of egret feathers freed other groups of South American Indians from virtual slavery.

Nowhere has the forest Indian of Latin America willingly entered the economic structure of the nation. He is unaccustomed to the sus-

tained effort and restraints on his personal liberty and tribal customs
that are inseparable from the condition of wage earner. If he is tricked
into such a state or tempted into debt slavery by his longing for some
of the white man's gadgets or finery, his spirit is either broken or becomes rebellious. It is only by a long and patient process of adaptation,
if at all, that he can ever be made an integral part of the national life
and accept the full responsibilities of membership in an industrial
society. Yet the alternative is almost certain to be eventual extinction,
or at least miscegenation with the whites and disappearance of all
tribal identity.

The Brazilian government has made some interesting experiments in the cultural assimilation of the Indian. Unlike the Andean
countries and Mexico, which have both types of Indian in their population, Brazil has only *Indios bravos*, or *bárbaros*, as they are known, in
contrast to the *Indios mansos*, or "tame" Indians of the west-coast
republics. Dozens of tribes are scattered through the vast forested
area of the interior from the Brazilian Guiana to Espírito Santo and
the western part of the State of São Paulo. Among the largest of these
groups are the Mundurucus and Nhambiquaras of Mato Grosso, the
Omaguas of Amazonas, the Parintintins of the Madeira basin, and the
Xavantes of the Araguaia country. Though no effort has naturally
ever been made to count the forest Indians of Brazil, their combined
numbers doubtless run into the hundreds of thousands.

The Brazilian government has established a special commission
whose purpose is the protection of the right of the Indian population.
The commission was long headed by General Cândido Rondon, the
famous explorer and companion of Theodore Roosevelt in his travels
in western Brazil. General Rondon was almost a full-blooded Indian,
and, therefore, had the initial advantage of an intimate understanding
of the ways and mentality of his charges. His first objective was to
gain the confidence of the tribesmen, who from past experience with
rubber gatherers, diamond hunters, and others of the ruling race, had
good reason to distrust the whites and mixed breeds. Rondon and his
agents also showed an active interest in the well-being of the Indians,
taking measures for the improvement of their health conditions and of
their living conditions in general. No attempt was made to break down
the tribal organization or to impose customs that were foreign to the
Indians' background, but, without any show of compulsion, the way

was opened to those who might wish to identify themselves with the life of the nation. The policy of the Brazilian Indian Service has been characterized by remarkable understanding of the Indian problem and it has been carried out with a rare combination of humaneness and practical sense. Though the activities of the Service were originally confined to the State of Mato Grosso, they have since been extended to other parts of the interior where similar conditions existed.

Catholic friars, continuing the missionary tradition of early times, have also accomplished a great deal of excellent work on behalf of the Brazilian Indians. Their missions are stationed on several of the larger tributaries of the Amazon and at points on the main river itself, from which the priests travel far and wide among the Indian settlements. Though the mind of the primitive Indian is not susceptible to any but the most elementary religious teachings, the missionaries administer medical care to the savages and also strive to hold in check some of the more violent manifestations of the native character. However, they often show a disposition to meddle with some of the more harmless customs of the Indian, such as their habit of going naked. In other South American countries, including Colombia, Venezuela, Peru, and Chile, the Catholic missions have also been an important factor in the movement for the protection of the aboriginal population. In some instances the Church has been officially designated as the representative of the state in its dealings with the Indians; elsewhere the work is conducted on the initiative of the various Catholic orders.

In its main features, Argentina's experience with its Indian population roughly parallels that of the United States. The plains Indians, who wiped out the first colony on the River Plate in the sixteenth century, continued to be intractable and to oppose the inland advance of white settlement. Though gradually pushed back, the Indians waged a perennial warfare against the settlers of the pampa, that was only ended with General Roca's campaign of virtual extermination in the last century. South of the pampa, the Patagonian tribes have been decimated by disease and the increasingly hard conditions of their existence, as their hunting grounds have been turned into sheep ranges. The government has done little to better their lot and their early extinction appears inevitable. Efforts have been made to employ the Indians of the Argentine Chaco in lumbering and cotton raising, but with the usual indifferent results and the abuses attendant on all attempts at the regular employment of the wild Indian. Similar efforts in the Paraguayan, or Gran, Chaco to industrialize nomadic Indians of a low order of culture have proved little, if any, more promising.

The Araucanians of Chile are noted as the only Indians who successfully resisted the force of the Spanish Conquest. The colonial authorities finally recognized their independent status within the province, but on condition that they remain within the wooded zone south of Concepción known as *La Frontera*. Under the Chilean Republic this "Indian Territory" became a center of disaffection against the central government, where defeated political leaders were accustomed to take refuge and incite the Indians against the party in power in Santiago. On one occasion the Araucanians were stirred to revolt by a remarkable French adventurer, who assumed the title of "Aurélie Antonine I, Emperor of Araucania and Patagonia." After a series of uprisings, the Indians were removed from their hereditary lands and confined to a reservation. Today the survivors of the Araucanian race comprise only a small minority of the Chilean population.

The five countries with large populations of civilized or sedentary Indians are Mexico, Guatemala, Ecuador, Peru, and Bolivia. In varying degrees, and with different basic policies, all have endeavored to deal with the important problem presented by this underprivileged and socially static group. In all there is a fundamental conflict of interest between those who would continue the Indian in his present dependent status as a cheap, if inefficient, labor force, and those more liberal leaders of opinion who would raise the Indian to full political and economic citizenship. Between these two opinions are those extreme partisans of *Indianismo* who would recognize the Indians as a group apart from the normal currents of national life, and who would stimulate a revival of their native culture, to be based on a self-sufficient Indian economy. Meanwhile, for some time the Anthropology Department of Cornell University has conducted a research program of on-the-ground study, on a site in the Peruvian Andes, into the problems and possibilities of the indigenous population.

Mexico presents an outstanding example of these attempts to reestablish the Indians in a position that conforms with their relative numbers in the population and with their early importance in the history of the land. In Mexico, as elsewhere, this policy represents a

radical reversal of the economic and social trends that have long governed national society. In adopting this policy, the Mexican Revolution, which began in 1911, has not only restored the natural unity
and sequence of Mexican history that was broken by the Spanish Conquest, but has thereby given realistic expression to the fact that Mexico has remained a predominantly Indian country. The policy has
been haltingly followed at times by the various governments of the
republic, but took its most clear-cut form in the Zapatista revolt in
Morelos and was uncompromisingly promoted by the Cárdenas regime.

The Mayas of Yucatán had risen in revolt in the late forties of
the last century and there had been minor outbreaks of Indian discontent in other parts of the country. However, it was the repressive
rule of Porfirio Díaz, himself a mestizo, which brought the Indian
problem to a head. Díaz permitted the large landowners to take over
the communal lands of the Indians, who gradually lost most of whatever economic independence they had been able to hold through the
turbulent history of the republic. Large numbers of the proud and
unruly Yaquis of Sonora were moved to the henequen fields of Yucatán
as punishment for their opposition to the will of the dictator, and cruel
measures were taken against the Tehuanas of the isthmus. Though the
large mass of Indians remained in a state of inert serfdom, a heritage
of hate was being accumulated that was soon to threaten the social
peace of the nation.

While many compromises have been made with the old aristocratic and capitalistic order, which culminated in the highly stratified
system of the Díaz era, the Indian is an important beneficiary of the
social revolution which began rather half-heartedly with Madero. It
was only under President Lázaro Cárdenas, himself a descendant of
Tarascan Indians, that the movement made any substantial headway
toward the realization of its pro-Indian ideals. Its concrete accomplishments to date include the restoration of lands to the Indian peasantry,
the virtual end of peonage, the introduction of public-school education
in the rural districts, the stimulation by the state of the Indians' remarkable cultural instincts, and a miscellaneous body of labor and
social legislation. The permanence of the gains depends on many
factors in the complex and contradictory political and economic structure of present-day Mexico.

Meanwhile, the Indian stamp is indelibly fixed on Mexico. It not

only colors every phase of contemporary life, but has given a new
perspective to the country's history. This is especially evidenced in
the prevailing attitude toward the Spanish Conquest. In contrast to
the disparagement of Cortés and his fellow conquerors is the glorifica-
tion of Cuauhtemoc, the Aztec hero. The new attitude also finds expression in an intensification of the old rivalry between the devotees
of the Spanish madonna, Nuestra Señora de los Remedios, and the
Indian Virgin, Guadalupe, whose cult is more than ever in the ascendant in the religious life of Mexico. Much is being done to revive the
Indian's pride in his past, and scholars like Manuel Gamio have furthered the process by the reconstruction of pre-Spanish cultural patterns around the great archaeological remains of the country.

Over the southern border of Mexico lies the overwhelmingly
Indian republic of Guatemala, peopled by descendants of the great
Maya-Quiché stocks. The lives of these Indians are regulated by a
body of ancient customs and beliefs that have been little affected by
conquest or time. Taciturn and secretive, though not unfriendly, they
avoid, so far as possible, the whites and *ladinos*, or mixed breeds, and
their modern ways. While many cultivate small patches of land of
their own, they also constitute the permanent or seasonal labor force
of the coffee plantations.

Regarding the Aymará and Quechua peoples, who constitute
the great mass of the Indian population in the three republics of the
central Andes, the writer quotes from an earlier work of his. Although
the statements quoted refer to the Indians of Bolivia, they are substantially applicable to conditions in Ecuador and Peru. However, the
Aymarás are not found in Ecuador, but dwell in the region of southern
Peru around Lake Titicaca, as well as on the Bolivian plateau beyond
the lake.

"The habitat of the Aymarás is the plateau region of the Department of La Paz and the northern part of the Department of Oruro.
They are a people of rugged appearance, and many are of robust build,
being above the average of the Indian races in stature. The hard struggle for existence eliminates the weaker individuals early in life, and
those who survive the first trying years are sturdy and well fitted for
coping with their rigorous environment. Their language, which may
be heard in the streets of La Paz, is harsh and guttural and is still in a
rudimentary state of development.

"The Aymará is disposed to be sullen and taciturn and has an air of habitual melancholy. Though normally servile in his attitude toward his white superiors, he is given to vindictive revolts when he feels that his communal or traditional rights have been too long violated. He is then cruel and relentless. Local risings of the *indiada* occur every few years and are put down by the government forces. The last of these troubles occurred in July, 1920, in the neighborhood of Lake Titicaca. Because of his fighting qualities, the Aymará (with *cholos* of Aymará admixture) forms the backbone of the Bolivian army. He is given to the drinking of liquor; only when he is under its influence does he laugh or become loquacious and communicative. His intelligence, which is naturally dwarfed by his environment and the monotony of his surroundings, is further impaired by his constant use of coca. Though the chewing of the strongly narcotic coca leaves endows him with inordinate powers of enduring fatigue and hunger, it is undoubtedly a factor for the physical degeneration of the race.

"The normal environment in which the Aymará lives, and which accounts for his peculiar temperament, is highly unfavorable to human life, when unaided by the resources of modern civilization, which are beyond the reach of the Indian. The Aymará's existence has been a continuous struggle against the environment of the bleak and inhospitable plateau—against cold and hunger and the lack of oxygen. The hard conditions of life have left little place in him for affection or any other of the finer feelings. One of his strongest sentiments is his ineradicable attachment to the *ayllú*, the community in which he was born and in which his ancestors lived. So strong is this attachment to his traditional home that he refuses to migrate to the warmer valleys beyond the Andes where the conditions of life are much more favorable. His music is in accord with the dreary circumstances of his life and consists of the melancholy and monotonous minor notes of the *quina* or reed flute. His few songs are mournful chants that are seldom heard.

"The country-dwelling Aymará lives in a hut made of mud or stones, where he sleeps on a sheep pelt on the bare floor or on the floor itself. His clothing consists of a peaked woolen cap with long 'ear flaps' that hang down over the side of his face; a homespun woolen poncho, generally of great age; rough trousers split part way up the back of the leg; and crude sandals, which he wears over the rocky roads of the mountain country or the sharp cobblestones of La Paz, but which are generally discarded. His sparse diet is made up of potatoes, usually in the desiccated form known as *chuño*, a stew made of vegetables and barley, or *quinua*, and parched corn. He eats little meat or bread, though he may kill a sheep to celebrate a fiesta.

"The Aymará is the agricultural laborer of the *altiplano*, though seldom a proprietor, save where the ancient communal tenure has been permitted to survive in some distant localities. He also does the rough work of the city and can always be seen carrying burdens about the streets of La Paz. He cares for the herds and flocks of the plateau and drives the pack trains of mules, burros, or llamas from place to place. He is often the owner of small flocks of sheep or droves of pack animals, whose life he shares in a strange intimacy. Most of the workers in the mines are also drawn from his class. He has no place in the political life of the nation, and sharp barriers of caste separate him from those who own and rule the country. Even the majority of the *cholos*, who have sprung from a mixture of his race with the Spaniard, look down on him and refuse to speak his language.

"The much more numerous Quechua race is spread over a wide area from Ecuador south into Argentina and Chile, as attested by such names as Cajabamba in the former country, Catamarca in Argentina, and Chuquicamata in Chile. In Bolivia the Quechuas constitute the aboriginal race in part of the Department of Oruro and in Cochamamba, Chuquisaca, and Potosí. Their language forms one of the great lingual stocks of South America and is much more highly developed than the rude speech of the Aymarás.

"The Quechua is smaller in stature than the Aymará, less robust and of finer features, some of the men of the Sucre district being of quite handsome appearance. However, the Aymará *cholos*, particularly the *cholos* of La Paz, are generally superior, as regards stamina and appearance, to the majority of the Quechua mixed breeds.

"There is a vast difference in the character of the two races. The Aymará, at the time of the Spanish Conquest, had lived under the Incaic dominion only a comparatively short time and still lived in a semibarbarous state. The Quechua, on the other hand, had long been subjected to the peculiar civilizing regime of the Incas, which had given him certain fundamental elements of culture and a settled order of society, even though it had deprived him of all personal initiative. The Incaic institutions have disappeared, save in the survival of a few customs, but the Quechua still preserves in his temper much of the heritage of pre-Spanish days. He is eminently docile and passive, whereas the submissiveness of the Aymará can never be taken for granted. He also is taciturn and uncommunicative, but never defiantly or sullenly so. His temper is in general much gentler and kindlier than that of the Aymará. However, he has the same propensity for drink, which he shares with the other Indian races of South America. Except in the high mountain districts of Oruro and Potosí, he prefers the milder *chicha* to the strong liquors that serve the Aymará. This is particularly true in the valleys of Cochabamba and Chuquisaca, where large areas of corn are devoted to the making of *chicha*.

"The Quechua's manner of life varies considerably in different districts. In the valleys of Cochambaba and Sucre, which are the favorite habitats of the race, it is much superior to the conditions in the more unfavorable environment of the Oruro and Potosí highlands. In the former he is an agriculturalist, working in a good soil and a temperate climate. There he has enough to eat of corn and vegetables and often of meat, and the climate makes few demands in the way of clothing and housing. In Potosí and Oruro he is a worker in the mines, or farms the barren and rocky soil of the mountains. Here his conditions of life are much like those of the Aymará of the La Paz *altiplano*.

"Like the Aymará, he lives apart from the political life of the Republic but is less esteemed as a soldier. Yet with the Aymará he forms the very basis of the whole economic life of the country."

The Quechua-speaking Indians are found under the most favorable conditions in certain parts of Ecuador, particularly in the Imbabura valley, north of Quito.[2] The Indians of that locality are actually descendants of the Cara stock, which was subject to the Incaic domination for only a short period before the Spanish Conquest, but, like many other peoples subjugated by the Incas, adopted Quechua as their own tongue. The Indians of the Urubamba valley, in the neighborhood

---

[2] "The Indians of the valleys south of Quito—Ambato, Riobamba, Cuenca— are second only to the Otavaleños (of the Imbabura valley) in thrift and general well-being. They too are of the happy, *sympatico* disposition that is in such marked contrast with the southern Andeans, the dour, disagreeable Aymará ... with their genial climate, ample food, varied domestic resources, arts to occupy their hands and minds; they should be, and are, a contented people." Edgar L. Hewett, *Ancient Andean Life* (Indianapolis: Bobbs-Merrill, 1939), p. 116.

of Cuzco, the old Inca capital, are typical of the Peruvian Quechuas, though nowhere are the Indians of Peru seen to such advantage as at the great fair at Huancayo, in the high plateau country to the east of Lima. However, these Indians lived so long in the strict mold of the Incaic society that they lacked the spirit to assert at least their cultural or spiritual independence against the Spanish conquerors and the subsequent generations of white or mestizo overlords. While they have kept many of their ancient customs, they have generally less economic freedom than the Ecuadorean Indians and to an outsider give an impression of habitual melancholy.

Of the three countries in question, the Ecuadorean government has probably pursued the most intelligent Indian policy. In this respect, Ecuador has had the initial advantage of a superior Indian population and the absence of a mining industry with heavy demands for labor. Its program has been a relatively passive one, designed to protect the Indian communities from undue interference with their traditional life and from abuse of the agricultural laborers who work on the large estates of the plateau. In 1915 peonage was legally abolished in Peru, but, in spite of improved conditions in some localities, the law largely remained a dead letter and the Indian continued to be bound to the land. Under the dictatorship of President Leguia an ostentatious Indian program was inaugurated, but with similar lack of results. The Indian was raised to full citizenship in the Republic, but remained disqualified from voting by standards of literacy which he could not meet. In an outburst of *Indianismo* the dictator proclaimed the establishment of a "day of the aborigine," which was to be celebrated each year with elaborate ceremonies calculated to impress the Indians with their importance in the nation. Little of the social legislation which has since been passed by the Peruvian government affects the status of the agricultural Indians of the *Sierra*, who comprise the large majority of the aboriginal population. In Bolivia most of the government efforts on behalf of the Indians have likewise aimed at improving conditions among the workers in the towns and in the mines, and, in recent years, in the distribution of lands to the Indian peasantry.

In April, 1940 the First Inter-American Congress on Indian Life was held at Patzcuaro in the Mexican State of Michoacán. The Congress was attended by delegates from practically all the Latin-American countries which have large Indian populations, as well as from the

United States. There were also representatives of Indian tribes from Chile, Panama, and the United States, and from eleven Indian groups in Mexico. A comprehensive series of resolutions were agreed upon, touching every phase of Indian welfare, and including recommendations on economic status, political rights, health conditions, folk arts, and education. In fact, the body of resolutions adopted by the Congress represented a veritable charter of Indian rights for the guidance of the American republics in formulating their Indian policies. The liberal spirit in which the Congress conducted its discussions is illustrated by the following extract from its "Declaration of Fundamental Principles":

> All measures and provisions prescribed for the purpose of guaranteeing the rights and the protection, when necssary, of the Indian groups, should be based on a respect for the positive values of the historic and cultural personality of the Indian and should be directed toward facilitating his economic advancement and his assimilation and utilization of modern technique and universal culture.

Since the establishment of the quota system by the United States, Latin America has become the world's largest field for immigration. The combination of attractions which it offers to immigrants from the Old World includes the availability of large areas of land suitable for settlement; opportunities for economic advancement; liberal naturalization policies; a favorable climate; a spirit of tolerance; a state of continental peace that is rarely broken by war; and governments which, though not always democratic in practice, at least interfere little with the personal life of the law-abiding citizen. The inducements are unequally distributed. They are greatest in Argentina and southern Brazil and are negligible in the "Indian" countries, including the three central Andean republics, Central America, and Mexico. Competition with the low living standards of the mass of the population, as also in the predominantly mulatto and mestizo regions of northern Brazil, is out of the question for the agricultural immigrant from Europe unless he is willing to accept the economic level of his neighbors. Moreover, there is almost no available land suitable for farming. An exception is the plains of Santa Cruz in eastern Bolivia, where, in lieu of money crops, at least a life of rude plenty and a larger degree of personal freedom is possible for the hardy colonist. While

Chile and Uruguay possess most of the elements listed above, they are lacking in the essential factor of land. Though Paraguay has a bountiful supply of good land to the east of the main river, a climate in which Europeans can flourish, and an unusually tolerant attitude toward foreigners, its full possibilities as a field for colonization have not been realized. Its economic backwardness has been a drawback and the current of immigration which might normally have reached its hospitable territory has been drained off by the more highly developed and publicized attractions of Argentina. Venezuela is greatly underpopulated and large tracts are suited for occupancy by European settlers. In Colombia, on the other hand, opportunities for the acquisition of productive land in the plateau country are very limited.

Total immigration into the four countries which have received the largest numbers of foreigners within the period for which records have been kept has been as follows: Argentina, 4,169,951 (1857–1938); Brazil, 4,603,414 (1820–1937); Cuba, 1,261,788 (1903–1932); Uruguay, 509,366 (1900–1937).

Large tracts of land otherwise desirable for colonization may suffer from a lack of markets for the settler's surplus production, the high cost of initial transportation for the immigrant and his family, the difficulty of establishing land titles, or a total absence of the institutional machinery of civilized society, such as educational and medical facilities. Also, governments may desire to give priority in the occupancy of such lands to their own landless nationals. The existence of latifundia, or large estates, whether actually developed or held fallow by their owners, is a further obstacle to the settling of immigrants on lands that would promise an early return for their labors. This condition is common throughout Latin America. In Argentina, for example, the immigrant without capital is forced either to become a farm hand or a tenant farmer on one of the big *estancias;* his alternative is to take up land somewhere on the outer fringe of the rich Argentine plains, as in the near-by irrigated regions in the south or in the wooded zone along the upper Paraná, above its junction with the Paraguay. Those with more capital than the average newcomer or who by thrift have accumulated sufficient savings as laborers or "sharecroppers" in the country can buy small parcels of fertile land whenever one of the large *estancias* is broken up.

Whereas the vast Amazon basin contains an apparently unlimited area for settlement within the six republics of Brazil, Bolivia, Peru, Ecuador, Colombia, and Venezuela, only well-financed plantation developments or subsistence farming under the hardest pioneering conditions is practicable in most of the area. In the remote Acre Territory of Brazil and elsewhere on high lands along the river margins one finds virtually self-sufficient farms that bear witness to the industry and resourcefulness of the settlers who literally carved them out of the wilderness and then labored incessantly to hold them against the encroachment of a too exuberant nature. The individual immigrant who attempts to emulate them has also to contend with a tropical climate that is especially trying to women from temperate lands and with the psychological burden of isolation from his kind in the confinement of the jungle. For these reasons, Amazonia may be considered as an enormous reserve of land, only to be drawn on to any appreciable extent as other parts of the world more easily brought under cultivation are occupied. In the meanwhile, a wide belt lying within the southern part of the Brazilian State of Mato Grosso offers real opportunities to the settler who is not too exigent in the matter of comforts and cultural advantages.

The immigration policies of the important Latin-American countries have undergone considerable modification in recent years. They have generally adopted as their standards the test of the immigrant's ease of assimilation and his utility to the development of the country. Governments are now more discriminating in the admission of immigrants and their strong nationalistic tendencies do not tolerate the entrance of elements which cannot be easily absorbed into the native population. Some governments forbid schools to conduct their instruction in a foreign language. There is a tendency to prevent the concentration of immigrants in separate localities, where they might resist assimilation and become potential nuclei of foreign attachments. Thus, Brazilian law requires that 30 percent of the colonists in any settlement of foreign immigrants shall be native Brazilians or Portuguese, and that not more than 25 percent of any colony shall be of any foreign nationality. By a decree-law of 1938, a quota system was established limiting annual entries from any country to 2 percent of the total immigration from that source for the period 1884-1938. Based on a total immigration of 3,951,015 for that period, the total annual quota is 79,020 persons. Of the quota for any nation, at least 80 percent must

consist of farmers. Official control over immigration and consolidation
is exercised by the Federal Directorate of Land and Colonization. Agricultural immigrants certified by consular officials are usually placed
in one of the government *núcleos* or colonies, where they are compelled
to remain until they have liquidated their monetary obligation to the
state for the cost of the land and any advances made for the purchase
of seeds, stock, or equipment. Early naturalization is expected of immigrants, and willingness to intermarry with women of the country
is considered the ultimate test of assimilation. For the Latin-American
woman, with her passive strength and her impermeability to foreign
ideas, is a potent force for national cohesion and her children are liable
to have their spiritual roots deep in the country of her birth.

As a rule the republics welcome agricultural immigrants. They
desire, above all, experienced farmers who will remain on the soil.
They are willing to accept some technical men and skilled workmen,
experienced in industrial processes that are of interest to the development of the national economies. But, generally, they are opposed to
the introduction of immigrants who would swell the population of
their already overgrown cities. They do not want professional men or
merchants, for their own professional classes are well organized and
jealous of their monopoly, and the mercantile field is overcrowded.
In the latter respect, Havana, with retail stores sufficient for twice its
population, is typical of most Latin-American cities. The governments also scan carefully the political ideas of prospective immigrants.
They have had unfortunate experiences with foreign agitators, ranging from old-style Catalan anarchists to Russian Communists and
Fascist propagandists of the totalitarian powers, and they deeply resent the disturbance of their domestic tranquillity by such alien influences. In the same way, they are extremely careful to ban foreigners
with criminal records or those who are liable to become public
charges.

As might be expected, the largest volume of immigration into
Latin America has originated in the Latin countries of Europe, especially in the two mother countries and Italy. Similarity of language,
religion, legal systems, and basic customs, and, in the case of Spain and
Portugal, a common historical tradition, greatly facilitate the process
of assimilation. Thus, an immigrant from Lombardy loses his original
racial identity and merges himself into the life of Argentina or of

Brazil almost as quickly and easily as does an immigrant from Andalusia or Alemtejo.

Most of the Spanish migration to the New World since Independence has been directed to Argentina, Brazil, and Cuba. About 2,000,000 Spaniards have entered Argentina since the middle of the last century, over half a million have settled in Brazil, and nearly 800,000 in Cuba. They also constitute by far the largest foreign element in Mexico, which offered asylum to many Loyalist refugees from the Spanish Civil War. Large numbers of Spaniards have migrated to Uruguay, and in 1930 Chile had over 23,000 residents of Spanish nationality.

Brazil has received about 1,200,000 immigrants from the Portuguese mother country since the end of the Empire. In consideration of the strong ties between the two peoples, the Brazilian government has exempted the Portuguese from the application of the quota system which governs the entry of immigrants. About 40,000 Portuguese have also settled in Argentina.

Italian immigration into Argentina has totaled over 2,600,000, and into Brazil, over 1,400,000. The Italians have been a highly important factor in the industrial and cultural development of both countries. In Argentina they have even given a special complexion to the language, and a particular stamp to the large city of Rosario. In the Brazilian State of São Paulo, Italian business interests, represented by such names as Mattarazzo, Martinelli, and Crespi, hold a pre-eminent position in the field of manufacturing and trade. Italians occupy first place among Uruguay's immigrant population and are found in considerable numbers in Chile and Peru. Men of Italian blood have risen to high position in the life of Latin America, and include such names as Alberdi, the great Argentine political thinker, Pellegrini, a president of that country, and the Alessandris in Chile.

For some time a special phase of Italian, and to a lesser extent of Spanish, immigration into the River Plate region was the seasonal migration of workers known in Argentina as "*golondrinas*" or "swallows." Formerly large numbers of peasants from Italy and eastern Spain were accustomed to go out in steerage to Buenos Aires and Rosario, to help in gathering the annual harvest, returning to Europe with their savings at the end of the harvest season. During the Fascist regime, Italian emigration to South America, both of permanent and seasonal character, virtually ceased. For example, in 1937 fewer than 3,000 Italian immigrants entered Brazil, and these entries were almost balanced by the number of Italians who returned home in the same year. Following the almost complete suspension of European immigration to Latin America during the Second World War, the movement of Italians to the River Plate was renewed on a considerable scale. However, with the improvement of economic conditions in the home country and in the Common Market area of western Europe in general, Italian migration to South America has decreased to a trickle. During the war the small current of immigration to the New World was largely confined to Jewish and Polish refugees, many of whom settled in the Dominican Republic, Cuba, Mexico, Colombia, and Bolivia.

While few Frenchmen have gone out to Latin America as agricultural colonists, the number who have migrated thither is not inconsiderable. For example, about 230,000 have entered Argentina and about one-fourth as many have settled in Brazil. There is also much French blood in Uruguay. The French element has contributed a great deal to the industrial development of Latin America, as well as to its scientific and cultural advancement.

At the beginning of the Second World War, the German-born in Latin America numbered over 250,000, and there were probably over 1,300,000 descendants of German immigrants. The largest German communities are in Brazil, Argentina, Chile, and Paraguay. Nearly three-fourths of all persons of German blood live in Brazil, largely in the four southern States of São Paulo, Paraná, Santa Catarina, and Rio Grande do Sul. There is a large and influential German-Brazilian population in Pôrto Alegre, capital of the latter state, and the towns of Blumenau and Joinville, in the State of Santa Catarina, are centers of predominant German influence. There are also strong German business houses in São Paulo and Rio de Janeiro. The first German immigrants arrived in Rio Grande do Sul in 1824, and, though less than 100,000 Germans have since entered that state, its population now includes over a half million persons of German blood. The majority of the immigrants who came during the period of the Brazilian Empire were peasant farmers, laborers, and craftsmen, and most of their descendants still live on the land. The Brazilian governments under whose authority they lived made little effort to integrate them into the life of the nation, and, left largely to their own devices, the German communities tended to retain the cultural and institutional pattern of "the Fatherland." They spoke German, read German newspapers, of which about ten dailies were published in Brazil, attended German churches, sent their children to their local German schools, and belonged to a variety of musical and social organizations, and sometimes to marching and shooting clubs that could easily be converted to military ends. While they generally felt little loyalty to the Brazilian government, after the first generation in the country, their attachments to Germany were largely sentimental. However, the German settlements in Latin America fitted too well into the dreams and designs of German imperialists from Bismarck to Hitler for them to be permitted to remain aloof from the two world wars which Germany has precipitated. Agents of German power politics made every effort to enlist the active support of all those of German blood, and in some circles met with considerable success. The more zealous and recalcitrant German sympathizers created serious problems of control for the Brazilian government during both wars, as they did for other governments in Latin America. On the other hand, there have been outstanding examples of men of German blood who have become thoroughly identified with the fortunes and life of Brazil, such as Lauro Müller, Brazilian Minister of Foreign Affairs during the First World War, the Konder brothers in Santa Catarina, and the Schmidt family in the State of São Paulo.

About 100,000 Germans entered Argentina prior to 1925. Net entries during the years 1933–38 amounted to about 13,800. Though a disproportionate share of the German population lives in Buenos Aires, German immigrants are well scattered over most of the country, a considerable contingent of them being established in the northern Territory of Misiones. The first movement of Germans into Chile began in the late forties of the last century. Part of this immigration was similar to those who sought a refuge in the United States after the abortive revolutionary movement of 1848; most of them were peasant farmers, interested in improving their material condition. This excellent colonizing material has been largely responsible for the development of the country to the south of Concepción, but particularly of the region about Valdivia. While German is still widely spoken in that area, its use and the survival of German customs cannot be said to have any special political significance, but is rather due to the long relative isolation of these German settlements. The ratio of this element to the total Chilean population is very low. The absorption of later arrivals has not proceeded so far, and the assertion of racial consciousness among the members of this group is liable to be more outspoken. The census of 1930 gave the number of unnaturalized Germans in Chile as 10,860. At the time of the Second World War, it was estimated that there were about 20,000 persons of German birth in Chile and about 75,000 descendants of earlier German immigrants.

Of the other Latin countries, Colombia had over 3,600 German residents in 1939. Some 2,700 Germans were residing in Mexico in 1930, and about 1,000 more entered the country during the following six years. There were relatively large and very influential German groups in Guatemala and El Salvador, most of whom were engaged in business or in the operation of coffee plantations.

Most of those who have migrated to Latin America from the United States have gone as individuals in search of business opportunities or mining prospects, or of cheap land in out-of-the-way corners of the southern republics. However, there have been a few attempts at organized colonization of Americans. The first of these were made by Southerners during the Reconstruction era that followed the Civil War. Except for a number of former Confederate soldiers and their families who migrated to Mexico, the most important movement of this kind was from the Southern States to Brazil. Brazil was then an empire, and, though abolitionist sentiment was widespread, Negro slavery still prevailed. One group settled on lands set apart by the imperial government near Santarém, at the junction of the Tapajóz River with the Amazon; the other established the community known as Villa Americana, on the temperate plateau of São Paulo. Although the northern colony was located on one of the best sites in the Amazon valley, many of the immigrants drifted back to the United States. Later generations of those who remained have intermarried with the Brazilians of the vicinity, and though American family names are common in the neighborhood of Santarém, their bearers speak Portuguese and have otherwise been completely absorbed into the local population. The settlement in the Paulista highlands prospered reasonably and by the enterprise of its members occupied a high position in the rapidly growing state. While the name

of the town that was the center of the colony still survives, intermar-
riage with the native population has proceeded until the community
has lost most of its original character. However, a veritable dynasty of
physicians and dentists sprang from the colony, and long held a
prominent place in professional circles in São Paulo and Rio de
Janeiro.

During the present century, at least three attempts at systematic
colonization by Americans have been made in the west-coast countries of South America. Two groups were settled in the heavily
forested belt of the Peruvian *montaña* on the eastern watershed of the
Andes, and the third colony, which was promoted by former Governor William Murray, of Oklahoma, was established in the basin of the
middle Pilcomayo, in southeastern Bolivia. All three undertakings
failed miserably and most of the unfortunate colonists had to be repatriated. The breakup of the Peruvian colonies was due partly to
mismanagement, and partly to disillusionment of the immigrants at
the slight prospect of early returns for the isolation and hard labor
involved in clearing the wilderness. Natural conditions in the more
open country along the Pilcomayo held out considerable promise for
stock raising, but the long distance to profitable markets, and other
special circumstances inherent in the situation of the colony, militated
against the success of the venture.

After the Spanish-American War several hundred Americans
settled in Cuba, where they embarked in the cultivation of tropical
fruits and in a variety of other farming and business enterprises. Some
of the immigrants were disbanded soldiers and others crossed from
the mainland during the American occupation that followed the attainment of Cuban independence. For lack of the necessary capital
and because of the development of subtropical agriculture in Florida
and California, few of them prospered. A minor problem was created
in Cuban-American relations by a small group who remained on the
Isle of Pines, in the belief that that island would eventually revert to
the United States.

A company of Americans also joined the socialistic colony of
Nueva Australia, founded in Paraguay, in 1893, by the Australian
Cooperative Society, under the leadership of the famous William
Lane.

In South American immigration statistics all citizens of the Brit-

ish Empire are classified as either "English" or "British." Except for
some 65,000 "English," who entered the Argentine Republic between
1857 and 1924, migration from the United Kingdom to Latin America
has been relatively small. It includes about 21,000 immigrants into
Brazil, and a very considerable movement into Uruguay, for which
country the English are accustomed to form a strong attachment.
These figures do not include the thousands of British who have been
engaged at any one time in the operation of British-owned railways,
mines, ranches, banks, and other enterprises in Latin America. There
is a very large group of Irish in Argentina, most of whom have been
in the country so long that they have little but their names to distinguish them from the mass of native Argentines. This community
of Irish-Argentines is distinct from the descendants of those His-
panicized Irish who went out to Spanish America during the colonial
period, and who left such distinguished names as O'Reilly and
O'Higgins and O'Donoju strewn through the history of the viceroyalties. Some Scotch have settled in Patagonia, and even in Tierra del
Fuego, where they are engaged in sheep raising. The Falkland Islands,
to which Argentina lays claim as the Maluinas, are populated almost
entirely by Scotch. There is also an interesting Welsh colony in the
valley of the Rio Chubut, in Patagonia, dating from the middle of the
last century.[3]

The largest Slavic element in South America is found in Argentina and Brazil. About 215,000 Russians, Poles, Lithuanians, and Yugo-
slavs entered the former country between 1820 and 1937, and many
Slavs were probably included among the 94,000 "Austro-Hungarians"
who arrived during the same period. Forty-two thousand Poles, including many Polish Jews, entered Argentina in the six-year period
1933–1938. Brazil admitted over 150,000 immigrants of six Slavic
nationalities between 1884 and 1933. The largest single group was
composed of over 61,000 Poles, many of whom settled in the State of
Paraná. On the west coast, there is a numerous and influential Yugo-
slav colony in the vicinity of Antofagasta in northern Chile. Some of
this group have penetrated into Bolivia, where they operate a number
of retail grocery and hardware stores in the leading cities. A White

[3] See A. F. Tschiffely, *This Way Southward* (New York: W. W. Norton,
1940), Ch. V.

Russian colony, composed largely of Cossacks, was settled beyond Tarma in eastern Peru after the overthrow of the Imperial Russian government, but proved a disastrous failure. A similar colony was established in Paraguay at about the same time, and there was a White Russian settlement in the State of São Paulo, in Brazil. Over 38,000 Roumanians have entered Brazil; many of these, like the Polish immigrants into Latin America, have doubtless been Jewish. One of the most interesting attempts at colonization so far made in Latin America is the large Mennonite settlement in the Gran Chaco. Though most of the industrious members of this colony came to Paraguay from Canada, their original home was in Russia.

Of Oriental immigrants into Latin America, the earliest to arrive were the Chinese. Large numbers of Chinese coolies were imported during the last century, to work the guano deposits in the islands off the Peruvian coast, after the tragic impressment of Polynesian islanders from the south Pacific. For a long time Chinese have comprised an important element in the retail trade of Peru, though restrictions against their further entry are now in force. There are many Chinese merchants in Central America and in northern Mexico, where they suffered many indignities during the early years of the Mexican Revolution, and there is a long-established colony in Cuba.

The largest Japanese group in Latin America, and, in fact, outside Asia, is in Brazil. 800 Japanese immigrants arrived at Santos in 1908, and in 1934, just before the quota system became effective, over 22,000 were introduced. In the intervening years, a total of probably 180,000 entered Brazil, many of them clandestinely. These Japanese colonists were introduced under agreements made between the state government of São Paulo and Japanese immigration companies. Though a vast colonization project for the settlement of Japanese in the Amazon valley was disapproved by the Brazilian Congress, many Japanese immigrated to the State of Amazonas, where they initiated plantation enterprises. Most of these who entered through the port of Santos were employed for a time as workers on the coffee *fazendas* of the State of São Paulo. Many of these gravitated into the state capital, where they operated small businesses or worked in the service trades. Others settled in the coastal plain of the state, where they engaged in fishing or farming. Most of them ultimately settled in the numerous Japanese agricultural communities in the state, where they lived apart from the mass of the Brazilian population. The misgivings which many Brazilians had as to the wisdom of permitting this immigration were increasingly confirmed as the Japanese colonists resisted assimilation and clung to their racial pattern of living. Disloyalty was active and widespread during the Second World War, and for a long time after the war the more fanatical elements refused to accept the fact of Japanese defeat. In recent years Japanese immigration into Brazil has been resumed. In the State of São Paulo Japanese are a very important element in the production of fruit and vegetables. They are engaged in large industrial enterprises in the vicinity of Belo Horizonte and Rio de Janeiro, in trawler fishing off the northeast coast, and in pioneer plantation ventures in the Amazon valley.

Japanese also became an important element in Peru, particularly in the agricultural regions along the coast, where they comprised a cohesive racial group, as in Brazil. Others crossed the Andes to work in the rubber forests of the Beni country, where many of them later drifted into the towns of the Bolivian lowlands. Several thousand Japanese settled in northwestern Mexico, chiefly along the coast of Sinaloa and Sonora, where many of them engaged in deep-sea fishing in the Gulf of California and in waters outside the peninsula.

One of the most enterprising groups of immigrants who have entered Latin America is that popularly known as "Turks," but most of whom are Syrians, with a sprinkling of Armenians and Lebanese. With a strong instinct for trade, they generally start on a modest scale in retail business in the towns or as itinerant merchants. Many of them have accumulated a large capital and become an important element in commerce and manufacturing. The second generation usually enters wholeheartedly into the life of the country, and sometimes attains to posts of importance. Of the 157,000 "Ottomans" listed by the Argentine government as having entered that country as immigrants, the great majority are doubtless of Syrian blood, as were most of the 78,000 immigrants of "Turkish nationality" admitted into Brazil under the Republic. The Mexican census of 1930 reported 6,836 Levantines, divided into six groups, as living within the country. Less than 300 have entered Mexico since that year. The Chilean census of 1930 reported the presence of 1,345 Syrians, 3,156 "Palestinians," and 1,634 "Arabians" in that country.

The extent to which foreign blood has been disseminated through the population of Latin America is suggested by the Hispanic names of many men prominent in the public life of the republics during 1962: Among them were five presidents. The list also included Luis MacKay, Eduardo Moore, and Gonzalo Abad, Ministers of Education of, respectively, Argentina, Chile, and Ecuador; three ambassadors to the United States, named Berckmeyer, Clulow, and Müller Hess; three Ministers of Finance—Azzini, MacKenna, and Zarak; Faustino Harrison, member of the Uruguayan National Council of Government; Manuel Stolyk Novygrod, Cuban Chargé d'Affaires in London; and Prado Kelly, a Brazilian politico.

Part IV

GOVERNMENT

AFTER the attainment of independence, Latin America faced the problem of finding a workable system of government. In the solution of this problem its past offered little guidance for its future. Behind it stretched centuries of absolutist rule and habits of obedience to an authority imposed from above and directed from overseas. In this unfortunate heritage the only vestige of democratic tradition was the limited right of the colonials to participate in the government of their cities. Otherwise they were subjects of a vice-king, who ruled by proxy for an all-powerful king in Spain. Loyalty to the crown was so strong, in spite of the individual inadequacy of most of the monarchs since Philip II, that paradoxically enough the movement for independence actually originated in colonial protests against the treatment of the unworthy Ferdinand VII by the French conquerors of Spain. The customary line of authority had been broken for the moment and the first impulse of the creoles was to demand that it be restored to its familiar form. It was only because the reactionary monarch failed to rise to the occasion by a display of gratitude and appreciation and, instead, lectured his loyal subjects for their political initiative, that the bolder colonial leaders questioned the whole system of government. But now that the kings and their viceroys had been eliminated, those who took their place in the political scheme had surprisingly little by which to go.

The great Bolívar, who lived long enough to observe the full trend of events, toyed for a time with ideas of New World monarchy, in which the Brazilians were to find refuge from the disorders that afflicted their neighbors. But Spanish America was committed by destiny and example to the republican form of government and to the ideal of democracy. Free men, the Spanish Americans reasoned from history, could live only under a republic; the United States furnished an example from the present. The founders of the new states ignored the circumstance that the French Revolution had ended with Napoleon and the Bourbon Restoration, and that the North American colonists had an active tradition of self-government before they declared their independence. The Spanish Americans believed that, by borrowing the original ideology of the French Revolution and the machinery of American republicanism, they could rationalize and implement their dream of democracy.

They took too little account of the realities of the situation wherein they built an exotic framework of government. The stabilizing influence of a middle class was lacking. In most of the republics a large and inert Indian population remained outside the political life of the nation, and regarded all governments alike as potential oppressors, to be given as wide a berth as possible. Thus, by a process of elimination an oligarchy of landowners and lawyer-politicians was inevitable. Oligarchy was tempered by pretorianism, for the veterans of the wars of independence were a power to be reckoned with, and the habits of violence bred by the long struggle with Spain created an atmosphere that was favorable to the ambitions of the military. Those who had the responsibility for rule lacked the knowledge of administrative organization and processes that might have enabled the governments to function with some degree of order and regularity in spite of this incubus of the past. The only tried administrative capacity was in the hierarchy of the Church, but that powerful institution refused to reconcile itself to the new order and long remained monarchical in its sympathies.

On the credit side were the nationalism born of the accomplished fact of independence and a deep faith in the republican ideal. That is, there were definite political sovereignties of their own making, to which men could give their loyalties, and which might become real democracies within their own qualified understanding of the term.

Yet, in the early republican period, the very nationalisms were ill-defined and variable entities. Nations were in flux, and it was long before the geographical limits of all the new sovereignties were fixed with any approach to finality. By a process of division, republics fell apart, to give birth to other states, as the young peoples sought some common denominator of nationality and became conscious of the differentia which distinguished them from their neighbors.

When the last Spanish force in the American continent surrendered to the patriots in January, 1826, there were ten independent nations in Latin America—Mexico, the United Provinces of Central America, Great Colombia, Peru, Bolivia, Chile, the United Provinces of the River Plate, Paraguay, Brazil, and Haiti. The Central American federation had been a part of Mexico from 1822 to 1824, and was to break up into its five component states in 1838. Bolívar's creation, the Republic of Great Colombia, was dissolved in 1830 into the three republics of New Granada, or Colombia, Venezuela, and Ecuador. At the first revolutionary movement in Buenos Aires, in 1811, Paraguay set up an independent government and thereafter refused the overtures of the Argentine patriots to join the United Provinces of the River Plate. The present Republic of Uruguay, then known as the Banda Oriental, was part of Brazil, as the Cisplatine Province, between 1821 and 1835. A confused struggle for independence, in which a rude but valiant countryman named José Artigas distinguished himself, was unsuccessful, and Uruguay owed her freedom as a nation to the rivalries of her larger neighbors. For a brief period Uruguay was a part of the loose federation of provinces beyond the River Plate. At the end of a war between Argentina and Brazil both recognized the independence of the Banda Oriental in 1828. After a prolonged and cruel conflict, that had as much the character of a class struggle as of a war of independence, the Haitians attained their independence from France in 1803. From 1822 to 1844, the Spanish-speaking eastern end of the island was a part of the black republic of Haiti. In the latter year it gained its freedom as the Dominican Republic. Of the other states of present-day Latin America, the Cuban Republic dates from 1898 and the Republic of Panama from 1903.

History played an important part in determining the eventual scheme of Latin-American nationalism. Mexico was the logical successor of the Viceroyalty of New Spain, as Colombia was of that of New Granada, Argentina, of the Viceroyalty of La Plata, and Peru of the second of the original viceroyalties. The more important of the outlying provinces of the viceroyalties also became republics under the new order. Sometimes the new states followed the lines of an old captaincy-general, as Chile and Venezuela did, and as Central America did until the dissolution of the confederation. Others succeeded to the colonial *audiencias* or administrative courts. Among these, Ecuador was the republican heir to the former jurisdiction of the *Audiencia* of Quito and Bolivia took over most of the territory that had been governed by the *Audiencia* of Charcas. Also, before the creation of the last two viceroyalties in the eighteenth century, there had been an *audiencia* in Bogotá, and, for a short time, in Buenos Aires.

Other factors contributed to the influence of the past in deciding the course of nationality. By virtue of her Portuguese background and language, Brazil's right to nationhood was unquestioned. Similarly, Haitian nationality was founded on her distinctive race and speech. Sometimes a fundamental ethnic unity bound a people together as a nation. Perhaps it was a predominance of Spanish blood, as in Costa Rica and Argentina and Uruguay, or the unifying leaven may have been supplied by the aboriginal race, as the Maya-Quiché stock gave a certain unity to Guatemala, the Guaranis to Paraguay, and the virile Araucanian-Spanish mixture to the Chilean masses. Uruguayan nationality has also been strengthened by the consciousness of the Oriental Republic's strategic and dangerous position as a buffer state between her two powerful neighbors.

Paraguay offers an interesting example of the development of nationality in Latin America. She possesses in unusual degree the basic elements of nationality. She is unified ethnically. The mass of her people are a mixture of Spaniard and Guarani Indian. The Guarani tongue, which is the idiom of the people, is another expression of this racial unity. The minorities within the country are too insignificant in numbers and influence to affect this essential oneness of the Paraguayan people. The Paraguayan race was also molded by the common experience of a series of remarkable mass disciplines, which were applied intermittently, but for long periods, over a period of three centuries. These were, by order of their appearance, the communal theocracy of the Jesuit "reductions," and the dictatorships of Francia and the López family. As the processes of history have made of Paraguay a true nation, so have the facts of geography. The real Paraguay, cohesive and integrated, is a natural fortress, with a wide, forest-lined moat on three sides, where the two great rivers almost encircle her. On the north the frontier follows the fosse of the Apa River and to the northeast the ramparts are constituted by the broken highlands of Ambaya and Mbaracajú.

Some of the other Latin-American republics, like Bolivia and Ecuador, Honduras and Nicaragua, though in varying degree, still lack a real basis of nationality. They are afterthoughts of history, conceived with little regard to the factors that make of a country a nation. They have governments and flags and the other trappings of sovereignty. On occasion their populations manifest a rather bellicose patriotism. But all these do not make them nations. Only time and accumulated tradition, and common effort and wise leadership can evolve these amorphous states into organized peoples with a collective consciousness and personality. The fruition of that development will justify the privileges of independent existence, as it will fit them for its obligations. Until then, they will play, rather seriously at times, at nationhood. Perhaps some of the states of Latin America may remain anachronous political entities, never to attain a true spatiotemporal position which might justify the perpetuation of their sovereignty. Eleven or twelve nations could deal more effectively with the problems with which governments are assumed to concern themselves than do the existing twenty, too many of whom lack the substance, material or spiritual, of nationality. For example, the Incas probably did a better "job" of managing their empire than do their present-day successors.

Most of the Latin-American constitutions are very new. The most extreme case of political ephemerae is represented by Haiti, which has had nineteen constitutions, the latest in 1957, since its independence in 1804. Bolivia has had thirteen. Until annulled by the Peronist regime in 1948, the Argentine constitution of 1853 was the oldest in Latin

America, but it was reinstated and given a new lease of life nine years later. Nine other countries adopted new constitutions in the period 1944–48. Brazil has had three constitutions since 1933, one of which was promulgated in 1937 by President Vargas and promptly suspended by him. After a five years' trial, El Salvador abrogated the constitution of 1939 and returned to an amended document of 1886. Chile, Cuba, and Paraguay promulgated new constitutions in 1940. The famous Mexican constitution of 1917 has remained in force ever since. Sometimes a comprehensive series of amendments has radically altered the existing constitution, as happened in 1943 with the Costa Rican constitution of 1871. Also the Colombian constitution of 1886 underwent substantial alterations in 1944–45.

The constitutions of the Latin-American nations have not only been relatively short-lived; they have certain other features which reflect the political restlessness of those peoples. A distrust of legislative processes has resulted in the incorporation in national constitutions of much that should normally be a matter for statutory enactment—a tendency that is by no means confined to Latin America. The lengthy Mexican Constitution of 1917 and the short-lived Brazilian Constitution of 1934 are cases in point. The former aimed to give definitive form to the fundamental ideals of the Mexican Revolution, which began with the overthrow of the Díaz regime, and the latter not only provided for recasting the framework of the Brazilian government, but contained the bases for a whole system of social reforms. Accordingly, the new constitutions are liable to express the prevailing political and economic philosophy of the moment, rather than such political ideas as may be deeply grounded in the nation's history. Also, realizing the fallibility of constitutional conventions and the excessive rigidity of constitutional checks in the face of political realities, provision is often made for the suspension of the constitution, or at least of the constitutional guarantees of the individual rights of the citizen, in the event of a political emergency. In such an event, the chief executive is the judge of what circumstances comprise a state of crisis or abnormal condition in the nation.

Conditions in several Latin-American republics were favorable to a federal system of government. Strong local attachments and interests had grown up through the centuries about certain cities and their dependent territory. Centrifugal forces were fostered by geographical barriers and difficulties of communication. Remote and isolated cities, like Mérida, in Mexico, and the Venezuelan city of the same name, had little in common with the rest of the country. In spite of the centralized rule of Spain under the Hapsburgs and the Bourbons, the mother country had never been unified spiritually, and Spaniards had brought to the New World their traditions of separatism and provincial patriotism.

By reason of their very size, if by virtue of no other considerations, Argentina and Mexico were destined to federalism from the beginning. Yet it was only after long and bitter struggles between the partisans of a strong central government and of the federal principle that the latter triumphed. For a time the conflict between Buenos Aires and the Argentine provinces resulted in virtual anarchy and the disintegration of all national authority. The United Provinces of the River Plate was but a loose confederation, whose members went their separate ways and even waged war on one another. The dictatorship of Rosas was an interval of tyranny in this period of confusion and disunion. Meanwhile, several attempts to adopt a constitution on the general model of the United States were defeated by the opposition of the Porteños, as the citizens of Buenos Aires were known. A decisive step was finally taken in 1880 toward settling the long-contested issue between "the port" and the provinces by federalizing the municipal area of Buenos Aires and making it the capital of the nation.

When, after the end of Iturbide's short-lived empire, the question arose as to the permanent form of the Mexican government, Centralists and Federalists carried on an active controversy for the control of the new state. The constitution of 1824 represented a victory for the federal idea, but twelve years later another constitution, dictated by the famous Santa Anna, abolished the states and made Mexico a unitarian republic. The centralist interregnum ended in 1840, and in 1857 a federal system of government was definitely incorporated in the constitution under which Mexico was to live for another sixty years.

Long before the breakup of Bolívar's republic of Gran Colombia in 1832 the issue between federalism and centralized government had developed in acute form. The first constitution of New Granada, as the independent republic of Colombia was known, provided for a centralized state in which the provincial governors were appointed from Bogotá. The process was reversed in 1857, when the new constitution of the Granadine Confederation left to the states all powers not expressly delegated to the confederate government. In practice the result was to render the central authority virtually impotent. In 1861 the name of the republic was changed to the United States of New Granada, and two years later, to the United States of Colombia. In the latter year the autonomy of the states was considerably curtailed, and in 1886 the present centralized republic was established under a constitution that was the basic law of the country for another half-century.

The first constitution of Venezuela represented a compromise on the basic issue which plagued the political life of her neighbor and former partner in the Bolivarian republic. However, the question arose again during the turbulent period which followed and led to armed conflict between Centralists and Federalists. In 1864 a new constitution established "the United States of Venezuela" as a confederation with large independent powers for the states. It was not until 1904 that the Venezuelan government received its present federal form in its entirety.

Central America presents an interesting example of the problem of coordinating the political life of neighboring peoples whose common heritage would appear to contain more elements of similarity than of divergence. The five original Central American republics—with British Honduras and the Mexican State of Chiapas—are heirs of the lands that comprised the old Captaincy-General of Guatemala. As an administrative appanage of the Viceroyalty of New Spain, it was for a brief period a part of Iturbide's Mexican Empire. In 1824 a congress of representatives of the five provinces declared their joint independence as the United Provinces of Central America. Discord early arose among the members of the federation, which was, however, held together for a time by the ability and moderation of President Francisco Morazán. The union signed its own death warrant in 1838, when it agreed to permit any state to withdraw from the federation. Nicaragua, Honduras, and Costa Rica were prompt to take advantage of the authorization and seceded from the union. A few years later El Salvador, Honduras, and Nicaragua set up the tripartite "Central American Confederation," but the process of disintegration had already proceeded too far and the league shortly broke up with war between two of its members. Attempts to revive the persistent idea in 1849 and again in 1862 failed as completely. A fresh impetus was given to the movement for Central American federalism in 1876, when delegates of all five countries met at Guatemala City at the invitation of General Justo Rufino Barrios, President of Guatemala. Accumulated animosities and jealousies proved to be too strong to permit the re-establishment of the now long-defunct union. Other subsequent projects for voluntary federation had no better fate, nor did the efforts of President Zelaya, of Nicaragua, in 1907 to bring about union by force.

In the same year all the states sent delegates to Washington to confer on plans for partial union. Several agreements were reached on subjects of common interest, but very little was accomplished toward the curtailment of national sovereignties in favor of a closer administrative union. In fact, the Central American Court of Justice, which sat until 1918, was the only tangible move in this direction. However, in spite of repeated setbacks, the idea of union still had so much vitality and made so strong an appeal to the imagination of Central Americans that three years later all the republics, except El Salvador, agreed on a union to be known as the Federation of Central America. The government of Costa Rica refused to ratify the pact and so condemned the move to failure. Meanwhile, the United States had given its encouragement to the general movement, but a second conference held at Washington in 1922 largely confined its deliberations to the international plane.

The obstacles to the consummation of the great design for a combination of the Central American states have grown with time. The independent republics have developed pronounced political personalities and their ruling classes have a strong vested interest in national independence. There is general distrust of Guatemala as the largest member of the group, and Costa Rica is reluctant to compromise its superior political progress by a closer tie with her less-advanced neighbors. In the meantime, a highway, imperfect though it may be, and a system of airlines link the five countries. To reduce the physical barriers that have separated them, a growing economic unity is in the making and wiser leaders accept the inevitability of a federal solution to the separation that has long plagued mid-America.

Of the other Latin-American countries, Peru, broken up into a number of widely separated communities, had all the natural conditions that were propitious for a federal system. However, a tradition of government from Lima, set by centuries of viceregal rule, determined the unitarian pattern which Peru has followed from independence. Brazil, whom history and circumstances of geography predisposed to a federalist system, had to pass through a long period of unitary rule under the Empire before she realized her natural role as the United States of Brazil.

Certain states of the federal republics have manifested separatist tendencies at one period or another of their history. Disgusted with Santa Anna's arbitrary attempts to centralize all authority in his own person, the State of Yucatán attempted in 1839 to secede from Mexico, and for all practical purposes remained independent of the central government for several years. The Colombian province of Nariño long conducted its affairs as though it were a sovereign nation, and for a period even refused to honor the currency of the Bogotá government. The Province of Panama, separated from the body of the country by the swamps and jungles of the Atrato region and conscious of its strategic position on the isthmus, showed an attitude of independence long before the fateful events of 1903. It revolted against Colombia in 1830, and during most of 1840–41 its name of the Free State of Isthmus was scarcely a misnomer. Throughout the various changes in the form of the national government Panama retained a certain autonomous status that was conceded to no other part of the country.

In Brazil, the rich and progressive State of São Paulo has twice revolted against the federal government during the present century. The Paulistas, as the citizens of the state are called, complained that they carried an undue share of the country's cost of government. Though the state occupied a privileged position in the federation, some of its leaders held the view that its interests would be better served by independence and seriously considered the possibility of secession. Meanwhile, the state had built up a large and well-equipped army that was more than a mere militia. The state flag was often displayed in the public schools above the emblem of the nation. The state government maintained quasi-diplomatic relations with foreign countries and sent its agents abroad to treat with foreign governments on matters pertaining to immigration and the all-important coffee trade. Civil war broke out in 1924 between São Paulo and the federal government. Again, in 1932, two years after a widespread revolt had overthrown the Washington Luís government, the State of São Paulo rose in arms against the dictatorship of Getúlio Vargas and the new political regime which had been enforced on the proud state. The largest armies so far engaged in the history of the continent fought for several months, but the rebellion was finally crushed by the superior forces of the federal government, which was able to cut off the Paulistas from their outside sources of supply.

In view of the strong position of the executive in most Latin-American governments, it was to be expected that ways would be found for controlling the members of a federal union of states. Thus, the president has become the instrument of counter-tendencies of centralization in the federal republics. Occasion for the assertion of the presidential or central authority against the government of a state may originate in any one of a number of circumstances. A state government may oppose certain fundamental federal policies to the point where its attitude constitutes incipient revolution, and so form a rallying point for discontent throughout the country, as happened in 1939 in the case of Governor Saturnino Cedillo, of the Mexican State of Aguas Calientes. A state governor may be so patently a candidate for the presidency that, unless he has the previous approval of the central administration, the realities of Latin-American politics would not permit a president passively to accept the situation. A state government may make such commitments or contract such obligations abroad as would compromise the federal authority, if the state should fail to fulfill its agreements. The large borrowing powers which were left to the Colombian departments as a survival from the federal period of that nation's past were to create an embarrassing problem for the central government of Colombia, with the result that restraints were later placed on the fiscal independence of the departments. Due either to corruption, administrative inefficiency, or public disorders resulting from the struggles of political factions, a collapse of the regular processes of government within a state may require the central power to undertake extraordinary measures of control, temporarily restricting the sovereignty of the state.

A regular technique for meeting most of these situations exists within the constitutions of Argentina and Brazil. The federal government may *intervene* in the internal affairs of the state in question and supplant the ordinary machinery of administration until normal conditions are restored. During the interim of federal control the state is governed by a federal *interventor*, who is appointed by the president and responsible to him. This device has been resorted to several times in the history of both nations, but generally during periods of political crisis. Thus, in 1937, President Vargas of Brazil removed all state governors, except that of Minas Gerais, from office. Though some were reappointed as federal interventors in their states, others were replaced by special representatives of the president. As a phase of the same general overturn of the Brazilian federal system all state legislatures and municipal assemblies were dissolved.

In Mexico and Venezuela, the two other federal republics, other methods, usually extra-legal, have been invoked in order to accomplish the same end. Porfirio Díaz and Juan Vicente Gómez, long-time dictators, effectively controlled the state governments of their respective countries by dictating the choice of governors. In Mexico, troublesome state governors have sometimes been intimidated into conformity by a display of federal force or have been removed from their local vantage point by appointment to some federal post of honor, usually in a foreign country.

Chile can be considered as typical of the centralized republics. She is geographically compact and unified to a high degree, since the ocean binds together the parts of the long, narrow country, and no serious natural obstacles separate the outlying parts of the republic from the capital and the important Central Valley. This natural unity has been further strengthened by the construction of a north-and-south railway, much of whose length serves a strategic, rather than commercial, purpose. In these respects she differs greatly from Bolivia, Ecuador, and Colombia, whose widely separated and distinctive regions have not been adequately linked together by railroads or other means of communication. Similarly, the authority of the central government is much more effective throughout a tightly knit country like El Salvador, which has a good network of internal transportation lines, than in the neighboring republic of Honduras, whose system of land communications is still primitive.

The *intendentes* or administrative heads of the Chilean provinces are appointed by the president and hold office at his will. The *intendentes*, in turn, select the "governors" of the departments under their jurisdiction, and, in accordance with the descending order of appointive power, the governors name the local officials of the administrative subdivisions within their territory. In other countries, the names of the administrative divisions and titles of the various categories of the governing hierarchy differ one from another, but the basic pattern is everywhere similar, and, regardless of the variations of political nomenclature, the ultimate authority stems from the presidential palace in the capital of the republic. At the opposite end of the centralized administrative process, considerable influence is wielded by the *jefe político,* or "political chieftain," who, as the political "boss" of the community, is also ever-mindful of his position in the dominant party machine of the nation. Many of the worst abuses in Latin-American government have been connected with the prevalence of *caciquismo,* as the rule of these petty political bosses is sometimes called, after a West Indian word for "chief."

Except in the national capitals or other large cities, whose mayors are generally appointees of the central government, there is liable to be more political independence and vitality in the municipal governments of Latin America than in the rural districts and in the field of provincial administration. There is not only a persistent tradition of city government from colonial times, but the urban citizenry is superior in respect to literacy and political education. It has a capacity for common action that is lacking in other groups of the national population, and which on occasion acts as a check on the more arbitrary exercise of power by superior authority. Sometimes this influence is wielded through the elective municipal councils; at other times it is exerted through an assertive public opinion, or even by more direct methods of protest.

The Latin-American constitutions have frequently aimed to place restrictions on the great power of the presidency. As the president often dominates the deliberations of those who draft these charters of government, efforts are usually ineffectual. However, the re-election of a president for two consecutive terms is now prohibited in virtually all the republics. In Guatemala a president must wait twelve years before he can again become a candidate. This safeguard is partially counteracted by the circumstance that in almost half the republics the presidential term is six years. Sentiment in Mexico for this constitutional provision has been so strong that for a time every official communication of the Mexican government closed with the words: "Effective suffrage; no re-election."

Various devices have been found for defeating the purpose of this restriction on the presidential power. An ex-president may continue to control the actions of his successors, as Rafael Trujillo did during an interregnum in the Dominican Republic, though the attempt of General Calles to dominate Mexican politics after his retirement failed before the uncalculated independence of Lázaro Cárdenas. Also, while there were several interims in the long presidency of Juan Vicente Gómez in Venezuela, during which the dictator apparently retired to private life, the actual sequence of his absolute authority was unbroken by these hiatuses. The real seat of power continued to be the country estate of Gómez at Maracay and not the presidential palace in Caracas.

Several examples of arbitrary action will illustrate the methods by which ambitious presidents may circumvent the constitutional limitations on their terms of office. The late President Busch of Bolivia dissolved the national congress, declared the constitution nonoperative, and set up a totalitarian state, which was only terminated by his death and the restoration of the *status quo ante* by his provisional successor, President Quintanilla. President Vargas of Brazil ruled without a constitution for much of his dictatorship. In the case of President Ubico of Guatemala, who first took office in 1931, the constitutional ban on a second term was suspended by a "plebiscite" which continued the president's term until 1943, but General Ubico was not permitted to serve out his extended term. In Honduras, Dr. Tiburcio Carias Andino, elected president for the term 1933–37, was reappointed by the national congress for an additional six years, and still occupied the presidential palace in 1948. In the neighboring republic of El Salvador, the six-year term of General Maximiliano Hernández Martínez was extended by a constitutional convention from 1937 to 1943. General Anastasio Somoza, after serving as president of Nicaragua from 1936 to 1940, was re-elected under the new constitution of 1939 to serve a further eight-year term expiring in 1947. On the conclusion of his second term, he removed his successor from office and reassumed the executive power, only to be re-elected in 1950 and assassinated six years later, thereby terminating a 20-year dictatorship. He was succeeded by his son, Luís, who went through the forms of an election in 1957 for a six-year term.

The most radical step taken in any country to curtail the prerogatives of the presidency was embodied in the Uruguayan constitution of 1917. This constitution was largely inspired by the brilliant José Batlle y Ordoñez, president from 1903 to 1907, and again in 1911–15. It provided for a dual executive, whereby power was divided between the president and an Administrative Council of nine men. Under this plan the president appointed three ministers of the government and the Administrative Council appointed four. In the skilled hands of Baltasar Brum, president from 1919 to 1923, the scheme appeared workable, but the inevitable impasse in the executive gradually came to a head after his guiding influence was removed. Gabriel Terra, president from 1931 to 1935, resolved the problem by dismissing the congress and the Administrative Council, and starting thence with a clean slate. The constituent assembly, which met at his call, prepared the constitution of 1934, which restored the presidency to substantially its former position in the government, while retaining the framework of the Administrative Council as an advisory body in matters of policy. Then, in 1951 the country returned to the Swiss-type of collegiate executive with the nine-member National Council of Government as planned by Batlle Ordoñez. Departments of the government are headed by nine cabinet-rank ministers.

In most countries the president is elected by direct popular vote. Argentina has a system of electors on the American plan, and in Haiti, Uruguay, and Venezuela the president is chosen by the national congress.

There is nothing comparable to the American party convention, and candidates are generally selected by the leaders of the respective parties, sometimes acting as a party caucus in the national legislature. The president sometimes dictates the choice of his successor, in support of whose candidacy he then uses the existing machinery of government. In Brazil, it was long the custom to alternate the presidency between the two dominant States of Minas Gerais and São Paulo, with an occasional candidate from Rio Grande do Sul or the northern states of the republic. As the official candidate of the government, his election largely became a formality.

Though party politics are very active in Latin America, they have certain characteristics not found in the United States. Parties tend to depend on the personality of some prominent leader and are frequently known by his name. Thus, the Irigoyenistas in Argentina were partisans of Hipólyto Irigoyen, who was the Radical party's president during the period 1916–1922 and again from 1928 to 1930, and the Monttvaristas in Chile represented the traditions of the Montt family and of Antonio Varas, a leader of the Montt faction. In these cases, the personal loyalties of the leader's followers are of more importance than any political issues. In Mexico the dominant political element is the *Partido Revolucionario Institutional*, or Party of Revolutionary Institutions, which purports to have a monopoly as representative of the major social revolution that began in 1910. For all practical purposes, Mexico is a one-party country, and the *Partido Acción Nacional* or Party of National Action, is only tolerated for the sake of appearances.

Sometimes party names are truly indicative of real divisions of opinion on fundamental issues. Thus, the Conservative party usually represents the traditional vested interests of the country, such as the Catholic Church and the large landowners, while the Liberal party represents those who would institute certain reforms at the expense of those interests. Specific issues in the struggles between these parties may involve such matters as civil marriages, separation of church and state, control of public education, extension of the suffrage, taxation of landed property and incomes, and social legislation. Such a division exists in Colombia, where it gives party lines a special significance seldom found elsewhere in Latin America. In Latin America political parties are generally known by the names Democratic, Republican, Socialist, or Radical, or by various combinations of the four. However, the names seldom give a clue to the special principles represented by the particular party, a practice by no means confined to Latin America.

Parties whose platforms embody more or less radical programs of legislation have become increasingly common in Latin America. One of the most interesting of these is the so-called APRA, or Aprista party, in Peru, now known as the People's party, which was founded by Raul Haya de la Torre, and whose original name was an abbreviation of the significant words "Alianza Popular Revolucionaria Americana." The conservative elements who have traditionally ruled the country long succeeded in keeping the party's candidates off the election ballots, or nullified its political influence by other methods. However, on the accession of the Bustamante Rivero government to power in 1945 the Aprista party was legalized and thereupon became for a time an important factor in the political affairs of the republic.

Communist parties are now very common in Latin America. They operate openly in at least eight countries, and Bolivia even has two, including one of the Trotskyite variety. In Cuba, the official party, the only one tolerated in the country, is Communist. In other countries the Communist parties come and go, as they are alternately tolerated or outlawed. In Mexico the Communist party of Vicente Lombardo Toledano persists as the Popular Socialist party, but it is not a major influence in national politics. In Brazil, the Communist party was licensed by President Vargas and suppressed shortly thereafter by order of the Supreme Court. Though presumably driven underground, the party apparatus has continued to function without effective interference or control by the tolerant authority of the superior government.

The Communist parties are singularly uniform in their policies and programs. Beyond acceptance of conventional Marxist dogma as an ideological "cushion" for their activities, they are accustomed to support the cause of extreme nationalism, particularly as it gives them a stronger leverage in their attacks on foreign, i.e. American, "imperialism." They work diligently for closer relations with Russia and China, while they oppose any efforts for strengthening ties with the United States. They aim to elect enough party members to the national congress to constitute an obstructive bloc of sufficient strength to influence the course of legislation in a "popular front" government. They stage demonstrations and disorders in order to harass and embarrass the existing authority of the state. Meanwhile, they endorse and proclaim revolutionary programs designed to shift the burden of economic and political power to their supporters, yet they do not concern themselves with quick solutions to the current social ills of the nation, whose cure would nullify their own appeal to the citizenry and remove the very *raison d'être* of their political existence.

The appeal of Communism is primarily to the mass of low-class mestizos, particularly in large distressed areas like northeast Brazil, and to the growing urban "proletariat" of slum dwellers, as in Caracas, Lima, and Santiago. It capitalizes on the obvious inequities in Latin-American life and on the frequent social callousness of the conservatives.

The most persistent Communist movement in Latin America has probably been in Chile. Under tough leadership, it has survived outlawry and other setbacks and, now legalized, in the turbulent political atmosphere of the country it could become a major influence in government.

Until its triumph in Castroite Cuba, Communism had its most sensational success in Guatemala. Never an exhibit of democracy, opinion in the dominant *ladino* class was softened up, for a change, by the revolutionary administration of Juan José Arévalo between 1944 and 1951. On the groundwork laid by Arévalo there was built the openly pro-Communist regime of Colonel Jacobo Arbenz, which was overthrown in 1954 by an armed invasion of Guatemalans from Honduras. Colonel Carlos Castillo Armas, leader of the expeditionary force, assumed control of the government and remained president until his assassination three years later.

In Cuba, a guerrilla rebellion, headed by Fidel Castro, succeeded in overthrowing the dictatorship of General Fulgencio Batista, and at the beginning of 1959 took over the government of the republic. Once firmly established in power, the Castro regime moved rapidly to the left and formed a close working relationship with the Soviet Union, its acknowledged model and sponsor. Moreover, propaganda agents of the Communist government in Cuba fomented discontent and disorders wherever in Latin America the local situation lent itself to their machinations.

In the early history of the Argentine Republic the country was torn by violent conflicts between the advocates of a strong centralized state dominated by the capital and the Province of Buenos Aires and those who favored a federal system of semi-autonomous provinces. This important issue long gave a meaning to political parties that overshadowed all other considerations. While partisan strife in Uruguay was even more prolonged and bitter than in Argentina, the division between the two dominant parties of the Oriental Republic early lost most of its original significance. The *Blancos*, or Whites, and *Colorados*, or Reds, first comprised the followers of Manuel Oribe and of

Fructuoso Rivera, who carried pennons of those colors on their lances at the Battle of Carpintaria in 1836. For a time the *Blancos* were the party of traditionalism and were strongest in the country districts, while the *Colorados* were at least reputed to favor progressive measures of government and had their greatest strength in Montevideo and the other towns. As time went on, the two became only contestants in a chronic and meaningless civil war, with the *Colorados* holding the ascendency during the latter part of the century.[1]

In contrast to the relatively simple partisan divisions of these countries is the complex party history of Chile. Party rivalries in that country originally followed the conventional formula of conservatives and liberals. The Conservative party represented the most powerful of the old landed families, and was strongly clerical in its policies. Under the able leadership of Diego Portales it incorporated its ideas of government in the constitution of 1833, which was the basic law of Chile for nearly a century. Except for a short Liberal interregnum, it dominated Chilean political life until the Balmaceda regime in the eighties. Meanwhile, party lines had lost some of their clearness, as certain groups espoused varying degrees of liberalism or conservatism, or as strong personal followings displaced the normal party attachments. As a consequence, when the Chilean party system appeared to attain its ultimate complexity toward the end of the last century there were six well-defined party groups. In addition to the two classical parties, these consisted of the Radicals, who had strong anti-clerical leanings, the Democrats, who championed the growing laboring class, the Nationalists, who represented the traditions of the Montt-Varas

---

[1] For a picture of life in Uruguay during the civil wars between the *Blancos* and *Colorados*, see W. H. Hudson, *The Purple Land*, first published in London in 1885 and since reprinted in several editions. In it the famous English naturalist writes: "It is the perfect republic: the sense of emancipation experienced in it by a wanderer from the Old World is indescribably sweet and novel . . . where all men are absolutely free and equal . . . I fancy I hear some wise person exclaiming, 'In name only is your Purple Land a republic; its constitution is a piece of waste paper, its government an oligarchy tempered by assassinations and revolution.' True; but the lust of ambitious rulers all striving to pluck each other down have no power to make the people miserable. The unwritten constitution, mightier than the written one, is in the heart of every man to make him still a republican and free with a freedom it would be hard to match anywhere else on the globe. . . . If this absolute equality is inconsistent with perfect political order, I for one should grieve to see such order established." (The New Reader's Library edition; London: Duckworth, 1927), pp. 334-35.

regime, and the Liberal Democrats, who were the political heirs of
President Balmaceda. Due to the breakup of the old party system,
congressional action became possible only by resort to blocs or combinations of parties, as in pre-war France. This resulted in much log-
rolling and maneuvering at the expense of established political policies
and principles, and set a lower tone for the parliamentarianism that
was the outstanding feature of Chilean government during that
period. Meanwhile, the number of political parties has continued to
grow, and seventeen parties participated in the congressional elections
of 1957.

The United States system of ministerial responsibility to the
executive is the rule among Latin-American governments, in contrast
to the European system of responsibility to the parliament. That is, the
president appoints the members of his own cabinet and may remove
them on his own volition. The former complex cabinet system of
Chile, which was designed to hold the president in check, has been
materially changed, but any cabinet member is still privileged to address the national congress in connection with the work of his department. There is considerable variety in the composition of Latin-American cabinets. Except in the larger countries, responsibility for the
national defense is usually concentrated in a single ministry. In
Mexico, several heads of independent government agencies have full
cabinet rank. The minister of interior, or "government," has an unusual position in the Latin-American cabinet, as is customary in
Europe. Except for serious disorders which may call for the use of the
military, he is generally charged with the maintenance of order in the
country, which may include surveillance of the political opposition.
In addition to his police functions, he normally dispenses political
patronage in the provinces, and through the *jefes políticos,* or political
bosses, who often have the position of local governors, he controls the
ruling party's political machine. Though the minister of foreign affairs
is usually the ranking member of the cabinet, in the Cuban and
Peruvian systems the head of the cabinet has a status in some respects
analogous to that of a European prime minister. Also, as an improvised
measure of political expediency, Brazil substituted a similar arrangement for its conventional executive in 1961. A minister of economy,
who is responsible for the execution of official policies designed to
improve the economic life of the country or to regulate its economic

activities, is found in the cabinets of several governments. As Argentine Minister of Economy, Alvaro Alsogaray held a particularly important place in the Frondizi administration during the early 1960's.

A bicameral body, made up of a senate and a chamber of deputies, is the normal legislative pattern of Latin-American governments, though most of the legislatures of the Central American republics are composed of a single chamber, commonly known as the National Assembly. The trend is now toward the popular election of the members of both houses, but Argentina still clings to the plan, which it borrowed from the United States (before enactment of the XVIIth Amendment), of selecting its senators by vote of the provincial legislatures. The term of office of members of the lower chamber is generally longer than in the United States. For example, a Chilean deputy holds office for four years, and a Mexican deputy for three years. On the other hand, the members of the unicameral legislature of El Salvador are re-elected annually. At the other extreme, Chilean senators are elected for an eight-year term. An interesting feature of the Nicaraguan constitution makes all former presidents of the republic ex-officio members of the National Assembly for life. However, since the Somoza family has ruled Nicaragua since 1937, and its most enduring member is dead, the provision is really an empty letter.

Some of the republics, including Mexico, make provision for a permanent commission of the national legislature, which sits during the recesses between the regular sessions of the congress. This device not only gives continuity to the life of the legislative body, but serves as a check on the decree-making tendencies of the executive.

The idea of proportional representation has gained some ground in Latin-American countries, notably in Chile and Uruguay. Important minorities are thereby given a place in the government in relation to their numerical strength, and share in the responsibility of rule, instead of harassing the current administration from the outside as an opposition party. For example, the important Uruguayan Council of Ministers is made up of nine members, selected in a ratio of six to three from the two political parties with the largest vote at the preceding elections.

Though the enforcement of electoral laws often leaves much to be desired, there is a growing tendency to surround elections with safeguards against the corruption or duress of voters or against the

inertia of the voters themselves. Balloting is also secret in a number of
the republics, where it is a strong influence for honest elections. It is
customary to hold elections on Sunday, and, in order to reduce the
chance of disorders at the polls, all places where strong liquor is dis-
pensed are generally closed from the preceding evening until the votes
are all in.

Until recently, suffrage was limited to men over 21, who were
able to read and write. The literacy qualification had the effect of
disfranchising the majority of adult males in countries with a large
Indian population, as in Peru, and wherever the restriction is still in
force it materially reduces the size of the voting registers. In Bolivia
the literacy requirement was annulled in 1952 by the revolutionary
government of the MNR, thereby enfranchising the great mass of
ignorant Indians. In Brazil and Chile illiterates are still denied the
vote, and in Venezuela, where they comprise the majority of the
adult population, they cast their votes by special colored ballots. In several countries the voting age is 18. In Mexico boys may vote at that
age if they are the heads of families, but bachelors and those without
an "honorable means of livelihood" are not eligible until they are 21.
In Costa Rica, married males and school teachers may vote at 18, but
bachelors are required to wait until they are 20.

Though sentiment in more conservative circles is still strong
against the active participation of women in politics, female suffrage
is now practically universal. But even progressive Argentina did not
enfranchise its women until 1947, Mexico five years later, and Peru
in 1955.

Compulsory voting is in effect, at least theoretically, in Argentina, Brazil, Costa Rica, Guatemala, Peru, and Venezuela, but in
Brazil voting is optional for unemployed women and for men over 65.
In Guatemala, women and illiterate males may remain away from the
polls if they desire. In Honduras, all men over 21 as well as all married
men and all literate men over 18 are required to vote, but voting is
optional for women.

Such has been the scheme of government; its working-out has
proven very different. The plan—and much of its philosophy—was
borrowed from the United States and France. It bore little relation to
the experience of the peoples whose framework of rule it was to be.
Realities quickly asserted themselves over constitutions and theories

and ideals, and it is only in our own time that the two have anywhere approximated one another. Meanwhile, history, geography, and the state of society foredoomed the republics to a long period in which inexorable facts took precedence over forms.

It was in the nature of things that the republic should be monocracies and not democracies. The demos or sovereign people were still too backward and inchoate to rule. One-man government was the natural alternative, except in Chile, where the landed oligarchs held all power tightly within their class and ruled through the national congress. Therefore, the political history of Latin America has been too largely a story of the cycle of dictatorship and revolution. Some of the countries have definitely freed themselves from the traditional formula; others have escaped for a time, only to relapse into the old ways.

Bolívar had foreseen the trend of events toward presidential autocracy, for the process took shape before his death. "My funerals," he predicted, "will be as bloody as those of Alexander." The South American counterparts of Ptolemy, Seleucus, and the rest of the Macedonian Diadochi were the generals of the Liberator—Santander, Paez, Flores, and Santa Cruz—who ruled the lands which he had freed. They were the first *caudillos,* and set the basic pattern for an age in which absolutism alternated with anarchy.

The power of the president-dictators rested on a combination of conditions and methods. They represented a colonial tradition of personal rule—of obedience to a viceroy or a captain-general—which was the only system of government within the experience of their peoples, and so the only system whose elements the public understood. As such, their rule did not constitute a break in the political evolution of Latin America, but rather a logical stage in that development. Under new names and forms, they only embodied habits of action and ways of thinking that were deeply grounded in the custom of centuries. The peoples still mistrusted the efficacy of their own concerted endeavors, as they doubted the confused wisdom of legislatures, and preferred to trust their political fortunes to a strong and untrammeled individual who would satisfy their urge to get things done.

The national congress, which the constitutions designed to be a check on the executive, was only too often subservient to the dictator. Autocrats, like Díaz of Mexico, Estrada Cabrera of Guatemala, and

Gómez of Venezuela, dominated their legislatures by manipulation or intimidation. The congress thus became a pliant instrument for giving legal validity to the arbitrary actions of the dictators, for the modern *caudillo* generally shared the colonial Spaniard's awe of the letter of the law.

A centralized scheme of public administration, with large appointive powers for the president, favored the position of the *caudillos*. It was particularly important to the dictator that he should control directly the treasury, the secret police, and the army. Only loyal henchmen could be trusted in charge of the customs houses, for import duties were usually the most substantial source of the government's revenues. It was the principal function of the national police to keep the president informed of the state of public opinion, especially among his enemies, so that revolts against his power might be forestalled and punishment meted out to conspirators.

Pretorianism was inseparable from *caudillismo*. Most of the early dictators were soldiers, many of whom had risen to power by barrack revolutions. In that event they carried with them to the presidential palace a nucleus of armed support. It was good policy to pamper the garrisons in the capital and in other key positions with good, or at least regular, pay and other favors, while keeping watch on the allegiance of their officers. One Haitian president is said to have locked up the national army in the palace courtyard every night, in order to prevent any rivals from tampering with its loyalty. Civilian presidents, though handicapped by the lack of military experience, often become, by their superior astuteness, as complete masters of the country's armed forces as any of the generals. While soldier-presidents have been the rule in some of the republics, like Mexico, Ecuador, and Guatemala, others, like Chile, Colombia, and Costa Rica, have drawn a majority of their chief executives from among the class of "doctors" or educated civilians. It is significant of the shift of power from the military that in the middle of 1962 only three Latin-American presidents were soldiers. In Uruguay none of the nine members of the National Council of Government was a military man.

The national courts have done little to restrain the activities of arbitrary and strong-willed presidents, but in matters which involved the prerogatives of the executive have usually been docile instruments of the current dictatorship, placing a judicial seal on his extra-legal or unconstitutional actions. Other sources of executive authority have been control of the electoral machinery and censorship of the press and of other agencies of public information. With the growing restiveness of the electorate in certain countries these devices have become important concerns of presidents who are desirous of perpetuating their power. Not only is editorial comment or news detrimental to the interests of the dictator banned from domestic circulation, but sensitiveness to foreign opinion may prevent news agencies or correspondents from sending out news unfavorable to the president or his policies. Foreign newspaper men who refuse to accept the official version of important events in their dispatches may be expelled from the country, as has occurred in Brazil and Mexico. Another source of control over the economic life of the country, which is sometimes utilized by the dictators, is through their participation in the direction of certain public monopolies of essential commodities or services. The notorious President Zelaya, of Nicaragua, resorted freely to this form of exploitation, and the famous Gómez, of Venezuela, took advantage of his position to indulge his stockman's instincts to the point where he controlled the cattle industry of the country.

There have been as many varieties of Latin-American dictators as there were of their early prototypes, the Greek tyrants of Sicily and the despots of the Italian city-states. Some, usually the military *caudillos,* based their power on downright force, a certain elemental cunning, the appeal of soldierly bluffness, and the dramatization of their authority by pomp and ceremony calculated to impress the populace. These men represented dictatorship in its crudest form, and were as liable to be found among the early governors of the Argentine provinces as among the presidents of Central America or the Andean republics. Some of them were barbaric chieftains, like the second López of Paraguay, Carrera of Guatemala, Daza of Bolivia, and Melgarejo of the same country, who killed his predecessor and rival, General Belzú, with his own hand. These men were vain and capricious, often given to bizarre and fantastic display, and to sadistic cruelty, but sometimes had a dashing manner that commended them to the hero-worshiping masses. Of the same general type were such inept and bombastic leaders as Santa Anna, who bedeviled the political life of Mexico for a long period, and as Castro, of Venezuela, became in the latter years of his rule.

As opposed to the more violent breed of *caudillos,* there were dictators of a sinister type, who ruled by craft rather than by force. Their power was based on a highly developed system of espionage and on terroristic methods that were more insidious and refined than those of their brutal fellows. Among their weapons were deception and intrigue, corruption and confiscation, secrecy and mystery.

Archetype of this more subtle category of autocrats was José Gaspar Rodríguez Francia, who was absolute lord of the Guarani Republic of Paraguay almost from its inception until his death—in bed— in 1840. Dr. Francia, known to his subjects and to history as *El Supremo,* embodied in his own person practically all the attributes of government. He was a solitary figure, without ministers or confidants, of superior intellectual attainments, plain living and incorruptible, who gave the same meticulous attention to the details of administration as had Philip II of Spain, and as much later the dour and lonely Hipólyto Irigoyen was to give to the complex government of Argentina.

Francia cut his country off from the rest of the world and the disorders of the time, and personally supervised the very limited trading operations which were authorized at the few ports of entry. Within the closed frontiers he gave the country domestic peace and a degree of well-being consistent with its primitive standards of living. But the local aristocracy, from whose members opposition to his rule might arise, was kept in subjection by a peculiarly oppressive technique of terror designed to break down its consciousness and cohesion as a class. Similarly, he stripped the Church of its privileges and bound its weakened organization to himself in a humiliating dependence.

His younger contemporary, Juan Manuel de Rosas, master of Argentina from 1829 to 1852, though of a more active temperament, employed many of the principles of rule so effectively practiced by Francia in a smaller sphere of action. Rosas rose to power by way of the bloody civil wars between Federalists and Unitarians, which long divided the Argentine population into two irreconcilable factions. Though a well-born Porteño, or native of Buenos Aires, he threw in his fortunes with the partisans of federalism against the metropolis. The richest Argentine of his day, an excellent horseman and experienced Indian fighter, he had qualities of leadership that won him complete ascendency over the wild and undisciplined Gaucho lancers of the pampa. Even Facundo Quiroga, half-savage chieftain of these centaurs of the plains, recognized his supremacy, as Paez, leader of the Venezuelan *llaneros,* had yielded to the mastery of Bolívar. As governor of the key province of Buenos Aires, Rosas, though champion of the federal cause, enforced on the divided nation its first unity. An able administrator, bold and enterprising in action, he was a ruthless autocrat, who would have no compromise with his opponents or, in fact, tolerate them within the bounds of the state. A secret group of his followers was the instrument of a terror that sent his most irreconcilable enemies to death or drove them into exile, while a proud people yielded him an obedience that bordered on servility. When his despotism was finally overthrown by General Urquiza, Rosas retired to England, where he lived as a country gentleman for another twenty-five years.

Some of the dictators were noted for their contributions to the material development of their countries. Their methods were no less arbitrary than those of the more destructive *caudillos* and their repression of democratic forces was as complete. But they had a sense of responsibility for the modernization of the nation's economy. They promoted the building of railroads and public works, the introduction of foreign capital for the development of the country's resources, the extension of foreign trade, and the financial stability and credit of the government. Among these "benevolent despots" of the Latin-American republics were Montes, of Bolivia, Díaz, of Mexico, the brilliant Guzmán Blanco, of Venezuela, the pro-clerical García Moreno, of Ecuador, and Barrios, of Guatemala. In the balance against the infamies of the long dictatorship of Gómez in Venezuela were his liquidation of the foreign debt, his construction of an elaborate network of highways, and the impetus which he gave to the petroleum industry of Maracaibo.[2] Some of these rulers were patrons of the arts, and Estrada Cabrera, who governed Guatemala with an iron hand for twenty-two years, was doubtless prouder of his ostentatious Temple of Minerva than of any of the other achievements of his autocracy.

By the middle of the century the conventional pattern of Latin-American politics had noticeably altered. The age of dictatorships and the revolutions that alternated with them had by no means ended.

---

[2] For the career of Gómez, see *Gómez: Tyrant of the Andes,* by Thomas Rourke, pseudonym for D. J. Clinton (New York: William Morrow; 1937).

Colombia was still to experience two long and sanguinary civil wars. In Uruguay the perennial armed struggles between *Blancos* and *Colorados* were to continue for many years, and when President Latorre resigned from office in 1880 he declared that Uruguay, now one of the most orderly of Latin-American republics, was "ungovernable." The first Uruguayan president who completed his term without armed opposition to his administration was Julio Herrera y Obes, who governed that country in the early nineties. Paraguay was to pass from the control of one ephemeral *caudillo* to another in rapid succession. The Andean republics were yet to sink to new lows of political disorder and arbitrary government. Our own generation was to witness a widespread reappearance of the familiar cycle.

Nevertheless, there were definite signs of progress toward a better order of things. New forces of stability, if not of immediate significance to the faltering struggle for democracy, rose in the republics wherever the bases of national life were essentially healthy. Though *caudillismo* persisted, its manifestations henceforth tended to take a less violent form and to assume, at least in the more advanced countries, more of the characteristics of political bossism in the United States. Meanwhile, the appearance of the noble Juárez was symptomatic of the possibilities of Mexican democracy, even though he was to be followed by the long interlude of the Díaz absolutism. Under the aegis of her governing aristocracy, Chile had attained a political peace that was only to be interrupted by the civil war between President Balmaceda and the partisans of congressional authority.

Advancement was most notable in Argentina. Though the aftereffects were to continue for some time, the long struggle between the provinces and the capital had ended with a compromise that was finally to bring internal peace to the long distracted country. Buenos Aires was made a Federal District, on the model of Washington, Rio de Janeiro, and Mexico City, while the seat of government of the province was removed to the near-by city of La Plata. The people were weary of the disorders and political repression that accompanied the old regime. As across the estuary in the Banda Oriental, there was a strong popular revulsion against the endless fighting and raiding, with their interruption of normal business and farming and with the killing of herds and flocks by the undisciplined bands of partisans. The country was on the eve of its extraordinary economic development, and the new industrial and financial interests exerted all their rising influence in favor of internal political peace and adherence to constitutional processes of government. The government and the national economy proved strong enough to weather, without political disturbances, a series of crises brought on by too rapid expansion. An extensive railway system was built, and the network of lines radiating from Buenos Aires sealed the union of the country and also enabled the federal government to deal more quickly and effectively with any incipient outbreak of rebellion in the provinces. Meanwhile, as elsewhere in Latin America, the first steps were taken to place the armed forces of the nation on a professional basis and to inculcate into the newly disciplined soldiery loyalty to the state, instead of to individual leaders.

Argentina was also fortunate in having, during this period of transition and development, a succession of able and public-spirited presidents, most of whom were civilians. By their superior intellectual qualifications and devotion to the public welfare, some of them represented a new type of Latin-American statesmen. Bartolomé Mitre, who was president from 1862 to 1868, was an eminent publicist, author of a scholarly biography of San Martín, founder of *La Nación*, one of South America's great newspapers, and, on occasion, active commander of the national army. His successor, Domingo Faustino Sarmiento, was a voluminous writer, who was the author of *Facundo*, the classical work of the Gaucho era. He enthusiastically promoted the cause of popular education, and on his return from a term as Minister in the United States, not only took back with him the pedagogical ideas of Horace Mann, but a company of American school teachers, who were to introduce progressive methods of instruction into the new public schools of the Republic. Nicolás Avellaneda, a leader of unusual intelligence and eloquence, had been Minister of Public Instruction in Sarmiento's cabinet before he became president of the federation in 1874. General Julio Roca, who followed him in the presidency, was not only a distinguished soldier of a new order, but by his political skill and administrative ability consolidated the gains made by his predecessors and set a high standard of public service for future governments. That such men could rise to the highest post in the state and govern it without interruption for twenty-four years was indicative of a momentous change in the life of the nation. Some of the later presidents failed to live up to the traditions of wise and moderate administration set by these remarkable men, and there were recurrent outcroppings of old political habits in the interior to plague the central government. But it was much that the precedents had been established, and, for the time being at least, the nation was to prove itself so sound economically and politically that it could survive these relapses without serious damage to its fundamental interest.

At the beginning of the fourth decade of this century an epidemic of political disturbances occurred all over Latin America, from whose incidence few governments escaped. At first sight, it appeared to foreign observers that the widespread nature of the overturn signified a general return to old political habits and the abandonment of most of the gains made toward more ordered government. Though a few of the dictatorial regimes set up at that time persisted until recently, in other countries the disturbances were relatively short in duration and represented only a violent attempt at the settlement of certain persistent political problems. Some were in the nature of revolts against dictatorships which had outlived the public acceptance of their rule. Thus, a common pattern was lacking as to the precise motives and methods of the revolutions. The ground was prepared by popular suffering and discontent resulting from the world depression which had seriously affected the national economies of all the republics by cutting down the foreign demand for their exports. It was this factor which was responsible for introducing into the revolutionary movements of 1930-31 a strong element of organized radicalism. The early thirties were a period of more than customary disorder and political instability in Ecuador. In Bolivia, widespread distress due to the fall of tin prices, on which the country's economy largely depended, precipitated in 1930 the outbreak of popular unrest that forced President Siles from office. The same year the eleven-year-old dictatorship of President Leguia of Peru was ended by a military revolt headed by Colonel Sánchez Cerro, commander of the garrison at Arequipa. In 1931, General Carlos Ibáñez, "strong man" of Chile, resigned in the face of a popular demonstration.

On the east coast, the movement everywhere had serious repercussions, and left in its wake a number of fallen governments. In Argentina, the second term of President Hipólyto Irigoyen, who had been elected by a large majority of the voters, was brought to a close by a *coup d'état* directed by General Uriburu, a leader of the

Conservative party. The aged president's peculiarly personal methods of rule, which involved his consideration of the minutiae of public administration, had led to a virtual stagnation of the national government before the opposition against him had crystallized into revolt. In protest against the political system whereby presidential elections were arranged by an understanding between the States of São Paulo and Minas Gerais, the government of the Paulista President of Brazil, Washington Luíz, was overthrown in 1930 by Getulio Vargas, Governor of Rio Grande do Sul. At the same time Vargas laid the foundations of the dictatorship which endured, with a break of six years, for almost a quarter of a century. A year later Gabriel Terra assumed the virtually dictatorial powers, which he was to exercise in Uruguay until 1938.

In Central America there were political upsets in nearly all the republics. Uprisings took place against the government of President Mejia Colindres, of Honduras. The outbreak of the famous Sandino's guerrilla warfare against the American-supported rule of President Moncada, of Nicaragua, dates from the same period. In Panama, President Harmodio Arosemena was ousted from office by a revolution led by Harmodio Arias. In El Salvador, Arturo Araujo lost the presidency to General Hernández Martínez. Even in Costa Rica, a rare armed demonstration took place against the government. In the Antilles, Rafael Leonidas Trujillo Molina began his long-lived Dominican dictatorship in 1932.

During most of this period the Brazilian Empire presented a remarkable contrast to the disordered conditions of the seven Spanish-American nations which adjoined her. For a few years after the separation from Portugal in 1822, there was a certain amount of confusion and turmoil, inevitable in a time of transition and adjustment to a new political order. However, the dislocations of normal life occasioned by the change were short-lived and unattended by the violence which accompanied the similar era in the former colonies of Spain. Much of the internal peace of Brazil was due to the relative mildness of the Portuguese character, which was naturally averse to sanguinary and extreme measures and disposed to believe in the efficacy of time and conciliation for the settlement of problems. The vast Oriental inertia of Brazil has always been a passive force for peace, and without resort to definite action the Brazilians have often talked themselves through what was apparently a serious crisis in their affairs. Also, the device of a constitutional monarchy offered a more gradual means of bridging the gap between the colonial status and eventual republican forms than was represented by the Spanish republics' abrupt break with the past. Thus, the processes of political evolution had an opportunity under the liberal Empire to prepare the nation for self-government without undergoing the shock of revolution.

The first Emperor, Pedro I, exerted little influence on the trend of events during his short reign. A man of more than ordinary physical vitality and of a certain rough charm of personality, his natural impulses would have found a larger field in the cruder atmosphere of the colony. Frequently ill-advised by some of his Portuguese intimates, he tended to vacillate between a sincere desire to serve the best interests of the country and resentment at the limitations on his prerogative which were embodied in the Imperial Constitution of 1824. He especially resented the strong control of government affairs which was exercised at times by the Andrada brothers, particularly by the able José Bonifacio, who was leader of the Conservative faction. Meanwhile, the most important influence in the government of the Empire was the opinions of the large planters, who were primarily concerned with a government that would give the maximum security to their interests. Widespread dissatisfaction with the conduct of certain military adventures in the River Plate region and with the Emperor's opposition to certain liberal measures and suspicion of his ambitions for a dual Portuguese-Brazilian monarchy forced the abdication of Pedro I in 1831.

He was succeeded by his five-year-old son, Pedro de Alcântara, who was to reign as Pedro II for fifty-eight years. In that time he gained such a deep hold on the affections of his subjects that aging Brazilians often expressed their *saudades* or nostalgia for the days of "the good gray Emperor." Dom Pedro, as he is familiarly and reverently spoken of by the Brazilians of the Republic, was a moderate and liberal ruler. His position was not only that of a moderator between opposing factions and forces in the country; he actively promoted its economic and cultural development. He foresaw the inevitability of republicanism and shrewdly avoided any move which might precipitate political rancor or conflict. In his personal life, he was a kindly man of scholarly instincts and democratic habits, and, unlike his rakish father, a model of the domestic virtues. No modern head of a state has been better fitted to meet the special needs of his time and his people.

During the Emperor's minority the stability of the country owed much to the strong hand of a priest, Diogo Antonio Feijó, who was for a time regent and Minister of Justice. Later the Empire had the services of a group of able and public-spirited statesmen and publicists, like Saraiva and Nabuco de Araujo. In the sixties Brazil was drawn into a costly and long-drawn-out foreign war by the ambitions of the Paraguayan dictator, Francisco Solano López. The war strengthened the position of the military element in the state, with the result that the army increasingly became a disturbing factor in the politics of the Empire. Republican sentiment, which had been slowly growing for some time, found support among the younger officers of the army. Meanwhile, considerable discontent had been aroused among the influential landholding class by the abolition of slavery in 1888. The Emperor's daughter, who had acted as regent during his absence abroad, and who held reactionary political and religious views, was held responsible for the act of emancipation and provided an object for the grievances of the opposition groups in the country. On the night of November 14, 1889, the Empire was overthrown by a *coup d'état* headed by General Deodoro da Fonseca, who was to be first president of the Republic. Dom Pedro, against whose person no hostility was expressed, was nevertheless expelled from the country within two days, in order that the Republic might start its existence unencumbered by the popularity of the Emperor.

The first years of the young Republic were stormy. The administrations of General Fonseca and Marshal Floriano Peixoto were troubled by civil war and by the paralysis and corruption of public administration. The civilian presidents who followed the regime of the militarists had to contend not only with the problem of restoring political equilibrium but with grave economic questions involving the financial credit and industrial development of the nation. Whatever progress has been made in the meantime toward the solution of these problems has been due more to the private initiative of the people and the natural riches of the country than to the efforts of her leaders. Meanwhile, the frustrating efforts of Jânio Quadros, a much-publicized reformist president, to deal with the accumulation of massive problems, ended in his voluntary resignation and temporary self-imposed exile in 1961.

In spite of local setbacks, as in Brazil, democracy has made very substantial, though unequal, gains in Latin America. This progress has been the result of a variety of factors. The decline of illiteracy, due to extension of the public-school system, has widened the electoral base of democracy, since the ability to read and write is a common qualification for voting. The growth of literacy has also had the effect of producing a better-informed public opinion, which is less responsive to the old appeals for its favor. The more public-spirited newspapers have taken full advantage of this opportunity to extend their influence on the side of good government, and the independent members of the press have become increasingly a power to be reckoned with by the politicians. The introduction of the secret ballot in Argentina and a few other countries has removed the customary pressures from voters and made elections a more effective expression of the popular will. Wherever industrialization has proceeded on a considerable scale, factory workers and allied labor groups have become conscious of their political interests and assertive of their rights. The rise of a middle class of citizens, consisting largely of members of the professions, small businessmen, and independent farmers, has formed a strong nucleus of democratic opinion in the more advanced republics. However, the middle class is still too conscious of its own economic problems, too new to the methodology of political struggle, too unaware of its potential strength, to occupy its proper position in the arenas of national politics.

Though numerically small, one of the most active groups in support of the democratic movement has been the body of university students. What they frequently lacked in matured judgment and in patience with the evolutionary processes of political change the students made up in zeal and boldness of action. Their demonstrations against flagrant political abuses and violations of the constitutional order have several times precipitated crises of government, often at the cost of imprisonment or death for many of their numbers. The tradition of student liberalism, characterized though it has been by much imprudent knight-errantry, was long one of the brightest phases of the long struggle for democracy in Latin America. The educated youth of the republics were at least free from the cynicism and time-serving that have so often accounted for the inertia of their elders in the face of arbitrary government. Yet, in recent years the quality of student participation in the political life of Latin America has deteriorated. Students have been too ignorant of the fundamental issues at stake, particularly where economic problems are involved. They have adopted too many of the tactics of their more seasoned and wilier adversaries and thus sacrificed much of their reputation for idealism. They have relied too much on emotional appeal and on frenetic and senseless public demonstrations to the discredit of whatever cause they purport to represent. Not only has higher education suffered as a consequence but so have the sounder interests of political progress.

Certain countries have made much more progress than others toward the realization of the common democratic ideals of the Latin-American peoples. Backsliding into the old ways is still possible in all these countries, and during the 1950's there were recurrences, often prolonged, of dictatorship in nearly all the republics.

In Chile a period of instability, accompanied by considerable experimentation with new political formulae, including state socialism, followed the weakening of the old oligarchial regime which prevailed during most of the last century. During the Aguirre Cerda administration (1938–41) Chile was ruled by a Popular Front government, representing a combination of liberal and radical elements, which was committed to a program of advanced social legislation. Due to the extremes of wealth and poverty in Chile, and to the excessive fragmentation of parties that represent every level of opinion from communism to ultramontanism, political and social tensions are strong and debate is acrimonious. To have avoided the occasion of violence in an atmosphere so highly charged is no small tribute to the skill and moderation of those who have ruled Chile during most of her history. However, the elements which condition this atmosphere are potentially so tempestuous that only the future can determine her eventual course.

Colombia has shown a remarkable growth in sound and orderly methods of government. Even during its long periods of disorder in the last century, the contending parties fought over issues rather than personalities, and the dictatorships so common in the neighboring republics were singularly lacking in Colombia. Under a succession of presidents after 1930, improved standards of public administration prevailed and government leaders displayed unusual political sense and moderation. Elections were free, the press uncensored, and the government more and more responsive to public opinion. However, Colombia's creditable record of political peace was suddenly and violently broken by an uprising which occurred in April, 1948. The occasion for the wave of terror which engulfed Bogotá and swept over the country was the assassination of the leader of the left-wing branch of the Liberal party. However, it was later charged by the government that Communist elements had quickly taken advantage of the initial confusion to obstruct the deliberations of the Pan-American Conference then meeting in Bogotá. The *Bogotazo*, or riot which rocked the capital city and added a new term to the political terminology of Latin America, was put down after a few days by loyal forces, but its consequences still bedevil the land. For, ever since the mountain valleys of Colombia have been the scene of a bloody civil war, compounded of partisan strife, large-scale brigandage, and bitter personal vendetta. To this witch's brew has been added the poison of Communist infiltration and intrigue. Over 100,000 persons have been slaughtered in the accursed hills, or more than all the Franco-Moslem killings in Algeria.

Meanwhile, following the archaic government of Laureano Gomez, patriarch of the Conservative party, and the military dictatorship of General Rojas Pinilla, an impasse in the central government has made it impossible to deal effectively with the long-chronic disorders in the interior. A joint administration of the two dominant parties, alternating in the presidency, has prevented any action that might restore peace to the stricken nation which has lost most of the political gains of thirty years.

The Central American republic of Costa Rica is one of the few genuinely democratic states of Latin America. Costa Rican democracy is based on the existence of a large body of small independent farmers of predominantly Spanish blood. Its civic life is not burdened with the incubus of a heavy population of economically dependent and politically inert Indians. It is relatively free from extremes of wealth and poverty, and its hard-headed citizens refuse to tolerate any curtailment of their political liberties by the government. Until the Second World War the national army was a small token force of a few hundred men and so conscious of its proper position in the state that pretorianism was impossible. In fact, it was a proud boast of the nation that it had more school teachers than soldiers. However, a dispute over the presidential succession in 1948 led to considerable armed disorder and a regrettable departure from the country's excellent record of political peace. Of the other Central American states, El Salvador possesses nearly all the elements necessary for a democratic system of government, but has been prevented from realizing its possibilities in that direction by the repressive influence of conservative army officers and large landholders. Democracy in Guatemala is only a relative term.

The political education of Central America, with the exception of Costa Rica, and of the island republics is a long-drawn-out process. There are too many bad habits to live down, like the ever-present hazard of dictatorship. For example, Rafael Leonidas Trujillo, one of the world's three "generalissimos," ruled the Dominican Republic from 1930 until his assassination in 1961. At his death, his subjects had lost whatever aptitude for self-government they may ever have possessed. His dictatorship was as sadistically brutal as any tyranny in the history of Latin America. There are dynasties, like the Somozas in Nicaragua, or social groups, like the mulatto aristocracy in Haiti or the coffee oligarchy in El Salvador, who have the habit of rule. Party organization has too little relation to the trying realities of politics.

Illiteracy is generally high, and in Honduras, a country of nearly 2,000,000, the combined circulation of newspapers is less than 40,000. Poverty is widespread and national economies generally have a base inadequate to raise living standards appreciably. A superior leader, like President Villeda Morales of Honduras, may be plagued by irrational and violent opposition from a number of sources. Of Haiti, overcrowded by an illiterate and impoverished peasantry, an authority has said: "Haiti has never known stable, constitutional and democratic government. Chaos, alternating with short dictatorships, has been the political rule." Basic conditions in Argentina would appear to be unusually favorable to the development of political democracy. It is peopled by a predominantly white race. It is free from the dead weight of a heavy Indian population, the too mercurial influence of the Negro, and the disturbing leaven of mixed peoples, who move in an uncertain political and social world between the fixed status of the pure bloods. The large foreign-born elements, who came late into the national life, have no part in the country's early traditions of revolution and *caudillismo* but have not yet been molded into a single people. A relatively high rate of literacy; an excellent press; an urban standard of living well above the average of Latin-American cities; considerable administrative capacity and experience for the conduct of public business; and an intense pride in the country's accomplishments and sensitiveness to its good name among nations—all these are sources of strength in Argentina's struggle for a political life in line with its constitutional design and the ideas of its political philosophers. These forces have to contend against the persistent incubus of personalism, that made possible Irigoyen's return to power, and against the sharp practices of the politicians, and the pressures of the military. But the outlook appeared, nevertheless, to be fundamentally promising for a government at once ordered and democratic.

However, since the overthrow of the second Irigoyen regime in 1930 Argentina has passed through a period of serious political disturbances that culminated in the dictatorship of President Juan Domingo Perón (1940–55). The presidential term of office is six years. Between 1942 and 1962 there were eight presidents. Six were generals, one of whom served two days, another two months, and Perón ruled nine years.

The uneasy years between 1942 and 1946 were characterized by the gradual rise to power of Colonel Perón, the outstanding member of a group of younger army officers who were discontented with current conditions in Argentine politics. As Vice President, War Minister, and Minister of Labor in the government of President Edelmiro J. Farrell, Perón early became the dominant figure in that administration. An extraordinarily shrewd politician and master demagogue, Perón used his position as Minister of Labor to build up the voting strength among the Argentine masses that was to sweep him into the presidency in the elections of February, 1946. As president, he initiated an ambitious program for the further industrialization of the country, the creation of a strong army, the regulation of the nation's cultural life, and for a political revolution that would transfer the traditional balance of power in Argentina from the landholding aristocracy to the lower classes of the population. When he was finally deposed, the once prosperous and sound country had been set back economically and financially for many years and its political life was to be long confused and embittered by irreconcilable passions.

The circumstances which have determined the present direction of Uruguay's political life are similar to those in Argentina. The common denominators are a stable racial stock, a healthy economic base, which, however, lacks the variety of Argentina's more diversified resources, and a sound popular sense of political values; on the other side is a like heritage of long civil disorders that finally burned themselves out, leaving as a force for orderly processes of government a profound distaste for methods of violence. Though partisan feelings may run high in Uruguay, political manners are better than formerly. The principal points of divergence are a more compact and homogeneous physical setting, lesser extremes of wealth with a less conservative national society, a more independent and assertive electorate, and an urge for legislative experimentation in the social and economic field. As a democracy, Uruguay easily ranks in first place among South American countries.

The factors which have conditioned the present stage of democratic development in Mexico are peculiar to that country. Mexican democracy, imperfect as it still is, is a concomitant of a far-reaching social revolution, and its main features are colored by its relation to that movement. Its characteristics are also deeply impressed by the prevailing Indian motif of Mexico's political life. Though the revolutionary movement is directed largely by men of white or mixed blood, its participants and beneficiaries are overwhelmingly Indian—as is the population of the country. In this sense it represents a democracy of the national proletariat, but none the less, a democracy. As a correlate phase of the class struggle inherent in the movement, it implies a corresponding abridgement of the position of the former privileged minority. Among the principal needs of Mexico in the present stage of her development are improved standards of public morality, a healthy opposition party, and a generally higher level of disagreement in political contests. Perhaps, by reason of its "imperial" and viceregal background, the supreme government in Mexico is destined to be autocratic, so that by the very nature of things the president of the republic exercises dictatorial power. Also, a thread of violence runs through the tapestry of its history, so that the hand of authority tends to be repressive and impatient of disagreement or resistance.

After the first outbreak of popular vengeance, Venezuela's reaction from the death of President Gómez, who had ruled the country from 1908 to 1935, was to assert the pent-up aspirations of her people for self-government. The younger element in the population showed great eagerness to undo in a few years the effects of political repression and stagnation during the long period of dictatorship. For a time, their natural enthusiasm was moderated and guided within feasible limits by the prudent government of President López Contreras, who was sympathetic with the national desire for comprehensive reforms and was, at the same time, cognizant of the difficulties involved in a rapid transformation of the country's institutions. Impatient with the apparent caution with which the government was being democratized, a popular movement forced the next president, General Medina Angarita, out of office in 1945 and substituted an interim administration headed by Rómulo Betancourt, a prominent journalist. Free general elections, the first in many years, were held in 1948, and resulted in the election as president of Rómulo Gallegos, Venezuela's foremost literary figure, who was committed to continue the liberal policies of the Betancourt provisional government. The novelist-president survived the harassments of the office for only nine months. Then, after a four years' interim, the presidency was taken over in 1952 by Colonel Marcos Perez Jiménez, who instituted a gaudy dictatorship that lasted for five years. Rómulo Betancourt, reinstated for a five-year term as president in 1959, undertook to bring political peace to the harried nation, but had to contend with an aggressive Communist organization, an unworkable party system, an undependable military, mobs of students and slum dwellers on the loose, and with attendant riots and armed revolts.

Brazil's very size has accounted for some of the major defects of her political evolution. For lack of an adequate system of transportation the various parts of the vast union have never been effectively coordinated, either as a nation or as a democracy. Regionalism persists, fostered by geographical isolation, ethnic differences, and great economic inequalities as between the states. The federal government has not yet created an administrative system which could bind together all these divergent elements and direct for the common interest of the nation the latent loyalties and energies of the Brazilian people. The authority of the federation has been either too fitfully or too unworthily represented by its agents, or imposed by dictatorial fiat from Rio de Janeiro, as it was under the long dictatorship of Getúlio Vargas.

A masterly politician, if not a great political philosopher, Vargas attempted to revolutionize the whole political system of Brazil. He broke down the federal pattern of government by substituting his agents, or "interventors," for the elected governors of all but one of the states, though he was forced to suppress an armed revolt by the proud State of São Paulo. He disbanded state legislatures and the federal congress and ruled the newly centralized republic by decree, until the confusing mass of decree legislation became the despair of lawyers, litigants, and judges. Through the special department known as D.A.S.P., he not only controlled the vast machinery of government of the *Estado Novo*, or New State, but improved its administrative personnel and procedures with a thoroughness which had never been known under the more easy-going regime that was so congenial to the political genius of the Brazilian people. His return to the presidency in early 1951, after six years, was ill-advised. He had lost much of his grip on the country and the glamor had worn off the *Estado Novo*. He made too many mistakes, and, confronted with an ultimatum by military and political leaders, he committed suicide on the night of August 24, 1954. Brazil returned to a certain "normalcy," but his ghost still walked and somehow many things would never be the same again. He had become a legend as the benefactor of the little people, and on the anniversary of his death they smother his statues with floral offerings and pay a sentimental homage to his memory. Meanwhile, João Goulart, ex-Governor of Rio Grande do Sul, head of the Labor party founded by Vargas, vice-president in the short-lived regime of Jânio Quadros, and president of Brazil since the temperamental Jânio's renunciation in 1961, is the political heir to the former dictator. Because of reputed "leftist" leanings, his occupancy of the Palace of the Dawn at Brasília was not congenial to certain elements in the high command of the armed services and to other political leaders. The resulting crisis, which in a Spanish-American country would probably have ended in violence, was settled by the typical Brazilian device of "talking things out." The constitution was changed overnight, and Goulart emerged as a representational president, with much of the real executive power in the hands of a newly created premier.

In the early decades of the republic, the central government of Brazil was cursed by the barrack influences common to Latin-American politics. However, with the establishment of better discipline in the armed forces and a growing realization of its responsibilities as the self-appointed guardian of constitutional processes in the state, the military has ceased to be a source of disorder.

Much of the root of Brazil's political troubles lies in the indifference of her cynical and fatalistic people, who refuse to take their civic rights and duties seriously enough, so long as their personal liberties are not appreciably curtailed. Where Brazilian democracy has failed or faltered, it was by default, and for a time it was in abeyance. The general acceptance of the suspension of normal political life by President Vargas was symptomatic of this deep-seated public apathy. However, in the past few years there have been widespread indications of a greater political consciousness in the Brazilian people that should augur well for the country's future.

Part V

THE ECONOMY

General Characteristics

FOR ALMOST half a century after Independence the economy of Latin America remained much as it had been during the colonial period. The unenlightened control of the royal governments of Spain and Portugal had been removed, but no new forces gave any substantial impetus to the development of the continent's resources. Some of the old mines continued to be worked, the farms supplied food to the near-by towns, and the herds and flocks increased in numbers and declined in quality. The economic life of the young republics was stagnant and lacking in the vitality needed to break with the routine methods of the colonial era. The political disorders of the period discouraged whatever industrial initiative may have been latent in the population, and the rulers were singularly lacking in a sense of the economic needs and possibilities of their countries. Isolation and lack of communications confirmed the universal backwardness of communities that became more ingrown than ever. The Industrial Revolution, which so profoundly altered the economics of the United States and western Europe, still passed Latin America by. The only hopeful sign was the increased commercial activity along the coasts, but this was due rather to the enterprise of British trading houses and of the captains of American sailing ships than to the initiative of the local inhabitants. The volume of this trade was small and the range of commodities very limited, but it was significant of the direction which the future industrial growth of Latin America was to take.

After the middle of the century a reorientation of economic life began to take place, though its full effects were not generally apparent until the eighties. The transformation came earlier in some countries than in others and the progress made was very uneven as between the various republics, but no country escaped altogether its revivifying influence. A number of factors contributed to this movement. Some of the basic political issues which had divided the republics into warring camps had been settled, as in Argentina and Chile. Where the civil wars continued, they were generally less devastating and interfered less with the daily life of the peoples. A new breed of rulers appeared who promoted the opening up of their countries' fallow resources and favored closer trade relations with the outside world. Government became cognizant of its economic responsibilities, as it found longer breathing spells from urgent considerations of self-defense which it might devote to measures for the increase of the national wealth. The first railroads were built and other works of public utility were undertaken, often financed by foreign capital. New industries arose and banking facilities were introduced. Currents of immigration began that were to bring in a steady and heavy flow of population before the end of the century. Meanwhile, the expanding industrialization of the United States and western Europe not only created a demand for Latin-American minerals and other raw materials, but the problem of feeding the growing industrial population of Europe's cities opened vast opportunities to Latin-American agriculture. Artificial refrigeration made possible the transportation of meats from South America to the warehouses of Europe and of bananas from the Caribbean countries to the United States. Under the impetus provided by these factors, Latin America became during the present century one of the world's greatest sources of raw materials and a correspondingly important market for the manufactures of the industrialized nations.

Unfortunately, for the stability of their newly augmented economies, most of the Latin-American republics have depended on one or two staples for their prosperity. In spite of attempts to avoid the consequences of excessive specialization, the percentage of total exports represented by foreign shipments of certain products in recent years has been approximately as follows:

Bolivia	tin	70–80
Brazil	coffee	35
Chile	copper	50
Colombia	coffee	70
Costa Rica	coffee	65
Cuba	sugar and by-products	80
El Salvador	coffee	80
Honduras	bananas	55
Nicaragua	gold	50
Venezula	petroleum	90

Variations in world demand and prices of these products distort the local economy to a degree that is not possible in a country with a well-balanced internal economy or which is less dependent on export trade. Examples of countries that have felt the disastrous effects of violent fluctuations in the world market for their basic staples are Cuba (sugar), Chile (nitrate), Bolivia (tin), and Brazil (coffee). When serious slumps occur in the market for any of these products, not only is the general standard of living quickly depressed, but government revenues fall off heavily and all government activities, except the army, are curtailed for the duration of the "crisis."

A very few countries have never been so dependent on the returns from a limited number of products. Of such are Paraguay and Peru. Others have made real, and partially successful, efforts to diversify their production and thus to place their national economies on a less precarious base. Thus, the banana industry has served as a partial counterpoise to the uncertainties of coffee production in the Caribbean republics. Brazil offers an interesting example of the same trend. The proportion of total exports represented by coffee has been steadily declining for some time and has fallen to between 35 and 40 percent, as exports of cotton have risen proportionately. A number of other products, none of which accounted for over 5 percent of exports, have, nevertheless, contributed much to a healthy spreading of Brazil's export business, and at the same time have served as the industrial mainstay of certain regions within the country. Among these products are hides and skins, cacao, meats, oranges, carnauba wax, lumber, and tobacco. In Argentina, a few products of her agricultural and pastoral industries comprise nearly 95 percent of all her exports. Of the former group, wheat, corn, and linseed hold a pre-eminent place; of her livestock industries, the principal products exported are chilled beef, wool, hides, and canned meat.

Few of the products of Latin America's mines, forests, and fields have enjoyed an uninterrupted demand or a reasonably firm price level. Sugar is a case in point. Once the most profitable of all tropical cultures, the cane sugar of Latin America now has to meet the competition of beet sugar, which is produced in practically every European country, as well as in the United States. As a rule, the domestic sugar industries of foreign countries are protected by abnormally high import tariffs, and sometimes by bounties to producers. As a result, the world market available to Latin-American sugar has steadily declined, and is now largely confined to supplying the deficiencies of home production abroad. Cuban sugar production has fluctuated by fifty percent during this period, with the inevitable repercussions on the economy of the nation. For a time the establishment of a quota on imports of Cuban sugar by the United States and the Cuban government's regulation of total grinding of cane did something to control the industry within the bounds of prospective demand.

Coffee presents a somewhat different problem in the Latin-American economy. For a long time Brazil held a dominant position in this industry comparable to that held by Cuba in respect to sugar. The prosperity of her coffee industry was sustained by the vast demand from the United States, into which coffee has always had free entry. A certain balance was maintained between the production of Brazilian coffee and the "mild" coffees of the Caribbean countries by the customary proportions of each employed in the blends of American roasters. Meanwhile, a natural succession of large and short crops in Brazil normally prevented overproduction, as the surplus from one crop was counted upon to make up the deficit of the succeeding year. When the alternating formula failed and the industry was threatened with a glut, the Brazilian government intervened with the process known as "valorization," whereby the excess production was withdrawn from the market and later released as the demand justified. The support of the world price of coffee by the Brazilian government not only encouraged further planting at home, but stimulated production in the Caribbean area. Policies of the United States government in holding up the price of cotton against depressive forces in the world market later had a similar effect in increasing the acreage of cotton in Latin America. In spite of government efforts, overproduction of coffee became almost chronic in Brazil, thereby presenting a serious problem, not only to the producing states, but also to the normal fiscal commitments of the federal and state governments. Because of the large amount of money required to finance the operations, as well as because of the declining influence of São Paulo in the federal government, resort to the device of valorization was no longer feasible. Government then adopted the radical measures of a "sacrifice quota," by which the excess production was permanently removed from the market. Nearly 80,000,000 bags of coffee were destroyed, either by burning, by dumping in the ocean, or by its utilization as fuel for locomotives. New plantings were restricted and an unprecedented freeze in the State of Paraná temporarily restricted Brazilian production. But, in spite of everything, output continued to rise and the 1960–61 crop amounted to 30,000,000 bags. Conventions between the Latin-American republics for the regulation of production and the fixing of import quotas by the United States in agreement with the producing countries tended somewhat to stabilize conditions in the industry. Meanwhile, the collapse of European buying power, resulting from the Second World War, greatly reduced the volume of coffee exports to these markets until full economic recovery was attained.

Along with Brazil, the sixteen other coffee-producing nations of Latin America were affected by overproduction and the consequent drop in coffee prices. Colombia, the world's second producer, with a crop of nearly 8,000,000 bags in 1960–61, was especially hard hit. In order of output the next largest producers are Mexico, Guatemala, and El Salvador. The total production of Latin America is normally 50,000,000 bags, or approximately three-fourths of world output. Meanwhile, growing and formidable competition now comes from Africa, where fourteen countries, headed by the Ivory Coast and Angola, produced nearly 14,000,000 bags in the crop year of 1960–61. Other Latin-American products have been seriously hit by the competition of new producing areas in other parts of the world. Sisal and henequen, two hard agave fibers used in the cordage industry, were originally a monopoly of the Mexican State of Yucatán. While Mexico still produces most of the world's henequen, the first producer of sisal is now Tanganyika, whose economy is largely dependent on exports of the fiber. Brazil ranks second. Similarly, cinchona bark, the source of quinine, was formerly a product exclusively of the tropical forests of the Andean countries. However, the bulk of the world's production came to be derived from plantations in Indonesia. The serious shortage of quinine for treatment of troops in malarial areas during the Second World War, which resulted from the Japanese occupation of the Dutch East Indies, led the United States government to undertake an energetic program for the gathering of the wild bark in South America and for the establishment of *cinchona* plantations. On a larger scale, the same fate befell the wild rubber industry of Brazil. The *Hevea brasiliensis* tree, which is the standard source of commercial rubber, is a native of the Amazon valley. Stimulated by the demand which was created by the new automobile industry, the Amazonian industry experienced a "boom" of fantastic proportions between 1908 and 1910, but collapsed as disastrously when the plantations of the Middle East began to come into full production. These plantations are located in Ceylon, the Federated Malay States, and Sumatra, and were developed from seeds originally obtained on the Tapajós River in Brazil. After a futile attempt to apply the principle of valorization to the industry, the Brazilian government undertook an ambitious project known as the "Defense of Rubber," but with similar lack of results. An intensified development of the Brazil nut industry in the lower Amazon country and of cotton growing in eastern Peru served in part to compensate for the loss of the profitable crude rubber monopoly. The establishment of the Ford plantations on the lower Tapajós and the costly efforts of the Rubber Development Corporation during the Second World War failed to give the expected impetus to the revival of the Amazonian industry, largely because of difficulties of transportation from the best wild rubber areas and the lack of an adequate and dependable labor supply.

Another indigenous product of Latin America which has lost its former predominance in world markets is cacao, or cocoa, the basic ingredient of chocolate. Ecuador, once the principal producer, now ranks sixth in world production. It is the mainstay of the economy of

Ghana, which now produces over a third of the world supply. The second producer is Nigeria and the third is Brazil.

Some other Latin-American products have lost much of their market to synthetic or other substitutions, or as the result of changes in consumer habits. These include indigo, chicle, the essential ingredient of chewing gum, balata, used in the manufacture of machine belting, certain types of cabinet woods and tropical hardwoods in general, Panama hats, egret feathers for women's hats, and vanilla beans.

A much more important case in point is that of Chilean nitrate, which is extracted from the *salitre* deposits of the northern desert that lies between the coast range and the Andes. The four nitrate provinces were taken from Peru and Bolivia in the War of the Pacific, and for a long time thereafter the output of their *oficinas* or extraction plants was the principal basis of Chile's economy. The heavy export tax was by far the largest source of national revenues and much of the yield from foreign sales of nitrate returned to the country in the form of wages and of profits for the domestic operators in the industry.

This condition prevailed until the appearance of a formidable competitor in synthetic nitrate, based on the process for the fixation of atmospheric nitrogen, which was developed by German chemists. The end of the First World War found the industry with large unsold stocks and prices falling to unprecedented lows. The situation of the industry became progressively worse and was little improved by the establishment of the Compañía Salitrera de Chile, or COSACH, as it is known in that country. This semi-governmental corporation was granted a monopoly of the export of nitrate and its by-product, iodine, and was endowed with certain other measures of control over the industry. During the second administration of President Alessandri, which began in 1932, the nitrate industry was reorganized and placed under the tutelage of the Chilean Nitrate and Iodine Sales Corporation. However, nitrate has never regained its former position in the economy of Chile. Production is about half the rate of the 1920s and exports normally comprise less than one-tenth of Chile's total outgoing trade. It is only by a progressive reduction of operating costs that the industry has been able to survive at all.

Markets for some other Latin-American staples have been heavily curtailed by the monetary or tariff policies of importing countries.

For example, the demonetization of silver has dealt a severe blow to the mining industries of Mexico, Peru, and Bolivia, even though they profited indirectly and temporarily from American purchases designed to benefit the silver-producing states of the Union. The American protective tariff reduced imports of leaf tobacco and cigars from Cuba long before all Cuban-American trade was suspended in 1961. Also, other Cuban products which meanwhile lost a large part of their promising markets in the United States because of import restrictions in favor of domestic industries were rum, and fruits and vegetables. Preference agreements between the United Kingdom and the British Dominions caused serious concern to Argentine producers of wheat and meats.

Some of the Latin-American republics have made determined efforts to free themselves from the vicissitudes of an export trade limited to a very few staples. To this end, they have promoted the diversification of production, encouraged the establishment of manufactures, stimulated the production of foodstuffs which are now imported, extended the control of the state over production and distribution, and attempted to stabilize their too precarious foreign commerce by means of reciprocal trade treaties. Their larger purposes are the increase of their trade balances by cutting down the drain of money for foreign imports and a greater degree of self-sufficiency for their national economies. The former would leave a larger surplus for the development of the second phase of their basic objectives. They realize the importance of a rich domestic market built on local production, and increasingly free from dependence on an export trade which is at the mercy of foreign tariff policies, unorthodox trade devices, fluctuations of the currency and prices, and the influence of destructive wars which cripple their leading customers or cut them off altogether from their sources of supply.

Due to a variety of circumstances, very few countries are in a position to realize such an economic ideal within a reasonably near future. They may lack the natural foundations of a well-balanced economy, including certain essential raw materials or basic sources of power, such as coal, petroleum, or hydroelectric energy. The very *quantity* of the resources on which they can draw may be limited, as in the case of Chile, which is a country otherwise favored by the possession of a virile and enterprising population. Their reputed natural wealth may be deceptive, as in the case of Mexico. Their population may not yet possess the necessary industrial or technical knowledge, or even an interest in acquiring them. In competition with politics and the law and other professions, business tends to attract too little of the best talents in the country. Practical industrial and technical education is woefully deficient. Certain countries have not yet attained the degree of political cohesion and stability needed for the undivided prosecution of a comprehensive industrial program. In some countries the survival of an antiquated social system is an obstacle to the attainment of a sound and realistic economic policy.

An Indian psychosis seems to dominate the subconscious spirit of three of the Andean nations, like a specter out of the Incaic past. An apparently irreconcilable dichotomy exists between the two racial elements in the population, which not even the large mestizo class can bridge. The endless "Indian problem" is an obstacle to the unified national effort necessary for any substantial and long-range economic progress. Meanwhile, while social tensions increase, as in Lima, the economic potential of the Andes declines, both for the Indian and for those who rule Peru, though for the time being the country has, to all appearances, a remarkably well-balanced economy. As for Bolivia, she is little more than a large mining camp, dependent on the demand for a single mineral, of which she is a high-cost, and minority, producer. The same situation exists in many parts of Latin America, though advances have been made in some countries, like Mexico and Chile.

For all her reputation, overglamorized by her capital city, Argentina is essentially the prize farm of the world. She is, above all, a vast source and storehouse of foodstuffs. She lacks many of the indispensable elements for industrialization—sufficient oil, coal, and hydroelectric potential, and virtually all the metallic bases of metallurgy. She has deteriorated politically, and there is too much confusion and discord in her national councils. She is still a land of very considerable promise, but currently her rate of economic growth has declined out of all relation to her true possibilities. Brazil, too, is short of coal and petroleum, though her hydroelectric potential is among the world's highest. But she has nearly everything else that is needed to make her economic destiny one of great promise. Her natural wealth is so vast and varied that all the impediments to her development inherent in the customary state of Brazilian affairs cannot prevent for long the inevitable progress of the normal economy.

Of the Andean republics, Colombia would appear to have the brightest future. She has a considerable diversity of resources, a favorable geographical position, an unusual collection of cities as local centers of her national life, and an attractive culture. There is much strength in her people, but they need to temper the virulence of their political passions.

Though basically a vast oil field, Venezuela has made a creditable beginning toward industrialization. For a young country, she has many mistakes in her brief past to live down and she has much to learn of economic and political rules before she can reach the place to which her resources entitle her. The future of the Central American republics largely rests with the regional "common market" whose construction is now under way, and with the manner in which their peoples accept its responsibilities and prospects.

Industries

Agriculture. In spite of the fame of its mines, agriculture is the basic industry of Latin America. Even in Bolivia, which is pre-eminently a mining country, less than 40,000 persons, in a total population of 3,000,000-odd, are regularly employed by the mining industry of the plateau. Latin America's total exports of agricultural products far exceed in value the exports of minerals. In all but Bolivia, Chile, and Venezuela, agricultural products are the nations' leading exports. In some countries, they are the only exports. The part of the population engaged in agriculture varies from 25 percent in Argentina and 30 percent in Chile to 84 percent in Honduras. About six out of every ten Brazilians and Mexicans make a living from the land. In Argentina about three-fourths of the "gross national product" is derived from agriculture. While imports of foodstuffs are relatively large in most of the republics, they generally originate in the neighboring countries and supply a deficiency of production in the importing country, as in the Argentine-Brazilian exchange of wheat for coffee. Otherwise, agricultural imports largely represent purchases in Europe of foodstuffs, such as olive oil and codfish, to which certain immigrant groups are accustomed, or of luxury foods, such as canned goods and caviar, for the upper class of the population.

The character of the agricultural industry throughout Latin America is closely bound up with the prevailing systems of land tenure. The republics inherited from the colonial era the practice of large landholdings, many of which dated from the *encomiendas* of the original conquerors, and, in Brazil, from the early *capitanias*. For example, the *Marquesado del Valle*, which was the royal grant to Cortés, covered 25,000 square miles of the best lands in southern Mexico. In an aristocratic society, land was the measure of the individual's position in the community. Though the actual money return from the operation of these properties was sometimes meager, it was usually sufficient to maintain the owners and their families in a state of rude plenty and to permit the indulgence of a considerable degree of display and luxury, especially when supplemented by trade or mining. For the more enterprising creoles, especially in Peru, often combined a variety of economic activities and profited accordingly.[1] After the wars of independence, the patriot leaders and their principal followers sometimes seized the lands of royalist sympathizers and frequently acquired large holdings by other means.

This process of building up large estates has continued down to our own time in some countries, sometimes by purchase, by grants from the government, by the arbitrary pre-emption of undeveloped public lands of potential value, i.e., by the large-scale exercise of "squatter's rights," or by pressure on the Indian occupants of communal lands. Land-hungry dictators, like Gómez of Venezuela, sometimes accumulated enormous holdings; other dictators, like Díaz of Mexico, promoted the acquisition of large estates by their supporters, frequently at the expense of the Indian owners of the soil.

As a result of these forces, by the beginning of the present century the characteristic form of land ownership in Latin America was the *latifundia*. This was particularly true in the more productive

---

[1] "There are, however, many families who . . . support a proper splendor entirely by the revenue of their estates, without joining in the cares and hurry of commerce. But a greater number with estates, add the advantages of commerce, in order to preserve them. These . . . find the benefit of having abandoned those scruples brought by their ancestors from Spain, namely, that trade would tarnish the lustre of their nobility." Juan and Ulloa, *A Voyage to South America* (fourth English edition, 2 vols., London, 1806), Vol. II, p. 113.

regions, such as the Central Valley of Chile, the Argentine pampa, the irrigated valleys of northern Peru, the red soil country of São Paulo, the valleys of the Mexican plateau, and the coffee-producing highlands of Guatemala. In Mexico, in the sugar-producing lands of Morelos, the wide valley of Jalisco, centering on Guadalajara, and in the country about Puebla, large *haciendas*, aggregating thousands of acres in extent, were the rule. Similar conditions prevailed in the henequen zone of Yucatán, and in the cattle country of the far north, where the famous Terrazas and Creel estates comprised millions of acres in Chihuahua. In the State of Durango, ten landowners held over 4,700,000 acres in 1905, and in Michoacán ten estates measured a total of 1,229,000 acres. At the other extreme, 97 percent of all rural families in either state had no land. In the three States of Mexico, Morelos, and Oaxaca, over 99 percent of the families owned no land. In the meantime, several American companies and individuals had acquired large tracts of land in northern Mexico. The Church, which Humboldt estimated to own four-fifths of the real estate in the country at the time of his visit to the viceroyalty, had been deprived of its holdings during the period of the *Reforma*. Its lands had found their way into the hands of laymen and constituted the original basis for some of the largest properties in the country.

The movement toward *latifundismo* in Latin America has received further impetus wherever certain tropical cultures were undertaken on a plantation scale. Concentration of landholdings has always followed the cane-sugar industry, whether in Cuba, Morelos, Pernambuco, Tucumán, or the Chicama Valley in Peru. The problem of insuring a regular flow of cane for the mill during the grinding season and of controlling the price of their cane supply in a highly competitive industry has everywhere led large sugar producers to the acquisition of suitable cane lands in the neighborhood. Similarly, in the lowlands around the Caribbean the tendency of the large fruit companies has been to increase the area of their own banana plantings, instead of depending on the small growers of the locality.

Except in the field of the cost-conscious corporate plantation, the average large landholding in Latin America has seldom been efficiently operated. Its owner has too often had little incentive for the improvement of his methods and the per-acre yield of his fields has usually been less than that of the small independent farmer, who was driven by necessity to extract as much as possible from his soil. This was particularly true in Mexico and Chile, where large-scale agriculture had become thoroughly unprogressive. Conditions on the large Argentine *estancias* and Brazilian coffee *fazendas* have been much better in these respects, but still leave much to be desired in efficient operation.

After all, the old-fashioned landed estate was fundamentally a social institution, to which its economic functions were incidental. Its organization was feudal and the position of the *hacendado* or *estanciero* in relation to his laborers and tenants was that of a baronial overlord. For all practical purposes, he was lawmaker and judge as well as employer, and the regularly constituted government authorities in the region stood ready to carry out his wishes, while the local priest impressed on the inhabitants of the estate the obligation of respect and obedience to the *patrón*. At its best, under a humane and far-sighted proprietor, the system had many redeeming features. It might become a fairly self-sufficient community, where the workers were assured of at least the minimum essentials of existence, regardless of conditions in the competitive world on the outside. To the owner, as a member of a definite ruling class, the system gave a sense of prestige and power, as well as an opportunity for spacious and graceful living. At its worst, the system bordered on slavery. This might be due to an inhuman *hacendado* or to the character of the major-domo or overseer who managed the estate in the owner's absence, and who felt no personal responsibility for the welfare of the *peonada*. Under this system the lot of the peon, who was systematically kept in debt to the *hacendado*, was liable to be a very hard one.

For absentee landlordism has carried with it some of the greatest evils, social and economic, that are associated with the system of *latifundia*. As an example, until recently the Pignatelli de Aragon family, who are descendants of Cortés, lived in Europe on the income derived from a part of the former estates of the conqueror of Mexico. It is customary for the better-to-do proprietors to maintain a city house in the capital or in the nearest large center of population, where they live much of the year, sometimes visiting their country place but infrequently. The wealthier Argentine *estancieros* also kept establishments in Paris or at the watering places of southern France. While these large landowners thus have an opportunity to participate in the superior social life of the cities or to take part in politics at the seat of government, they thereby neglect their position as the natural leaders of the rural districts of the country. They also fail to give their constant personal attention to the administration and improvement of their properties, but leave them for much of the year to the dubious care of a paid manager, who naturally lacks the incentive to develop them to their fullest capacity.

In recent years much attention has been given to so-called "land reform" in Latin America, meaning the break-up of large holdings and their distribution to the landless. The Chilean constitution of 1925 contained the noncommittal provision: "The State shall incline toward the suitable division of estates and the creation of family holdings." The charter of the Alliance for Progress in 1961 declared for "programs of comprehensive agrarian reform" that would bring about "an equitable system of land tenure." A half century earlier the Mexican Revolution had initiated its vast plan for turning over the hacienda lands to the peons. The famous Article 27 of the Mexican constitution of 1917 declared that "the necessary measures shall be taken for the subdivision of large rural estates, and for the development of small agricultural properties under cultivation." Revolutionary movements in Guatemala and Bolivia later parceled large properties among the Indian tenantry. Perón hoped to bring about the dissolution of the large *estancias* on the Argentine pampa by a shift in the incidence of taxation that would force large-scale selling by their owners. In Cuba the Castro regime was to turn over the bulk of the island's farmlands to a special agency of the government for operation on a communal basis. In Brazil, Colombia, and Venezuela, the state endeavored to accomplish some of the same purpose by the establishment of agricultural colonies on public lands. In the meantime, the number of small subsistence farms was growing generally throughout Latin America by normal processes of acquisition. Almost a quarter of the farms in Guatemala are of less than 20 hectares (about 50 acres). In Ecuador, another country with a large Indian population, the ratio is about 12 percent; in Costa Rica between 6 and 7 percent; and in Colombia approximately 12 percent. In the latter two countries farms of this size may be well above the subsistence level.

In some countries there is a large body of medium-sized independent farms, worked by their owners and families, whose economic and social position tends to correspond to that of the traditional "quarter-section" farmer of the American Middle West. Typical of this element are the mixed farms in the so-called "zone of the colonies" in the Argentine Province of Santa Fé, where they are the prevailing form of agricultural development. Here, immigrants from Spain, Italy, and other European countries have taken root, while others have moved into the area from the high-priced lands of the Province of Buenos Aires in search of greater independence. These farms generally have well-kept properties, where the owners cultivate cereals and a variety of miscellaneous food crops, and keep small herds of cattle. Small ownership is also spreading in Brazil, even in the heart of the coffee *fazenda* area in the State of São Paulo.

The classical display of *latifundismo* in Latin America is probably in Argentina. Vast properties were accumulated after the Indian wars in the last century, to become the base of the Porteño aristocracy. Most of these were in the Province of Buenos Aires, but there are also large holdings of less desirable lands in Patagonia, where they serve as sheep ranches. In Argentina there are about 30,000 farms of over 1,000 hectares. In number they comprise only 5 percent of all farms in the country, but they occupy about three-fourths of the arable land, or some 60,000,000 hectares. In Brazil, where no land shortage is imminent, about half the registered farmland is in tracts of the same general size, but they constitute a much smaller proportion of all farms than in Argentina. Large *fazendas* are especially common in the northern states, in the open frontier spaces of Goiás and Mato Grosso, and there are still many in São Paulo and Rio Grande do Sul. In Chile, there are only about one-tenth as many thousand-hectare farms as in Argentina, but they include practically the same proportion of the country's good farmlands, chiefly in the rich Central Valley. In Peru large estates predominate—some of the largest in the irrigated river valleys along the north coast. Even in little middle-class Uruguay there are substantially as many large farms as in Peru, which has an aristocratic social structure, but fewer sheep. In Paraguay, *latifundia* would appear to prevail to a degree found nowhere else in Latin America. However, the statistics of land ownership in the small backward republic are deceptive. For many of the larger properties include lands of little immediate potential value, and there is, moreover, no "landed aristocracy" in the sense that one exists in Chile or Guatemala.

While individual landholding is generally held to be socially desirable and a "guarantee of freedom and dignity," a sudden and large-scale transformation of the traditional land systems of Latin America would entail serious problems. Probably the most important would be that of financing the new landholders' purchases of equipment, livestock, and seeds, and construction of farm buildings. There is no precedent, even in Mexico, for a credit operation of such magnitude—and novelty. Since the national impulse of the new farm owner would be to increase his own food supply, regardless of export or even domestic urban markets, the volume of produce available for shipment abroad or for city demands might be seriously affected. Other problems are the nomadic farmer, so common in Brazil, who might prefer his freedom to roam to the satisfaction of settling down once for all on his own parcel of land, and the urban-minded countryman, who would sell his new home and move into the nearest big city. It may develop that better results could eventually be obtained by internal reform of the present land system rather than by programs of mass distribution of the larger properties.

The oldest land system in Latin America is the Indian commune. It prevailed in pre-Spanish Mexico as the Aztec *atlepetalli* or *calpullali* and was the very basis of the agricultural economy of the Incas. The Spanish government made efforts to insure the possession of these common fields and pastures by the Indian communities, and, in spite of the encroachments of the *encomiendas,* the system continued fairly intact in many localities down into the republican period. In Mexico, under the Díaz regime, the communal lands of the *ejidos* were systematically absorbed by the *hacendados* with the blessing and active complicity of the government.

The similar *ayllú* of the Andean countries has met the same fate as the Mexican *ejido,* though it survives in much of its original form in parts of Ecuador. In Peru and Bolivia the independent Indian communities have been pushed by the large landowners ever farther into the high recesses of the mountains. There, at altitudes from 12,000 feet up to the edge of the zone where cultivation is no longer possible, they cling desperately and precariously to areas of rocky ground that afford the barest living. The traditional hunting grounds of the forest Indians and of the fast-disappearing tribes in Patagonia present another aspect of the land question of Latin America. The same principle of group possession of the common source of food supply is involved, though in a more primitive and lower form than among the sedentary agricultural peoples of the mountain regions.

Irrigation is a very important factor in the agriculture of Latin America, but particularly in Mexico, Argentina, Chile, Peru, and Venezuela. Over 6,000,000 acres are under irrigation in Mexico. The fine valley of Jalisco in the region of Guadalajara and the newer cotton lands of the Laguna district near Torreón are examples of the intensive use of irrigation. The Mexican government has also constructed several dams in recent years to bring water to new areas where only dry farming was formerly possible.

Similar conditions are found along the arid west coast of South America and in the Andes. Throughout the Inca dominions, both in the *Sierra* and in the coastal belt south of the Gulf of Guayaquil, irrigation was the principal basis of agriculture, for which the melting snows of the Andes furnished a dependable supply of water. The streams which flow down the western slopes of the Andes and trickle across the desert to the Pacific are still bordered with fringes of intensive cultivation, as they were before the Spaniards came to Peru. The important cotton and sugar industries of northern Peru are dependent on this source of water, which has been further developed during the later period of the republic. The oases of Arequipa and Tacna in the south of the country are other examples of irrigated districts. From the border between Peru and Chile down to the vale of Coquimbo the desert is absolute, and agriculture is only possible in a few small pockets, as at Calama on the Antofagasta and Bolivia Railway. In the Central Valley of Chile, the near-by Andes provide an ample supply of water that has made possible the intensive agricultural development of that favored region.

On the opposite side of the Andes, there are a series of irrigated districts in Argentina, the most famous of which are those about Mendoza and Tucumán, with many smaller centers in the valleys of the Andean foothills that lie between these cities. In localities where the water supply is precarious, as in some of the oases in the Province of Catamarca, an elaborate set of local customs and regulations, enforced by the community of farmers, controls the use of the water.

In northeastern Brazil there is a large area of small and highly uncertain rainfall, where agriculture, in spite of the fertile soil, is carried on with great difficulty. Prolonged drouths, sometimes lasting two years or more, occur in this arid country, which includes the State of Ceará and parts of the neighboring states. Yet, in the periods between the long *sêcas* or "drynesses," large numbers of cattle and goats are raised and the best cotton in Brazil is grown. In 1922 the federal government of Brazil undertook the construction of a series of vast storage reservoirs that were to be used for the irrigation of this region of the *sertão*. The original project was never completed, but a series of small unconnected catch basins have been constructed to serve for the watering of stock and for restricted local irrigation. The uneven topography of much of Brazil makes it difficult to develop an effective irrigation system with the network of necessary canals and ditches for distributing the water.

Farming methods in Latin America range from the most primitive to the most advanced. They are generally most backward in the Indian countries and most progressive in Argentina and some of the better immigrant colonies in Brazil. Despite improvements made by this generation, hand farming is practiced over vast areas of the land, and the standard tools of agriculture in much of Latin America are a heavy hoe and the machete. The one is used for preparing the ground for planting and for cultivating; the other, for clearing and a variety of other purposes. In the Andean countries, the wooden plow is common and the small subsistence farmer in any part of Latin America is seldom able to buy any implement more advanced than a small steel plowshare. Horses and mules are little used as draft animals, except in southern Brazil and the River Plate countries, but oxen take their place at the plow in most of Latin America. The use of modern agricultural implements, including cultivators, reapers, and mowers, is common in Argentina and growing steadily. Uruguay and southern Brazil are also relatively advanced in this respect. Power machinery, such as tractors, is found only on large-scale farming operations in a few countries. Of some 300,000-odd farm tractors in Latin America, over half are in Argentina, Brazil, and Mexico. In 1957 their number ranged from 20 in Bolivia to over 80,000 in Argentina. American threshing machines are common in the wheat-growing regions of Argentina, but in the more backward countries, where farm labor is cheap, grain is generally threshed by flailing or by driving mules or oxen in a circle over a plot of hardened earth. While in Argentina, Uruguay, and parts of southern Brazil farm produce is usually hauled to market in wagons or motor trucks, in most other countries it is transported on the backs of mules or burros, and in the Andean lands by llamas. Even where the farmers keep draft animals, manure is seldom plowed back into the ground as fertilizer. On the west coast of South America, where a source of supply is at hand, guano and nitrate are widely used as fertilizer. Crop rotation is little used as a means of maintaining the fertility of soil. Except on the big estates, where capital is available for improvements or there is a large force of labor bound to the land, or in the more progressive immigrant communities, farm buildings are liable to be much below generally acceptable standards.

Some of the most interesting farming communities in Latin America are the small Indian farms in the Andes. In contrast to the irrigated and intensively cultivated belts along such streams as the Urubamba, are the vestiges of ancient terrace cultivation on the mountain sides above the valleys. Hillside farming is probably seen at its highest state of development in the terraced fields devoted to growing the coca plant in the Bolivian Yungas. In some places in the same region there are plots of cultivated land on ledges overhanging deep chasms in the mountains, where the slope of the ground is so steep that a foothold appears scarcely possible. On the Tibetan-like heights of the *páramos*, the Indian grows potatoes under some of the most unfavorable conditions to be found anywhere in the world. With rocks picked off the ground which he intends to cultivate he first builds a stone fence around a little patch of land. This wall is designed to protect the growing plants against the force of the cold winds that blow down from the region of eternal snow across the bleak floor of the tableland. Without the compensating warmth of the vertical sun in these low latitudes all cultivation would be impossible at such altitudes. There are also a few localities in the *tierra fria* of Mexico, as in the high country about Toluca, where agriculture is carried on under difficulties almost as severe as prevail in these inhospitable parts of the Andes.

One of the obstacles to the advancement of agriculture in Latin America is the lack of capital available to the small farmer. This problem is all the more serious in view of the high cost of implements, which results from the accumulated transportation charges between the point of manufacture in a foreign country and the warehouse of the local dealer and from the extra burden of import duties. Interest rates on loans from the regular banks generally range from 12 to 24 percent a year, and even at these rates the average small farmer is not considered a safe risk. The speculative values placed on land in the best farming districts also make more difficult the situation of the native or immigrant farmer who wishes to acquire a piece of land. In many districts farmers depend on local storekeepers or commission merchants for advances, either in money or goods, on their crops, which are then marketed through the lender and on conditions that are likely to be most profitable to him. Several of the governments have made efforts to deal with this question by the establishment of rural credit banks, but the resources placed at the disposal of these institutions are generally inadequate for the purpose. One of the most serious problems which the Mexican government has faced in its program for shifting the Indian farm workers from peonage to a status of independent or communal ownership has been in connection with the necessity for financing the former peons during their initial period of adjustment to new conditions. This requires keeping the Indians, who were lately released from a state of peonage, in a relation of tutelage to the government, pending the satisfaction of their obligations to the treasury and the demonstration of their ability to shift for themselves.

The Latin-American governments have taken an increasing interest in the promotion of agriculture. The national department of agriculture—where one exists—has generally served as the medium for these activities, which include the operation of experimental stations and agricultural schools, the standardization of products for export markets, measures against plant and animal diseases, agricultural extension work, the establishment of semi-official bodies devoted to the interests of particular industries, such as the special services for the Brazilian coffee and cacao industries, and even the fixing of prices for farm products. Much good work has also been done by associations of stockmen and farmers and by cooperatives.

One of the most promising elements in promoting better agricultural standards is the agricultural schools and experimental stations which are found all over Latin America. Some of these are administered by private organizations, like the excellent Agricultural College at Lavras, in the Brazilian State of Minas Gerais, and the well-equipped school at Zamorano, in Honduras, which is supported by the United

Fruit Company. Most such institutions are operated by the various national or state governments, like the schools at Piracicaba and Viçosa, in Brazil; Damien, in Haiti; and Chapingo, in Mexico. Colombia and several other republics have a system of farm schools at the elementary or secondary level of instruction. The Inter-American Institute of Agricultural Sciences at Turrialba, Costa Rica, is the most important center for agricultural research in tropical crops and represents an initiative of the official Pan-American system. Agricultural experimental stations like that at Tingo Maria, in Peru, are part of a chain of cooperative institutions supported by the United States Department of Agriculture and the governments of the respective countries. Many Latin-American youths are enrolled in the agricultural colleges of the United States. A large number of American agricultural experts have contributed in various ways to the improvement of Latin-American farming methods, either as private individuals or while engaged in official missions to those countries. The roster of this distinguished company includes, among many others, Wilson Popenoe, Hugh H. Bennett, Ross Moore, F. Spencer Hatch, William Vogt, P. H. Rolfs, and Edward J. Kyle. To the list have been added many agricultural specialists of the federal technical assistance or "Point 4" missions.

In the twelve republics of the Caribbean area the staple products of agriculture are similar. Their principal products which are largely destined for export are sugar, coffee, bananas, and cacao. The four largest producers of each important commodity are as follows:

Bananas—Venezuela, Honduras, Panama, Colombia
Cacao—Colombia, Dominican Republic, Mexico, Venezuela
Coffee—Colombia, Mexico, Guatemala, El Salvador
Corn—Mexico, Colombia, Guatemala, Venezuela
Cotton—Mexico, Colombia, Nicaragua, El Salvador
Rice—Colombia, Mexico, Central America, Cuba
Sugar—Cuba, Mexico, Dominican Republic, Colombia
Tobacco—Mexico, Cuba, Colombia, Dominican Republic, Venezuela

Colombia is the leading producer of "mild" coffees. The crop is normally between 7,000,000 and 8,000,000 bags, the bulk of which is shipped to the United States. The Caribbean area has lost its dominant position in the banana trade to Ecuador. Mexico has greatly increased

her production of cotton, sugar, and coffee in recent years, and is the
only important wheat producer in the area. All the other countries
are accustomed to import wheat or flour to supplement local production, which is usually small. Corn is the basis of the popular diet in
much of the region and a correspondingly large area is devoted to its
cultivation; over half the farmland in Mexico is planted to corn. Large
crops of beans and sweet potatoes are grown for local consumption,
and Mexico produces considerable quantities of vegetables for the
off-season market in the United States.

Of the four west-coast republics of South America, only Ecuador
and Peru produce any significant quantities of agricultural commodities for export. It is interesting that there are no minerals among the
first three exports of either country: 85 percent of Ecuador's exports
consist of bananas, cacao, and coffee, of which bananas provide almost half the total income from exports. The first three exports of
Peru are cotton, the products of deep-sea fisheries, and sugar. She
usually produces about a half million bales of Pima-type cotton. Crops
largely consumed within the country include about a million tons of
potatoes, a tuber native to Peru, tobacco for the state monopoly, and
some 5,000,000 bushels of wheat. Yet one of her biggest imports is
wheat. Excellent melons, strawberries, grapes, and navel oranges are
raised for the Lima market. She also produces both coffee and tea.
Bolivia is an importer, not an exporter, of foodstuffs, for the impoverished nation does not feed herself and is dependent on the
bounty of the United States to fill the subsistence gap. Chile, primarily
an exporter of minerals, produces yearly some 40,000,000 bushels of
wheat, of which a minimum surplus may be exported. Large quantities
of barley, rye, oats, corn, beans, lentils, and potatoes are also grown in
Chile for the local market, and a wide variety of fruits of excellent
quality are an increasingly important item in Chilean production and
export trade.

Brazil, as one of the two leading agricultural nations in South
America, has a highly diversified production. She is the world's largest
producer of coffee, bananas, beans, and manioc (cassava), and the third
producer of cacao and corn. She ranks fourth in the production of
cotton and sugar and fifth in tobacco. She grows more rice than any
country outside of Asia. Yet only about 4 percent of her vast area is
under cultivation. While some of her important staples, like bananas,

beans, corn, and manioc, are mostly consumed by the large domestic market, others are chiefly grown for export.

Coffee, which comprised over 70 percent of all Brazilian exports in 1929, still accounts for about half the total and no other single commodity represents more than 5 percent of all exports. In view of world overproduction and the consequent slump in coffee prices, this situation represents a major economic problem for the country. Coffee is grown largely in the states of São Paulo, Paraná, Minas Gerais, and Rio de Janeiro. The newest and most productive coffee zone is in northeastern Paraná, where it centers around the city of Londrina. Chief ports for shipment are Santos, Paranaguá—through which Paraguayan coffee is also exported—Rio de Janeiro, and Vitória.

Cotton farming, an old colonial industry in Brazil, now yields about 2,000,000 bales a year. Formerly centered in the dry states of the northeast, where much of the cultivation is primitive in method, production of the southern states, particularly of São Paulo, has increased to the point where the yield of that region now greatly exceeds the output of the northern farms. Some long-staple fiber is grown in the north, but most of the Paulista cotton is medium staple, or shorter. Though the large national textile industry takes the bulk of the production, some cotton finds its way into the highly competitive import markets of western Europe.

Cacao is mainly produced in a rainy zone of southern Bahia, centering on the port of Ilhéus. Though tobacco is grown in considerable quantities in other parts of the country, even including a tropical belt in the State of Pará, the three States of Bahia, Rio de Janeiro, and Minas Gerais account for about three-fourths of all Brazilian production. The large domestic cigar and cigarette industry, which produces goods of excellent quality, generally takes about half the tobacco crop, but some of the leaf is shipped to Argentina and western Europe.

Sugar is the oldest industry in Brazil and during the colonial period the crude *engenhos* of Pernambuco and Campos made the fortunes of many planters. Like tobacco, sugar cane is grown in all the states of the Brazilian Union, but the largest producers are now Minas Gerais, Rio de Janeiro, and Pernambuco. The total production generally runs well over 3,000,000 tons, a large part of which is centrifugal sugar, produced by the larger mills, or *usinas*, with modern equipment. Many small establishments account for a large production of crude brown sugar, sold in cakes, which is used as sweetening, and often as an important item of diet, by the poor classes of the population. Total output and exports of sugar tend to fluctuate very widely, so that there is little stability in the industry. A large production of alcohol is an important by-product of the industry.

Brazil's production of corn is over 300,000,000 bushels a year, which places it in third rank among the world's producers, after the United States and Argentina. With better seed and improved methods of cultivation, production could easily be doubled without a proportionate increase in acreage. While much of the crop is used for feeding hogs and other livestock, corn products are an important factor in the diet of the Brazilian population.

No other Brazilian crop has equaled the rate of increase for rice culture. Annual production has reached a total of 4,000,000 tons, and prospects are for future expansion of the crop, most of which is dry-land rice. On the other hand, Brazil, a large consumer of white bread, has not succeeded in her efforts to increase her output of wheat. An ambitious program to that end in Rio Grande do Sul has failed since 1960, with the result that the country has become more and more dependent on imports, chiefly from Argentina.

Brazilian fruits are always a major item in the national food supply. There is little large-scale commercial fruit growing, and most of the crop is a product of small groves. The business has suffered from bad management, speculative tendencies, particularly in orange growing, insect pests, shortages of transport and refrigeration facilities, and lack of quality standards. Yet total production of fruits is enormous. An orange industry that once ranked second in the world has declined, though the general quality of oranges and tangerines is excellent. A wide variety of other tropical and subtropical fruits provide a much-needed diversification of the Brazilian diet. These include grapes in Rio Grande do Sul, guavas, mangoes that grow wild, avocados, melons, probably the world's best pineapples, excellent Japanese-grown strawberries, the mamão or papaya, a native of Brazil, and a number of indigenous fruits not found outside Brazil. Apples are inferior, and most of the apples sold in Brazil are products of the Rio Negro country in Argentina. A once promising export trade in citrus fruits has failed to materialize. Argentina has developed a large citrus industry of her own and is no longer dependent on imports from Brazil and Paraguay.

The same fate befell the export of Brazilian bananas. Except for the coastal plain of São Paulo, where plantations were established, most bananas would appear to be derived from the small patches of the plant that seem to surround virtually every rural cabin in Brazil. The fruit ranges from the small and delicate-flavored *banana de ouro* to large plantains for frying.

In volume of production, among the most important of other Brazilian food crops are beans, manioc or cassava, and sweet potatoes. The production of beans is nearly twice that of the United States, and unaccountable millions of tons of manioc (the common or bitter cassava) are produced annually. This prodigious tuber (*Manihot esculenta*) is of great economic importance in Brazil. A coarse meal known as *farinha de mandioca* is made from this species, the tubers of which must first be ground and roasted to expel the poisonous hydrocyanic acid. It is also the source of tapioca. Another species (*Manihot aipi*) is nonpoisonous and its tubers are boiled and eaten like potatoes.

Argentina's principal asset as an agricultural nation is the deep soil of the pampa. A secondary advantage is a climate that is generally favorable to the growing of crops. Of the cereals, she is by far the largest wheat producer in Latin America. The crop normally varies between 175,000,000 and 215,000,000 bushels, less than half the Canadian yield. But Canada grows more wheat than all Latin America combined. The Argentine wheat belt almost rings the capital beyond an intervening zone of pasture lands. It extends around from the southern rim of the Province of Buenos Aires, by the important port of Bahia Blanca, spreading widely over the western part of the province and spilling over into the territory of La Pampa, thence northward deep into Córdoba and Santa Fé, from whence it turns eastward in a narrow strip across Entre Rios to the Uruguayan border. While Argentina's total corn production is only about half that of Brazil, only the United States exports more corn. Corn growing is most heavily concentrated in the southern part of the Province of Santa Fé in the region tributary to the river port of Rosario, but, thinning out, it reaches well down into the Province of Buenos Aires.

Among other important cereal crops are barley, oats, and rye, to whose cultivation over 7,000,000 acres of land are devoted. Cotton is an increasingly important crop, which produced a yield of about 550,000 bales in 1961. The industry is largely concentrated in the

Chaco Territory and is primarily designed to serve as a source of supply for the national textile industry. Sugar is an old and highly protected—and regulated—industry, which is largely centered in the Province of Tucumán. Efforts are made to restrict output to domestic needs, and production normally ranges from 500,000 to 650,000 tons of raw sugar, reaching nearly 1,000,000 tons in the crop year 1959-60. Argentina also produces around 150,000 tons of rice a year, and is the largest potato-growing country in Latin America.

The growing, processing, and export of fruits has become a major industry in Argentina. The oldest branch of this industry is the cultivation of grapes in the irrigated Mendoza and San Juan regions. About 200,000 tons of table grapes and 1,000,000 tons of wine grapes are produced in a normal year. There is a very large production of wine, some of which is exported. A considerable citrus industry has developed in Corrientes, Entre Rios, and the Territory of Misiones. In 1960, the yield totaled 20,000,000 boxes of oranges, 850 boxes of grapefruit, and 2,500,000 boxes of lemons. The Rio Negro and Neuquen districts to the southwest of the pampa are the center of a flourishing industry that specializes in the temperate-zone fruits such as apples, pears, and peaches. The export of fresh and dried fruits has reached a total of about 40,000 tons a year.

Argentina produces in quantity a wide variety of vegetable-oil materials, for both industrial and cooking purposes. She is the world's principal source of linseed, a derivative of flax. There is a very large output of sunflower-seed oil, which is consumed within the country. Other sources of vegetable oils are sesame, soybeans, olives, palm seed, and peanuts.

Brazil's position in the same field shows a similar diversification of raw materials. She is the world's largest producer of castor beans. Of a normal production of 200,000 tons, a large part is exported, but over 10,000 tons of castor oil are normally produced. Cottonseed oil is an important by-product of the cotton industry, production being generally in excess of 100,000 tons. The export of babassu palm kernels from the State of Maranhão to Europe was formerly a business of large proportions. The economic collapse of Germany after the war dealt a severe blow to the industry, from which it has not fully recovered. Other valuable sources of vegetable oils in Brazil include *oiticica* (for the paint industry), linseed, coconuts, and a variety of other palm nuts, such as *curuá* and *murumuru*, peanuts, corn, and sesame. Over 4,000,000 tung trees have been planted in the country.

Of the smaller east-coast countries, Uruguay's agriculture holds a very secondary place to her all-important stock-raising industry, which occupies nearly two-thirds of the land. The most important crop is wheat, but her normal 8,000,000-bushel annual crop does not meet domestic requirements. Considerable corn is grown, and a large variety of fruits and vegetables, including peaches, oranges, grapes, and potatoes, are cultivated for the local market.

Though Paraguay is essentially a rural nation, the products of her agriculture do not appear among her first three exports, but meats comprise almost a third of the total. The true Paraguay to the east of the main river, as distinguished from the Gran Chaco, provides an excellent setting for a varied farm economy. Yet agriculture is generally backward, and has made little progress toward the realization of its bright potential. She produces modest quantities of corn and sugar, strong tobacco, and cotton. There are orange trees everywhere, even in the great forest, whither birds have carried the seeds, and in the north along the Brazilian border, there are new coffee plantations. Everyone drinks the traditional tea of the country, and no one need go hungry in a land where nature is benign and bountiful.

Stockraising. Stockraising is an important adjunct of agriculture in most Latin-American countries. Sometimes, as in Argentina, it is its coequal in the national economy, or even, as in Uruguay, its superior. Except for the breeding of llamas, which have long been used as a beast of burden by the Indians of the Andes, the roots of Latin America's pastoral industry do not go beyond the Spanish and Portuguese conquests. All the domestic animals common to the peninsula were introduced early into the New World, where, save in the tropical lands, they flourished and greatly multiplied in numbers. Life in the colonies, for both aborigines and creoles, was enriched by the valuable contributions which the herds and flocks made, not only to the food supply of the population, but to the means of transport, and by virtue of leather and wool, to many other purposes in the local scheme of things. The industry suffered severely during the wars of independence and the civil wars which followed, when the herds of cattle were decimated by a soldiery that lived off the country. After the middle of

the last century conditions became more favorable for the industry,
which grew rapidly in importance and in the quality of its products.
The principal factors which have been responsible for the remarkable
growth of the livestock industry during the past fifty years have been
the importation of improved breeding stock from Europe and the
United States, and the development of artificial refrigeration, which
made it possible to ship South American beef and mutton to European
markets. Previous to that period the industry had only entered into
international trade through the shipments of jerked beef[2] from one
country to another and in the exportation of hides, skins, and tallow,
largely from Buenos Aires and Montevideo.

On a commercial scale, cattle raising has been most highly developed in Argentina and Uruguay, and more recently in Brazil.
Paraguay, Venezuela, and Mexico are also important cattle countries.
Due to the vast expanses of natural grazing lands and to the mild
winter climate, the Argentine plains were destined to be one of the
foremost cattle regions of the world. As everywhere else in Latin
America, no efforts were made for hundreds of years to improve the
original Spanish stock, which had meantime run to legs and horns.
Large herds of wild cattle roamed the open range of the pampas,
where they were captured by the plains Indians or slaughtered for
their hides. The introduction of a purebred Durham bull in 1848
marked the beginning of a new era in the Argentine cattle industry.
Large numbers of breeding animals, mostly Herefords and Shorthorns,
were imported and rapid improvement of the herds resulted, while the
zone of the long-legged creole stock was pushed out farther toward
the frontiers. Though the government actively promoted the welfare
of the industry, much of this progress was due to the initiative of the
Sociedad Rural, an organization of stockmen and farmers founded in
1875, which has been the leader in every movement for the advancement of the country's pastoral and agricultural industries. For example, it sponsors the annual stock show in Buenos Aires, which at-
tracts breeders from all over the world. Meanwhile, the pastures have

2 Jerked beef, the original sun-dried *boucan* of Haiti, which gave its name to
the buccaneers, is called *charqui* in the Spanish-speaking countries and *xarque* in
Brazil. Largely produced by the *saladeros* of the River Plate countries, it is still
eaten widely, usually with beans and rice, and has long been an important article
of diet among workers in the Cuban cane fields.

been fenced, and alfalfa, which is cut three or four times a year, and other forage crops substituted for the native grasses of the plains. The picturesque and primitive *Gauchos*, who became famous in the days of the longhorns and the open range, have either been trained in the more exacting methods of the new industry or their place has been taken by cowboys of a new type.

Argentina now has over 44,000,000 head of cattle. This number is exceeded only by India, the United States, Russia, and Brazil, but, on the basis of the quality of her herds, Argentina's standing is even higher. Though cattle are raised in all parts of Argentina, the largest herds are in the Provinces of Buenos Aires, Santa Fé, Entre Rios, Corrientes, and Córdoba. Meats, both beef and mutton, comprise about a quarter of the country's total exports, and wool, another 12 percent. In Uruguay wool accounts for over half her exports, and, with meat and hides, her pastoral industry accounts for about 80 percent of her export business. The Oriental Republic has over 8,000,000 head of high-grade cattle and some 20,000,000-odd sheep. Natural conditions are highly favorable to stockraising and the same standards are generally observed in the industry as in Argentina.

Brazil's livestock population is the fourth largest in the world, and is surpassed in total numbers only by the United States, Russia, and the low-grade herds and flocks of India. Of the total, more than 75,000,000 head are cattle. Except in Rio Grande do Sul, whose stockmen have been greatly influenced by Uruguayan methods, the general quality of Brazil's herds is not so high as in the River Plate countries. However, the government and the more enterprising breeders are doing a great deal to promote the introduction of better breeding stock and the demand of the packing plants for a better grade of beef for the export trade has had the same effect. In the more tropical parts of the country inferior national breeds, such as the Caracú, predominate. These districts include the hinterland of the northeastern states, especially of Piauí and Bahia, the island of Marajó, the open *campos gerais* of northern Amazonas, northern Minas Gerais, and the vast ranges of Goiás and southern Mato Grosso. In addition to Herefords, Durhams, and Polled Angus, a number of other European breeds of beef cattle have been introduced, until no country in the world has so great a variety of cattle. Also, because of their hardiness and adaptability to the climate, a large number of humped zebu cattle

have been brought in from India. Some of the zebu herds have been
kept intact, but there has been considerable cross-breeding of zebu
and creole stock. On the lowlands along the Amazon in the State of
Pará there is even a large herd of semi-amphibious *carabao* or water
buffaloes.

Paraguay has long been a cattle country, but the industry, due
to the ravages of two major wars in less than a century, has actually
declined. There is good natural pasturage and the native *vaquero* has
no superior in South America, but little has been done to improve the
stock. The principal market is for canned beef and the manufacture of
beef extract, though the *saladeros* still slaughter a large number of
cattle for the production of jerked beef.

While the other South American countries have from 1,000,000
to 12,000,000 head of cattle, they generally serve only as a source of
meat for the local population or for use as oxen. In recent years there
has been a remarkable development of the cattle industry in Colombia,
which now has about 16,000,000 head, putting the country in third
place in Latin America. As a rule, the only product of the cattle industry to enter into foreign trade is hides, which constitutes an important export in several countries, especially from Chile, Colombia,
and Venezuela. An interesting exception was the survival until recent
times of the old trade in live cattle between the Mojos plains of eastern
Bolivia and the nitrate and shipping centers of northern Chile. These
wild cattle were formerly driven around by way of northern Argentina
and thence over the barren Atacama sector of the Andes into the
Chilean desert. Another famous cattle industry is that of the Venezuelan *llanos*, portrayed by Rómulo Gallegos, the former president
of Venezuela, in his novel *Doña Barbara*. The locale of this backward
and picturesque industry is the low savannas which cover the upper
basin of the Orinoco and its confluent, the Apure, and which are
alternately dried up and flooded from one season of the year to another.
There is also a sizable cattle industry in eastern Cuba, and another, of
varied fortunes, in northern Mexico. Until the appearance of the hoof-
and-mouth disease in Mexico in 1947, large numbers of cattle were
shipped from the States of Chihuahua and Sonora into our southwest
for fattening.

An increasingly important branch of the cattle industry in Latin
America is that of dairy products. It is not long since it was a com-

mon experience to find Swiss canned milk served at the tables of Argentine *estancieros*, who were the owners of tens of thousands of cattle. Foreigners, including Swiss, Basque, and Danish immigrants, were pioneers in this industry, which has now assumed large proportions in Argentina, Uruguay, and southern Brazil. Beginnings have been made in the other countries, but the supply of fresh milk and butter is still inadequate to meet the local demand in most of them. Thousands of Guernseys, Jerseys, Holsteins, and Frisians have been introduced as the basis of the new dairy industries, which produce large quantities of cheese as well as of fresh, condensed, and powdered milk, and butter. Argentina now produces over 50,000 tons of butter and 80,000 tons of cheese a year, and exports over 60,000 tons of cheese, butter, and casein. The output of the long-established Brazilian cheese industry is about 60,000 tons of cheese per year.

Argentina, Uruguay, and Brazil are the principal sheep-raising countries of Latin America, followed in order by Peru, Chile, Bolivia, and Mexico. Argentina's flocks, which number about 48,000,000, are the largest in the world, after Australia and Russia. The heaviest concentrations of sheep are found in the southern part of the Province of Buenos Aires and along the Uruguayan border in Entre Rios. The sheep country spreads south from the pampa the length of Patagonia and across the Straits of Magellan into Tierra del Fuego, which it shares with the Chilean flocks. Basques gave the first impetus to the industry in the last century, and Scotch breeders are prominent in the Patagonian field. By 1895 there were nearly 75,000,000 sheep in Argentina, but as the flocks were pushed off the pampas by the advance of the cattle and grain industries, the sheep industry declined in relative importance. Merinos predominate where wool is the first consideration, but in regions where the emphasis is on mutton, as in the far south, the Lincoln and Romney Marsh have largely supplanted the Merino. The raising of sheep for wool is Uruguay's principal industry. Brazil has over 20,000,000 sheep, most of them in Rio Grande do Sul; Peru, about 14,000,000; and Chile and Bolivia, over 6,000,000 each.

With nearly 50,000,000 swine, Brazil is the fourth hog-producing country in the world, after the United States, the Soviet Union, and China. About one out of nine hogs is Brazilian. While large numbers are raised in all parts of the republic, the States of Minas Gerais and Rio Grande do Sul account for over half the national production.

Something has been done to improve the stock by the introduction of Berkshires, Poland Chinas, and Duroc Jerseys, but the native types, particularly the *canastrão*, still predominate. Pork is an important food of the Brazilian people and most of the meat is consumed locally. Argentina, Venezuela, and Mexico also raise many hogs, and the former country exports about 60,000 tons of hams and frozen carcasses a year.

Meat packing has become an important accessory to the cattle- and sheep-raising industries of South America, especially of the River Plate republics and Brazil. The first refrigerated beef was shipped from Buenos Aires in 1877, but the *frigorífico* industry did not attain important proportions until the present century. The later development of the industry was due to the investment of large amounts of American and British capital in chilling and freezing plants, which coincided with the opening up of European markets to South American beef. The chilled, frozen, and canned beef of Argentina accounts for over half the total volume of this business. Brazil, Uruguay, and—intermittently—Paraguay also contribute to the packing of beef products for export, while mutton is frozen for export in Argentina, Uruguay, and the southern Chilean province of Magallanes. American interests still operate in the meat-packing industry of Latin America, but their relative position in the business has declined as a result of nationalist pressures and other influences. However, there are still American-controlled plants in the Buenos Aires area in Argentina, and in Rio Grande do Sul, Paraná, and São Paulo in Brazil.

One of the oldest animal industries in Latin America is the breeding of horses and mules. It has about 40 percent of all the horses on earth and over half the mules. The first horses and mules which the Spaniards brought to the New World were small, but hardy, and adapted themselves easily to their new environment. A good many horses of Arab strain were introduced from time to time, to breed up the original stock. During the present century much has been done to improve the breed of both draft and saddle horses, particularly in Argentina, by importing thoroughbred stallions from England and other foreign countries. In Latin America horses are still used much more than in the United States for getting from one place to another, though less used as draft animals on the farms. In the interior of the southern continent and in Mexico, mules have long been extensively used as pack animals and are an indispensable factor in the transportation of farm and mine production in many localities. The smaller donkeys, like the little *jerico* of northern Brazil and the Mexican burro, are also important in carrying local produce on short runs.

Brazil and Mexico each have some 10,000,000 goats, or about four times the caprine population of the United States. In northern Brazil, particularly in the States of Bahia and Pernambuco, they are bred for meat and for their skins. Brazil ranks third in world production of goatskins.

Mining. Mining was the basis of Spain's colonial economy, to which all other industries were subordinated. For centuries great mining centers, like Potosí, in Upper Peru, and Guanajuato and Zacatecas, in Mexico, poured out a stream of wealth that made their names fabled for riches. The Spaniards were interested only in gold and silver, and paid little attention to the baser metals which they found all about them and mingled with gold or silver in the ores which they extracted. Thus, the tin which they ignored in the tailings of the silver mines at Potosí has only been worked in our own time.

Most mining operations were suspended during the disorders of the wars of independence, and many mines which could be worked at a profit under the low labor costs of the colonial regime were never reopened. As the industry revived during the last century, its emphasis was shifted from gold and silver to the industrial metals, and, later, to the non-metallic minerals. At the same time, the industry became dependent upon the demands of the industrialized economies of the United States and western Europe, instead of on those of the royal treasury of Spain.

The reorganized mining industry of Latin America has faced a variety of special problems, some of which were only recurrences of problems which had tried the ingenuity of the colonial miners. There was a lack of exact geological knowledge of the highly mineralized Andes and of its lower prolongation into Central and North America, as well as of the eastern plateaus of the southern continent. Much exploratory work has been done by both prospectors and geologists, but the resources of large areas are still imperfectly known. A remarkable group of American geologists, including Branner, Derby, Crandall, Hartt, and Leith, have made extensive surveys of Brazil's mineral deposits, and their work has been supplemented by valuable reconnaissance studies of native geologists.

The scope of the colonial industry was strictly limited by the accessibility of the richer lodes to mule transportation. The ores were smelted as close to the mines as possible, and the high value of gold and silver in relation to their volume and weight made it feasible to use mules, and even llamas, to carry the bars of bullion to seaboard. Since the possibilities of using pack animals for transporting the ores and concentrates of the baser metals are limited, transportation is a major problem of the later phase of the industry. Only a few large deposits, like the Chilean iron mines at El Tofo, the coal mines of Brazil and Chile, and some of the petroleum fields, are within easy reach of ocean transportation. Most of the important fields are situated well inland, usually in the high Cordillera Real of the Andes or in the Mexican *Sierras*. Where modern mining methods are used, this involves the transportation of heavy machinery and supplies from the coast and the hauling of the mines' production in the opposite direction. It also may require the foreign managerial and technical staffs to live at altitudes where existence is difficult for those unaccustomed to life at such heights. For some of the largest mining camps in South America are located at over 15,000 feet above the sea, or higher than any point in the United States. Even with the resources of modern engineering, some of the most promising fields are too inaccessible to justify their development at normal price levels in the world market for their product.

Though railroads have done much to remedy this condition, the building of railroads in the Andes is extremely expensive and, at best, the prospective volume of freight is small in relation to the cost of construction and maintenance. However, the building of the Antofagasta and Bolivia Railway, and of its extension, the Bolivia Railway, opened up the mineral resources of the Bolivian plateau to systematic development. This rail system, later supplemented by the construction of long spurs into the eastern Cordillera, and of the Arica-La Paz Railway, and the Guaqui-La Paz branch of the Southern Railway of Peru, afforded excellent outlets for many important mining centers that would otherwise have remained unworked. The Central Railway of Peru has made possible the operation of the rich properties owned by the Cerro de Pasco Copper Corporation, whose business accounts for over 90 percent of the traffic of that line.

The airplane has also facilitated the development of certain isolated districts, such as the mines of Honduras, and the petroleum lands in Colombia. Heavy equipment is first dismantled into loads that can be carried by plane and reassembled at the mine or oil field.

Improvements in the technology of mining have been an important factor in the later growth of Latin America's mining industry. These include the utilization of such mechanical devices as the link belt for carrying ores from the mines to the mill. Steam shovels are used for surface mining, as at Chuquicamata in Chile. Bucket or suction dredges have enabled the working of alluvial gold and tin deposits. Power drills have made it possible to work the hard primary lodes, whose extraction would have been impracticable with hand tools. Hydroelectric power has been substituted for steam or more primitive forms of power. New reduction or smelting methods for the treatment of ores have been introduced, and the electrolytic process for the separation of copper has made possible the commercial utilization of the low-grade ores of northern Chile.

The recruiting of an adequate labor force is a major problem in many mining districts. In the Andes, the Indians and *Cholos*, or mixed breeds, of the region are the only source of labor, since workers from lower altitudes would be incapable of sustained physical effort at such altitudes. The nitrate *oficinas* and copper mines in the Chilean desert country have had to draw a sufficient working force from the excess population of the central provinces. In order to attract and hold enough laborers, the larger companies offer inducements in the form of a higher wage scale than prevails in the locality, and provide housing and recreational facilities and medical services for their workers. The large petroleum companies, in particular, have done much for the welfare of their employees, and have also generally followed a policy of training and advancing their native workers to positions of responsibility. Nevertheless, serious and prolonged labor troubles have occurred in some mining districts, particularly in the Andean countries. The majority of the workers in the mining industries of Latin America have been organized and in some fields comprehensive contracts between companies and unions regulate working conditions in great detail. In Mexico, working conditions in the mining industry, involving questions of employment, tenure, pay and hours, housing, union status, and other phases of the employer-employee relationship, are prescribed by the advanced labor legislation of that country.

Government policies have entered increasingly into the calculations of the mining companies. In this connection, Mexico has been a pioneer in asserting the right of the state to ownership of all subsoil products, thereby reducing the original mine owners to the position of operating concessionaires, and, in the case of petroleum, bringing the issue to the point of expropriation of the foreign-owned properties. Due to its strategic value in considerations of national defense and to the lack of alternative sources of fuel and power, petroleum has been the object of an unusual amount of regulatory legislation. Bolivia, in fact, preceded Mexico in the nationalization of her petroleum industry. In 1952, the three principal tin-mining companies of Bolivia were nationalized by the government, which has since operated them through the medium of a special corporation. The oil industry in Venezuela has operated under arrangements which, while highly lucrative to the governments of that country, have formed a satisfactory, if precarious, working basis for the private companies. Most of the oil fields in Argentina have been exploited by the national government from the beginning. The mining industry is also the object of much special taxation which is generally levied in the form of either export taxes or production royalties. Revenues derived from the petroleum industry are the principal support of the Venezuelan government, as the tax on nitrate was for a long time the mainstay of Chile's fiscal system.

Most of the capital employed in mining has been invested by foreigners, and any considerable expansion of the industry is dependent not only on the prospects in the world markets for minerals, but on the treatment of foreign investments by the various governments. As a rule, official policies are now highly nationalistic, and in many places foreign investments continue on sufferance. Their position is liable to become increasingly precarious, as the demands of government become more exacting and the sphere of regulation steadily widens.

The principal mining countries of Latin America are Bolivia, Chile, Mexico, and Peru, followed by Brazil, Colombia, and Ecuador. Bolivia, Chile, and Venezuela are the only countries where mineral products constitute the bulk of principal exports. On the other hand, lead represents less than 5 percent of Mexico's exports. With the exception of Honduras and Nicaragua, none of the Central American republics has any mines of importance. Of the three West Indian countries, Cuba is the only one whose mining industry is worthy of consideration. Except for petroleum, Argentina's mineral production is small, both in absolute terms and in relation to the national economy as a whole. Uruguay's mines are negligible, and though Paraguay has deposits of iron and manganese, they are not worked. Though certain areas are well mineralized, Venezuela's mineral development is restricted to her great petroleum industry and the mining of gold in the far east of the country and of iron ore in the zone of the lower Orinoco.

Latin America is no longer an important factor in world gold production. In a "normal" year the combined production of its first five producing countries—Colombia, Mexico, Nicaragua, Brazil and Peru—is less than 6 percent of that of South Africa. The largest producer, Colombia, generally yields about 400,000 fine ounces, mostly from dredging operations in the lower Cauca Valley. There is considerable small-scale placer mining in remote Andean valleys and in the beds of some tributaries of the Marañón, but much of the gold production is a by-product of other mining. Some of the old gold camps, like São João del Rey in Brazil, El Callao in Venezuela, and Zaruma in Ecuador, have declined in importance. Mines may be worked out or the ratio of operating costs to yield may have made their continued operation uneconomical.

Mexico is the world's largest producer of silver, normally accounting for about 40 percent of the total output. Due to the general demonetization of silver, the industry has undergone severe vicissitudes in recent years, but has been partly sustained by American purchases of silver designed for the relief of the silver-mining industry in the western states. Peru and Bolivia are the only other countries which produce appreciable amounts of silver.

Of the industrial metals, Latin America's position in the production of copper is especially strong. Its total output is usually over 600,000 metric tons, or about one-fifth of world production. The most important producers are Chile, Mexico, and Peru. Chile's output of nearly 500,000 tons a year is second only to that of the United States and larger than that of the Soviet Union or Congolese Katanga. In the three Latin-American countries the industry is controlled by

American capital. The largest camps in Chile are the vast open-pit workings of the Chile Exploration company at Chuquicamata, on the line of the Antofagasta and Bolivia Railway, the Braden Copper Company's mines near Rancagua in the south, and the Potrerillos property of the Andes Copper Mining Company, which lies inland from the northern port of Chañaral. Most of Peru's copper is produced by the famous Cerro de Pasco Copper Corporation whose mines also produce lead, zinc, gold, silver, tin, antimony, tungsten, coal, bismuth, and arsenic. The Cerro de Pasco company's operations are located in the Province of Junín in the high Andes, and are served by the Central Railway. The company's smelter is situated at Oroya, from which a spur of the railroad climbs to nearly 16,000 feet above sea level on its way to Cerro de Pasco. An important new mining center has been opened at Toquepala in the Province of Tacna in southern Peru. Most of Mexico's copper mines are in the northern States of Coahuila, Sonora, and Baja California, from which the bulk of the output is exported to the United States. In Cuba, copper was long mined fairly continuously at Matahambre, in the western part of the island, and only intermittently at Cobre, in the Province of Oriente. Bolivia's industry is peculiar in that the Corocoro mines, which are the only producers of any volume, yield some copper in a pure state.

Though northwestern Argentina now produces over 2,000 tons of tin a year, Bolivia is the only Latin-American country in which tin mining is a major industry. In fact, tin dominates the depressed economy of that country, and to an unusual degree determines her prosperity. Though Bolivia ranks second as a producer of tin, her production is only a small part of that of Malaya. A world cartel allocates production among the producing regions, but Bolivia's output is usually well short of her quota. It is a high-cost industry under any circumstances, but, as now operated by the government, it suffers from other conditions incidental to control by an extremist political regime, and from labor costs out of all reasonable relation to value of output.

Most of Bolivia's production was accounted for by three groups of mining interests, those of Patiño, Hochschild, and Aramayo. The most important element in the industry was the Patiño Mines and Enterprises Consolidated, a Delaware corporation. This company was founded by the late Simón J. Patiño, who from the humblest beginnings became one of the world's richest men and resided in Paris and Buenos Aires. The second of the so-called Big Producers was Mauricio Hochschild, a former ore buyer from Argentina. The group of foreign investors which he headed controlled the mines of the legendary Cerro de Potosí and other valuable properties. The Aramayo interests, which were incorporated in Europe, were built around the original holdings of a Bolivian family of that name and controlled a considerable number of minor properties.

Mexico and Peru are the only countries which produce sizable quantities of lead and zinc. Their combined output of the two metals is respectively about 350,000 and 325,000 metric tons. The United States, which produces only a little more zinc and substantially less lead, habitually causes considerable irritation in both countries by its protective tariffs in the interest of the home industry. The American-owned Cerro de Pasco company, in Peru, ships large quantities of electrolytic lead to the United States.

Large reserves of iron ore exist in seven of the Latin-American republics—Brazil, Chile, Colombia, Cuba, Mexico, Peru, and Venezuela. The ore fields in all these countries are being worked, some of them intensively. The ore serves as the basis of an existing metallurgical industry in nearly all the seven countries, or as a potential source of raw material for future industrialization. Also, considerable quantities of ore are being shipped to the United States or western Europe. In Brazil, in the well-known Itabira zone of Minas Gerais, there are solid mountains of hematite ore, whose iron content ranges from 65 to 70 percent. Belo Horizonte, the capital of the state, is ringed by iron-bearing hills that are the seat of a growing steel industry. A complex of steel mills, including the large operation at Volta Redonda in the State of Rio de Janeiro, and several plants in the State of São Paulo and elsewhere in Minas, as at Sabará, are dependent on the vast deposits for their supplies of ore. Exports of iron ore are largely made through the port of Vitória.

Iron occurs in several parts of the Atacama region of northern Chile, but the most important field is that of El Tofo, situated in the Province of Coquimbo a short distance from the port of Cruz Grande. The deposits are extensive and of good quality, and are mined by quarrying. The Bethlehem Steel Company, which owns the deposits, has installed the most modern equipment for handling the ore, which is shipped to its plant near Baltimore. Ocean shipments from northern Chilean ports may reach a total of over 4,000,000 tons a year. Quantities of ore are also sent southward to supply the needs of the national steel mill at Huachipato near Concepción.

Mexico has large reserves of iron ore, but some of those located in the western part of the country are still too inaccessible to be worked on a commercial scale. Commercial production of iron in Mexico is largely limited to the States of Durango and Nuevo León. Most of the output is derived from the famous Cerro del Mercado in the former state. This rich mine, and the deposits at Lampazos, in Nuevo León, are the property of the Monterrey Iron and Steel Smelting Company, which utilizes most of the production in its steel mill at Monterrey.

There are considerable deposits of iron ore in the Cuban Province of Oriente, formerly held as a reserve by American steel interests, though shipments were made intermittently to supplement local American supplies. Peru is estimated to have over 500,000,000 tons of iron ore in the vicinity of Marcona, in the coastal Department of Ica. This ore is located near the sea and offers good possibilities for future development. Other deposits exist in the inland region to the north of Lima and are, therefore, more accessible to the government's steel plant at Chimbote. American steel manufacturing interests have acquired and are developing two large ore fields on either side of the lower Orinoco. Ore is transported down river and out by the delta to steel plants in the United States. Iron ore from this source is now Venezuela's third export. Production now runs at an annual rate of nearly 20,000,000 tons.

Latin America also has valuable reserves of other minerals used in steelmaking. Most important of these are the manganese resources of Brazil. The oldest of the manganese ore fields in point of development is located in Minas Gerais, where the United States Steel Corporation began operations about half a century ago. Due to transportation problems, a large deposit of ore in an isolated hill at Urucúm near Corumbá on the Paraguay River was not developed until much later. The newest field, worked by the Bethlehem Steel Company, is located in the Territory of Amapá north of the Amazon River estuary. Its development has been responsible for a large increase in exports of the mineral, which now exceed a million tons. Another potential source of manganese is Cuba, now closed to trade with the United States.

Other steel-alloy metals found in commercial quantities in Latin America are vanadium, molybdenum, tungsten, chrome, and nickel. The Minasragra mine of the Vanadium Corporation of America is located at a height of 16,500 feet in the Peruvian Department of Junín. It is the world's largest source of the metal. Mexico and Chile are producers of molybdenum and Bolivia, Brazil, and Peru produce small quantities of wolframite or tungsten ore. Deposits of chromite and nickel oxide in eastern Cuba were developed during World War II and there was a considerable production thereafter until the mines were seized by the Castro government. Brazil also has large reserves of chrome ore, which are being developed on a modest scale, and deposits of beryllium, titanium, and zirconium. Antimony, which has a variety of industrial uses as an alloy, including the manufacture of battery plates, is produced in Bolivia and Peru, mainly in small workings in the mountains.

The low Atrato basin of northwestern Colombia ranks next to the Ural zone of Russia in the production of platinum. Annual exports are normally at a rate of about 16,000 troy ounces.

Mexico still ranks high among the mercury-producing countries of the world. On the other hand, the Santa Barbara mine, near Huancavelica in Peru, which was a large producer in colonial times, has been worked only intermittently and on a small scale during this century. Mercury is also found in Brazil, Chile, Venezuela, and Colombia.

The Cerro de Pasco company in Peru produces between 20 and 25 percent of the world's bismuth, and is the decisive factor in the international market for this mineral. Smaller producers are Bolivia, Chile, and Mexico.

Due to the frequency of volcanic formations, sulphur occurs widely in Latin America. Important deposits are found in Colombia and Mexico, but Chile is the largest producer. One mine is located at 18,500 feet, on the volcano of Aucanquilcha in the Ollague region near the Bolivian border. This is the highest mine in the world. The government of Chile has made large loans to the industry and has promoted its interests in other ways. Peruvian deposits in the Department of Tacna yield about one-tenth as much as the Chilean mines.

Bauxite, the basis of the aluminum industry, is found in Brazil,

Cuba, and Venezuela. Several companies have been organized in Brazil for the development of aluminum manufacture.

The most important producers of gem stones in Latin America are Colombia and Brazil. The Muzo and Cusquez deposits of emeralds in Colombia, which are worked by the government, control the world market for these gems. Brazil ranks next to the Union of South Africa as a producer of diamonds. There are rich fields in Minas Gerais and Mato Grosso, which have produced some of the world's largest and finest stones. The State of Bahia also has a considerable industry in the production of carbonados or black diamonds, which are used for industrial purposes. Brazil also produces a variety of semi-precious stones, including aquamarines, tourmalines, topazes, beryls, and amethysts. Mexico yields opals, tourmalines, and turquoises. An interesting Brazilian industry is represented by the mining of quartz crystals in the State of Minas Gerais. The use of these crystals in optical and radio manufacture led to an intensive development of the Minas deposits during both World Wars.

One of the most defective branches of the mining industry in Latin America is that of coal. The product is mostly low-grade bituminous, with high ash content. For example, coal from the mines in southern Brazil must be pulverized, washed, mixed with imported coal, and pressed into briquettes before it is suitable for use by industrial plants, like the Volta Redonda steel mill. In its original state it is not even fit for use in locomotives. Peru has the only known deposits of true anthracite in Latin America, but there are also reserves of high-grade bituminous in that country and in Mexico. Though reserves may be large, as in the Brazilian fields, actual production is everywhere low in relation to the potential market and the level of fuel requirements in general. In the four major producing countries, Brazil, Colombia, Chile, and Mexico, output runs between highs of 1,600,000 and 2,200,000 tons. Minor producers are Peru, Argentina, and Venezuela. Some of the largest coal reserves are inaccessible to existing transportation facilities, as in Colombia and Mexico, and the high cost of railway construction in mountainous country would apparently preclude an early solution of the transportation problem involved in their development. At the other extreme, the old Vulcan mines in the vicinity of Lota, Coronel, and other localities to the south of Concepción are closer to the sea. The established coal-mining industry in Mexico is largely concentrated in the State of Coahuila, and its most serious transportation problems have been solved.

Nine countries produce oil in commercial quantities. Their output of crude oil in 1960 was as follows:

	BARRELS
Venezuela	1,041,000,000
Mexico	99,050,000
Argentina	64,200,000
Colombia	55,700,000
Brazil	30,000,000
Peru	20,000,000
Chile	7,200,000
Bolivia	3,500,000
Ecuador	2,700,000
Total	1,323,350,000

Venezuela now ranks, after the United States, as the second oil-producing country in the world. Her output exceeds that of the Soviet Union and she is the largest exporter of petroleum. Petroleum is produced in both the eastern and the western end of the country. The older, and major, field, in which the first wells were opened in 1917, lies in the low inland basin bordering Lake Maracaibo. A newer field, which is being actively developed, is located in the eastern part of the republic between the lower Orinoco and the Caribbean coast and extending well up toward the Orinoco delta. Crude oil from the Maracaibo zone is refined on the near-by Dutch-owned islands of Aruba and Curaçao or in a national refinery.

The Venezuelan industry is almost entirely controlled by American and British capital. The history of the corporate ramifications of the various concessionaries is complex, but the principal operating interests are represented by a number of Standard, Gulf, and Royal Dutch-Shell subsidiaries known locally as Creole, Mene Grande, Caribbean, etc. The investment is very large and the installations are correspondingly elaborate and efficiently managed. In spite of its extraordinary statistical position, the oil industry has not been an unmixed blessing to Venezuela. The large revenues derived by the national treasury from the high production royalties have not been spent to the best advantage of the nation. Too much of the income has gone to make a showplace of Caracas, while neglecting the development of the interior. Dominance by the petroleum industry has unbalanced the national economy at the expense of agriculture and a healthy growth of manufacturing, though efforts have been made by the government to correct this imbalance and with some gratifying results. The magnitude and strategic implications of the industry, the general tendency in Latin America toward extreme national control of petroleum resources, the potential menace of radical elements in labor and politics, have made necessary a delicately balanced relationship between the government and the oil companies. That this relationship has generally been so satisfactory through successive changes of government is testimony to the practical sense and diplomatic skill of the high management of the oil companies.

The Mexican oil industry dates from about 1901. In 1910 the yield was 3,600,000 barrels, and by 1921 it was producing 193,000,000 barrels in a year, or about twice its present yield. The oil fields are located in the lowlands along the Gulf coast, within the States of Tamaulipas and Vera Cruz. The southernmost field is that at Minatitlán, in the northern part of the Isthmus of Tehuantepec. The oldest producing wells are in the basin of the Panuco River, where they supply oil to the large refineries at Tampico.

The pioneers in the Mexican industry were an Englishman named Pearson, later ennobled as Lord Cowdray, and the American, Edward L. Doheny. In the mid-twenties, the Standard Oil Company of Indiana acquired the Doheny concessions, and in 1932 its interests were taken over by the Standard's New Jersey Company. In the meantime, the Sinclair interests had bought out the rights of the old Pierce company, which was one of the earliest operators. European holdings were largely represented by the Royal Dutch-Shell group, known in Mexico as "El Aguila," or "The Eagle."

The war-time boom in Mexican oil began to collapse in 1922. The Tampico wells had already passed their peak of production and salt water from the Gulf had penetrated into some of them. The Mexican Constitution of 1917, by declaring all subsoil products the property of the nation, made the future prospects of the foreign companies highly uncertain. Also, the counter-attractions of the new Venezuelan fields and the favorable petroleum laws of that country turned the attention of foreign operators from Mexico. However, the

British development of the highly productive Poza Rica field later gave a new spurt to the industry.

Government opposition to the foreign oil companies came to a head under the administration of President Cárdenas. Meanwhile, with the backing of the government, the petroleum unions began to press their demands for a series of advanced labor conditions, which led to a general strike of oil workers in May, 1937. The impasse between the foreign operators, on one side, and the petroleum workers, supported by the government, on the other, grew steadily worse, until a settlement that might serve as a basis for continued operations became impossible. Finally, on March 18, 1938, President Cárdenas invoked the expropriation law of 1936 by signing a decree which expropriated the properties of seventeen American and British oil companies. The foreign companies later made unsuccessful representations to the Mexican government for indemnification, and the British government went to the length of breaking off diplomatic relations with Mexico. Since then the operation of the major fields has been turned over to the state-owned *Petróleos Mexicanos*, known locally as "Pemex." This government corporation also acts as the distributing agency for products of the national petroleum agency.

The beginnings of the Colombian oil industry date from about 1919. The two major producing fields are located well inland in the middle of the Magdalena basin, and serious transportation difficulties long retarded their development. Two pipelines, one 262 miles long and the other 335 miles long, were built through jungle country to provide an outlet to the Caribbean coast for the product of the fields. The bulk of production is supplied by two concerns, the Tropical Oil Company and the Colombia Petroleum Company, which works the deposits of the famous Barco Concession.

The Argentine petroleum industry began with the opening of the Comodoro Rivadavia field in the Province of Chubut in 1907. While this area still accounts for most of the Argentine production, several widely separated fields have been opened up in other parts of the country. These include the Plaza Huincul field in Neuquen, the Tupungato field in Mendoza, and, in the north, the minor Tartagal area in the Province of Salta. Much of the industry has been nationalized from the beginning and the bulk of the output is derived from wells operated by the official corporation known as *Yacimientos Petro-*

líferos Fiscales. Though under restrictions, private enterprise, American and British, has been permitted to continue in control of a minority interest in the industry. In spite of all efforts to make the country self-sufficient in petroleum, a considerable deficit in the national supply is represented by imports from Venezuela.

The origin of the Latin-American petroleum industry dates from the opening of a well at Zorritos, Peru, in 1878. The Peruvian oil zone extends for about 100 miles along the desert coast, from the vicinity of Paita to Tumbés, near the Ecuadorean border. There are three distinct producing areas within that region—Zorritos, Negritos, and Lobitos. Zorritos, the pioneer field, is now a very small producer. It is owned by the Peruvian government. The Negritos-Talara field accounts for the great bulk of Peruvian output. It belongs to the International Petroleum Company, a subsidiary of the Standard Oil Company of New Jersey. The Lobitos field is a property of the British company, Lobitos Oilfields, Ltd. There has been considerable interest in a field on the eastern side of the Andes, but little progress has been made in the exploitation of those deposits.

Ecuador's only operating oil field is located at Ancón in the Santa Elena peninsula, north of the Gulf of Guayaquil. Development is in the hands of the Anglo-Ecuadorean Oil Fields, Ltd.

The present Bolivian petroleum industry began with a grant of development rights to the Richmond Levering Company, of New York, in 1920. The Standard Oil Company of New Jersey early acquired the Levering concession, and through the purchase of a number of smaller concessions came to control the entire Bolivian field on the eastern side of the Andes, extending from the Argentine border to the Rio Grande district in the Department of Santa Cruz. Between 1922 and 1928 twenty-two wells were drilled. In 1936, the Bolivian government created a state corporation, on lines similar to the Argentine YPF, for the purpose of developing the nation's oil resources. Early the next year, the government of President Busch expropriated the Standard's concessions, thus antedating the final action of Mexico in nationalizing the Mexican petroleum industry. The industry has been stagnant under state operation and, in the meantime, efforts to attract foreign capital into the development of new petroleum areas have failed.

Production is confined to small camps located in the low country in the southeastern part of the country. Connections with the populated districts of the plateau are difficult and much of the small production is diverted into Argentina, which has a financial stake in the Bolivian industry. In the meantime, a rivalry developed between Argentina and Brazil for control of the oil output of Bolivia. The Brazilian government had already begun construction of a railroad across the country with the object of tapping the Bolivian fields from the east. This line was to connect with the Brazilian Noroeste Railway near Corumbá, thus providing an outlet to the industrial region of São Paulo. The Argentine government, meanwhile, countered with a proposal for the extension of the state railway beyond its terminus at Yacuiba, with the important center of Santa Cruz de la Sierra as its ultimate destination. During the Chaco War between Bolivia and Paraguay, possession of the Bolivian oil fields was evidently one of the aims of Paraguayan strategy, but the peace settlement left the fields in Bolivian hands, with Argentina in the strongest position to profit eventually from their fuller development.

The Brazilian government has been greatly concerned over the lack of a substantial domestic source of petroleum and has made strenuous efforts to locate oil resources within the country. Meanwhile, geological reconnaissance has covered only a relatively small part of its vast area, and the only field of any immediate promise which has been found is in the State of Bahia, where the industry is now concentrated. Considerable progress has been made in the development of this limited area, but it is still necessary to import the bulk of the country's oil requirements. As a result of President Vargas' nationalistic dictum, "The oil is ours" ("*O petroleo é nosso!*"), a government monopoly, known as *Petrobrás*, assumed control over the operation of the industry. However, gasoline and other petroleum products are distributed through American and European outlets.

Oil has been found in southern Chile in the remote Province of Magallanes, on the large island of Tierra del Fuego. The field is being developed by a special government agency, similar to those in Argentina and Brazil. The crude oil is refined at Concón, north of Valparaiso. The industry now fills over 30 percent of the country's petroleum requirements.

One of the most important non-metallic mineral industries in Latin America involves the extraction of sodium nitrate in northern

Chile, whose deposits comprise the only important natural source of this material. Sodium nitrate is used as a fertilizer, as a raw material in the making of nitric acid, and in the manufacture of explosives. The Chilean nitrate deposits are situated in the arid northern part of the country, and lie within the so-called *pampa* belt between the Andes and the coastal range. The belt extends north and south for about 400 miles in width. This region was formerly a part of Bolivia and Peru, but was taken from those countries in the War of the Pacific, which was fought between 1879 and 1881. The original capital in the industry was British, Spanish, and Chilean, but American interests later gained a strong position in the industry. The Chilean nitrate industry had a profitable history until German scientific research succeeded in developing a competitive product, as described earlier in this book.

Forest industries. The forest products of Latin America are an important source of wealth, and the forest resources of the southern republics constitute an enormous reserve for future development. Most of these raw materials are native to the New World, but some of them have been transplanted to other continents, thereby introducing new elements of competition. The market for some has been reduced by the substitution of other products, sometimes of synthetic manufacture.

The principal products of these extractive industries are as follows:

Lumber. Latin America has the largest area of forest land in the world. Over 3,000,000 square miles, or about 40 percent of the entire land area, is in timber. Yet in spite of the vast extent of its forests, the timbering industry of Latin America accounts for only 5 to 7 percent of the world production of sawn lumber.

Brazil produces well over half of all Latin-American lumber. Other countries which produce more than 100,000,000 board feet are Paraguay, Colombia, Bolivia, Guatemala, Haiti, Argentina, Mexico, Venezuela, Chile, Peru, and Honduras. Except in Paraguay, it is nowhere a major factor in a country's economy or in its export trade.

This circumstance is largely due to the prevailing nature of the Latin-American forests and to the lack of local demand for lumber for building and other purposes. The tropical rain forests, which comprise the bulk of the forested area, are rich in hardwoods, but poor in

the softwoods that are in general demand for construction and industrial uses.

In the Amazon jungle, which is typical of conditions elsewhere,
solid stands of any particular tree do not exist, but an acre of forest
may contain a dozen species. As a result, the timberman in search of
enough logs to make up a shipment of a certain hardwood may have to
cut over a large section of the forest. This makes timbering a difficult
and time-consuming operation. Moreover, transportation is generally
difficult. Jungle trails are liable to be muddy, and while the hardwood
trees grow on the *terra firme* or high ground, the swampy belt along
the river banks may offer serious obstacles in getting out logs to the
nearest navigable stream. As the common hardwoods have a specific
gravity higher than water, rafting the logs to the sawmill presents a
special problem, which is sometimes met by mixing logs of lighter
wood with those of hardwood. Throughout most of the west-coast
countries of South America the Andes present a virtually impassable
barrier to the transport of lumber from the forests on the eastern side
of the mountains to the industrialized regions on the plateau or the
coast.

Stands of softwoods, chiefly of pine, are well localized, the largest
areas being located in Mexico, which has a well-developed lumbering
industry, using modern sawmill equipment. The Brazilian softwood
industry is largely concentrated in the Paraná pine region of the state
of that name. Large quantities of this valuable lumber are normally
exported in a year, largely to Argentina, where it has a multitude of
uses.

Excellent cabinet woods have been exported from Latin America
for hundreds of years. It was the retired buccaneers who, as cutters
of logwood or mahogany in the forests of northern Central America
in the seventeenth century, secured England's title to the present
district of Belize or British Honduras. While the original stands of
mahogany, known locally as *caoba*, have largely been cut off, there
is considerable production from second-growth trees in Honduras and
other Central American countries. Mahogany also grows in the forests
of the Amazon. The wood is widely used for the manufacture of
furniture for local use, and declining amounts are exported to the
United States and Europe.

The common terms applied to the principal hardwoods vary

considerably from one country to another, so that it is sometimes difficult to identify certain species by their local names. In addition to mahogany, among the cabinet woods which enter most largely into the export trade in lumber or into the domestic manufacture of furniture are the Brazilian jacarandá (*Dalbergia nigra*), the rosewood of Demerara and *palissandre* of Cayenne; andiroba (*Carapa guianensis*), the crabwood of Demerara; the Amazonian *pau-marfim*, or "ivory wood" (*Agonandra brasiliensis*); and the dark red muirapiranga (*Brosimum paraense*), of Brazil. The increasing use of veneers and of other special finishes, as well as changes in furniture fashions, has considerably reduced the demand for the fine cabinet woods of tropical Latin America. The tough, dark green lignum vitae, or guayacán sometimes called *palo santo*, or "holy wood," is still in demand for a number of special purposes, including propeller-shaft bearings for ships, for which it is much superior to steel or bronze. Other hardwoods have a wide use in wagon and boat building, railroad ties, piling, and for flooring, beams, and other construction purposes.

The most useful of all Latin-American woods is the so-called Spanish cedar (*Cedrela brasiliensis*), which is widely scattered throughout Latin America. It is a medium-weight wood, which occurs in large logs, and is easily worked. It has a large market for interior finishing in construction purposes and for a variety of other uses. There is an extensive export trade in this valuable wood from regions as remote as eastern Peru. Another group of medium-weight construction woods of wide occurrence consists of the several species of laurel, of the Lauraceae family. This includes the *laurel blanco*, of Paraguay, the various *louros* of the Brazilian Amazonia, the "greenheart" of northern South America, and the Chilean laurel, in which there has been a considerable export trade to Germany, Argentina, and Peru.

One of the most interesting woods of northern Latin America is the *balsa* or well-known corkwood which, in spite of extreme lightness (about one-sixth the weight of water and half that of cork), is unusually strong. It is worked extensively in the forests of Ecuador, which carries on an export business in the wood, largely to the United States. It has many uses in industry, especially in insulation for refrigerators and cold storage rooms and in airplane construction.

Rubber. During the few decades between Charles Goodyear's discovery of the vulcanizing process and the beginning of the automobile era, the Amazon valley dominated the world's rubber industry. Though Brazil was the most important factor in the wild rubber industry, Bolivia, Colombia, Ecuador, Peru, and Venezuela also shipped out appreciable quantities of smoked latex by the Amazon. But even before Amazonian exports reached their peak in 1912, with total shipments of 45,000 tons, plantation rubber from the Middle East had become a serious competitor in the international market. The next year plantation rubber production exceeded the output of wild rubber from South America for the first time. Thereafter, the disparity between the two sources of supply continued to widen as the production of automobile tires increased, until Amazon rubber became an insignificant factor in the world market. In 1938, the Amazon valley accounted for less than 2 percent of all crude-rubber exports, which in that year totaled 895,000 tons. In spite of the costly program undertaken by the Rubber Development Corporation during the Second World War, when the Japanese occupation of Malaya cut off the principal sources of world supply, production of the Amazon area proved to be much below expectations. It has reached a total of 30,000 tons again, but the large deficit in supplies for the domestic manufacturing industry is now made up by imports from the Orient, by way of Rotterdam. In the meantime, the Ford plantations on the Tapajós River have been acquired by the Brazilian government, but companies which maintain branch tire factories in Brazil are now required to develop plantations in the country. There are two or three such plantations in the vicinity of Belém and another in the rain belt of southern Bahia.

As its name indicates, the *Hevea brasiliensis* tree, which is the basis of the world's crude-rubber industry, is a native of the Amazon valley. It occurs widely through the forest to the south of the main river, its habitat extending from the delta of the Amazon west to the valley of the Huallaga in eastern Peru and south into the Beni country of Bolivia. The best districts are the remote Acre Territory in Brazil and the continuation of the same area in northern Bolivia, which produce the superior grade of rubber known in the trade as "upriver fine." To the north of the Amazon an inferior variety of the *Hevea* family is the source of rubber production. Except where the example of the

Ford plantations on the Tapajós and the influence of the Brazilian Agronomic Institute at Belém reached into the jungle, methods used in the Amazonian industry have continued to be primitive.

In addition to the *Hevea brasiliensis*, there are several minor sources of rubber in Latin America. These include the *Castilloa* (or *Castilla*) *ulei* tree of the Amazon valley and the *elastica* of the same genus, which is found in Mexico and Central America; the maniçoba (*Manihot glaziovii*), of the dry *sertão* country of northeastern Brazil; and the guayule shrub of the north Mexican desert, which has also been planted in the southwestern part of the United States. However, in terms of world production the combined output from these sources is negligible, and insufficient to supply the tire industry of the United States for an hour.

Tanning materials. The most important tanning material found in Latin America is quebracho extract. This is the crystallized sap of the hard *quebracho colorado* tree, which occurs only in the Chaco country to the west of the Paraná-Paraguay river. Argentina is the largest producer, followed by Paraguay. Arrangements between the producers in both countries restrict production, fix prices, and allocate markets among the members of the group. The strong position held by quebracho extract in the leather industry, by virtue of its superiority to all other tanning materials, makes it possible for this highly localized business to determine conditions of production and sale. However, the threatened exhaustion of the supply of the slow-growing trees has put a definite period to the future of the industry. The decline is already apparent; Argentine production fell off by more than a third between 1951 and 1958, and the output of the Paraguayan mills decreased by almost 20 percent.

Another Latin-American source of tanning materials is various trees of the *Caesalpinia* genus. The best known of these is the dividivi, which is widely encountered in the Caribbean countries. Others are the algarobilla of Chile, and the cascalote, which is widely employed for tanning leather in Mexico. In all three, the tannin is extracted from the seed pods of the tree.

Paraguay tea. Maté, or Paraguay tea, is made from the leaves of a tree (*Ilex paraguayensis*) of the holly family. The natural habitat of the tree is in the upper basin of the River Plate system. Though it is generally associated with Paraguay and occurs widely in the eastern part of that country, Brazil is the largest producer. It grows in the States of Mato Grosso and Santa Catarina, but the center of the Brazilian industry is in Paraná. In Brazil the product is known as herva mate or Brazilian tea. In Argentina, the tree is cultivated on a large scale in the Province of Corrientes and the Territory of Misiones. Due to the destructive methods of harvesting the leaves in some districts, reliance may have to be increasingly placed on plantations. The tea, which is a healthful stimulant, has long had a large market in Argentina, Uruguay, and Chile, and in recent years has gained a limited vogue in the United States and in some European countries.

Vegetable oils, nuts, and resins. Though total production, except of a few products, is smaller than that of Africa and the Orient, the vegetable-oil industry of Latin America has attained large proportions and its possibilities of expansion are virtually unlimited. In addition to the oils derived from cultivated plants, there is a wide range of oils which are extracted primarily from the immense variety of palm nuts common to tropical America. Production for domestic use is already large in several countries and exports are considerable.

Coconut palms are found in the coastal regions of Latin America from Mexico down to southern Brazil on the east side of the continent and as far south as Ecuador on the west coast of South America. Plantations have been developed in Panama, Honduras, and Brazil, but most of the production of nuts, copra, and coconut oil comes from wild trees. Mexico produces considerable copra a year from her national soap industry, but imports even larger quantities. In spite of its great potentialities, very little has been done to develop the coconut industry in Brazil. While the Brazilian government estimates the annual production at over 140,000,000 nuts a year, most of these are consumed locally, large numbers of them being opened solely for the water which they contain.

Babassu nuts are another source of vegetable oil in Brazil. There are vast stands of the babassu palm over the north of Brazil, particularly in the States of Maranhão and Piauhý. They cover probably one-fourth of the 134,000 square miles of the former state, which accounts for about 95 percent of all Brazilian production. The oil which is extracted from the kernel of the babassu nut has wide uses in the manufacture of oleomargarine, as a substitute for olive oil in cooking, and in soap production. The nuts have a high value as fuel, and have been extensively used for stoking locomotives on the railroads in the vicinity. The principal obstacle with which the industry has had to contend is the difficulty of breaking the extremely hard nuts and extracting the kernels in an unbroken state. In spite of repeated efforts to devise a profitable machine for this purpose, most of this work is still done by hand labor. The kernels contain about 65 percent of oil.

Both in the lowlands along the Amazon and its tributaries and in the drier regions between the States of Pará and Pernambuco there are many other species of oil-bearing palms. The traveler among the islands of the Amazon delta and about the mouths of the Xingu and the Tocantins is amazed by the profusion and variety of palms. In proportion to the extent of these resources, the state of their development is still negligible. However, there are a few small oil mills in the lower Amazon, which work the *curuá* and other palm nuts, and a promising beginning has been made in exporting the kernels of the murumuru, ouricuri, and tucum nuts.

There is also a small development of the palm-oil industry in the lands about the Caribbean, though production and exports are nowhere large. Due to the confusion in the popular names applied to the various oil-bearing palms, it is difficult to appraise the relative importance of each source of supply. The most common palms whose nuts have an industrial value for their oil content are the cohune, corozo, and coquito.

Brazil is now the world's largest supplier of castor beans, whose oil has a wide diversity of uses, including the preparation of soluble oils for the textile industry, the manufacture of synthetic resins, the preparation of leather, linoleum, paints, varnishes, and lacquers, the lubrication of high-speed engines, and medicinal purposes. In spite of the fact that little has been done to cultivate the castor plant and the primitive and unsystematic organization of the industry, production of castor beans generally reaches a prodigious total of between 150,000 and 200,000 tons a year, most of which is exported to the United States.

A Brazilian product of related uses is carnauba wax. This bright yellowish substance is an important ingredient in the manufacture of floor polishes, and also has a variety of other industrial uses, including the manufacture of phonograph records and electrical insulation. It is derived from a resinous coating which covers the leaves of the remarkable carnauba palm, and which serves to retain the moisture in the tree against evaporation in the dry atmosphere of its habitat in northeastern Brazil. Production of the wax is an old and well-established industry. Exports of the wax, chiefly to the United States, normally amount to from 7,000 to 10,000 tons. Its value is high in proportion to volume, and it now holds a well-established place in Brazilian exports.

Brazil nuts, known locally as *castanha-do-pará*, still constitute a well-known but declining export from the Amazon valley. They are practically unknown in southern Brazil and most of the crop is shipped to the United States. The nuts are the seeds of the *Bertholletia excelsa*, which is the largest tree in the American tropics.

Among other Latin-American edible nuts of importance are the cashew and the *sapucaia*, or Paradise nut, of the lower Amazon, which is exported largely to Great Britain.

Fibers. A number of useful fibers are derived from the many varieties of palm trees found in tropical Latin America. The most important of these is piassava, a product of the Amazon valley, of which over 5,000 tons are generally exported each year. The caroa palm in Brazil and the mocara palm in Ecuador are other sources of industrial fibers. Uncertainty of the Middle East as a source of jute for sacking for coffee, wheat, corn, rice, and other products, has led to a diligent search for substitute fibers. Both Brazil and Argentina are now growing jute as a source of materials for bags. There are large jute plantations near Manaus on the Rio Negro, operated by Japanese. The fiber of the caroa palm offers good possibilities in the same field and Mexico uses large quantities of sisal in the manufacture of sacking. Colombia is almost completely dependent on the locally grown fique fiber for the same purpose. Abacá, or Manila hemp, is now grown in Panama, Peru, and Colombia. A considerable acreage is devoted to the cultivation of flax in Argentina and Peru, as a source of material for the manufacture of linen. Other fiber plants, either wild or cultivated, which are utilized in various countries are ramie, in Argentina and Brazil; pita, in Colombia and Mexico; the ixtle hemp and zacatón, in Mexico. The jipija-pa fiber (*Carludovica palmata*) is employed in Ecuador and Colombia in the manufacture of "Panama" hats. The tucum fiber of the Amazon valley is used for the production of the world's finest hammocks.

Medicinal plants. The forests of Latin America are rich in plants which have a definite therapeutic value. The natives of those regions have developed, by pragmatic methods, a large body of *materia medica.* Knowledge of these plants and their curative powers, except for such well-known examples as the febrifuge, cinchona bark, has been very slow in reaching the outside world, though the early Catholic missionaries were familiar with their usefulness in the treatment of disease. Also, among the Indians their use by the medicine men of the tribe is often accompanied by a certain amount of extraneous ritual or professional hocus-pocus, which has tended to obscure the real efficacy of many of these jungle remedies. A few years ago the Mulford Drug Company, of Philadelphia, made a scientific survey of the native pharmacopoeia of the Amazon valley, with the object of determining the possibilities of its commercial utilization. The principal obstacle to the development of these medicinal resources is the difficulty of obtaining an adequate and continuous supply of the raw materials and of standardizing their quality.

Among the many plants which are regularly employed by the native population of the Amazon valley in the treatment of their ailments are pichurim (*Nectandra pichurim*), used against dysentery and other digestive complaints; pau-para-tudo (*Simaruba cedron*), or "a stick for everything," which is employed in a variety of cases; copaiba oil, a powerful astringent used in cicatrizing wounds. During the past few years, the value of curare, the famous Indian poison of the upper Amazon, in the treatment of spastic paralysis has been clinically demonstrated in American hospitals.

There has been a marked development of the rotenone industry in the Amazon valley. Rotenone is the active ingredient of several members of the *Lonchocarpus* genus of plants, which are known locally, largely depending on the locality, as timbó, cururu-apé and barbasco. The crushed roots of these plants have long been used by the natives for the purpose of stunning the fish in a stream, so that they could be easily gathered. The need for insecticide materials for the use of American troops in the western Pacific during the Second World War led to a large increase in rotenone exports from the Amazon valley, particularly from the Peruvian river port of Iquitos.

Other parts of Latin America—Mexico and Central America, the Andean countries, and the old Guarani lands of Paraguay—have their distinctive pharmacopoeia. One of the most famous of such drugs is the coca plant, whose leaves are widely chewed for their narcotic purposes by the Indians of Bolivia, Peru, and Ecuador. In modern medicine it is the basis of the local anesthetic, cocaine, and considerable quantities of the coca leaf and of the drug itself are exported for that purpose. Other medicinal products and plants are balsam of Peru, which is actually produced in El Salvador, balsams of copaiba and tolu, ipecacuanha, nux vomica, digitalis, and senna.

Other products. Among other forest products of Latin America which are exploited on a commercial scale are: balata, the coagulated latex of a tree related to the source of chicle and found in northern South America (used in the manufacture of machinery belting); oil of petitgrain, a distillation from the leaves of the apepú or bitter orange tree, of Paraguay (used as a base for Florida water and other lotions and perfumes); aromatic tonka beans; and tagua or corozo nuts derived from the ivory palm (*Phytelephas macrocarpa*) common in the upper Amazon region and constituting an export from Ecuador, Peru, and Colombia (used largely in the manufacture of buttons and as a substitute for animal ivory in the manufacture of other small articles). Animal products of the Latin-American forest which enter into the realm of trade are parakeets and toucans, marmosets and alligator skins, and the blue wings of the Morpho butterfly.

Fisheries. Commercial fishing is a major industry and important source of protein food in many Latin-American countries. Fish products—canned and frozen fish, fish meals and oils—comprise the second export of Peru. The waters off its coast are extraordinarily rich fishing grounds, which abound with tuna and swordfish, bonito and pompano, anchovies and mackerel, and a host of other species. The annual catch now amounts to around a half million tons. The United States Bureau of Fisheries contributed much to the establishment of this now flourishing industry, as it did to the stocking of Andean streams and lakes, in which the world's largest trout are now found. There is much big game fishing off the north coast, centering in the oil port of Talara.

Chile's long strip of coastal waters has formed a natural scene for the most thalassic of all Latin-American peoples. Fish is an important item of diet and a lucrative source of national income. A large fleet of fishing craft accounts for an annual catch of nearly 200,000 tons. About 60,000 tons of shellfish are yearly hauled in at Robinson Crusoe's Juan Fernandez Islands, of which large quantities of lobster are shipped to Buenos Aires by air. In no other city in Latin America is high-quality seafood so great a feature of restaurant fare as in Santiago. Canneries are also an import factor in the fishing industry.

Venezuela represents a different kind of fishing industry. Though there is considerable sport fishing for tarpon, marlin, and sailfish off its Caribbean coast, the principal emphasis in its fisheries is on sardine canning. Fresh fish are also an important article of diet in Caracas and other coastal towns. The per capita consumption of fish is the highest in Latin America and about three times that of the United States. A development program, financed and organized by the Venezuelan Basic Economy Corporation, supported by Rockefeller interests, did a great deal to promote the national fisheries industry, particularly in providing a supply of fresh fish for the capital. The annual Venezuelan catch runs at a rate of about 60,000 tons. Among products of Venezuela's fisheries are pearls, obtained in waters near the offshore island of Margarita, which was a center of pearl fishing in colonial times.

Mexican fisheries off both coasts are very large. Specialties of the industry are tuna and shrimp. The annual yield of shrimp is over 50,000 tons, much of which is exported to the United States. Abalone, mackerel, red snapper, and sardines are other important items in the fishing business.

In relation to its potential, the fisheries of Brazil are inadequately developed, and the total catch is probably around only 75,000 tons a year. There is much regional variation in the industry. Off the northeast coast the picturesque *jangadeiros* ply the near-by waters on their sail-borne rafts, while farther out Japanese trawlers work the sea lanes for lobster, some of which is exported to the United States. In the waters of the northern states of Paraíba and Rio Grande do Norte there is fishing for swordfish, albacore, and shrimp, and off the far southern coast tuna is caught. In the intermediate area, centering on

Rio de Janeiro and Santos, the government has developed a state-controlled branch of the industry, supplying boats to the fishermen. While the Amazonian rivers are a vast fresh-fish aquarium, beyond a small amount of local fishing to supply the city of Manaus the commercial fishing is largely limited to the salting of the huge pirarucu, a competitor of codfish, which is still imported in large quantities for the Portuguese element in the population.

The Argentines, who are the largest beef-eaters on earth, are little interested in fish. However, the government, in order to cut down local meat consumption for the benefit of the export trade, has encouraged fishing, and with unexpectedly gratifying results. The annual catch has risen to over 80,000 tons a year, much of it mackerel-type pejerrey and the gilded *dorado*, which is similar to salmon.

Cuba has long had a flourishing fishing industry, now operated by government-controlled cooperatives. Ecuador has rich tuna fishing grounds about the Galapagos Islands, but has done little to develop the industry beyond the establishment of a small cannery. Fishing is very important to the Panamanian economy and shrimp is one of the republic's exports.

At the opposite extreme are some of the smaller Caribbean countries. Nicaraguans eat less than a pound per capita annually and the Guatemalan industry is unimportant. Haitian production of fish is reported to be between 70 and 100 tons a year. Although the waters which border the island teem with fish, the natives shun the sea.

An interesting survival of early deep-sea fisheries in the waters off Latin America is represented by the whaling industry. In a recent year Argentine, Chilean, and Peruvian whalers caught a total of nearly 6,000 of the big *ballenas*.

Manufacturing. One of the most significant factors in the economic life of Latin America is the trend toward industrialization. In its present proportions, this trend is relatively new. The First World War, which cut Latin America off from many of its customary sources of supply, gave a decisive impetus to the movement for the establishment of domestic manufactures. The Second World War greatly strengthened the trend and promoted the establishment of many new industries. The growing spirit of nationalism in the republics has fostered the desire for a greater degree of economic self-sufficiency, for greater freedom from the uncertainties of export markets, and for a curtailment of the heavy overseas payments for imported goods, with their pressure on the exchange value of the national currencies. When exports to the United States and Europe fell off heavily during the depression years 1931–36, imports from those sources declined correspondingly. During that period, several of the countries, notably Brazil, Chile, and Uruguay, made feverish efforts to build up manufactures that would insure a domestic supply of necessary consumer goods at all times. The movement was facilitated by the readiness of foreign interests to invest their capital in the establishment of factories. In fact, by increases in the import tariffs, the governments deliberately promoted the opening of branch factories by foreign concerns, which were faced with the alternative of losing a considerable part of their business in these countries. Other devices were adopted to attain the same ends. As a part of its program for the economic rehabilitation of the country, the Venezuelan government made loans to national interests for the establishment of a sisal-bag factory, a fish-processing industry, a button factory using mother-of-pearl, and a cement plant. It also gave a monopoly to the Compañía Ganadera Industrial Venezolana for the production of fresh meats, dried salt meat, beef extract, canned tongues and sausage, corned beef, and lard. The Peruvian government had previously granted a number of monopolistic concessions for the manufacture of specified lines of goods. In 1933, all such monopolies, except those directly administered by the state, were abolished. However, the government of Peru retained the exclusive right to produce tobacco products, matches, salt, explosives, and industrial alcohol. Government exchange and import controls have also been widely used for the encouragement and protection of national manufactures. Chile has allocated foreign exchange to importers of goods which did not compete with the output of domestic factories and has withheld it from importers of competitive products. While exemptions from import duties on industrial machinery and equipment have long been used as an inducement to the founding of new industries, the governments are quick to remove such exemptions when over-expansion of the industry is threatened. Both Brazil and Peru have resorted to this means of safeguarding the competitive position of their cotton textile industries. Special import permits may be required, and there is a growing tendency to impose import quotas, or on occasion to suspend altogether the importation of particular goods. However, the motive for measures of this kind may be either the protection of a domestic industry, the strengthening of the exchange position of the national currency, or retaliation for foreign discrimination against the country's export staples.

In Chile, considerable impetus has been given to her manufacturing industry and auxiliary power services by the government organization known as *Corporación del Fomento de la Producción* (CORFO). CORFO invests special public funds in the development of any industries that in its judgment might increase the national income and promote the economic independence of the nation. It acts in the capacity, not only of a lending agency, but of a substantial stockholder in enterprises which it has furthered. A somewhat similar institution exists in Colombia, and the general trend toward state planning and participation in the economy will doubtless increase the incidence of this type of government corporation. In Mexico, an autonomous agency of the central government, known as *Nacional Financiera, S.A.*, serves as an official clearing house for the financing of business enterprises. A large part of the funds which it distributes is derived from loans by the Export-Import Bank and the World Bank.

There has long been an elementary manufacturing industry in most of the republics. In some cases its origins, as in the tanning of leather, were in the crafts of the colonial period, or, like weaving and the making of pottery, in the traditional industries of the aboriginal peoples. The relatively backward countries, like Paraguay and the Central American nations, are still largely in this stage of industrial evolution, which is characterized by the production of primary consumer goods. These manufacturing industries are engaged in the processing of local raw materials, and their operations do not involve the use of complex or costly equipment and production methods. Among the products of these industries are laundry soap, cigars and cigarettes, saddlery, jerked beef, matches, wooden furniture, alcohol, and brick and tile.

The secondary stage of industrial development saw the introduction of textile manufacturing on a modern scale, and the establishment of breweries, commercial wine production, large iron foundries, shoe factories, meat-packing plants, and flour mills. From this stage, manufacturing has progressed in a few countries to industries which employ more elaborate machine processes and techniques. These include steel production, metal fabricating, automobile assembly plants, and the production of heavy chemicals and pharmaceuticals, the higher grades of paper, and automobile tires and industrial rubber goods.

In no other part of the world has industrialization ever proceeded so far in so short a time. The result has been that several of the republics have freed themselves altogether or in large part from dependence on foreign imports of many lines of consumer goods, such as boots and shoes, cotton piece goods, glass, flour, and a wide variety of other processed foodstuffs, cement, and the lower grades of paper. Some of this development is sound, especially where the home market is sufficiently large to absorb the output of the national industry and the country's economy has otherwise attained a relatively advanced state of evolution; some of it is premature and forced, an artificial growth imposed upon an economy whose basic elements are still very simple. The population may be too small and its buying power too low, so that costs represented by the initial capital investment and the necessary administrative overhead have to be spread over a very restricted market. Under such conditions, operating expenses are inevitably high, with the result that price levels may be beyond the majority of consumers. High import tariffs may also widen the margin within which the products of national industry may be priced without having to contend with the competition of foreign goods. Even where manufacturing industry is wisely confined to small plants, with a capacity in line with the potential market, these conditions are liable to prevail. Yet, in a world of unorthodox economic policies and increasingly dominated by the isolationist philosophy of autarchy, the resolve of these small countries to promote their economic independence beyond apparently sound limits is, at least, comprehensible, if not always wise.

While the Latin-American governments at first displayed a liberal attitude toward the investment of foreign capital in manufacturing, the trend has recently been toward greater national control of industry. The more radical political groups are everywhere opposed in principle to foreign investments, and governments are sometimes ready to bid for their favor at the expense of these outside interests. They may harass the foreign companies with excessive regulations and high taxes. Foreign investors without a voice in the affairs of the country may have to bear the principal burden of costly welfare and labor legislation, for which the credit and the political advantages redound to the benefit of the government in power. In Mexico, enforcement of extreme labor legislation paved the way for the expropriation of certain industries. The workings of the official exchange control may prevent foreign companies from taking any profits they make out of the country. Other restrictions on the operations of foreign concerns are in the form of price-fixing devices in the interests of the consumers, and of limitations on the proportion of foreigners who may be employed even in managerial and technical capacities. Also, the dominant agricultural and mining interests in a country are generally adverse to its industrialization, except as manufacturing may provide a sizable market for their products, and whenever a conflict of interests occurs the government may have to decide against the domestic manufacturing industry. Thus, attractive barter deals with other countries for the exchange of raw materials and foodstuffs for manufactured goods may be made at the temporary expense of local manufacturing interests.

Under these conditions, the survival of a foreign manufacturing concern in a Latin-American country may become dependent on its almost complete operating divorcement from the parent company and its close identity with the interests of local nationalism. This generally involves the admission of local capital into the concern and of local personnel into its management. It is these circumstances which make the character of the foreign manager of paramount importance in the success of his firm's business. To an unusual degree he must possess the personal qualities necessary for dealing harmoniously and skillfully with any elements in the country which may be in a position to affect the fortunes of his company. Such competence can only be acquired by one who has lived long enough among Latin Americans to be familiar with their language and their ways, and at the same time is sufficiently open-minded to make the necessary concessions to the sometimes trying demands of local sentiment and ways of thinking. In other words, he must be a diplomat as well as a businessman and technician, for public relations may assume a special significance unknown at home.

In the degree of their industrialization the republics vary from

Haiti and Honduras to Brazil and Mexico. Other countries which
have made considerable progress in manufacturing are Argentina,
Chile, and Colombia. Argentina and Brazil and Mexico have entered
the field of heavy industry, and others have taken steps in the same
direction. An example is the production of steel, which has become a
symbol of economic independence. The oldest steel industry in Latin
America is located at Monterrey in Mexico. Much the largest is in
Brazil, where it is dispersed in a growing number of plants in four
different states of the Union. There is another in Argentina, though
the country has inadequate supplies of either good ore or coal. Chile
has a steel plant at Huachipato near the important city of Concepción.
Colombia has one at Paz del Rio, and in 1958 the Peruvian government opened a small steel mill at Chimbote on the coast above Lima.
However, the combined output of the six national steel industries,
mostly operated by the respective governments, is much smaller than
that of Canada. Reinforcing bars and other construction materials
constitute a large part of production, which also includes sheets, tubes,
as at Belo Horizonte, rails, wire, ingots, and shapes for specialized
treatment.

The production of other basic construction materials, such as
cement, brick and tile, glass and lumber, is a very large industry in
much of Latin America. Heavy metallurgical industries produce a
wide variety of industrial goods that include railroad rolling stock,
ships (in Brazil), industrial machinery, motors and other electrical
equipment, and automobile bodies. A growing percentage of the component parts of motor vehicles is being produced in the several automobile assembly industries. São Paulo and surrounding towns are the
center of a flourishing automotive industry represented by branch
factories of about nine different American and European firms. Metal
fabricating now includes a multitude of lines, from farm implements,
machine tools, refrigeration, and sewing machines to small hardware
and notions.

An expanding chemical industry turns out a wide diversity of
products that range from sulphuric acid to aspirin. Much of the output consists of products of the coke oven, of a new and large-scale
petrochemical industry, in which the W. R. Grace interests are
heavily involved, and of derivatives of native extractive products, like

sodium nitrate and sulphur. Paints, plastics, pharmaceuticals, fertilizers, and chemicals for the use of the textile and paper industries are among the large assortment of products of the chemical industry in Argentina, Brazil, Chile, Mexico, and Peru.

The textile industry, with food processing, is the most widespread branch of Latin-American manufacturing. Even a relatively "underdeveloped" country like Paraguay may have a mechanized cotton mill. The industry is especially large and varied in Argentina, Colombia, and Mexico, while Chile excels in the manufacture of woolens. The Brazilian textile industry is the oldest and largest segment of the manufacturing economy. Pioneers in establishing cotton mills were chiefly Manchester spinners, and there was formerly a substantial English investment in the business. Other lines produced in the diversified Brazilian industry include woolens, natural silk, rayon and other synthetic cloths, and jute bagging. Examples of native textiles in Latin America are alpaca and vicuña fabrics in Peru and Chile and sisal rugs in Haiti. Traditional weaving handicrafts produce attractive and serviceable woolen garments and cloth in Guatemala, Ecuador, Mexico, and Peru.

Tributary branches of the clothing industry are correspondingly important in the principal textile manufacturing countries. Shoe manufacturing, long a handicraft industry, has now been largely mechanized. The manufacture of rubber footwear and other garments is still carried on in Brazil. Most of the larger American and European rubber companies operate branch factories, chiefly for tire production, in several of the republics.

Food processing, utilizing the products of native agriculture and stockraising, is a highly developed business in practically all Latin-American republics. Its branches include flour milling, baking and sugar refining, meat slaughtering and packing, the canning and preserving of fruits and vegetables, coffee roasting, and the preparation of alcoholic beverages and soft drinks. Frozen foods, long unpopular, are also being produced. There is a large output of beer, of particularly high quality in Mexico. Wines, some of very good quality, are produced in Argentina, Brazil, and Chile. An important by-product of the sugar industry is generally the distilling of rum. Alcoholic liquors peculiar to the country are produced in Mexico. In Brazil, a soft drink which competes with Coca-Cola is guaraná, the effective ingredient of which is a powder made from the dried seeds of a native climbing shrub (*Paullinia cupana*).

The principal industrial areas in Latin America are well localized. São Paulo, a city of 4,000,000, is the most important manufacturing center in the southern half of the world. There is a complex of large industrial plants in its "A B C" suburbs, as well as in small near-by cities like Campinas and São José dos Campos. Secondary centers of manufacturing in Brazil are Pôrto Alegre in Rio Grande do Sul, Belo Horizonte in Minas Gerais, Recife in the State of Pernambuco, and Rio de Janeiro, the former federal capital.

In Argentina, there is a heavy concentration of industry in Buenos Aires and its suburbs, and up country in Rosario and Córdoba. In Chile three-fourths of production is in the Santiago-Valparaiso area, and in Peru there is almost as great a concentration of manufacturing in the Lima-Callao zone. Medellín and Cali are the foremost industrial centers of Colombia. In Mexico, 40 percent of manufacturing industry is located in the Federal District, including towns like Tlalnepantla. The other leading factory centers are Guadalajara and Monterrey.

Transportation

Nature has placed serious obstacles in the way of the movement of men and goods from one part of Latin America to another. From northern Mexico to Tierra del Fuego a mountain wall, whether low and jungle-covered, as in Central America, or high and snow-covered, as in the central Andes, interposes a barrier between the narrow strip of land along the Pacific and the body of the continent to the east. For long distances the outworks of the coastal range may rise directly from the sea, so that even an initial foothold is difficult to gain. Within the area of the Cordillera, except for short distances where a mountain valley can be followed, communication between localities on a north-and-south line may encounter impediments as formidable as those offered by the main axis of the Andes or of its northern extension. Two communities located in mountain pockets only a short distance apart, as the crow—or the condor—flies, may be entirely isolated from each other, except by a long and roundabout road by way of the lower country on either side. For among the chaos of the mountain knots the ridges of the Cordillera may lose all orderly direction, so that only mules and men on foot can make their way among their tangled heights.

Along segments of the Spanish Main a high and rugged coast, such as overhangs the Venezuelan port of La Guayra, presents an immediate obstacle to communication with the interior. Similarly, on the far-away coast of southeastern Brazil the precipitous escarpment of the Serra do Mar had first to be scaled before penetration of the important plateau country was possible. The ascent of the coastal range is so steep that the first railroad which climbed from the port of Santos to the highlands of São Paulo had to use a system of inclined planes and cables. The railroad from Paranaguá to Curitiba is an engineering marvel of steep grades, bridges, hairpin curves, and numerous tunnels on mountain sides.

The tropical jungle which covers so much of Latin America is as great an obstacle to communication as are the mountain ranges on the periphery of the southern continent. The initial clearing of the heavy forest and the continuous struggle necessary to keep the jungle from reclaiming the right of way, the wear and tear of torrential rains, the bridging of rivers bordered by swamps or a wide flood plain—all these make the building and maintenance of roads or railroads a difficult and costly matter. In the several million square miles of the Amazon valley and of the contiguous forested areas on either side, the rivers are the roads, supplemented by trails that lead back from their margins into the forest. The problems connected with the establishment of other means of transportation in the forests and lowlands of the tropics are well illustrated by those which were met in constructing the famous Madeira-Mamoré Railway in the interior of Brazil, in building roads across the Gran Chaco during the war between Bolivia and Paraguay, and in laying the pipelines from the oil fields in Colombia to the Caribbean coast. It is the same natural conditions which isolate the Yucatán peninsula from the rest of Mexico, and which effectively cut off Colombia from its former State of Panama, thereby facilitating the growth of the separatist movement on the isthmus which culminated in the events of 1903.

Of the major economic areas of Latin America, the Argentine

plains offer the greatest facility for the establishment of modern communications. The ease with which railroads can be built on the pampas is indicated by the largest stretch of straight track in the world. Though the topography presents no obstacles, the lack of stone and gravel for roadbeds is a problem in rail and highway construction. Other important regions in which the "lay of the land" offers few difficulties to the development of a transportation system are Chile from the level of Antofagasta south to that of Valdivia, the favored Brazilian plateau of Minas Gerais, São Paulo, and Paraná, and the rolling country of Uruguay and Rio Grande do Sul. Also, in much of northern Mexico the building of roads and railroads has met few serious technical difficulties, in spite of the rough character of much of that country. The regions in which the topography is highly unfavorable to the opening up of modern lines of communication are the approaches to the heart of the Mexican tableland, the snarled maze of deep valleys from which Honduras derives its name, and the settled Andean plateau from Colombia south into Bolivia.

No other country in Latin America is so handicapped by the configuration of its surface as is Colombia. The two large rivers which flow down from the plateau are too broken by rapids or shallows to provide satisfactory outlets for the interior. With the exception of Barranquilla, none of the important cities of the country is located on either the Cauca or the Magdalena. A very high range of the Andes separates the valleys of the two rivers. Bogotá and the departmental capitals, like Medellín, Bucaramanga, and the distant city of Pasto, are separated from each other by wide areas of rugged mountain country. Due to these enormous obstacles of topography, Colombia's transportation system is a piecemeal composite of many local railroads and roads, linking isolated centers of population or providing connections with a navigable sector of one of the two main rivers. There is no central trunk highway or railway to bind together all the inhabited parts of the republic in any direction. To reach the Caribbean from Bogotá by surface transportation formerly involved several changes between train and Magdalena River boat. Bogotá and the other cities of the Cundinamarca plateau have now been linked to the Caribbean coast by a railroad, providing an alternative to the old route. There is a through land route between Bogotá and the Pacific by way of the railroad through Girardot and Espinal to Ibagué, thence by automobile over the divide to the terminus of the Pacific Railway at Armenia. This rail connection leads up the Cauca valley via Palmira and Cali and down to the west-coast port of Buenaventura.

Similar difficulties attend the problem of linking up the regions of the Peruvian *Sierra* served by the Central and Southern Railways, due to the tangle of high mountains and deep valleys that separate Huancavelica and Ayacucho to the north from Cuzco in the south.

Though the rail link between Salta, in Argentina, and Antofogasta has been completed, there is no direct through transcontinental railway connection north of the Transandine Railway, which bridges the mountain gap between the Chilean state system and the Argentine rail network. A few railroads pass the divide, to end at points on the eastern side of the cordillera, but none reaches the plains country beyond. At Ambato, the lowest point on the mountain section of the Guayaquil and Quito Railway, from which a road leads down into the Ecuadorean Oriente, the line descends to an altitude of only 8,430 feet. At its lowest point on the eastern side of the mountains the Central Railway of Peru is nearly 11,000 feet above sea level. According to a leading authority on Latin-American railroads, this line is "one of the most remarkable railways in the world, not only because of the altitude attained at its highest point (16,000 feet above sea level) but as a feat of engineering unequaled in railway construction." In the 106 miles of the main Callao-Lima-Oroya section there are 57 tunnels, over 60 bridges, and 16 switchbacks. A through road connection now exists between Lima and navigable water on the Ucayali at Pucalpa, from where there is steamer service down-river to Iquitos and on to Belém. This highway crosses the Andes by way of Oroya and Huánuco, from where it falls down through the montaña to Tingo Maria, on the Huallaga and beyond. Previous to the building of this road the most traveled land route between the Peruvian coast and the Amazon was via the old Pichis trail, which led from the railroad at Oroya to La Merced in the Chanchamayo Valley. From La Merced the traveler eventually reached Iquitos, over 1,100 miles away, by a combination of mule, dugout canoe, and river launch. Until a few years ago, the Peruvian government maintained steamer communications between Callao, the port of Lima, and Iquitos, by way of the Panama Canal and the Amazon River. Government officials bound for posts at Iquitos sometimes found that the most convenient route to that city lay roundabout by way of New York and Pará. The Southern Railway of Peru comes to an end near the site of the Incaic ruins of Machu Picchu, a short distance down the valley of the Urubamba below Cuzco, from which there is no practicable route into the Peruvian Amazonia.

In Bolivia, the Yungas Railway from La Paz, after crossing the divide at nearly 16,000 feet, was only completed as far as the hill town of Chulumani, which is far short of its ultimate destination in the plains of the Beni. Two spurs of the Bolivia Railway connect the main north-and-south line with the important cities of Cochabamba and Sucre, both of which are situated at an altitude of about 9,000 feet. For the important connection between Cochabamba and the eastern plains city of Santa Cruz, dependence on a short narrow-gauge railroad across the floor of the valley and a long mountain trail has been superseded by a through truck road built by American engineers. From the end of the railroad at Sucre, a road, developed during the Chaco war, leads into the area of the Bolivian oil fields.

The transportation system of the colonial period left little on which the republics could build. Most land transport was by means of mules or llamas and the roads were laid out to accommodate these pack animals. In the Andes the Spaniards followed the remarkable roads of the Incas; elsewhere they developed new trade routes, like that between Upper Peru and the River Plate by way of Tucumán and Córdoba. Other important roads laid out by the Spaniards were those across the Isthmus of Panama and between Vera Cruz and Mexico City, from which the "China Road" led down to the Pacific at Acapulco. Lengths of occasional *camino real* or "royal highway" were paved with cobblestones to admit the passage of coaches in which high officials and their wives might ride. But for the most part the mule set the standards of colonial road building throughout Latin America.

Railroads. Latin America has approximately 90,000 miles of railroads. The distribution of mileage (mostly single-track) by countries is about as follows:

Argentina	27,672	Paraguay	673
Brazil	24,931	Ecuador	618
Mexico	12,683	Guatemala	455
Chile	7,965	El Salvador	385
Cuba	3,482	Dominican Republic	371
Peru	2,140	Panama	367
Bolivia	2,031	Honduras	349
Colombia	1,961	Venezuela	324
Uruguay	1,872	Nicaragua	216
Costa Rica	701	Haiti	187

These figures include not only common carriers, but some short lines which serve private mining, sugar, banana, and quebracho companies. In some countries, as in Honduras, their total mileage may exceed that of the public railroads. Important groups of similar private lines are found in the other Central American republics, Cuba, the oil regions of Venezuela, the Gran Chaco of Paraguay, and northern Chile. As new producing areas are developed or old ones abandoned, the mileage of these lines may vary considerably from one year to another. The only railroad systems which are truly national in scope are those of Cuba, Mexico, Argentina, Chile, and Uruguay. Of these, the Cuban system is the most complete and reached practically every locality in the island. In Mexico, all but five of the twenty-eight state capitals have rail connections with Mexico City. There are several rail connections between the American border and the heart of the Mexican plateau, and there are connections between Matamoros, Tampico, and Vera Cruz, on the Gulf, and Mazatlán, San Blas, and Manzanillo, on the Pacific. Also, for part of its way, the interoceanic route across the Isthmus of Tehuantepec serves as a link in a through connection with the railroad system of northern Central America.

The heart of the Argentine system, which is the seventh in mileage among the countries of the world, is the elaborate network of lines that radiates out from Buenos Aires. Few regions anywhere have been so well served by railroads as are the Province of Buenos Aires and the neighboring districts of Córdoba and Santa Fé. A north-and-south belt line between Rosario and Bahia Blanca binds the various lines together in the western part of the zone. Lines of the central network also reach west into San Luís and the Territory of La Pampa, and east of the Paraná they connect with the Entre Rios system of the Argentine Mesopotamia. From Bahia Blanca a line extends westward into the Neuquén country, and another from the same port leads around by Viedma to San Carlos de Bariloche on the Chilean border. Farther south, three isolated lines extend into the Patagonian hinterland from Puerto Madryn, Comodoro Rivadavia, and Puerto Deseado. The Argentine railway system connects with the lines of all the five adjoining countries. Besides the two rail links with the Chilean system, there is a through connection between Buenos Aires and La Paz by way of Córdoba, Tucumán, and Uyuni. A through service between Buenos Aires and Asunción is provided by the Argentine Northeastern and the Central Paraguay. The international trains are ferried across the Paraná at Posadas-Encarnación. At Uruguayana, the same line forms a junction with the Brazilian system, and at three points along the border there are connections between the Argentine and Uruguayan systems.

The Chilean rail system links every important city in the country, with the exception of Arica, in the extreme north, and Punta Arenas, on the Straits of Magellan. The northern terminal of the system is at Pisagua, above the 20th parallel; the southern end is at Puerto Montt, well below latitude 40 and 1,934 miles from Pisagua. The first railroad built in South America led inland from the north Chilean port of Caldera to the mining center of Copiapó. The line was constructed by the famous American promoter and builder, William Wheelwright, who also built the Rosario-Córdoba section of the Central Argentine, and was opened to traffic in January, 1852. The first step in the development of the Chilean government's railway program was the opening of a line between Santiago and Valparaiso. This was followed by the building of a railroad down the Central Valley, by Rancagua, Chillán, and Temuco, to the edge of the archipelago at Puerto Montt. Meanwhile, a number of short roads were built in the north as outlets for nitrate and mining camps. In accordance with its comprehensive plan, the Chilean government later extended the state system to the north, thereby tying together all these separate lines in a single network. The northern trunk line, known as the Longitudinal, which parallels the coast for a long distance, was built for strategic and political reasons as much as for commercial purposes. The Chilean State Railways operate over three-fifths of the total mileage in the country and practically all the lines outside the nitrate region. Throughout the length of the system numerous spurs have been built to ports on the coast or to centers of population in the Andean valleys.

Railroads cross the Chilean border into Peru, Bolivia, and Argentina. The northernmost of these is the short line from Arica to Tacna, in Peru. The Arica-La Paz Railway, the Chilean section of which is owned by the government, climbs up into Bolivia from the same port. The British-owned Antofagasta and Bolivia also links the Chilean coast with La Paz by way of Uyuni and the leased line of the Bolivia Railway through Oruro.

The Uruguayan railway system consists of a series of lines which converge, fan-like, on Montevideo. At three points on the border of Rio Grande do Sul the Uruguayan lines form a junction with the Brazilian rail system. There is now a through rail connection, over the different-gauge tracks of several lines, between Fortaleza on the remote northeastern coast of Brazil and the River Plate system of Argentina and Uruguay. For the hardy and unhurried traveler it is possible to continue ultimately from Uruguayana or Concordia around to the south Peruvian port of Mollendo-Matarani. The only break in the long and roundabout route is the overnight steamer trip across Lake Titicaca between Bolivia and Peru. Plans to replace this water link in the through international connection with a railway around the southern side of the lake have not been realized.

The important Brazilian States of Minas Gerais and São Paulo are well supplied with railway facilities. The state-owned Central of Brazil connects the federal capital with the city of São Paulo and with the Minas highlands. To the northeast of Rio de Janeiro the old Leopoldina system serves the state of the same name and part of Espírito Santo. Three distinct systems, the Paulista, the Mogiana, and the Sorocabana, provide the interior of São Paulo with excellent rail communications. The privately owned Paulista, in particular, ranks high among the railroads of Latin America in the quality of its service. From the outer fringe of São Paulo one line reaches up into the plateau of Goiás and another, the Northwestern Railway, extends from the Paraná River at Baurú across southern Mato Grosso to the Paraguay River near Corumbá. The western terminus of this frontier railroad is now linked with the Bolivian city of Santa Cruz de la Sierra.

North of Vitória, a number of local systems ramify out from such important coast cities as Salvador, Recife, and Fortaleza into the back country of the *sertão*. These various systems are loosely coordinated with each other, and are now connected by a circumambulatory route with the Rio de Janeiro-São Paulo network of lines in the south.

One of the most interesting railways in Latin America, and the most isolated line in the world, is the Madeira-Mamoré, which runs for 226 miles around the rapids of those rivers. Originally planned by the brilliant American engineer, Colonel George Church, in 1878, the project was soon abandoned and except for a few sporadic attempts by groups of Brazilians and others, lay dormant until 1907. It was then taken on by the remarkable American capitalist and promoter, Percival Farquhar, as one of his numerous large-scale enterprises in Brazil, and completed in 1913. This remarkable line was built in accordance with an agreement of the Brazilian government to provide an outlet for the rubber of the Beni River basin in compensation for Bolivia's cession of the Acre Territory to Brazil. Its construction was a difficult and costly enterprise and, due to the ravages of malaria, yellow fever, and beri-beri, was attended by heavy losses of life among its builders.

In proportion to its size, no country in Latin America is so deficient in railroad facilities as Venezuela. In the western end of the country, particularly in the region of Lake Maracaibo, there are about a dozen short lines, most of which are operated by the oil companies to meet their own local transport requirements. Of the lines in this area, the Great Railway of Tachira is 75 miles long and the Great Railway of La Ceiba, 53 miles long. Along the coastal rim of the central highlands are eight separate and infinitesimal railroads. There is a through connection between Ocumare in the east and Puerto Cabello in the west by way of Caracas, Maracay, and Valencia, with a short line linking Caracas and its port of La Guayra.

Railroad building, except in Guatemala and El Salvador, has been little developed in Central America. The International Railways of Central America, which serve both those countries, forms an interoceanic connection between Puerto Barrios on the Caribbean coast and San José de Guatemala on the Pacific, with an extension on one side to the Mexico border and on the other into El Salvador. No other Central American countries are linked by rail. There are two other transcontinental connections in Central America, one across Costa Rica, between Puerto Limón and Puntarenas by way of San José, and the other by the old Panama Railroad, which was completed in 1855. The other Central American railroads are local lines serving limited areas of country or the properties of the large fruit companies on the north coast.

Most of the early Latin-American railroads were built with foreign capital, usually with a guarantee of interest or some other form of subsidy on the part of the government of the country. While the original promoters and builders of the more important lines generally dealt honestly with the respective governments, some of the subsequent financial operations were characterized by bad faith on the part of either government or bankers, or both. One of the greatest scandals was in connection with the "Interoceanic" railway which was to be built from Puerto Cortéz on the Caribbean coast of Honduras to the Gulf of Amapala on the Pacific side. Various European banking houses participated at one time or another in bond issues of the Honduras government, designed to finance the construction of the railroad. One of these issues was offered at a rate of 80 and bearing interest at 10 percent. By 1873 a total of 57 miles had been built at an actual cost of around $1,500,000, but the corresponding debt already amounted to nearly $30,000,000, which represented a liability of the Honduran government. By the beginning of 1917, it was calculated that the total debt, including accrued interest, amounted to approximately $130,000,000.

The construction of some of the Latin-American railways is associated with the names of certain enterprising American promoters. Among these men were Henry Meiggs, who built the Central Railway of Peru and began the construction of other lines, including the Southern Railway of Peru, William Wheelwright, Henry Thorndyke, Allan Campbell, Archer Harman, of Guayaquil and Quito fame, Minor C. Keith, and Percival Farquhar, by whose initiative a number of connecting lines were built in southern Brazil, in addition to completion of the Madeira-Mamoré Railway previously mentioned.

The fine Argentine system, including the four major lines, the Central, the Western, the Pacific, and the Southern, and a number of minor lines such as the Central Córdoba and the Entre Rios, was largely the work of the British. The long-anticipated acquisition of these valuable properties by the Argentine government became a fact in 1948. The heavy accumulations of unliquidated sterling credits built up by Argentina during the Second World War, on account of shipments of meats and grain to England, placed the Argentine government in a favorable bargaining position, of which it availed itself to take over the British railways. Of other British properties, which included the United Railways of Cuba, the Leopoldina and the Great Western of Brazil, the Antofagasta and Bolivia, the Central Paraguay, the Central and the Midland of Uruguay, the Mexican Railway between Vera Cruz and Mexico City, and the rich São Paulo Railway in Brazil, all but two have been acquired by the respective governments. The Peruvian Corporation, a British concern, administers and operates, under contract with the government of Peru, a total of over 1,000 miles of lines, including the Central and the Southern.

American interests have been most active in railroad construction and operation in the North American republics. American lines included the Southern Pacific's Mexican branch from Nogales to Guadalajara, a large part of the Cuban system, and the International Railways of Central America. The first has been purchased by the government of Mexico, and the Western of Cuba was "nationalized" by the Castro regime. The lines of the Bolivia Railway, whose construction was financed by American capital, are now leased to the Antofagasta and Bolivia, and control of the Guayaquil and Quito, which was built by Americans, is now held by the Ecuadorean government.

Three important French railway properties in Argentina, the Province of Santa Fé, the Rosario-Puerto Belgrano, and the Central of Buenos Aires, the only standard-gauge line with tracks into the capital, have been purchased by the Argentine government, in connection with its program for the nationalization of all railways.

With the exception of Venezuela, and of some of the minor countries, the trend in Latin America is toward the increased state ownership of railways, as it is of all public utilities. Except for a few short industrial feeder lines, the entire Argentine system is owned and operated by the government. In Brazil, less than 10 percent of all track has been left to private ownership, but this includes the Paulista, the best railroad in Brazil. In Chile, about 70 percent of the system belongs to the government. The balance largely consists of short industrial lines. The Colombian system was acquired by the central government in 1954. The government has a railroad monopoly in Ecuador and Uruguay and owns a majority of the mileage in Nicaragua and Venezuela. Two-thirds of the large Mexican system is included in the government-owned lines of *Ferrocarriles Nacionales*.

Except in a very few countries, railroad construction in Latin America is virtually at a standstill. The only lines of any importance completed during the past few decades are the Atlantic Railway of Colombia, the extensions of the Brazilian and Argentine systems into the lowlands of eastern Bolivia, the Belo Horizonte-Salvador link between northern and southern Brazil, and the long-planned Mexican line over the western Sierra Madre between Chihuahua and Topolobampo on the Pacific.

The railroads share in the effects of the general hostility to foreign investments, and even in Argentina, whose development has owed so much to the British railways, the companies had to contend with adverse official policies and hostile public opinion long before the roads were taken over by the Argentine government. In order to implement their new economic controls, the governments desire the eventual nationalization of the railway lines. Only by centralized state administration, they reason, can the railroads be coordinated to serve the best interests of the nation as a whole. The diversity of gauges, which plagues the transportation systems of most of the republics, can then be corrected without regard to the cost of unifying the tracks of the various parts of the system. In fact, the ratio between revenues and expenditures gives little concern to most of the state railway systems, and operating deficits are chronic. Low passenger rates are frequently considered as a form of official bounty, from which the government in power enjoys large returns in public favor. Also, the organized railroad workers can expect greater concessions from the state than from private owners, and exert their pressure accordingly. The process of nationalization will proceed faster in some countries than in others and its methods will vary, but the ultimate issue is already settled.

In the meantime, service has deteriorated and the volume of business has decreased almost everywhere, including in the once-model Argentine system. The only major country which is making a serious effort to reverse the trend is Mexico. Otherwise there are railroads in Latin America that are literally falling apart.

In view of these conditions, it is highly unlikely that foreign capital can be attracted into further railroad construction. Experience such as the British-owned Mexican Railway had with the Carranza administration, the troubles of the British lines in Argentina, and the "squeeze" tactics used with certain other lines in Latin America, by means of taxation, regulation, and restrictions on earnings, will discourage additional investment in the future. The prospective returns are no longer commensurate with the risk involved. Very few of the foreign lines had a high earning record over a relatively long time. Among these was the Panama Railroad, whose monopoly of interoceanic transportation enabled it to pay a 40 percent stock dividend in 1865 and a 33 percent cash dividend three years later. The Buenos Aires Western consistently earned an annual 7 percent dividend for a long period before 1914. In 1918 it was said of the São Paulo Railway that it "normally produces more revenue per mile than any railroad in the Western Hemisphere." Other factors which are working increasingly to the disadvantage of the privately owned railroad lines is the growing competition from truck and airplane transportation. By undertaking large road-building projects which parallel existing rail lines, governments can easily aggravate the competitive position of the railways.

Roads. It is only during the past twenty years that the Latin-American republics have actively promoted the development of their highway systems. Previous to that there had been a considerable mileage of dirt roads and pack trails, some of which dated from early colonial times. Even on the Argentine plains these roads were generally deep in mud in the rainy season, and in the dry season a cloud of dust marked the passage of carts or pack animals. Virtually the only all-weather roads were to be found in the coastal desert zone of Peru and Chile, where the climate is uniformly rainless. Bridges were few, and varied as much as the hanging—and swaying—bridges of the Andes differ from the buttressed stone bridge which the Spaniards built over the dry bed of a stream at Arequipa. Rivers were generally crossed by fording or swimming one's horses or by means of a rope ferry. Persons bound from one place to another generally traveled on horseback, or, if in the mountains, by the more sure-footed mule. Sometimes, in low sandy country they rode on steers. Goods were hauled either on the backs of animals—and sometimes of men—or in carts. In Argentina covered high-wheeled carts were used until relatively recent times; elsewhere produce was carried in the solid-wheeled ox carts so destructive of roads. In a rural economy where money was scarce and labor was cheap and travel was an occasion for conversation, the pressure of time was of little consequence. This is still the common pattern of local transport over large parts of Latin America where the new roads have not yet reached, or the means are lacking the local population to avail itself of motor vehicles.

Nearly all countries have participated in the new road-building program of Latin America. Some have established public roads departments in their governments as an expression of the importance which they attach to highway development. Surveys of transportation needs have been made, ambitious four- and five-year plans of road construction have been drawn up, and considerable sums have been appropriated for their financing, sometimes on the basis of gasoline or other special taxes. Among the sources of revenue on which the Argentine Highway Fund depends is a 3 percent tax on net receipts of railroads fixed by the Mitre law of 1907. One of the first problems to be resolved is the relationship of the proposed highways to existing rail lines. In Argentina, the first roads were planned as feeders to the country's excellent railway system, and this remains an important factor in the calculations of the National Highway Board. However, the paralleling of railroad communications was inevitable in some places, especially between large neighboring cities like São Paulo and Rio de Janeiro, Buenos Aires and Rosario, and Santiago and Valparaiso. The pressure from associations of automobile dealers and owners was partly responsible for the decision to build such roads, as it has been a force for better roads in general. In Venezuela, the fine network of roads built under the Gómez regime was laid out as though with a deliberate purpose to offer competition with the country's railroads, particularly in the La Guayra-Caracas-Valencia-Puerto Cabello circuit. To governments whose earlier railroad-building programs had been suspended for lack of funds, automotive highways suited for truck traffic provided a solution for their transportation problems. For example, the new road from Cochabamba in Bolivia to the plains city of Santa Cruz has offered a satisfactory substitute for the long-projected rail link between these two localities. Also, in the mountainous republics of Colombia and Peru, where railroad building is inordinately expensive, highways have assumed a special importance. The former country has used roads to good advantage in tying together the parts of its disjointed rail system in sectors where the terrain discouraged further railroad construction. Honduras has at last found in highway construction the answer to the old problem of connecting her two coasts.

Among other influences which have favored the national road-building programs in Latin America have been the development of domestic cement industries, the existence of local supplies of petroleum, as in Mexico, Venezuela, Peru, and Argentina, the presence of a newly trained body of native engineers, with the required technical capacity, the prospect of attracting foreign tourists, as in Mexico, and, sometimes, the ability to use numbers of unemployed on road work.

For lack of any international agreement on road-building standards, there is no common denominator for classifying the roads of Latin America. For example, an all-purpose, all-weather road in one country might have a very different meaning from the accepted idea of such a road in another country. The kind of highway that is built may depend on the available materials, the prospective volume and kind of traffic, the topographic conditions along the route, and the chances of weathering, whether from freezing, as in the high Andes, or from heavy rains. In regions where the rainfall is relatively light, as in northeastern Brazil, the São Paulo highlands, central Chile, and northern Mexico, well-drained dirt roads with a good base are generally adequate, unless a considerable amount of heavy long-distance traffic develops on inter-city trunk highways. The better class of mountain roads, such as are found in Peru and Mexico, are well ballasted and paved and protected against washouts and landslides.

In spite of ambitious good-roads movements, progress in the development of modern highways systems has generally met neither expectations nor needs. Roads in major countries like Argentina, Brazil, Colombia, and Venezuela are still inadequate. Mexico and Peru have probably done most in terms of their transportation needs. There are generally good surfaced trunk highways leading out of the capital to important cities, as in Argentina, but maintenance is often neglected. The bulk of national road systems is made up of dirt roads, a large part of which may be seasonal, as in Colombia. The basic highway requirements of Mexico have been well met. Three long all-weather roads connect the capital with the American border and there is a network of good secondary roads. Brazil is estimated to have about 300,000 miles of "passable" roads. Highway-building projects have resulted in the construction of a series of paved trunk roads. Some of the first connected São Paulo and Rio de Janeiro, Santos and São Paulo, and Belo Horizonte and Rio. It is now possible to travel by car between the Uruguayan border and São Luiz in the State of Maranhão in the remote northeastern part of the country.

Though sections of the through road are very unequal in quality, buses ply regularly between Recife and other cities of the northeast and Rio-São Paulo. Brasília has become the nucleus of a greatly expanded road-building program in the interior of Brazil. It is connected, by way of Belo Horizonte, with São Paulo and Rio de Janeiro. Other roads, not yet completed, will link the new federal capital with Belém at the mouth of the Amazon and with Salvador to the east beyond the line of the Rio São Francisco. There are also plans for roads to open up vast areas far to the west and northwest of Brasília.

Peru embarked earlier than most Latin-American countries on a road-building program. Considerable progress was made during the Leguia regime, and a plan initiated in 1937 greatly extended the national road system. The Central Highway, completed in 1935, follows the railroad from Lima to Oroya and then descends on the eastern side of the cordillera to La Merced in the *montaña* country. Another road goes by Lima to Cerro de Pasco and thence north via Huánuco to Tinga María on the Hullaga, from where it has been extended to Pucalpa on the Ucayali, thus affording an alternative route into the tropical lands of eastern Peru. From Oroya another road goes south through rugged mountain country by Huancayo, Ayacucho, and Abancay to Cuzco, from where another road leads up the valley of the Urubamba and on to Puno on the lake. The coast highway now extends from Tumbés in the north via the inland city of Arequipa to the Chilean border. From Arequipa a road climbs up into the Sierra, where it connects at Puno with the road between Cuzco and La Paz. A road is also being built over a low pass in the Andes of northern Peru toward the upper reaches of the Marañón or Amazon. There is regular bus service between Lima and remote parts of the country.

In the face of serious engineering difficulties presented by its mountainous terrain and by the swamps and jungles, Colombia has made remarkable, if inadequate, progress in road building. The two main trunk roads consist of the Colombian section of the Simón Bolívar Highway, which extends from Caracas to Bogotá by way of Cúcuta and Bucaramanga, and the north-and-south road between Medellín and the Ecuadorean border by way of the Cauca Valley through Cali and Popayán. The latter road is being pushed down through the low rain forest of the Chocó to the Caribbean coast at the Gulf of Urabá. The two principal highways are linked by a road which crosses the central cordillera by the high Quindio pass. Another much-traveled route is the Cambao highway, which leads from the head of navigation on the Magdalena at La Dorada onto the plateau to Bogotá.

For many years plans have been under way for the construction of a Pan-American highway between the United States and Buenos Aires, with branches leading off from the main route into all the countries not on the direct line of the highway. Elaborate technical surveys have been made of various alternative routes, and governments and unofficial organizations have actively interested themselves in promoting the project. The United States government has provided funds to aid the Central American republics in constructing their respective segments of the through road particularly during the Second World War, when a land connection with the Canal Zone appeared desirable.

For most of its distance the route has been agreed upon. The through route has now been well defined and is passable all the year for most of the distance. The sections now in operation vary in quality from the so-called "washboard" and rutted dirt roads to the most modern paved highways. Beyond southern Peru there are two alternative routes to Buenos Aires, one continuing down the coast to Santiago and thence eastward across the Andes and the Argentine pampa, and the other crossing the high Bolivian plateau and descending into the plains of Argentina by Salta and Tucumán, from where there is a good highway into Buenos Aires. The total distance from Laredo, Texas, to Buenos Aires by way of the latter route is approximately 11,360 miles, of which about 3,300 miles are in the section between the Rio Grande and the Colombian border. A large number of travelers have succeeded in reaching Buenos Aires by making special provision for passing the unfinished sections.

The uncompleted, or deficient, sections of the through Pan-American Highway consist of a short gap between Mexican and Guatemalan systems; a mountainous stretch in southern Costa Rica; the route through the Darien Gap, between Panama and the Colombian network; and the low coastal region of Ecuador below Guayaquil. It is now possible to cross from Mexico into Guatemala, though not with ease, but the combination of low jungle and swamp in the Darien Gap has been an obstacle to road construction in that area. A Panamanian has crossed into Colombia, though there is not even a forest trail between the countries. Long stretches of road in southern Bolivia and northern Chile still leave much to be desired. Improvement of the road is progressing, particularly in southern Mexico and northern Colombia.

As there is at least a presumptive correlation between the mileage of good roads and the number of automobiles, the following table of motor vehicle registrations may be accepted as fairly indicative of the progress made by the highway movement in Latin America. However, important reservations must be made, for a heavy registration of automobiles in a large metropolitan area may account for the majority of cars reported in a particular country. A road system may be built far in advance of the capacity of the population to buy automobiles, as in the Dominican Republic. Automotive traffic is still extremely light on certain long stretches of paved highway, as in Peru, and mule trains and ox carts may be the principal beneficiaries of the new *carreteras*, as in parts of Central America. In Mexico, allowance would have to be made for the large number of tourist cars from the United States which traverse the road between the Texas border and Mexico City.

In four, and probably five, of the countries listed below over half the motor vehicles are registered in the national capital. The same conditions doubtless prevail in nearly all the nine countries for which corresponding data are not available. This is due not only to the customary concentration of private wealth in the capital cities, but to the superior avenues and roads to be found in their vicinity, and also to the large number of trucks operated by business concerns and government departments.

The registration of automobiles in the Latin-American republics in 1959 was approximately as follows:

Country	Total Vehicles	Passenger Cars	Trucks	Buses
Brazil	985,206	471,203	467,143	46,860
Mexico	736,100	411,200	297,100	27,800
Argentina	698,837	364,458	320,526	13,853
Venezuela	345,000	216,000	120,000	9,000
Cuba	221,358	174,129	42,923	4,306
Colombia	161,200	73,200	75,000	13,000
Uruguay	154,600	87,000	65,000	2,600
Peru	132,383	72,275	53,458	6,650
Chile	115,503	53,772	56,675	5,056
Bolivia	38,632	14,292	23,111	1,229
Guatemala	32,169	23,084	6,862	2,223
Costa Rica	29,631	19,198	8,943	1,490
Ecuador	26,435	10,240	16,170	25
Panama	22,978	15,262	7,716	
El Salvador	21,865	18,408	2,352	1,105
Dominican Republic	16,783	9,444	6,961	378
Nicaragua	13,305	8,455	4,200	650
Haiti	12,300	8,300	2,000	2,000
Honduras	11,828	3,431	7,894	503
Paraguay	7,700	4,300	3,000	400
Total	3,783,813	2,057,651	1,587,034	139,128

(*Note: The figure for truck registrations in Panama* (7,716) *included buses*)

Comparable totals for 1940 and 1946 were 823,969 and 1,022,428 respectively. Combined registrations in 1959 were approximately equal to that of the state of Illinois, or the Soviet Union. The highest rate of motor vehicles to population was in Uruguay and the lowest in Haiti.

Waterways. In spite of its great river systems, fluvial transportation is of relatively small importance in the internal trade of Latin America. Though the Amazon has the world's largest network of navigable rivers, its traffic is very small in proportion to its possibilities. The main stream of the great "river-sea" is navigable for ocean steamers to Iquitos, in eastern Peru, a distance of 2,032 miles from Pará, and there is a regular shipping service from Liverpool to that point. Manaus, situated near the confluence of the Negro and the Amazon, and 925 miles above Belém, is the terminus of steamship lines from southern Brazil, the United States, and Europe. However, the extensive and modern dock facilities of Manaus and Belém are still far in excess of the volume of shipping which uses them. Local transportation within the Amazon basin is carried on by a fleet of steamers, which ply up and down the central river and up the Amazonian tributaries to the first heads of navigation. Conditions of navigation vary greatly on these side rivers, but limits are definitely fixed on all of them by the low ranges of hills which cut transversally across their channels, creating a line of rapids. Sometimes these obstacles to navigation are relatively near their mouths, as in the Xingu and the Tocantins; other rivers, like the Madeira, the Purús, and the Negro, are navigable far from their confluence with the axis stream. Heavy rains in the interior and the melting of snows in the Andes cause great and sometimes sudden differences in the depths of these rivers. The normal variations in level in the larger rivers are from 30 to 60 feet. For example, during the season of high water large ocean-going freighters may reach Pôrto Velho, on the Madeira River, 690 miles from its mouth, whereas during part of the year certain reefs in the channel limit navigation to steamers drawing only six or eight feet of water. Among the many other branches of the Amazon whose lower courses are navigable by river steamers are the Trombetas, the fine Tapajós, the Maués, the Juruá, the Javari, and, in Peru, the Ucayali and the Huallaga. Above the usual line of rapids or *cachoeiras*, continuous navigation may be possible for long stretches of open water, as on the Tocantins-Araguaya and the upper tributaries of the Madeira. Sometimes, as on the upper reaches of the Tapajós and the Xingu, navigation is frequently interrupted by rapids or waterfalls, around which boats and goods have to be laboriously portaged. A large variety of craft are used for transportation, some of which are peculiar to certain rivers. These include small steamers, gasoline and steam launches, strongly built open boats, like the Brazilian *batelão* or Bolivian *batelón*, and dugout canoes, sometimes of great length and large carrying capacity. The *batelão* is a cargo lighter, with a capacity of from 10 to 25 tons. Sometimes huge rafts are seen moving down the upper Amazon, in the center of which is a thatched hut. Whole families drift downriver on these rafts, with their livestock and other possessions. On reaching their destination at Manaus, or some other town, the raft is broken up and its logs sold for lumber.

Aside from the Amazonian rivers, the upper reaches of the Paraguay, and the middle course of the Paraná, the only other Brazilian stream of commercial importance is the São Francisco, whose section above the Paulo Affonso falls has long provided a water road between the Minas highlands and the northeastern part of the country.

Due to the more advanced economic development of its basin, the River Plate fluvial system is far more important commercially than either the Orinoco or the Amazon. The two main arms of this river system are the Paraná-Paraguay and the smaller Uruguay. Their tributaries are either short, like the rivers of the true Paraguay, or sluggish and shallow, like the right-bank branches, the Bermejo and the long Pilcomayo. The north-south Paraná-Paraguay is navigable for steamers drawing six or seven feet of water to Corumbá, in Brazil, 1,800 miles above Buenos Aires, and regular service is maintained into the heart of the continent to that point. Above Corumbá smaller steamers ascend the Paraguay several hundred miles farther to Cuiabá, the capital of Mato Grosso. Except for a few low passes in the channel of the upper river, considerably larger vessels could ascend as far as Asunción and even higher. The upper course of the Paraná, above its junction with the Paraguay at the old trading center of Corrientes, is navigable by shallow-draft steamers to the foot of the great Guaíra falls, known as the Sete Quedas.

The course of the Paraná below Sante Fé is of major importance in Argentine transportation. Ocean-going steamers load wheat and other products at Santa Fé, Rosario, and intermediate ports, and there is heavy local traffic up and down this section of the river. Steamers drawing fourteen feet of water can reach Paysandú on the Uruguay and those of nine-feet draft can go up to Salto, whose falls set a limit to navigation. On the River Plate estuary large ferry boats provide an excellent service between Buenos Aires on the south bank and Colonia and Montevideo on the north bank.

Second in importance as a river highway, though its volume of traffic is much less than that of the River Plate system, is the Magdalena in Colombia, which empties into the Caribbean through a delta below the important river port of Barranquilla. Flat-bottom stern-wheeler steamboats, similar to those used on the Mississippi, ascend the Mag-

dalena to La Dorada, about 560 miles above Barranquilla. The channel
is interrupted by sandbars and by shallows that occasionally suspend
all steamer services until the river rises. From La Dorada or Puerto
Salgar passengers and freight bound upriver are transferred to a railroad or a motor road for the rest of the journey to Bogotá. Above the
rapids at La Dorada, there are navigable stretches of water on which
smaller boats ply. With all its defects, the Magdalena forms a fairly
continuous water road deep into the Plateau of Cundinamarca and the
traditional connection between Bogotá and the north coast of Colombia.

Formerly of relatively little importance in Venezuelan transportation, the Orinoco, from its branches in the Llanos to its mouth, has
gained considerable impetus as a commercial route. The growth of
Ciudad Bolívar or Angostura and the development of a large iron-ore
industry along its lower reaches have increased its volume of traffic. A
channel in the delta has been opened for the passage of large ocean-
going steamers, which can now ascend the main river for several
hundred miles.

Because of the narrowness of the western watershed of the Andes
and of the low rainfall in much of the zone, the rivers on the west
coast of South America are too short and their fall too rapid to permit of their navigation. An exception is the Guayas, in the forested
coastal plain of Ecuador, which is navigable by launches for a considerable distance. Similarly, the rivers of Mexico and Central America have little value for the transportation of goods, though launches
and canoes ply on some of the streams which empty into the Gulf
and the Caribbean.

Coastwise shipping plays an important role in the domestic commerce of the republics with a large frontage on the ocean. Brazil,
Argentina, and Chile have a considerable merchant marine, and
Mexico, Peru, and Venezuela possess a fleet of steamers, which are
engaged in the carrying trade along their coasts. The government-
owned Lóide Brasileiro and the Chilean Compañía Sud-Americana de
Vapores operate regular services to countries outside Latin America:
as do the Dodero and state merchant fleets of Argentina. A joint
shipping enterprise was established by the governments of Colombia,
Venezuela, and Ecuador under the name of the *Flota Mercante
Grancolombiana*. The west coast of South America has a dearth of
good harbors, though adequate docking facilities have been installed

at Callao and Valparaiso. Farther north, Guayaquil and Buenaventura have well-protected ports. Most of the other ports are open roadsteads on an indentation in the coast line and goods are lightered between ship and shore, as at Arica and Antofagasta. There are many excellent harbors on the east coast, such as Salvador, Vitória, Rio de Janeiro, and Santos. Others, like Recife, whose harbor is formed by a reef, Pôrto Alegre, Montevideo, and Buenos Aires, have been developed by dredging and the building of breakwaters, and by the installation of such modern systems of docks as serve shipping in the two leading ports of the River Plate. On the north coast, the only first-class natural harbor is that of Cartagena. In order to admit ocean shipping to Barranquilla, it has been necessary to dredge a channel across the bar at the mouth of the Magdalena. Though considerable sums have been spent on port works, the principal Venezuelan ports have few natural advantages. While the Pacific coast of North America has a few good natural harbors, like Acapulco and the large Gulf of Fonseca, on the Atlantic side good natural ports are almost non-existent. However, the harbor of Vera Cruz has been developed until it is adequate to the needs of the shipping which touches there.

Only five countries, Brazil, Argentina, Venezuela, Chile, and Mexico, have a merchant marine of over 200,000 gross tons. Of these, the total of Brazilian shipping is over 1,350,000 tons, but a major part of its fleet is represented by ancient bottoms of the state-owned Lóide Brasileiro. Ships of Panamanian registry, to a total of over 6,000,000 tons, are not nationally owned.

Airways. Air transport has had a remarkable development in Latin America. Commercial aviation has solved many of its long-standing communication problems, which had previously defied solution because of the physical difficulties and great cost involved in meeting them by traditional methods of transportation. Isolated areas have been opened to development, parts of countries divided by natural obstacles have been bound together, and connections between localities have been shortened in distance even more significantly than in time. To an unusual degree, airplanes have been used in Latin America in carrying freight in and out of otherwise inaccessible places. This growth of civil aeronautics has been the work of both foreign interests and the governments of the various republics. Though military aviation has expanded concurrently with the commercial airways, the balance is still heavily on the side of civil aviation, and the airplane has seldom been discredited in Latin America by its use for the destruction of life and property.

The oldest commercial aviation company in Latin America, and the second oldest in the world, was the Sociedad Colombo-Alemana de Transportes Aéreos, or Colombian-German Air Transport Company, popularly known as SCADTA. This company was organized in 1919 by an Austrian named Peter von Bauer. Starting with a line between Barranquilla and Bogotá, SCADTA early built up an extensive network of lines in Colombia, where the deficiency of other means of communication assured the commercial success of air transport. In the field of first-class passenger traffic and of express business its planes acquired a virtual monopoly of inter-city transportation in the republic. An interesting feature of the concession under which it operated was that its air-mail service was independent of the Colombian post office department.

In 1931 Pan American Airways bought 84 percent of SCADTA's stock from Peter von Bauer and his brother. As the Von Bauers owned 90 percent of the stock at that time, it left them with a minority interest of 6 percent. In spite of their acquisition of a strong controlling interest in SCADTA, Pan American left its management in Peter von Bauer's hands, with little change until 1939. The planes continued to be flown by German pilots, among whom were young Nazi zealots recently out of Germany, and the executive and technical staff was made up of Germans, while there were between 30 and 40 German clerks in the air-mail post offices of the company.

In view of the suspected designs of the Nazi government in Latin America, the existence of this compact German air organization so close to the Panama Canal and the southern borders of this country constituted a situation which could not be ignored by the United States. In 1940 a reorganization was carried out, whereby political control over the company's operations was vested in the Colombian government through its acquisition of 40 percent of the company's stock. It was further stipulated that an additional 20 percent of the stock must be held by Colombian citizens. The remaining 40 percent might be held by outside interests, which presumably included Pan American's remaining shares. The reorganized company is known as Aerovias Nacionales de Colombia, or AVIANCA, and is operated as an affiliate of the Pan American System.

International competition for through air traffic early developed between French, Germans, and Americans. Air France provided communications with Europe via Natal on the upper Brazilian coast and Dakar in Senegal. From Natal its line followed the coast cities south to Rio de Janeiro and Buenos Aires, from where it carried on a weekly round-trip service to Santiago, Chile, by way of Mendoza.[3] An Italian airline, popularly known as LATI, operated between Rome and Rio de Janeiro until long after the beginning of the Second World War.

The Deutsche Lufthansa provided a certain unity to the varied German air activities in South America during that period. The exact nature and extent of Lufthansa's interest in each of these separate activities was not always clear, but its position as a coordinating agent and representative of the national aviation policy of Germany was evident. Before the war, Lufthansa flew a mail service between Frankfurt a/M and Natal by way of Lisbon and Bathurst on the West African coast. At Natal its planes connected with those of its subsidiary, Sindicato Condor, which carried on a through mail and passenger service roughly paralleling the route of Air France into Buenos Aires, and thence across the Andes into Chile.

A series of links of the Lufthansa system also provided a transcontinental connection between Rio de Janeiro and Lima. A Condor line operated a weekly service from the Brazilian coast across southern Mato Grosso to Corumbá on the Paraguay River. At this point the line made a junction with the Lloyd Aéreo Boliviano, whose planes flew passengers and mail thence into La Paz, from where they were relayed to Lima by Lufthansa Peru. A majority of the capital stock of Lloyd Aéreo Boliviano was held by Bolivian interests, including a considerable share by the Bolivian government, and it is possible that some of those interests consisted of German business houses long established in the country. Lufthansa had only a minority holding in

---

[3] The brilliant French writer, Antoine de Saint Exupéry, was formerly a pilot on this line. An early work of his formed the basis for the movie *Night Flight*, and his later book, *Wind, Sand and Stars*, recounts incidents in his South American service.

the company, but the principal executive personnel and virtually the entire force of pilots consisted of Germans. The main center of operations was at Cochabamba, from which a line reached north into the Mamoré basin by Trinidad, eventually connecting with a branch line to Cobija on the border of the Brazilian Acre. An important secondary base was at Santa Cruz in the eastern plains country. Santa Cruz was the terminal of six lines which fanned out in every direction over eastern Bolivia, including one southward to the Argentine border at Yacuiba. No other aviation company, except SCADTA in Colombia and TACA in Central America, so completely revolutionized the transportation system of the territory which it served. Many of the towns then connected by Lloyd Aéreo Boliviano were previously accessible only by mule or by long and arduous river travel.

Though German interests had gained a foothold on the Pacific coast, with Lufthansa Peru's Lima-Arequipa-La Paz connection, they had made little further progress in extending their operations on that side of the continent when the war interfered with their ambitious plans for expansion. To the north were SCADTA's long-established activities in Colombia and the lesser operations of SEDTA in Ecuador, but there were still gaps between the areas served by these three west-coast concerns. SEDTA was a local Ecuadorean corporation, whose managerial and operating staff was German. It was taken over by the Ecuadorean government early in the war and was then operated by Panagra. It carried on a service between Guayaquil and Quito, with side runs to their coast and interior points, such as Manta and Cuenca.

As a pioneer in the field, Pan American Airways has long had a strong position in commercial aviation in Latin America. Its planes serve the east coast of South America by way of Caracas and Belém. Through its affiliate or subsidiary companies, especially Panagra, and including a series of national lines like Panair do Brasil, its total coverage is the largest of any air system. Panagra, or Pan American-Grace, partly owned by the important trading and shipping house of W. R. Grace and Co., covers the west coast of South America from Panama to Santiago, and thence to Buenos Aires, where it connects with the parent company. Other affiliates of Pan American include Avianca, which operated routes to New York and Europe, as well as an extensive local service in Colombia, the Compañía Mexicana de Aviación, LASCA in Costa Rica, and SAHSA in Honduras.

Braniff International Airways is the second largest American company operating in Latin America. Its planes fly to Buenos Aires through Panama, Guayaquil and Lima, La Paz and Asunción, with an important alternative route by Lima to São Paulo and Rio de Janeiro. American and western lines maintain services into Mexico from the United States.

A very important factor in Central American transportation is TACA or Transportes Aéreos Centro-Americanos.

This concern was founded in 1931 by Lowell Yerex, an enterprising New Zealander, who began operations with a single second-hand plane and virtually no working capital. From this small beginning he built up an organization which blankets all of Central America. TACA, which is now controlled by American aviation interests, has extended its lines from Guatemala north to Mexico City, by way of Belize and Havana to Miami. It has an elaborate network of local affiliated lines within Central America. Its service is especially noteworthy for its large and diversified volume of freight and express business. Its planes transport all kinds of cargo, including chicle from the Petén jungle of Guatemala, tractors and mining machinery, mineral concentrates, fresh meat and other provisions for the banana plantations on the north coast, supplies for isolated mining camps, and even orchids and fresh flowers.

In most of the twenty republics there are one or more national systems whose services are entirely or largely confined to the territory of the particular country. Some of these are small "barnstorming" outfits, flying one or two planes; others are relatively large operations, conducted by the air services of the respective governments or by private interests. PLUNA, a local Uruguayan line, is typical of these national services. Other national lines, some of which operate a service into the United States, include Aeronaves de Mexico, Aerolíneas Argentinas, Línea Aeropostal Venezolana (LAV), and Línea Aérea Nacional (LAN). The Mexican line, one of several in Mexico, flies planes to the American border at Tia Juana and Nogales, and has flights by Hermosillo into Tucson. It also operates a route to New York and Montreal. The Argentine system maintains separate services to Europe, Santiago, São Paulo and Rio, Bolivian cities, and a short daily shuttle service to Montevideo. The Venezuelan line, besides covering most interior cities out of Caracas, has routes to New York and western Europe. Chilean LAN conducts a regular service from Santiago through the northern part of the country as far as Arica, and south to Concepción and Puerto Montt, with flights through the archipelago to Punta Arenas on the Straits of Magellan, under some of the world's worst flying conditions. It also operates a daily plane to Buenos Aires.

The development of commercial aviation in Brazil has been particularly great, and in no other field has the Brazilian economy made such progress. Reflecting this growth, São Paulo's Congonhas has become one of the first airports of the world in the volume and international scope of its traffic. National lines, serving the most remote areas of the huge country, include, among others, VARIG, VASP, Real, Cruzeiro do Sul, Lóide Aéreo, and Panair do Brasil. VARIG (Viação Aérea Rio Grandense), a pioneer line in southern Brazil, now operates a jet plane service to New York in competition with American companies. VASP (Viação Aérea São Paulo), also a veteran in local aviation, maintains an hourly commuter service between São Paulo and Rio de Janeiro in cooperation with other lines. Brazilian air lines steadily extend the range of their international services. Real has a route, by way of Miami, into Chicago, and VARIG operates a service to Los Angeles. Brazilian planes fly into most of the countries of South America.

Most of the European air lines operate services into Latin America. In most cases the southern terminus of their east coast routes is at Buenos Aires, though some continue over the Andes to Santiago. KLM, pioneer in the area, still specializes in its original Caribbean field, but now has routes into Lima and Buenos Aires. Others include Air France and BOAC, both with wide coverage on both coasts; Alitalia, with service to Caracas and down the east coast; Lufthansa and SAS, with through routes to Santiago via Buenos Aires; Iberia, the Spanish line, with flights to Havana and Mexico City, and the usual Rio-São Paulo-Buenos Aires run.

One of the oldest and most successful of independent air-carrier enterprises is the Faucett Aviation Company. This company was founded in Peru in 1920 by E. J. Faucett, an American, but the majority capital is now Peruvian. Its planes fly from Lima south to Arequipa and Tacna, north as far as Talara and Tumbés, to Cuzco in the Sierra, and from Chiclayo over the Andes to Yurimaguas, on the

Huallaga, and thence on to Iquitos on the Marañón or upper Amazon.

Foreign Trade

Like its counterpart anywhere, the course of foreign trade in Latin America depends on a number of factors of changing impact on the volume and direction of its exports and imports. Besides the elemental influence of habit, price, and quality, a growing number of forces, some of them artificial, affect the statistical position of a nation's foreign commerce. Sometimes the facts of geography are an important factor, as in Mexican-American trade. Customer nations may change their buying habits, and, for example, shift from metals to plastics for certain purposes. A country may turn to the manufacture of its own radios or shoes, fountain pens or machine tools, and reduce proportionately the business of its foreign suppliers. Due to a production glut, prices for a commodity may fall below a profitable level, so that there is no longer a motive for growing or making it. The reciprocal advantages of exchanging certain merchandise may have a very special appeal to two countries, so that there is a "natural" basis for trade. Other influences may be the volume of a foreign nation's investment, the buying habits of immigrants, the existence of inflation that can upset any calculations of profit, the success of a seller's promotional efforts, and increasingly the policies and actions of government—import bans and quotas, exchange regulations, "dumping" practices, export subsidies, and formal international compacts or conventions, such as trade treaties. All of these influences have operated in Latin America, where the rate of flow and flux in international business is probably normal. In the background there are the pressures of a "revolution of rising expectations," impatient demands for higher living standards without the time lag incidental to evolutionary processes, accompanied by the growing assertiveness or meddlesomeness of government in the baffling arena of economics.

In both exports and imports, Latin America accounts for about one-twelfth of the world's total foreign commerce. In 1959, its combined volume of exports was approximately $8,300,000,000 and of imports roughly $8,000,000,000 or a little over half the corresponding totals for the United States.

For several years Latin-American trade with the United States has tended to decrease. In 1960, less than 20 percent of American exports went to Latin America, as against 27.2 percent two years before. In 1961, exports to the United States amounted to $3,200,300,000 and imports from the United States to $3,422,500,000, broken down by countries in round numbers as follows:

	Exports to U.S.	Imports from U.S.
Argentina	$102,000,000	424,000,000
Bolivia	9,900,000	26,200,000
Brazil	568,100,000	485,800,000
Chile	183,800,000	226,700,000
Colombia	274,800,000	244,000,000
Costa Rica	40,000,000	42,200,000
Cuba	34,900,000	13,700,000
Dominican Republic	90,100,000	29,400,000
Ecuador	53,700,000	49,000,000
El Salvador	36,500,000	35,500,000
Guatemala	63,200,000	60,500,000
Haiti	19,100,000	25,900,000
Honduras	29,700,000	36,600,000
Mexico	536,600,000	797,000,000
Nicaragua	25,400,000	32,300,000
Panama	22,700,000	107,100,000
Paraguay	8,500,000	55,500,000
Peru	176,400,000	173,300,000
Uruguay	22,600,000	47,900,000
Venezuela	902,300,000	509,900,000
Total	3,200,300,000	3,422,500,000

The two largest items in the exports of Latin America to the United States are coffee and petroleum, followed by sugar, copper, and iron ore. Bananas, cacao, and wool are important staples in this north-flowing trade. In 1960, the United States bought nearly $900,000,000 worth of coffee from Latin America, most of it from Brazil and Colombia, and over $800,000,000 in petroleum, largely from Venezuela. In the opposite direction, about two-thirds of Latin-American imports from the United States consist of machinery. In this category are included automobiles and parts to a total value of over $400,000,000 or somewhat more than American exports of chemicals and pharmaceutical derivatives.

About 75 percent of Mexico's trade is with the United States. While Argentina receives about 19 percent of her imports from the United States, only about 10 percent of Argentine exports are destined for the American market. Nearly half of all that Brazil exports comes to the United States, but this country supplies only about one-third of Brazilian imports. The United States takes about 70 percent of Colombia's exports and sells her about 60 percent of her imports.

Of European countries since World War II, Western Germany has regained a relatively high level of trade throughout Latin America. She sells more to Argentina than does Great Britain, a traditional supplier of the River Plate markets, but her strongest position is in Chile.

Although she has lost ground, Britain still maintains a substantial and well-distributed commercial position in Latin America. She still takes about a quarter of Argentine exports or over twice as much as any other country. In spite of isolated appearances, Japan has not yet gained an important place in Latin-American trade. Spain and Portugal, the mother countries of Hispanic America, hold only an insignificant position in its foreign commerce. Except for Cuba, the Communist countries are a very minor factor in the trade of Latin America. Their strongest position is in Uruguay, and new arrangements with the Brazilian government may result in an increase of trade with the Soviet Union.

Despite ambitious projects for its increase, trade between the Latin-American republics is seldom a major element in their national economies. The most important single item in this interchange is Venezuelan petroleum. Even geographical proximity does little to promote intracontinental trade. For example: Costa Rica takes only 4 percent of Nicaragua's exports, while El Salvador accounts for 9 percent of Honduranian shipments outside the country. Fourteen percent of Uruguay's imports and only a little more than 3 percent of Argentina's come from Brazil. About 8 percent of Argentina's exports are sold to Brazil. Argentina's disproportionate share of Paraguay's foreign trade is largely the result of her control of the approaches to the inland nation, now shared with Brazil. Mexico has remarkably little trade with other Latin-American countries and Peru's only important trade ties are with Chile.

Investments. Aside from the strictly commercial phase of economic relations, Latin America's principal problem is the lack of investment capital for the development of its resources. Where sizable accumulations of national capital exist, as in a few countries, too little of it finds its way into industrial channels. Old investment habits have favored real estate—land and urban property—over factories and utilities. Traditional social prestige attaches to the former. One individual can be lord of ten thousand acres of land, and even if indifferently farmed the income from them will enable him to live according to the gracious pattern that has always been the ambition of the Latin-American aristocracy. He can also understand the natural processes by which the land yields an income for him. If he invests his capital in an apartment house in a growing city, the returns come in quickly and regularly and with a minimum of effort on his part. A factory is an impersonal thing, whose complex production processes he may not understand. If he owns it outright, it may become an exacting master which sets the tempo of his life, instead of the reverse. If he is only a stockholder in an industrial concern his position in the anonymous machinery of control and management is foreign to his native individualism and to his personalized concepts of economic relationships. Thus, much of the industrialization which has taken place is the work of men of other breeds who have accepted the full implications of the industrial revolution and who do not labor under a racial economic inferiority complex. Hence the Latin-American's disposition to leave the unfamiliar responsibilities of industrialization to the state. But the state's collective knowledge is no greater than his own, and its methods are liable to be cursed with the dead hand of bureaucratic regulation and inefficiency. Moreover, its stock of investment capital is restricted, and, due to a generally antiquated system of taxation, its capacity to raise additional funds also has definite limitations. Faced with such a cycle of investment obstacles, the republics formerly relied on foreign capital to do what native capital could not—or would not—do. If in the early days some of that capital seemed to be overly speculative in its calculations of profit, the risks of political uncertainty and the lack of financial responsibility of governments provided ample explanation for the bargain which it sometimes drove, but from which it seldom reaped the anticipated returns. And, in spite of all the outcry of "economic imperialism" against the foreign investor in recent years, the political independence of the Latin-American republics has no more been threatened by these investments than that of the United States was menaced by the large volume of European capital that aided in the development of this country in the last century. After all, the foreign companies were—and still are—in the business of earning a reasonable profit on their investment and not in the extraneous occupation of operating an alien government.

Latin America has not yet reached the stage in its development where it can dispense with foreign investment capital. The wave of nationalistic restrictions which it has placed on such investment is premature and can only retard the economic evolution of those countries. Private investment capital, whatever its nationality, cannot be expected to accept the risks involved in the conditions that are now imposed by many Latin-American governments. Nor should intergovernmental loans endeavor to provide the developmental financing that is the proper field of private enterprise, except as an emergency measure and in circumstances where political considerations are so compelling and urgent as to outweigh the economic factor.

While American investments in Latin America are large, it is impossible to determine more than their approximate volume at any one time. This is particularly true of the direct investments of industrial corporations, such as public utilities and mining and petroleum companies. Not only does the true value of such investments fluctuate with the return on operations, but the valuations which the companies place on their properties are subject to a number of factors, which may bear little relation to the original dollar investment or to the current market value of their holdings.

In the case of dollar bonds, there is a wide disparity between par values and current market values, depending on the regularity with which the service on them has been met by the debtor governments. Also, an unknown quantity at any moment is the extent to which such bonds have been repatriated, that is, the degree to which they have passed into possession of the debtor nations or their citizens. For some governments have systematically reduced their par-value obligations by buying up the bonds of their country under especially favorable market conditions.

At the end of 1947, the estimated par value of dollar bonds held in the United States, still outstanding, was as shown below.

Eight years earlier, the total par value was $1,039,600,000 and the market value was $350,191,400. At that time, the ratio of defaults to investments was 14.2 percent for the West Indian republics, 82.2 percent for the Central American countries, and 67.6 percent for the debtor nations of South America. Due to the financial arrangements made during the American Occupation, only the Dominican Republic and Haiti were entirely current in meeting the service on their bonds. Argentina and Uruguay had maintained a very good record. Brazil was over 92 percent in default, Colombia almost 90 percent, and Bolivia and Peru were in complete default.

GOVERNMENT ISSUES

(MILLIONS OF DOLLARS)

Country	National	Provincial and Municipal	Government Guaranteed	Corporate Issues	Total
Argentina	—	.7	—	—	.7
Bolivia	38.4	—	—	—	38.4
Brazil	67.5	30.7	—	—	98.2
Chile	46.1	3.9	25.5	—	75.5
Colombia	31.7	39.6	1.3	1.6	74.2
Costa Rica	2.9	—	—	—	2.9
Cuba	4.6	—	—	1.5	6.1
Guatemala	.7	—	—	—	.7
Panama	9.6	—	—	—	9.6
Peru	32.6	1.9	—	—	34.5
El Salvador	4.2	—	—	—	4.2
Uruguay	13.8	.1	—	—	13.9
Total	252.1	76.9	26.8	3.1	358.9

Most of these dollar loans were contracted during the late twenties. Many of the issues were marketed at a considerable discount and bore interest at exaggerated rates. In some instances, as in the case of Bolivia, they represented obligations clearly beyond the capacity of the debtor country to service or eventually to liquidate, even under the most favorable economic conditions. Sometimes the uses to which the proceeds of the loans were put were as questionable as the methods by which they were contracted.

For a long time Latin America's principal source of investment capital was Great Britain, which financed the construction of railways, mines, cotton textile mills, and a wide variety of other enterprises. Many of these properties have been lost to the governments of the countries in which they were located, as it happened to the British railway system in Argentina. Sometimes mines were worked out, the equipment of the cotton mills became outdated, or the rate of profit on once lucrative ventures fell to the point of no return. Meanwhile, Britain has ceased to be a major factor in Latin America's market for development funds. Smaller quantities of French capital went into mines in Mexico and Peru, railways in Argentina, and textile mills and department stores in Mexico. There were also considerable investments of Canadian money in Brazilian and Mexican utilities and in Cuban sugar mills, while Canadian banks were important lending institutions in several of the republics.

The first American investments in Latin America were in mines, chiefly in Mexico, where they included the petroleum fields of Tampico, in railways in Cuba, Mexico, Central America, and Bolivia, in banana growing in Honduras, and in sugar milling in the West Indies. Central Trinidad in Cuba was founded before the Spanish-American War. After the second decade of the century, the principal field of investment was in Venezuelan oil. In the meantime, the operations of the fruit (banana) companies expanded in Central America, first on the initiative of Minor Keith and later under the leadership of Samuel Zumarray. The mines of Cerro de Pasco in Peru were acquired by American interests and others undertook the development of copper mines, like Chuquicamata in Chile, and other properties along the Mexican border. The W. R. Grace interests had already built up a vast enterprise on the west coast that included merchandising operations, manufacturing, mining, banking, and shipping. Among American entrepreneurs who went into manufacturing were Dayton Hedges in Cuba, Marvin in Brazil, and Bolling Wright in Mexico. Sanborn and Jenkins became important figures in the business life of Mexico, as L. C. Heilbronner did in manufacturing in São Paulo and John

Carriker in banking in Rio. American firms like General Electric, Goodyear, Armour and other meat-packing companies, Ford and General Motors, and Corn Products put up factories in Latin-American countries. The National City Bank of New York and the First National Bank of Boston established a large chain of branches, and the Rockefellers became interested in the development possibilities of Venezuela.

In 1936, the total book value of direct American investments in Latin America was about $2,847,000,000. In the next three years it grew very little and by the end of World War II it had scarcely changed. In 1961, it amounted to over $9,000,000,000. While the largest share of capital is still in Venezuelan oil, investment in manufacturing has increased from only 8 percent of the total, in 1940, to about 20 percent. Meanwhile, the proportion of capital invested in public utilities has decreased by a third, a trend which will probably continue. Considerably more money is now invested in manufacturing than in mining and smelting operations. New fields of investment in Latin America are in lands, hotels, department stores, and aviation facilities.

Investments in Venezuela represents almost a third of the total, in Brazil about one-eighth, and in Mexico approximately one-tenth, followed by Argentina, Peru, and Colombia. The former large investments in Cuba, amounting to nearly a billion dollars, were taken over by the Cuban government in 1961.

The investment climate for foreign capital has deteriorated perceptibly during the past few years, and the rate of investment in Latin America has declined accordingly. Though profit levels are generally lower than in comparable lines of business at home, there are growing limitations on the remittance of earnings. In 1960, almost a quarter of earnings in petroleum, mining, and manufacturing industries were reinvested locally. For utilities, expropriation is a growing hazard. Labor and tax laws are liable to be discriminatory where foreign interests are concerned and an undue proportion of Latin-American taxes is paid by American firms. Agitation by inflammatory elements against foreign investment has been particularly blatant since the establishment of a Communist regime in Cuba.

A widespread urge to speed up the rate of development has greatly intensified the need for investment capital in Latin America.

The result has been a large increase in government financing operations as distinct from direct private investment. The major sources of new capital have been the World Bank, or International Bank for Reconstruction and Development, the Export-Import Bank, an agency of the United States government, the Inter-American Development Bank, a cooperative institution, and various phases of the foreign-aid program of the United States.

The World Bank, a United Nations subsidiary, had 124 loans outstanding in fifteen countries in March, 1961, for a total of $1,124,000,000. Ten more loans totaling about $144,000,000 were added during the fiscal year 1960–61. Most of these loans were for highway construction and power development.

Between the inception of its lending operations in 1934 and the middle of 1960, the Export-Import Bank authorized a total volume of credits for disbursement in Latin America amounting to nearly $4,000,000,000. About a third of this amount represented credits opened for projects in Brazil, including the national steel mill at Volta Redonda and rehabilitation of the railroad system. Mexico received about half as much as Brazil, all of which was distributed by Nacional Financiera, S.A. for use in a wide variety of projects. Other recipients of large Export-Import Bank credits were Argentina, Chile, Colombia, and Peru.

The Inter-American Development Bank was the result of the Act of Bogotá, signed by representatives of nineteen nations in October, 1960. It is a multi-nation institution, with the Latin-American republics providing 53 percent of its capital. In 1961, its first year of operations, the new bank made loan commitments for a total of $294,000,000, over half of which was to private borrowers. The IADB has three departments. One for "ordinary operations" requires repayment in the currency in which the loan is made. In addition to loans to private business, the bank also lends directly to special government development agencies for re-lending, and to governments themselves. The second or "soft" loan department handles the affairs of a "Fund for Special Operations," which examines each request for capital on its specific merits instead of by the more general rules applicable to most of the bank's business. The third phase of the bank's activities is represented by the Social Progress Trust Fund, which is responsible for the disbursement of special development grants made by the United States government.

The first of such major grants was the $500,000,000 credit authorized by Congress in September, 1960, to help finance the program of social progress which was announced by the Bogotá Conference earlier in the same month. This was the precedent for the larger program proclaimed by President Kennedy in March of the following year as the "Alliance for Progress." In the declaration signed by the foreign ministers at Punta del Este, Uruguay in August, 1961, the Alliance was announced as "a vast effort to bring a better life to all the peoples of the Continent." A comprehensive list of specific objectives included the strengthening of democratic institutions, the acceleration of economic and social development, designed to raise living standards, the construction of urban and rural housing, the reform of agricultural methods, improvement of the worker's lot, the extirpation of illiteracy, the betterment of health conditions, the modernization of tax systems, the curbing of inflation, the stimulation of private enterprise, price stabilization, and "the integration of Latin America," already in process in Central America, and as planned by the Latin America Free Trade Association.

The United States agreed to finance the over-all program to the extent of $10,000,000,000 of the $20,000,000,000 ten-year goal. The presumption was that the balance would be supplied by other governments and private investors. Other official contributions to the solution of Latin-American problems have been made by the AID (formerly ICA), which has earmarked $100,000,000 of its funds for use by the Alliance, by the "Food for Peace" program, under the Agriculture Trade Act, which dispenses surplus farm crops in distress areas of the world, and by the International Monetary Fund, which provides capital for the stabilization of currencies. The government of the United States also provided $100,000,000 for Chilean earthquake relief after the cataclysmic disaster of 1960.

Part VI

INTERNATIONAL RELATIONS

꧁꧁꧁꧁꧁꧁꧁꧁꧁꧁꧁꧁꧁꧁꧁꧁꧁꧁꧁꧁꧁꧁꧁꧁꧁꧁꧁꧁꧁꧁꧁꧁꧁꧁꧁

Relations between the Republics

THE PRINCIPAL source of friction between the republics of Latin America has been their ill-defined boundaries. In colonial times, the exact delimitation of the various administrative subdivisions of the viceroyalties was not of serious importance. At any rate, all owed allegiance to a common ruler and perhaps recognized the authority of the same viceroy. Moreover, the lands of the colonial marches usually consisted of a sparsely populated wilderness, and that frequently inhabited by Indians who resisted any efforts at white intrusion or settlement. In view of the imperfect geographical knowledge of much of the colonial territory, any finality in the determination of frontiers was impossible. The existence of conflicting official maps of the same area was subsequently to furnish both parties to several boundary disputes with cartographical evidence in support of their respective claims.

When independent nations succeeded to the jurisdictions of the captains-general and the *audiencias*, it was inevitable that this indefiniteness would sooner or later complicate the relationships between neighboring states, possibly to the point of provoking wars. Meanwhile, as settlers pushed out into these border zones, the proverbial aggressiveness of frontier populations came to intensify these potential occasions of international conflict. Sometimes the disputed lands were of doubtful intrinsic value, either for economic or strategic purposes; sometimes the new importance of a certain product gave unexpected significance to areas in controversy. Examples are rubber in the Amazon valley, which precipitated the Acre crisis between Brazil and Bolivia, and petroleum in the lowlands on the eastern side of the Andes, which played its part in the Chaco dispute between Bolivia and Paraguay and colors the long-drawn-out boundary impasse between Ecuador and Peru. Whatever the value of the region at issue, once national pride became definitely involved in the controversy any reasonable settlement has generally been out of the question. Though politicians have sometimes used this tendency to their own advantage, other governments have been swept along by public clamor to take measures against which their better judgment counseled them, and until the situation was entirely out of their control. This element in international relations is well illustrated by the failure of the numerous attempts which were made by leaders of Bolivian and Paraguayan national policy to settle the Chaco question before it finally got out of hand and led to war between their countries. Here, as elsewhere, considerations of popular psychology, rather than of sound national interest, became the decisive factor in resolving a problem which had reached a degree of irritation where reason no longer had a hearing.

The thalassic urge is strong in the Latin-American nations, even in those like the Ecuadoreans, who are not a sea-faring people. For, as exporting countries, dependent to an unusual degree on their commercial contacts with the outside world, they wish to have an unrestricted road to salt water. Solano López, the famous Paraguayan dictator, attempted to slash a way through to the Atlantic for his pent-up country. Ever since Bolivia lost her coast provinces to Chile, much of her foreign policy has been dictated by the desire to recover a foothold on the Pacific, or, failing that, to obtain practicable outlets to navigation on the Amazon and the Paraguay. Access to the Amazon, that internationalized river highway which is virtually an arm of the sea, is also an important consideration for all the republics within its watershed. Thus, Colombia, after a controversy with Peru which led to brief hostilities, drove a wedge down to the Amazon between Peru and Brazil. Long before this incident, Peru, stung by her defeat in the War of the Pacific, had tried to find compensation for her lost prestige and wounded pride in the development of her vast Amazonian territory. In doing this, she had thrust her thin lines of occupation deep into regions claimed by Ecuador and Colombia and cut off the former country, perhaps irrevocably, from any direct frontage on the Amazon. Similarly, Bolivia, whose only outlets to the Paraguay River were through the shallow lagoons of Cáceres and Gaiba, long maneuvered for possession of the river port of Bahia Negra or Puerto Pacheo, where she would have tapped the navigable course of the north-and-south river connection with Buenos Aires and the Atlantic. The outcome of her war with Paraguay left that valuable transfer point in the hands of her enemy and definitely barred her from a place on the Platine system of rivers.

The most famous of Latin-American boundary disputes was the long-lived Tacna-Arica imbroglio between Chile and Peru. Although the War of the Pacific actually ended with the Chilean capture of Lima in January, 1881, it was nearly three years before a treaty of peace was signed. Then, by the terms of the Treaty of Ancón, Chile was to remain in occupation of the Peruvian provinces of Arica and Tacna for a period of ten years, at the end of which time a plebiscite was to be held in the provinces for the purpose of deciding their permanent disposition. When the date set for the plebiscite arrived in 1894, the parties could not agree on the conditions for the balloting and a poll was not taken. There followed 35 years of embittered relations between the two countries. Each charged the other with bad faith and with high-handed proceedings within the provinces, so that a reasonable settlement appeared impossible. Every effort to solve the question failed, until a new generation grew up that promised a more favorable environment for calm consideration of the now perennial problem. Yet, when an attempt was finally made in 1925 to hold the long-delayed plebiscite, the old bitterness flared up again and the proceedings broke up in an atmosphere of futility. Our own prestige suffered for the moment from the circumstance that the United States government had actively participated in the preparations for the referendum and no less a personage than General Pershing had been a member of the official supervisory commission at Arica. When the problem was settled four years later, it was by direct negotiations between diplomatic representatives of the two parties, though the United States had acted as a friendly and disinterested go-between in the preliminaries. An air of good will prevailed on both sides and the settlement agreed on was an eminently sound one. Chile retained Arica and the oasis-city of Tacna was restored to Peru. Peru was also to receive the equivalent of $6,000,000 in money and Chile agreed to build a special port to accommodate the commerce of Tacna. When the site chosen for the port was found to be unsatisfactory, Peru was compensated by an additional money indemnity.

In the arrangements between Chile and Peru, the claims of Bolivia to a corridor to the Pacific had been ignored. By a treaty signed in 1904 Bolivia had recognized the Chilean title to the Atacama coast. In return Chile bound herself to pay Bolivia an indemnity of £300,000, to consider Arica as a free port for the transit of goods into and out of Bolivia, and to build a railway between Arica and La Paz. In accordance with her agreement, Chile turned over to Bolivia the Bolivian section of the railroad fifteen years after its completion. Bolivia continued her efforts to gain an outlet to the Pacific, but since her unsuccessful protests against the Chilean-Peruvian arrangements of 1929, she has remained shut in on her high plateau. In the meantime, Chile had begun an interesting process of economic penetration of Bolivia, which for a time held serious threats for Bolivia's sovereignty over much of her territory.

Another survival of the inadequacies of colonial geography was the Gran Chaco or Chaco Boreal. Bolivia, whose centers of population were located far away in the mining regions of the Andean plateau, claimed it as a part of the old *Audiencia* of Charcas; Paraguay also based her contentions on equally plausible historical evidence. But Paraguay, facing the Chaco across the river of the same name, had begun the occupation of the zone along the river, which lent itself to the raising of cattle and the development of the quebracho extract industry.

Over a period of nearly half a century repeated attempts had been made by both governments to determine the frontier and several treaties had been made to that end, none of which was ratified by the national congresses. Meanwhile, both countries had continued to push a line of *fortines* or fortified outposts, deeper into the wilderness of the interior. The inevitable happened in 1928, when a small force of

Paraguayan frontier guards attacked a Bolivian outpost in the northern part of the Chaco. Realizing the gravity of the incident, the League of Nations and the Pan American Conference on Conciliation and Arbitration, which happened then to be meeting, both intervened to prevent the spread of hostilities. For a time the disputants agreed to accept the proposals of a five-power commission set up by the latter organization, but since the boundary question, which was the real crux of the problem, was not touched, the final reckoning was only delayed. War broke out in earnest in June, 1932 and continued for three years, when the exhaustion of both belligerents prepared the way for a truce and eventual peace. The struggle had been waged with great ferocity and under frightful natural conditions, which took a particularly heavy toll of the mountain-bred Bolivian soldiers. Hostilities had ended with the Paraguayans in possession of practically all of the disputed territory, and consequently in a strong bargaining position whenever her defeated rival should be ready to discuss the question of the ownership of the Chaco. Diplomatic relations were renewed in August, 1937, and in July of the next year, as a result of the good offices of the members of the special Chaco Peace Conference, representing Argentina, Brazil, Chile, Peru, the United States, and Uruguay, a treaty of peace was signed at Buenos Aires. A boundary line, giving Paraguay most of the disputed area, was later accepted by Bolivia and Paraguay.

The Leticia dispute between Peru and Colombia illustrates most of the elements common to Latin-American boundary controversies. By the terms of a treaty of 1922, the frontier between the two countries was delimited and, by means of the corridor known as the "Leticia trapezium," Colombia was granted access to the Amazon at a point adjoining the western limits of Brazil. Ten years later a band of Peruvians seized the village of Leticia and thereby precipitated a crisis in the relations between the two countries. The failure of the Sánchez Cerro government of Peru to disclaim the aggression of its nationals aggravated what should otherwise have been an insignificant border incident. Acting separately, the Ecuadorean government, the United States Department of State, and the League of Nations took prompt steps to forestall more serious developments. However, some local jungle fighting actually took place between small detachments of Colombian and Peruvian troops, and Colombia moved some of her armed forces around through the Caribbean and up the Amazon to

the scene of the dispute. The accession of General Benavides to the
presidency of Peru paved the way for an understanding between the
estranged nations. The actual machinery of conciliation was supplied
by a special committee of the League of Nations, which, pending the
outcome of direct negotiations in Rio de Janeiro, placed Leticia under
the administration of a commission of three. This Commission was
composed of a Brazilian, a Spaniard, and General Brown, Judge Ad-
vocate General of the United States. Through the good offices of the
Brazilian government, friendly relations were restored between Colombia and Peru, which reaffirmed the treaty of 1922.

A number of other Latin-American boundary disputes have been
settled peaceably, either by arbitration of a third power or by direct
negotiation. Chile, dissatisfied at being pent up behind the wall of the
Andes, had long aspired to an outlet to the Atlantic across Patagonia.
Though most of the groundwork for a settlement of the Argentine-
Chilean boundary was laid by a series of treaties between the two
countries, the final issue of the Patagonian section of the frontier was
referred to the arbitration of King Edward VII, who issued the
award in the case in 1902. To seal their pact of friendship, the famous
statue of the Christ of the Andes was set up on the border between
Argentina and Chile.

Brazil, which touches all the South American countries except
Chile and Ecuador, has been able to define her long border without
recourse to arms. Much of this remarkable record was due to the able
diplomacy of Brazil's great foreign minister, the Baron of Rio Branco,
as well as to the unusual combination of astuteness and restraint which
has generally characterized the conduct of Brazilian foreign policy.
Some of Brazil's boundary controversies were settled by direct negotiation; others, like that with Argentina, were settled by the arbitration
of a third power.

A number of boundary questions remain unsettled. A considerable belt of thinly populated land, lying between Honduras and Nicaragua, is claimed by both countries, and the former country also has
a frontier problem with Guatemala. A large strip of jungle country
between the Arauca and the Meta appears on Venezuelan maps as
part of the Province of Apure and on Colombian maps as the *Comisaria*
of Arauca. Argentina and Uruguay have always disagreed as to the
ownership of the River Plate estuary, the former claiming the river

to the north bank and the latter insisting on a line in mid-stream. None of these controversies has seriously affected the relations between the countries involved. A dispute that had greater possibilities of trouble was that between Ecuador and Peru. Peru's long-standing claims to the wedge-shaped Province of Oriente, which reached far out into the Amazonian lowlands, would have pushed Ecuador back onto the plateau. After several years of desultory and fruitless negotiations in Washington between emissaries of the two countries, the controversy was suddenly brought to a head by the Peruvian invasion of southern Ecuador. The Ecuadoreans were unable to resist the aggression of the Peruvian army and were only saved from further despoiling of their southern provinces by the peaceful intercession of other republics. The meeting of arbitrators, held in Rio de Janeiro, granted to Peru most of the territory in dispute and left Ecuador with a deep feeling of resentment that has had the effect of strengthening her ties with other member states of Bolívar's Republic of Gran Colombia.

Fortunately for the peace of the Americas, the forces for international harmony are much stronger than those for discord. In the first place, there is a common historical tradition and a similarity of basic customs and attitudes, at least among the ruling classes. The very existence of a common tongue, in which men can discuss their differences, is a powerful force for understanding. Nor does Portuguese constitute a serious obstacle to Brazil's sharing in this essential lingual unity, for Brazilians and their Spanish-speaking neighbors have little difficulty in communicating with one another. There are no ancient racial hatreds to poison the relationships between neighboring peoples. Quarrels between the republics are not seated deep in time, like those of Europe, and once they are definitely settled the peoples show a remarkable readiness to forget old scores, as Chileans and Peruvians have done. Latin Americans have a strong juridical sense and international law is not a dead letter, as it largely is in the Old World. No other group of nations has such a creditable record of arbitration as have these twenty republics. Except in Haiti, El Salvador, and Chile, there is no approach to overpopulation or pressure for land or natural resources. Consequently an urge for imperialistic expansion or aggression against their neighbors is generally lacking among the Latin-American countries in these times. Chile has passed through this phase and some of the Central American dictators have occasionally taken advantage of the internal difficulties of their neighbors.

Finally, the absence of a large armament industry in Latin America is a deterrent to war. In spite of the prevalence of "universal service" laws, armies and navies are relatively small according to European standards. With the exception of small-arm ammunition in a few countries, governments are dependent on American and European manufacturers for guns, munitions, planes, and most of the other paraphernalia of combat. Between wars in Europe—and especially just after their termination—they have no difficulty in obtaining all the equipment they need and can pay for. However, this is a precarious source of supply, which is liable to be cut off at any time for one reason or another. For example, during the Chaco War between Bolivia and Paraguay the United States government placed a ban on the shipment of arms to the combatants, thereby forcing a sudden readjustment of buying channels in certain lines of materials.[1] Embargoes of this kind may not have the effect of preventing wars or forcing an armistice on belligerents, but they can disrupt the plans of military extremists on the loose. During the Second World War, many of the Latin-American armies were provided with modern equipment by the United States. After the war, efforts were made to have the armaments of the Latin-American republics standardized, in order to facilitate their military cooperation with the United States in the event of a need for common hemispheric defense.

The existence of certain latent sources of international friction must be recognized. One of these, the survival of unsettled boundaries, has already been mentioned. Another is the potential rivalries for the territory of the weak countries. Thus, there can be little doubt that Bolivia's neighbors have all given careful, if not open, consideration to their course of action in the event of the disintegration of that feeble and loosely knit nation.[2] Unless Paraguay attains greater politi-

---

[1] In recognition of the efforts of the late Senator Huey Long in opposing the sale of war supplies to Bolivia, the Paraguayans named a site in the western Chaco "Mr. Long." A village in the eastern side of the Chaco is called Villa Hayes, for President Rutherford B. Hayes, who, as arbitrator in a boundary dispute with Argentina, rendered a decision favorable to Paraguay.

[2] A former Under Secretary of Foreign Affairs of Argentina once remarked to the writer, as he pointed to eastern Bolivia on a map of South America: "All this is Argentine."

cal stability and a sounder economy, a similar fate might ultimately threaten her national independence. Only the counterbalance of Brazil has restrained the gradual extension of Argentine hegemony over the Guaranian republic. Uruguay, on the other hand, once the battle-ground of her giant neighbors, has established such a strong position as a buffer between Brazil and Argentina that any aggression against her from either side appears highly improbable. Central American dis-union holds the possibilities of a New World Balkans. Permanent peace between Haiti and the Dominican Republic would seem un-likely, in view of the racial differences, the memory of past grievances, the lack of natural boundaries, and the overcrowded condition of the former country.

Democratic controls over national policy are generally weak in Latin America, and there is always the chance that some ambitious dictator may resort to a war of aggression in order to strengthen his position at home and to enhance his own personal glory.

Ideological differences among the predominant elements of the various republics have occasionally caused temporary rifts in their original spiritual solidarity. During the more radical and anticlerical phases of the Revolution, Mexico's relations with the more conserva-tive countries were sometimes strained. The Spanish Civil War not only divided opinion within the republics, but aligned the various governments according to the predominant official sympathies with either the Loyalists or the Nationalists. Thus, the Cárdenas administra-tion in Mexico and the Popular Front government in Chile were openly in favor of the republican regime in Spain, while others made no secret of their leanings toward the Franco cause. During the period of military superiority of the Axis powers in the early part of the Second World War there were violent and vocal cleavages of opinion among Latin Americans that generally followed their traditional patterns of social and political thinking. Nevertheless, in spite of po-tential factors of discord in the field of ideas and of material interest, the forces which work for peace among the Latin-American peoples are definitely in the ascendant.

While the basic international policies of the average republic are dictated by considerations of self-interest, there exist certain move-ments for the regional grouping of states within the framework of the Inter-American system. One of these, which has regained some momentum in recent years in Colombia, Ecuador, and Venezuela, represents a revival of the plan for the restoration of Bolívar's Gran Colombia. There are at all times protagonists of Central American union, who have refused to be disheartened by the progressive hardening of the realities that hinder the reconstitution of the early federation. In the southern part of the continent, Argentina, which aims at the leadership of Spanish America, has actively promoted an economic union with her neighbors that holds within it possibilities which are more than economic.

Acceptance of the "common market" principle of commercial integration is very general among Latin-American leaders, and growing disappointment with export prospects may further such a movement. In the late 1950s President Kubitschek of Brazil proposed a similar grouping of the nations of the hemisphere as "Operation Pan-America," and, meanwhile, a long-planned trading union of the Central American republics was on the point of realization.

Relations with Europe

The Latin-American nations have not been participants in the questionable game of world politics. They have not actively shared in the secular quarrels of Europe and have desired nothing so much as to remain aloof from them. On its side, Europe in general has secretly looked upon them as international parvenus, as unsophisticated colonials who practice a mongrel, half-Indian culture. Attracted by some of the more gracious and urbane aspects of its life, individual Latin Americans have long haunted the cities and watering places of western Europe. But these visitors, whatever their station or the motive of their sojourn, have had little concern with the alarums and goings-on of Europe's devious politics. The foreign policies of the republics continued to be singularly detached from European affairs.

During the First World War, eight of the Latin-American republics declared war against Germany. They were, in the order of their declarations, Cuba and Panama (April 7, 1917), Brazil, Nicaragua, Guatemala, Costa Rica, Haiti, and Honduras. Bolivia, the Dominican Republic, Ecuador, Peru, and Uruguay broke off diplomatic relations with Germany. In spite of considerable provocation, including the famous Luxburg despatch, Argentina remained neutral, as did the six other republics. Brazil was the only country which took steps leading toward actual participation in the conflict.

Though most of the Latin-American countries ventured into the League of Nations in its prime, it was because of their deep sympathy with its objectives and not because of any desire to intervene in the muddled affairs of the Old World. When they were disillusioned as to the League's ability to bring about a new order of international peace, the majority of them withdrew their membership. Some of them may have hoped to use the League as a counterpoise to the influence of the United States in the western hemisphere, but the fact that the original League Covenant recognized the binding force of the Monroe Doctrine was displeasing to the pride of the republics. Moreover, a turn in the Latin-American policy of the United States had the effect of restoring the principle of continental solidarity as the soundest basis of their collective security.

During the initial stages of the Second World War the sympathies of Latin Americans were deeply divided. Many conservative members of the clergy and of the officers' corps of the armies were openly pro-German, and within the large and influential Italian communities in Argentina and Brazil there were violent schisms of opinion. However, the leanings of the masses of the people everywhere were toward the Allied cause, and became increasingly pronounced as the war progressed.

A sudden and radical turn took place in Latin-American attitudes toward the war with the entry of the United States into the conflict in December, 1941. Panama declared war on Japan on the day of Pearl Harbor, the first nation in the western hemisphere to do so. Two days later all the Central American and West Indian republics had followed suit and on the 11th and 12th of December all of them declared war on Germany and Italy. The other countries moved more slowly. Colombia and Mexico broke off relations with the Axis powers very early and Mexico formally declared war in May of the next year. By the middle of 1942, Bolivia, Brazil, Ecuador, Paraguay, Peru, Uruguay, and Venezuela had severed their diplomatic ties with the Axis. In the early months of 1945, by which time the Axis was thoroughly defeated, there were "eleventh-hour" declarations of war by Argentina, Chile (against Japan only), Paraguay, Uruguay, and Venezuela, while Peru announced herself in a "state of belligerency," as Colombia had done over a year before. Brazil, which had declared war against Germany and Italy in August, 1942, did not declare war against Japan until June, 1945, or only two months before Russia took similar action.

Only two of the republics actively participated in the war. A Brazilian Expeditionary Force took a creditable part in the Italian campaign against the Germans and the Brazilians also performed a valuable service in patrolling the important sea lanes off their long coast. They also gave the United States the free use of invaluable bases at Natal and other points along their northern coast. Mexico sent a small airforce overseas and cooperated actively in controlling the Japanese communities in the northwestern part of the country. Most of the other republics had a largely passive role in the war and generally limited their belligerency to assistance in rounding up enemy nationals, to patrolling their own coasts, to cooperation, which was sometimes grudgingly given, in enforcing the so-called "Proclaimed List" against enemy businesses, and to the granting of bases and port privileges to the armed forces of the United States.

Throughout the war, Argentina refused to support the Allied cause, even passively. Her efforts at neutrality reacted in favor of the Axis powers, particularly of Germany, which continued to use Argentina as a base for propaganda and espionage almost until the end of the war. Even after Argentina had belatedly entered the war on the side of the Allies her participation was purely perfunctory and formalistic. Her refusal to cooperate with the United States led to strained official relations with this country that persisted for some time after the end of hostilities.

During the war, the United States had supplied large quantities of arms to the Latin-American republics and trained many Latin-American aviators at its airfields. After the war it made efforts for the establishment of an inter-American defense pact that would include all the republics of the hemisphere. Such a pact was agreed upon in principle at the Chapultepec meeting of foreign ministers in 1945, and was restated in the Inter-American Charter adopted at Bogotá in 1948.

Except for these excursions into the field of what the French rather poetically call *la haute politique*, Latin America's connections with Europe can be reduced to the relationships between certain individual European states and the New World republics:

Spain. For a long time after the end of the wars of independence, Spain grudgingly refused to recognize the heirs to her former empire. She clung to hopes of reconquering her lost colonies, and in 1864 attacked Peru on the slimmest of pretexts. Peru was joined by Chile, and before the Spanish fleet withdrew from South American waters it wantonly bombarded the city of Valparaiso. During most of the century the government of Spain was not such as to arouse the respect of foreigners of any nationality. The Spanish-American republics sympathized with the Cubans in their long and bitter struggle with the mother country, and it was not until after 1898 and the disappearance of Spain as a New World power that the estrangement gave way to a better understanding.

The new generation which gradually came into power after "the '98" made efforts to cultivate the good will of the Spanish Americans and its overtures were generously reciprocated. The institution of the *Dia de la Raza*, or "Day of the Race," in commemoration of the discovery of America by Columbus, was made the occasion for an annual assertion of the blood bond and cultural ties between Spain and the eighteen republics of Spanish speech. Organizations were founded to give expression to the *rapprochment*, Spanish intellectuals visited South America on lecture tours, and, as a token of the new feeling, Spain presented the city of Buenos Aires with what is perhaps the noblest piece of group statuary in the Americas. Pan-Hispanism, or Pan-Iberianism, became a definite movement, which was warmly received by those Spanish Americans who desired a counterpoise to Pan-Americanism. The founding of the Spanish Republic in 1931, by its abolition of monarchical forms, strengthened the movement for a time. However, the Civil War in Spain and the close involvement of the Franco government with Nazi Germany and Fascist Italy gave a setback to the movement and confused Spanish-American opinion as to the proper relationship with the mother country. Meanwhile, there was considerable loose talk among members of the dominant Falangist party, advocating the restoration of Spain's American empire. There were wide differences of opinion in Latin America on the merits of the Franco regime, and Guatemala and Mexico resorted to a break of relations with the Spanish government. Mexico not only admitted large numbers of Spanish Republican refugees, but permitted a Spanish "government in exile" to set up its headquarters in Mexico City.

Portugal. After the separation of Brazil from Portugal, there was no such prolonged estrangement as there was between Spain and her former colonies. As Brazil outdistanced the mother country in population, world influence, and wealth, she became the real head of the Lusitanian family. Brazilians are disposed to patronize the homeland and to laugh good-naturedly at its old-fashioned ways and threadbare gentility. But official relations between the two countries are extremely cordial and the Brazilian government has made special concessions to Portugal. Thus, Portuguese immigrants are exempted from the Brazilian quota. This heavy migration to the greater opportunities of Brazil represents a serious drain on the population of the older and more static country, but, in return, the remittances of immigrants constitute an important factor in the economic life of many a Portuguese village. To Brazil they bring a leaven of sturdy and industrious, if somewhat stolid and unimaginative, citizens, whose assimilation presents no problems.

Great Britain. British relations with the countries of Latin America are of earlier origin than those of any other outside power. British merchants had traded in the River Plate cities before the revolt against Spain. In 1806, a British force from Capetown took Buenos Aires, only to be driven out after a few weeks by an uprising of creoles under the command of an officer named Liniers. The next year a similar fate befell a much larger expedition, which had previously captured Montevideo. Though the British government remained officially neutral during the wars of independence, it did little to restrain the open recruiting efforts of the agents of the revolutionary juntas and otherwise gave its support to the patriot cause. When independence was attained, Great Britain followed the United States in recognizing the new governments, and it was Canning's firm stand and the British fleet which gave substance to President Monroe's warning to European powers against intervention in the Americas.

Except for activities on the Mosquito Coast of Central America, Britain made no further attempts at the acquisition of territory in

Latin America. On several occasions, ports were blockaded in order to enforce greater respect for British citizens, and there were controversies with Argentina, Brazil, and Venezuela, none of which reached serious proportions. In 1938 she severed her diplomatic relations with Mexico over the expropriation of British oil properties. She has had a perennial controversy with Argentina over the ownership of the Falkland Islands and another with Guatemala over the title to Belize. A long time ago she had a comic-opera quarrel with Melgarejo, the notorious Bolivian dictator, which is said to have resulted in the erasure of that country from official British maps of South America.[3]

Great Britain's principal preoccupation with Latin America was with the spread of her commercial and financial interests. Vast sums were invested in railroads and other enterprises in the republics, as well as in loans to the various governments. British trade, founded on the sound basis of an exchange of manufactures for agricultural products, came to assume a pre-eminent place in the commercial life of the republics, though American and German competition was later to threaten its supremacy. In all the important business centers were compact communities of British merchants, bankers, shipping agents, and administrators of utilities, who, in a strange environment, duplicated as nearly as they could their manner of life at home. In the larger cities, they set up little Britains, with clubs, churches, schools, newspapers, cricket fields, and cemeteries.[4] While the natives regarded their unemotional and stiff-necked attitude and the idiosyncrasies of their ways with a tolerant amusement, they admired their correct and punctilious business habits and their sense of fairness in sports and other activities.

France. In their dealings with France, Latin Americans have generally drawn a clear line between the French government and French cul-

---

[3] This incident is said to have occurred because of a slight to the dictator's mistress by the British minister, who was later ridden out of La Paz seated backwards on a mule.

[4] A guidebook to Rio de Janeiro, written in Brazilian-English, has this to say of the English Cemetery: "It is the oldest cemetery in the city. . . . Lord Strangford inaugurated the necropolis in 1809. . . . It is a small cemetery with very little movement." Angelo Orazi, *Rio de Janeiro and Environs* (Rio de Janeiro, 1939), p. 238.

ture. The former was a partner in the Holy Alliance, which would restore them to Spanish rule. Its fleets twice blockaded the River Plate for long periods, and it was responsible for placing Maximilian on the throne of Mexico. However, during the past half century or more, French political relations with Latin America have been uneventful. While French trade reached sizable proportions, particularly in certain lines of specialized manufactures, it never ranked in volume with that of Great Britain or the United States.

Franco-Latin-American relations have been primarily cultural, and France has exerted a great influence on the thought and imagination of the republics. Paris has been the mecca of writers and artists, scholars and professional men, as well as of the wealthy and leisured class. French has been the second language of most educated Latin Americans, who usually speak it with great fluency. French works have often been more common in the bookstores of South America than the writings of native authors, and much of the scientific and philosophical thinking of other European peoples has reached Latin-American readers through the medium of French translations. The various schools of French literature and art have at certain periods fixed the prevailing pattern of imaginative expression in Latin America. Prominent representatives of all branches of French culture and the leaders of the French stage have been acclaimed in Latin-American capitals. Organizations like the *Alliance Française* and the *Comité France-Amérique* and publications like the *Revue de l'Amérique Latine* and *France-Amérique* have actively promoted the infiltration of French culture, and for a time the more ardent followers of this cultural *rapprochement* sponsored a Pan-Latin movement, which recognized France as the head of the Latin world. France has affected other fields of thought and activity in Latin America, as in its strong impress on the architecture of Buenos Aires and on secondary education in some of the countries. French cultural influence has declined in recent years, partly to the advantage of that of Spain, but much more because of the rise of a strong national consciousness in art and literature, which rebelled against the excessive imitation of foreign models. Under the impetus of the revolutionary regime which began in 1911, Mexico's strongly nationalistic culture has led this move to find its inspiration in the native scene. Also, twice in this century war has cut off Latin America from her contacts with France and French cultural influence.

Germany. Germany was a late comer in Latin America. However, during the years preceding the First World War, Germans, with the obvious encouragement of the imperial government, made feverish and highly successful efforts to overcome the handicap of their late entry into the field. German trading houses and banks were established in the leading cities and German traders pushed their operations far into the interior of South America into areas previously neglected by the business interests of other nations. Germany became a formidable commercial rival of Great Britain and the United States, but as a result of the World War of 1914–18 lost much of the ground which she had gained in the previous decade. The movement to re-establish her former position was taken up with even greater intensity and with the employment of new methods under the National Socialist regime of the Third Reich, only to be as sharply curtailed on the outbreak of war in 1939.

German relations with Latin America have been essentially economic, whatever the eventual designs of German policy. German cultural influence has been remarkably small, and the incompatibility of the Teutonic genius with the Latin temperament would apparently preclude any considerable gains in this field in the future. Germany formerly exerted considerable influence in the military circles of several countries through the medium of special missions which trained their armies.

Participation in the United Nations

From the beginning, the Latin-American republics accepted with enthusiasm the idea of the United Nations as an instrument for world peace. They took an active part in the organizational meeting at San Francisco. Their representatives were given posts of responsibility in the hierarchy of its organization, including for a time that of President of the Assembly. Generally voting as a bloc, the twenty states threw their collective influence solidly against the more obvious and extreme manifestations of power politics and exerted all their efforts to increase the usefulness and prestige of the organization.

Relations with the United States

The Monroe Doctrine. When the Monroe Doctrine was proclaimed in 1823, it was 40 years since the American Revolution had ended. Most of Latin America was free, but Bolívar had not yet completed the liberation of Peru. The contrasts between the United States and the young nations to the south appeared to outweigh heavily their points of similarity. The one was Anglo-Saxon in race and predominantly Protestant in religion. Its people had a long and active tradition of democratic government. Its natural setting presented no serious obstacles, either to national unity or internal communications or to the physical and mental activity of the individual citizen. It had a secular educational system and a growing body of the population could read and write. Beyond the original bounds of the new federation extended an enormous area of rich and unoccupied land, into which settlers were pushing from the states along the Atlantic seaboard. Beyond the Mississippi nothing blocked their way to the Pacific except the Indian tribes, vague British claims to the northwest, and the thinly populated and lightly held territory which Mexico had inherited from Spain. The rampant individualism which already set the tone of the advancing frontier was to be equally contemptuous of Mexicans and Indians who tried to bar the path to what it considered the natural limits of its destiny. From Jackson's time the government rode with this unruly tide that rolled westward and framed its policies accordingly. And already inherent in the conditions of American life were the prospects of an immense growth in population and wealth.

The governing class of the new nations of the hemisphere were Latin in race, and the mass of the population were Indians or mixed breeds. Roman Catholicism was the universal religion. The political background was one of subjection to an absolute government, that offered no opportunity for the practice of democracy. Nature favored the isolation of communities and peoples and the growth of regionalism, and in the tropical regions discouraged orderly and continuous effort of brain and body. Education was dominated by the Church and was the privilege of a few. Though vast expanses of land still awaited settlement and a pioneer spirit existed in some of the new countries, expansion was limited by the boundaries, ill-defined as they were, of fellow peoples. And the Andes and the tropical jungle presented more serious obstacles to the Latin-American pioneers than did the Appalachians and the Rockies and the great plains to the frontiersmen of the north.

With the exception of the Brazilian Empire, all the independent states of the New World were republics, which had won their independence in a struggle against monarchical government. However broad the gap of experience which separated them, they had at least a common ideal of democracy. And they shared the same continent, between which and Europe lay what was then a very wide ocean.

It was these factors—differences and similarities—which were to decide the course of relations between the United States and Latin America. For the time being, it was the common factors which determined our attitude. They accounted for the good will which we extended to the young and untried republics, as they had called forth our sympathies during the wars of independence. They prompted our anxiety for their continued freedom from Europe. Later the factors of differentiation were to assert themselves, and our Latin-American relations at any period in the future would be the resultant of the workings of both sets of forces.

The enunciation of the Monroe Doctrine represented the first phase. The principle which is known by his name was not original with President Monroe. Fifteen years before, Thomas Jefferson had expressed a similar idea in a letter to Governor Claiborne at New Orleans. Other leaders, both in the United States and Latin America, had given thought to plans for preserving the independence of the New World states against the possibility of intervention from Europe. This possibility became acute when the powers of the Holy Alliance began to consider measures for the restoration of Spain's authority over her lost colonies. It was this threat that prompted President Monroe to declare the policy which, though its interpretation has varied, long governed our relations with Latin America. In his message to Congress on December 2, 1823, Monroe made this momentous statement:

". . . the occasion has been judged proper for asserting as a principle in which the rights and interests of the United States are involved, that the American continents, by the free and independent condition which they have assumed and maintain, are henceforth not to be considered as subjects for future colonization by any European powers. . . . We owe it, therefore, to candor, and to the amicable relations existing between the United States and those powers, to declare that we should consider any attempt on their part to extend their system to any portion of this hemisphere as dangerous to our peace and safety. With the existing colonies and dependencies of any European power we have not interfered and shall not interfere. . . ."

While the United States then lacked the military strength to enforce this bold warning, it realized that in an extremity it could count on the active cooperation of the British fleet. And though the stand of both governments was dictated by selfish considerations—"*our* peace and safety" and Canning's determination to maintain Britain's advantage in the trade of Latin America—the undeclared partnership proved none the less effective.

After the dissipation of the threat from the Holy Alliance, occasion for invoking the Monroe Doctrine was lacking for some time, during which the United States grew in numbers and strength. Then President Polk, who represented the assertive nationalism of the era of the annexation of Texas and the Mexican War, at least twice found opportunity for reminding Europe of the Doctrine's existence. In the sixties, Napoleon III took advantage of our preoccupation with the War Between the States to place a Hapsburg archduke on the Mexican throne and Spain embarked on a punitive war against Peru. When the end of the Civil War released the American army for possible action in Mexico, Maximilian's empire was already doomed. Spanish aggressions on the west coast of South America were ended as much by the strong stand taken by Chile as by the friendly intercession of the United States. In 1870, President Grant extended the original scope of the Monroe Doctrine by declaring that "hereafter no territory on this continent shall be regarded as subject to transfer to a European Power." This enlarged aspect of the Doctrine clearly implied our refusal to sanction the transfer of a European colony to a second European power. President Hayes proclaimed another corollary to the Doctrine in 1880, when he announced that the United States would not permit the construction and operation of an inter-oceanic canal by any other power, since such a canal would be "a great ocean thoroughfare between the Atlantic and Pacific shores, and virtually a part of the coast line of the United States." In 1895, Secretary of State Olney restated the original intent of the Doctrine in a communication to Lord Salisbury, on the occasion of the dispute between Great Britain and Venezuela over the boundary of British Guiana. However, it was Secretary Olney who gave the extreme and unwarranted interpretation of the Doctrine in his declaration that "Today the United States is practically sovereign on this continent, and its fiat is law upon the subjects to which it confines its interposition."

It was during this period that Great Britain definitely accepted the principle of the Monroe Doctrine as binding on herself, by tacitly acknowledging the primary interest of the United States in the defense of the western hemisphere. The rising power of the new Germany, however, showed no such acquiescence in the binding force of the Doctrine. Bismarck called it "an international impertinence" and "a species of arrogance peculiar to the American and quite inexcusable." Our intercession on the occasion of German efforts to enforce the collection of certain claims from Venezuela by a bombardment of Venezuelan ports rankled in the minds of German leaders. Also, it was the obvious designs of Germany on the Danish West Indies which decided the United States to acquire what are now the Virgin Islands.

As the nationalities of Latin America took more stable form after the anarchy of the civil wars, its peoples began to give more thoughtful consideration to the possible implications of the Monroe Doctrine. The expansionist activities of the United States in the Caribbean lands, which followed the Spanish-American War, led many Latin Americans to question the purpose of the Doctrine and to consider it as a cloak to the imperialistic designs of the United States. Since no European power had attempted aggressions against the territory of a Latin-American state for nearly half a century, the republics had a feeling of security which they ascribed as much to the lack of warlike intentions on the part of possible aggressors as to the protection of the Monroe Doctrine. Also, the stronger nations like Argentina considered the Doctrine as a reflection on their ability to defend themselves against an attack from Europe, and, therefore, as a humiliating form of tutelage.

The people of the United States, on the other hand, had long since unquestioningly accepted the Doctrine as the foundation of the country's Latin-American policy. Their uncritical acceptance of the Doctrine appeared justified by the fact that Latin America had remained intact ever since it was promulgated, and they naturally regarded this preservation of the territorial integrity of the republics as the fruit of the Doctrine. The Doctrine had gained the force of an international axiom, and, as something axiomatic, required no analysis.

Two distinct tendencies have colored the development of the Monroe Doctrine in the present century. Some Americans would have restricted the field of the Doctrine to the Caribbean area, or, at most, to the northern part of South America. As the "bulge" of Brazil is the logical landing place for planes flying from Africa, they favored including that section of coast in the sphere of its application. On the west coast, they would extend our zone of interest to the edge of Peru, or to cover that corner of the continent from which hostile aircraft might attack the Panama Canal. Those persons felt that any aggressions against the lower part of South America would not affect our national welfare, and that the defense of that portion of the hemisphere was the responsibility of the ABC powers. They argued that western Europe is nearer to the United States than are Rio de Janeiro or Buenos Aires, and that we should have less concern for the protection of Argentina or Brazil than for that of Ireland or Portugal.

Many Latin Americans had long protested against the unilateral character of the Doctrine, which, they contended, implied the existence of a virtual American protectorate over their countries. This sentiment was especially strong in Argentina, where the Doctrine was generally resented as an affront to the nation's pride and independence of action. Theodore Roosevelt, whose Latin-American policies often appeared inconsistent and unpredictable, believed in sharing responsibility for the Doctrine with the stronger states. In 1906, he said:

> "There are certain republics to the south of us which have already reached such a point of stability, order and prosperity that they themselves are guarantors of the Monroe Doctrine. If all the republics to the south of us will only grow as those to which I allude have already grown, all need for us to be the especial champions of the Doctrine will disappear. . . ."

President Baltasar Brum, of Uruguay, in 1909 recommended a

union of all the nations of the continent, which would be bound to come to the aid of any country attacked from overseas. The principle of collective action of the American republics as a guarantee of their individual and common security was agreed upon at the Pan American Conference at Lima in 1936, and has been definitely accepted by the government of the United States. Moreover, the principle has been recognized in various inter-American parleys held since the beginning of the Second World War. For all practical purposes, the Monroe Doctrine has thus become a phase of Pan-Americanism.

The United States and the Caribbean Area. Geography determined the special interest of the United States in the lands about the Caribbean. Early in the century the Louisiana Purchase had brought this country to the shores of the Gulf of Mexico, and the acquisition of Florida in 1819 pushed our southern frontier down to within a short distance of Cuba. For a long time the tone of our relations with Mexico was fixed by the secession and annexation of Texas and by our predatory war against that country. Though not sanctioned by the government of the United States, the filibustering adventures of William Walker in the fifties left a further heritage of anti-American feeling in Mexico and Central America.

Meanwhile, our seizure of California had called the attention of the American people to the importance of the Isthmus of Panama and the Nicaraguan portage. Great Britain was maneuvering to enlarge her sphere of influence on the east coast of Central America, particularly by means of dealings with the Indians of the Mosquito Territory. The conviction was growing in both the United States and Great Britain that the building of an interoceanic canal was only a question of time, and there followed considerable diplomatic sparring between the two countries over the control of the future isthmian waterway. It was not until 1901 that the British government renounced its claim to participate in the building and operation of a canal and left the United States free to carry out its plans in that area. Due to financial and sanitary difficulties, the French had abandoned their efforts to build a canal at Panama. For $40,000,000 the French company sold its concession and equipment to the United States, which about that time decided in favor of the Panama route as against that across Nicaragua. When the Colombian Congress refused to ratify the Hay-Herran

Treaty granting the United States virtual sovereignty over a strip across the isthmus on both sides of the canal, events moved swiftly toward the secession of Panama and the speedy recognition of the new Panamanian Republic by this country. The questionable propriety of American participation in this affair, which bore all the earmarks of having been engineered by the United States government, resulted in long-estranged relations between this country and Colombia.

The Panama revolution took place in November, 1903. After the necessary political arrangements, including the cession of the Canal Zone, had been made with the new government, the Americans promptly began work on the canal and completed it ten years later, in 1914. The Republic of Panama had emerged as a protectorate of the United States, with its independence guaranteed and certain controls established over its internal affairs and international relations.

However, Cuba was the first American protectorate in the Caribbean area. During the long and periodic revolts of the Cubans against Spanish rule, the American people had often given more than moral support to the Cuban patriots, and American sympathy became particularly active during the repressive governorship of General Valeriano Weyler. The short Spanish-American War of 1898 not only freed Cuba from Spain, but raised at once the difficult question of its future relations with the United States. The island remained under American administration until 1901, when the Cuban Republic was inaugurated. Though its essential sovereignty was recognized, the freedom of action of the Cuban government was considerably curtailed by the terms of the so-called Platt Amendment, which defined the relationship between the two countries. This appendix to the Military Appropriations Bill of March, 1901 was incorporated in the Cuban constitution and was later made the subject of a treaty.

By the Platt Amendment Cuba was definitely brought within the political orbit of the United States. In order to avoid the pretext for the interference of a third power in Cuban affairs, the United States was authorized to intervene for the maintenance of orderly government in the island and its permission was necessary for the contraction of any foreign loan. Cuba also granted the United States the use of Guantanamo Bay as a naval base. This harbor, which commands the Windward Passage and the waters of the mid-Caribbean, has become of increasing importance in the naval strategy of the United States.

As a result of the Spanish-American War, the United States acquired outright the smaller island of Puerto Rico, and thereby strengthened its position in the eastern end of the Caribbean. In 1916, the purchase of the Danish West Indies, with their fine harbor of St. Thomas, further confirmed our strategic domination of the American Mediterranean.

The third American protectorate was established under different circumstances. The Dominican Republic had been an independent nation since 1844, when the Dominicans freed themselves from Haitian domination, though Spanish rule was restored for a few years in the sixties. The history of the republic had been turbulent, and by the end of the century there seemed little prospect that it could attain political stability unaided. A series of unscrupulous and incompetent rulers had burdened the nation with a volume of foreign debt that was beyond its normal financial capacity to service. It was the growing insistence of European governments in pressing the claims of their nationals that precipitated the first American intervention in Dominican affairs in 1905. Theodore Roosevelt, who was president at the time, took the stand that this and similar situations about the Caribbean imposed on the United States, as guardian of the Monroe Doctrine, the duty of policing those republics in which political disorder and financial irresponsibility had become chronic. Under the protectorate set up in the Dominican Republic, the United States assumed the collection of Dominican customs, supervision of payments to foreign creditors, and general control of the fiscal and foreign affairs of the distracted country.

The classic formula of the Caribbean protectorates was not fully established in the Dominican Republic for several years. During the intervening period, the United States had to contend with the rapid shifting of political power from one leader to another. Some of the American agents, particularly Secretary of State Bryan's partisan appointees, were inept and unable to deal effectively with the baffling realities of Dominican politics. The end of this inglorious phase of the American intervention was not reached until late in 1916, when an impasse in the internal political situation of the republic provided the occasion for the military occupation of the country. The United States Navy took over the government for six years, while the marines remained until 1924.

Under Roosevelt's successors, the United States greatly extended its activities in the Caribbean area. There was much confusion in the motives which determined American policy during this period. There can be no doubt that a simultaneous climax of disorder and misgovernment in a number of the republics offered extreme provocation to the United States. A minority of frank imperialists talked loosely of our "manifest destiny" to rule the Caribbean lands, to push our real southern border once for all down through Mexico and Central America to the Canal, and across the sea to the Spanish Main. Many more, including those high in the government, were concerned with the promotion and protection of American business interests in the region. This policy took on the appearance of economic imperialism when American marines and bluejackets were used to guard the enterprises of bankers, investors, and traders, who were aware of the high speculative element in Caribbean business. The stigma of "dollar diplomacy" which was attached to this phase of American policy did much to discredit our activities during this era of interventions and protectorates. Strategic considerations doubtless played an important part in the calculations of the United States, which was anxious to remove the conditions that might provoke the interference of European powers in the Caribbean and so bring them within striking distance of the Panama Canal.

With these motives was mingled a large amount of missionary zeal for the welfare of the peoples of the Caribbean republics. Whether ill-timed and misdirected or not, the sincerity and unselfishness of much of this crusading ardor can scarcely be questioned. We desired to impose better political habits on the native populations, regardless of their wishes in the matter. We believed that the way to cure the evils and troubles of the Caribbean countries was to spread the American gospel of public schools, good roads, modern sanitation, internal order, and respect for elections, not to mention baseball as a counterpoise to the urge for revolution. In all this there was a purpose to make Nicaraguans and Cubans and Dominicans as much like Americans as possible. We were trying out such a program in Puerto Rico, and reasoned that it might have as good chances of success in Central America and the island republics.

The rest of Latin America saw in these plans only an attempt to force our customs and habits on peoples who preferred their own ways, however backward and trying they might appear according to American standards. Above all, they feared this expansionist movement in the Caribbean as a threat to their own political future, or at least as an affront to the racial solidarity of the Latin-American peoples. At no period in our relations has such a volume of anti-American literature appeared in Latin America or has the Latin-American press been so hostile to the United States. Throughout the era of the Caribbean protectorates a highly vocal and persistent group in this country continued to criticize our interventionist policy as imperialistic.

Our adventure in Nicaragua contained all the familiar elements of political disorder and threats to American interests, which characterized the earlier intervention in the Dominican Republic. That republic had been ruled for a long time by José Santos Zelaya, an example of the worst type of Latin-American dictator. His capricious and arbitrary rule, his flaunting of the rights of American citizens in his country, and his suspicious negotiations with European bankers all exasperated the patience of the United States government to the point where American action became inevitable. Theodore Roosevelt had shown considerable restraint under the provocations of Zelaya, but when Taft succeeded to the presidency, with Philander C. Knox as his secretary of state, Nicaragua was destined to be added to our growing list of protectorates. Knox roundly condemned the rule of Zelaya as a "blot on the history" of Nicaragua and prepared to undermine the dictator by encouraging his enemies to revolt. Matters came to a head in 1910 with the flight of Zelaya from the country and the assumption of the government by General Juan J. Estrada. The United States had not counted on the release of all the pent-up rivalries and ambitions of Nicaraguan politics and for several years was forced to juggle its policy to fit the rapidly changing political scene. It was 1913 before the internal situation had cleared sufficiently for a discussion of the formal terms of a protectorate. A system of financial controls was established, with American investment bankers among the interested parties to the arrangements. During Wilson's administration, William Jennings Bryan, as secretary of state, concluded a canal treaty, which, however, was not ratified by the United States Senate, though the existing fiscal supervision remained in effect. During the period 1911–28, the banking houses of Brown Brothers and the J. and

W. Seligman Company managed the public finances of Nicaragua.

In 1925, the force of marines, which had long been stationed in Managua as a "legation guard," was withdrawn from the country. The next year, in response to the requests of President Adolfo Díaz, six thousand marines and sailors were landed in Nicaragua and promptly became the real rulers of the country. In 1927 Henry L. Stimson was sent to Nicaragua as the representative of President Coolidge, with the object of reconciling the rival factions of the dominant Liberal party. Stimson was successful in his efforts, but a group of young irreconcilables under the leadership of Augusto Sandino took to the mountains and defied the new regime and its American supporters. This led to a long guerrilla war between the followers of Sandino and the marines, which made the name of the Nicaraguan chieftain a legend throughout Latin America and a rallying cry for the opponents of American "imperialism."

Haiti was doomed to follow sooner or later the road of its Dominican neighbor and fall under the hegemony of the United States. Since its independence from the French in 1803, the Negro republic had been ruled by an almost unbroken succession of barbarous tyrants. The nation had become accustomed to a regular pattern of revolution and its devastating consequences, from which there were only a few short respites of orderly government. The French had preserved an important economic stake in the country, and in the period before World War I the Germans had made efforts to establish their influence in the distracted republic. By 1915 the Haitian national debt had become dangerously large, and the current financial operations of the government were being conducted on a precarious hand-to-mouth basis that made it the prey of foreign moneylenders. American control over Haiti began in 1910 with the plan for the reorganization of the national bank, which Secretary Knox forced on the Haitian government over the protests of the French and Germans. In 1914 the United States proposed a customs convention along the general lines of our arrangements with the Dominican Republic and other conditions leading to the establishment of a protectorate. However, the customary cycle of revolutions was moving with more than ordinary speed and no government succeeded in remaining in power long enough to conclude the necessary agreements with the United States. Events were brought to a head by the occurrences of July, 1915, which ended with the slaughter of the current president by a mob in Port-au-Prince and the landing of American marines from a warship in the harbor. The country was rapidly brought under military control and the scene prepared for the imposition of the long-delayed protectorate. A treaty of the same year provided for American control of the Haitian customs, the appointment of an American financial "adviser" with large powers, the substitution of an American-commanded native constabulary for the turbulent and revolution-minded national army, a commission to pass on the claims of the country's creditors, a loan to the new government, and a pledge against the alienation of Haitian territory to a third power. For several years the marines and the newly organized and efficient Haitian constabulary carried on operations in the hill country, aimed at the extermination of the famous *caco* mercenaries, who had long bedeviled the land by their revolutionary activities.

While our relations with Mexico have often seemed to follow a distinctive pattern, much the same influences have determined their course as operated in our dealings with the smaller countries of the Caribbean area. The major difference has been in the special circumstances arising out of the Mexican social revolution which began in 1911, particularly its anticlerical manifestations. As with the other republics of the region, until recent times, our policy toward Mexico was not consistent for long, and its application frequently reflected its amateurish handling. Our government alternately threatened and cajoled the Mexicans, often with a very bad sense of timing. It had to consider strong pressures at home from business interests affected by the radical activities of the Mexican governments and from the Catholic Church, whose co-religionists in Mexico had suffered from the anticlericalism of the Revolution. It had to adjust itself to frequent changes in Mexican leadership, and to the shifts of Mexican policy between the left and the right. For the course of the Revolution itself was tortuous and uncertain. It had to guard against the possibility of other countries fomenting anti-American feeling or using Mexico as a covert ally against the United States. Moreover, we had to reckon with Mexico's ability—and readiness—to appeal to the sympathies of the rest of Latin America against the United States. Although the conservative elements in countries like Argentina, Colombia, and Peru frowned upon the more radical aspects of the Mexican Revolution, public sentiment in those nations responded readily to Mexico's appeals for moral support in her difficulties with the United States. Finally, our policy always had to take account of powerful sympathies in the United States for the basic objectives of the Revolution, particularly as they aimed at improving the economic lot of the Mexican masses.

The long rule of Porfirio Díaz, which ended in 1911, was a period of unusually friendly Mexican-American relations. The dictator kept the peace, however harsh his measures at times, welcomed American investors as indispensable to the material development of the country, and raised the credit of the government by the scrupulous observance of its foreign obligations. It was natural that in the difficult era which followed, the State Department and American businessmen should often feel a profound nostalgia for that golden age.

Liberal opinion in the United States was at first favorable to Madero, who lacked both the strength and the opportunity to put into effect the reforms he had promised. Victoriano Huerta, his brutal successor, soon fell afoul of the United States and was forced out of office by the relentless opposition of the Wilson government to his rule. It was during the ignominious Huerta regime that the Americans occupied Vera Cruz, producing a crisis in the relations between the two countries, which was probably only saved from more extreme consequences by the friendly mediation of some of the other Latin-American countries.

Although the United States recognized the government of Venustiano Carranza, Mexico had already become the battleground of rival leaders, and it was increasingly difficult to chart a consistent course of policy toward a country which itself had seemed to lose all direction. In the north, the depredations of Villa created a local situation for the United States, with which we attempted to deal by means of General Pershing's futile punitive expedition across the border. This violation of Mexican sovereignty, though actually in the interests of his own precarious rule, had the effect of aggravating Carranza's anti-American attitude. He appealed for the support of the other Latin-American republics and baited the United States at every opportunity. The national constitution of 1917, which was drafted during Carranza's administration, laid the legal foundation for the subsequent troubles of American investors with the Mexican government.

Under Obregón, relations with Mexico tended to improve, but during the presidency of Calles the anti-religious policy of the government and its application of the land distribution features of the new constitution again brought affairs to an impasse, which was only broken for the time being by the personal diplomacy of Ambassador Dwight Morrow. After another period of drifting and wavering under Calles' immediate successors, the accession of Lázaro Cárdenas to the presidency precipitated an acute crisis in Mexican-American relations. By his uncompromising adherence to the principles of the Revolution, Cárdenas found himself in direct opposition to the large American business interests in the country, which had managed to survive all the vicissitudes of treatment by his more violent or opportunistic predecessors. The expropriation of the properties of the oil companies climaxed this period of extreme measures. Though the United States government protested vigorously on behalf of the oil companies, it showed an inclination to avoid an open break for fear of forcing Mexico into the hands of Japan or Germany. Both countries had long showed a disposition to profit by any strained relations between the United States and Mexico, so that strategic considerations dictated much of our leniency toward the Mexican government's obvious provocation. Also, the active sympathy of a large element in the United States with the social objectives of the Mexican Revolution influenced our official policy toward that country. The visits of President Roosevelt, Vice-President Wallace, and President Truman proved to be particularly felicitous gestures of good will toward the government and people of Mexico.

The adoption of the "Good Neighbor Policy" by the administration of President Franklin D. Roosevelt resulted in a remarkable improvement in our relations with the countries in the Caribbean area. This reversal of policy required our renunciation of the Wilsonian doctrine of the non-recognition of governments established by revolution or perpetuated by fraud and violence. We gave up all responsibility for maintaining orderly processes of rule within the republics, though it has involved the necessity of our dealing with certain dictatorships some of whose methods have been highly obnoxious. In practice the new policy also forced us to relinquish the ancient obligation to protect American business interests which were threatened by the action of Latin-American governments. And while we maintain the fiction of the solidarity of the "democracies" in the western hemisphere, we ceased to inquire too closely into the actual methods of government employed or the degree of popular participation.

The principal concrete manifestation of our new Caribbean policy was the complete restoration of national sovereignty and freedom of action to the former protectorates. Although this movement was initiated, even if haltingly and half-heartedly, by previous administrations, it was carried out unreservedly by the Roosevelt government. The first of the protectorates to be abandoned was that over the Dominican Republic. American forces left that country in 1924, though a certain measure of fiscal control was continued even after the Trujillo dictatorship, which began in 1930, had removed any further occasion for American occupation on behalf of the preservation of public order. American occupation of Haiti was definitely ended in 1934 by an arrangement made between President Roosevelt and the Haitian President Vincent. On the withdrawal of the marines, the national constabulary, known as the Garde d'Haiti, assumed full responsibility for policing the republic. The long period of American intervention in Nicaragua was ended in 1933, with the embarkation of the last marines from Nicaraguan ports. By a new agreement with Panama in 1936, the United States renounced its right to intervene in Panamanian affairs and to guarantee the nation's independence, as stipulated in the original treaty of 1903. In 1934, the United States took the radical step of abrogating the famous Platt Amendment, which had seriously circumscribed the independence of the Cuban government.

Pan Americanism. The idea of a New World amphictyony is founded in the circumstances of geography and history. The concept of the common interest of the American states as occupants of the same hemisphere and as confronted with similar dangers from Europe originated independently in the minds of several New World leaders, including Simón Bolívar, Henry Clay, and Francisco de Paula Santander. The example of the union of the thirteen North American colonies appeared to form a model for a larger, if looser, league of independent nations. Bolívar attempted to give concrete expression to what was yet but a tantalizing abstraction, by his summons to an international congress at Panama. Though the delegates of only a few states attended the meeting of 1826 and though the deliberations resulted in no plan of future action, the conference at Panama pointed the way to a movement which was eventually to have substantial significance.

For the time being, neither the Latin-American nations nor the United States were ready to take part in an organized movement for hemispheric confederation. The former were too immature politically, too preoccupied with their own internal problems and the possible designs of one another, to give serious consideration to the dream of internationalism. After the winning of independence, the latent forces of disunion and isolation asserted themselves. As in the United States at the same period, the conditions of the time favored the growth of a provincial outlook among the various peoples, and only a few leaders were capable of a vision of things beyond the national borders.

When the movement was resumed later in the first half of the century, its sphere was limited to the Spanish-American republics. The United States had embarked on its career of expansion at the expense of Mexico, which clearly disqualified it for participation in a program based on respect for the rights of the group. When the attainment of our "natural frontiers" and the disappearance of slavery as a motive for territorial expansion removed the immediate probability of further advances by the United States, it was superseded in the minds of Latin Americans by a vaguer fear of the material growth of this country. The remarkable development of American resources and population after the Civil War created an eventual disparity of power that was to be a real barrier to Pan-Americanism. Meanwhile, several conferences of local groups of states had been held in South America and for a time it seemed that international cooperation might be limited to the Latin countries, definitely excluding the United States from the New World partnership of nations.

However, all was not harmony among the Latin-American countries during this transitional period in the evolution of Pan-Americanism. Between the end of our Civil War and 1883, two of the bloodiest wars in the history of Latin America were fought, involving the participation of seven South American states. The United States had again become conscious of the importance of cultivating a better understanding and closer cooperation with the countries to the south, and during this time generally abstained from any move likely to arouse the dormant suspicions of its motives. Moreover, our action in invoking the Monroe Doctrine against the French in Mexico had brought us much good will which had not yet been dissipated.

The moment appeared propitious for the United States to espouse the principle of Pan-Americanism and to assume the leadership in the movement. James G. Blaine, as secretary of state under President Garfield, took the initiative and in 1881 invited all the states of Latin America to send representatives to a conference in Washington. Due to a number of reasons, the conference was not held as scheduled, but the United States did not abandon its plans for such a meeting. The first International Conference of American States, now more commonly known as Pan-American Conferences, was held in Washington in the winter of 1889–90. Though President Cleveland was responsible for summoning the conference, it met under the auspices of his successor and under the chairmanship of Blaine, again secretary of state. The conference accomplished a vast amount of work in both the political and economic fields, and agreed on recommendations for arbitration of international disputes and for the common adoption of measures designed to further commercial intercourse within the Americas. Though few of the agreements reached at the Congress were ratified by the respective governments, nevertheless the conference can, paradoxically enough, be considered highly successful. It marked the real beginning of the Pan-American movement on a truly continental scale, and set a precedent and a pattern which have never since been broken.

The most substantial of its tangible results was the establishment of the International Office of the American Republics, now known as the Pan American Union. For some time this organization served only as an office for the collection and dissemination of commercial statistics and information. It was at first under the exclusive direction of the United States government and its usefulness and prestige suffered from the exercise of political patronage by several administrations. It was later placed under the joint control of all the twenty-one republics and given a status compatible with its new position as the permanent and official center of the Pan-American movement. While the Union has no authority over the actions of its members, it serves an indispensable function by providing the organizational basis of Pan-Americanism and now serves as the secretariat of the Organization of American

States. It has charge of the arrangements for the large number of special inter-American conferences in the United States. Through the medium of its publications, its large library, its widespread extension work, its promotion of Latin-American music, and in many other ways, the Pan American Union is a major force in the spread of a better understanding among all the peoples of the Americas. To great numbers of Americans who have visited Washington, a tour of its attractive building has served as a practical introduction to Pan-Americanism and the beginning of a real interest in the other peoples of the continent.

The position of the Pan American Union in the Inter-American system was considerably strengthened by the Act of Chapultepec, of 1945, and by the Charter of the Organization of American States adopted at the Bogotá Conference in 1948. Its status has been dignified by the assignment to its Council of full-time representatives of each member republic with ambassadorial rank. For the first time in its history, Latin Americans held the position of Director General. Three special organs of the Union are provided for: an Inter-American Economic and Social Council, an Inter-American Council of Jurists, and an Inter-American Cultural Council. The occasional Councils of Foreign Ministers are now recognized as an integral part of the superior organization. A large number of special organizations serve as the subsidiary institutional machinery of Pan-Americanism. These include, among many others, the Pan American Sanitary Bureau and the Pan American Institute of Geography and History, with headquarters in Mexico City. By the terms of the Inter-American Charter of 1948, the Pan American Union is declared to be a "regional agency within the United Nations."

Since the Washington meeting of 1889, and particularly since the beginning of the century, Pan-American conferences have generally been held at five-year intervals. Among issues discussed at the meetings have been the use of arbitration and conciliation procedures in the settlement of international disputes; problems of hemispheric defense; the formulation of codes of public and private international law pertinent to inter-American relationships; the right of intervention by one country in the affairs of another; measures for the promotion of common economic interests; the relaxing of restrictions on travel; the standardization of commercial minutiae; and more recently, questions related to the Cold War and the challenge of Communism to the established order, including the alienation of Cuba from the Inter-American community.

Progress in the attainment of these objectives has sometimes been slow, but none the less real and, in some fields, very substantial. Deliberations have not always been harmonious and sometimes the atmosphere has been strained, but disagreements have been tempered by Latin-American good manners and by the usual restraint of the United States in pushing its views before the assembly. Latent factors of discord have had to be overcome, vested interests considered, and fears and prejudices conciliated. When pertinent to the discussions, potential sources of dissension have generally been handled with skill and with consideration for the feelings and dignity of the interested parties. Besides the consciousness of the overwhelming material superiority of the United States, at one period or another the following factors have, directly or indirectly, affected the tone and course of the discussions: the divided attitude of the Americas in the First World War; American interventions in the Caribbean countries; the counter-attraction of European attachments and interests; agitation by the intransigent Yankeephobes of Latin America; fear of the larger states of being outvoted by a coalition of the smaller republics; the counter-appeal of the larger sphere of the United Nations; the question of the defaulted Latin-American debts to American bond-holders; Latin-American policies toward foreign investments; disputes between Latin-American states, as between Paraguay and Bolivia; the special character of Mexican-American relations; and the grievances of individual countries against the United States.

During recent years, the tendency has been to remove many non-political matters from the sphere of action of the International Conferences of American States, and to make them the subject of special inter-American parleys. Probably the most important of such meetings was the Inter-American Conference for the Maintenance of Peace, held in Buenos Aires in 1936 at the suggestion of President Roosevelt, who opened the conference in person. On that occasion he declared: "In our determination to live at peace among ourselves, we in the Americas make it at the same time clear that we stand shoulder to shoulder in our final determinations that others who, driven by war madness or land hunger might seek to commit acts of aggression against us, will find a hemisphere wholly prepared to consult together for our mutual safety and our mutual good." Some of the most successful of these special meetings have been the Pan-American Scientific Congresses, the first of which met in Washington in 1915, and the most recent of which was held in the same place in 1940. Among the great variety of such non-political conferences have been congresses on child welfare, medicine, law, roads, education, art, music, history, bibliography, police, the civil status of women, Indian affairs, public finance, and student life.

The United States has generally been represented at the International Conferences of American States by the secretary of state. Some of these, notably Elihu Root, Charles Evans Hughes, and Cordell Hull, have contributed much to the success of the conferences. President Coolidge briefly addressed the Havana Conference of 1928. President Hoover was genuinely interested in promoting a better understanding between the United States and Latin America, and made a tour of the continent before his inauguration. However, he inherited the full force of the ill will and suspicion generated by our system of protectorates. He had, moreover, to deal with a Latin America which was then suffering from severe economic dislocations consequent on the world-wide economic crisis and torn by internal political upheavals. More than any other factor, the policies of President Franklin D. Roosevelt were responsible for the extraordinary improvement in inter-American relations during his administration. In his first inaugural address, the President enunciated the policy of the "good neighbor," which was to guide this country's relations with Latin America. Received at first with caution by the Latin-American nations, the "good neighbor" policy produced a remarkable change in their attitude toward the United States, as words were translated into deeds. This country rapidly wiped the slate clean of the remaining protectorates, accepted the full equality of the Latin-American states regardless of size or resources, definitely renounced the right of intervention, and agreed to joint responsibility for carrying out the principle of the Monroe Doctrine.

In spite of all the obstacles with which it has had to contend, the recognition of its obvious limitations and of the possibility of retrogression, and the cynicism of the advocates of a more "realistic" policy, Pan-Americanism, now generally referred to as "the Inter-American system," has in this generation become a powerful force for the peace and solidarity of the hemisphere. After all, nowhere else in the world is there such a concerted structure of international understanding and good will based on the principle of live and let live.

Cultural Relations with Latin America. Until recently Americans and Latin Americans knew remarkably little about each other. Except for businessmen and government officials, there was little north and south travel in the hemisphere, for the established lines of travel ran from both North and South America to Europe. Newspapers contributed little to the mutual enlightenment of the two peoples. Consequently, there existed not only a great deal of ignorance about one another's ways, but a disturbing mass of prejudice and misconception, which was a bar to a much-needed understanding. Idiosyncrasies and deviations from each other's standards of international and private conduct were magnified out of all proportion to the truth. Americans tended to picture all Latin America as a land of chronic revolutions and of romantic, dilatory, and generally unreliable habits; Latin Americans looked on this country as a materialistic colossus, whose people were given to disorderly living. Little had been done to popularize the work of a small group of American scholars and writers who were familiar with the civilization of Latin America and its historical background. At five-year intervals, as the time for another Pan-American Conference came around, the press built up a rather sensational and superficial interest in Latin America, after which the public attention promptly relapsed into customary indifference.

The first official recognition of the need to correct this condition was represented by the Convention for the Promotion of Inter-American Cultural Relations, which was agreed to at the Inter-American Conference for the Maintenance of Peace, in December, 1936. This, with seven other important conventions signed at the Buenos Aires conference, was ratified by the United States Senate in June of the following year, and has since served as a formal basis for the efforts of the American government in that field.

To implement this new departure in governmental activities, the secretary of state issued a Departmental Order on July 27, 1938, establishing the Division of Cultural Relations within that department. as provided for in an act of Congress of the previous month.

The State Department's Division of Cultural Relations began its operations with a small, but select, staff and a salary budget of only $33,800. Since the funds at its disposal were entirely incommensurate with the magnitude of its task, it had to rely very largely on the cooperation of private organizations. Its objectives were expressed in the following words of the official order of July, 1938:

> "The Division will have general charge of official international activities of this Department with respect to cultural relations, embracing the exchange of professors, teachers, and students; cooperation in the field of music, art, literature, and other intellectual and cultural attainments; the foundation and distribution of libraries of representative works of the United States and suitable translations thereof; the preparations for and management of the participation by this Government in international expositions in this field; supervision of participation by this Government in international radio broadcasts; encouragement of a closer relationship between unofficial organizations of this and of foreign governments engaged in cultural and intellectual activities; and, generally, the dissemination abroad of the representative intellectual and cultural works of the United States and the improvement and broadening of the scope of our cultural relations with other countries."

Though the scope of the Division's work was intended to be worldwide, its limited facilities and international circumstances of peculiar urgency forced it to confine most of its activities to the Latin-American field. In this endeavor, its work was later aided by allocations from other funds voted by Congress for similar purposes.

Long-range considerations guided the Division in its program of activities, which was planned on a commendably sound basis. It studiously avoided the techniques of high-power propaganda which would defeat its own purpose and confined its activities to the objective promotion of a better intelligence between the peoples of the Americas. These aims involved a wide variety of undertakings, which were sponsored by the Division and carried out either on its own initiative or with the cooperation of universities, foundations such as the Carnegie, Guggenheim, and Rockefeller, associations for cultural ends, and public-spirited business concerns and citizens' groups.

In May, 1938, an Inter-Departmental Committee on Cooperation with the American Republics was set up in Washington, for the purpose of drafting "a concrete program designed to render closer and more effective the relationship between the Government and people of the United States and our neighbors in the twenty republics in the south." This committee was composed of representatives of thirteen branches of the federal government, each of which was concerned with some phase of inter-American relations, but whose efforts in that sphere had hitherto been uncoordinated. The Inter-Departmental Committee submitted to the President a comprehensive report, containing detailed recommendations for specific projects to be undertaken by the various departments associated in the joint enterprise. Its recommendations were of both an economic and cultural nature and their application would have involved total expenditures of approximately $1,000,000. Though Congress did not immediately make available the funds necessary for carrying out the projects recommended, some of the 74 proposals made were later put into effect by the various departments. Known as the Inter-Departmental Committee on Scientific and Cultural Cooperation, this council of twelve federal agencies steadily enlarged the scope of its Inter-American activities and increased its annual expenditures to over $4,000,000. Appropriations were made by Congress to the State Department, which allocated the funds to the various departments. Much of the State Department's embryonic cultural relations program was financed by its share of the total appropriation. Other agencies carried on a wide range of projects in Latin America, that included agricultural experiment stations, surveys of mineral resources, and studies in child welfare, meteorology, anthropology, census methods, and other lines.

A new element was introduced into our relations with Latin America by the creation, in August, 1940, of the office of the Coordinator of Commercial and Cultural Relations. Its title was later changed to that of the Office of Inter-American Affairs. Until his appointment as assistant secretary of state, this organization, which was originally a part of the National Defense Advisory Commission, was headed by Nelson Rockefeller. It had a two-fold purpose—to aid the Latin-American republics to adjust their economies to the impact of the European war on their foreign trade, with its disturbances to their industrial life and public finances; and to mold into a concerted program the diversified activities and potentialities of public and private agencies for promoting a cultural *rapprochement* between the peoples of the Americas. The latter objective was founded on the assumption that a more intelligent and sympathetic understanding of each other's racial culture was necessary to the maintenance of continental solidarity. In other words, its purpose was to bring about the greater moral unity of the Americas, then threatened by the propaganda of the totalitarian states of Europe.

The Coordinator's Office originally had the responsibility for integrating all the official and private efforts in the Inter-American field into a well-balanced program. This not only involved the continuance of activities already under way, but their extension in many cases and the establishment of new lines of endeavor. This required the gathering together of a number of hitherto disassociated enterprises, through the medium of special liaison arrangements with the Departments of State, Agriculture, and Commerce, the Export-Import Bank, and other agencies of the Federal Government which had a special interest in Latin-American relations. Similarly, in its dealings with private groups, the Coordinator's Office worked through special committees, which were headed by business or professional men drawn from the particular field and familiar with its problems and methods. The cultural and informational phase of its dual functions was directed by a special section, whose work was further broken down along specific lines, such as press and radio, motion pictures, literature and publications, art, music, and education.

As the war progressed, the Office of Inter-American Affairs expanded its range of activities. It set up its own offices in the Latin-American capitals and enlisted the cooperation of local American businessmen whom it organized into Coordination Committees. It also had regional offices in many cities in the United States. In the economic field, it promoted the work of national Committees on Inter-American Development. It established in several countries a program for the promotion of additional food production, and undertook many other special projects of an economic nature, such as raising the working standards of the railway trainmen of Mexico. In the cultural and informational field, it published an attractive war propaganda magazine in Spanish and Portuguese; provided fellowships for the technical training of Latin Americans in the United States; conducted an Inter-American meteorological school at Medellín, Colombia; founded American libraries in Mexico, Nicaragua, and Uruguay, and "cultural institutes" in many cities, where English was taught to adults of the country and a wide variety of other cultural activities carried on; arranged for the translation of many American books into Spanish and Portuguese and of Spanish-American and Brazilian books into English; brought hundreds of Latin-American newspapermen, teachers, physicians, and other specialists to the United States for observation of methods used in their respective professions; and sent many American musicians, writers, scholars, educators, and technicians on special missions or assignments to Latin America. In the United States, it actively promoted the teaching of Spanish and Portuguese and did much to educate the American people to a better knowledge and understanding of Latin America and Latin Americans by means of lectures and publications.

It created two special corporations to administer its educational, public health, and food promotion programs. These subsidiary organizations made contractual arrangements with the various governments for setting up cooperative services in those fields. The Inter-American Educational Foundation occupied itself particularly with the improvement of rural and vocational education. The public-health branch of the other corporation carried out a wide diversity of projects, ranging from local mosquito control in malarial areas to a comprehensive sanitary plan for the Amazon valley. One of the most successful achievements of the food promotion branch of the Office of Inter-American Affairs was its efforts to raise the level of subsistence food farming in Paraguay. The three special corporations were eventually combined as the Institute of Inter-American Affairs, and at the end of the war this agency was made a dependency of the Department of State. Its legal existence was further prolonged by congressional action in 1947. In 1946 the cultural and informational activities of the Office of Inter-American Affairs were taken over by the State Department Office of International Information and Cultural Affairs. It had been one of the most unorthodox agencies in American political history. As an emergency organization forced to deal with difficult "spot" problems, it inevitably committed many mistakes, but in the sum total of its achievements it justified its creation and its expenditures.

During the period 1942–47, the cultural relations program of the State Department underwent radical changes. Due to congressional opposition, the word "cultural" was for a time eliminated from its organizational terminology. The functions of the original Division of Cultural Relations, which was later known as the Division of Science, Education and Art, were finally absorbed into the larger Office of International Information and Cultural Affairs. This bureau of the State Department represented a consolidation of the basic Division with two war-time agencies, the Office of Inter-American Affairs and the Office of War Information, resulting in a new emphasis on the use of "fast" informational media such as radio, press, and motion pictures, and the extension of the field of operations to other areas outside Latin America.

Reorganization of the machinery of the dual program brought about corresponding changes in the special field service. The State Department had been able to attract into this service on a temporary basis as cultural attachés to the various Latin-American embassies men of high caliber, like Herschel Brickell, the literary critic, George Vaillant, the anthropologist, and Hayward Keniston, head of the University of Michigan's Department of Romance Languages. When the Department took over the informational functions of the Office of Inter-American Affairs the members of the field staff of the joint program became known by the anomalous title of "public affairs officers." In 1946–47, as a result of congressional hostility to certain features of the informational program, both the departmental and field organizations were stripped to skeleton proportions. However, funds were later provided for the enlargement of this particular branch of the State Department's service. Eventually most of its informational and cultural activities were transferred to the jurisdiction of a new entity of the federal government known as the United States Information Agency, only supervision of the "exchange of persons" remaining with the original Department.

One of the oldest phases of the movement for the improvement of inter-American cultural relations is the interchange of professors and students. The official phase of the movement is the joint responsibility of the State Department, the USIA, the United States Office of Education, and a private organization known as the Institute of International Education. The system of Guggenheim Fellowships has enabled a number of Latin-American scholars, as well as artists and others, to prosecute special studies in the United States. Other organizations which have provided fellowships for study and research in this country, generally in specialized fields, are the Rockefeller Foundation, the Kellogg Foundation, and the Commonwealth Fund. Under the various official programs, hundreds of Latin Americans have been brought to the United States for work as research internes or trainees in agriculture, public administration, commercial aviation, statistical methods, and other fields. By the terms of the so-called Buenos Aires Convention and of other arrangements between the United States and certain Latin-American governments, this country undertook the interchange of both professors and students. The voluntary efforts of universities, foundations, and industrial corporations in offering scholarships have extended the scope of this movement. Though for many years there has been a considerable enrollment of Latin-American students in American schools of agriculture, engineering, medicine, and dentistry, most of these have been sons of well-to-do families, who could bear the high costs of education in the United States. The system of government and private fellowships, including the travel and maintenance grants offered by the State Department, have made these opportunities available to many worthy students at a lower economic level. In the academic year 1960–61, there were almost 10,000 Latin-American students in the United States, or about 18 percent of all foreign students in this country at that time. The largest number came from Mexico and Venezuela and the smallest contingent (49) from Paraguay. The 1,540 American students in Mexico represented the only considerable enrollment in any foreign country.

Another important phase of the State Department's work in the field of cultural interchange is its system of travel grants to Latin-American scholars, writers, educators, and leaders in other lines of endeavor. The recipients of these grants are enabled to spend from three to six months or longer in travel and observation in the United States. Some of the foremost figures in the cultural and professional life of Latin America have visited this country under the auspices of the State Department. Some of these, like the Brazilian novelist, Erico Verissimo, later contributed to a wider knowledge of the United States in their own countries by books describing their impressions of this country.

The expansion of the government phase of the interchange program has been made possible by the authority of the Smith-Mundt Act of Congress and by provisions for financing the so-called Fulbright fellowships. Many groups of journalists and legislators have also visited the United States as "grantees" of the State Department. While the movement in the opposite direction has not been heavy, it has enabled many American educators to teach in Latin-American universities or to carry on research in their particular field of study.

One of the most useful forces in promoting a better understanding of the United States in Latin America is the series of cultural institutes or "bi-national centers." Official participation in this program was originally on the initiative of the Office of Inter-American Affairs, but for several years it has been a responsibility of the United States Information Agency. These organizations are generally the result of the joint action of local American citizens and nationals of the country. In addition to providing an attractive meeting place for the two peoples, they give instruction in the English language to many thousands of persons, and offer concerts, lectures, art exhibits, motion picture showings, and the facilities of large and representative libraries of American books.

An important, though so far little popularized, phase of American intellectual interest in Latin America has been the extensive research work carried on by American historical scholars, usually in conjunction with university instruction in Latin-American history. Important centers of Latin-American historical studies in the United States have been the University of California, Harvard University, the University of Texas, and the University of North Carolina. Among outstanding scholars in the field are the names of Bolton, Chapman, C. H. Haring, Hubert Herring, Martin, Means, Rippy, J. A. and W. S. Robertson, and Wilgus. For many years, this large group has used the *Hispanic-American Historical Review* as an organ for the publication of their findings. Their influence in the professional historical circles of Latin America has been profound. Several hundred colleges and universities now offer courses in Latin-American history, geography, government, and literature. Special centers of Latin-American regional studies are established in many schools notably at Stanford, University of Wisconsin, New York University, University of Texas, and University of Florida. An interesting innovation in this field of studies is the American Institute for Foreign Trade, located near Phoenix, Arizona, which trains students for work in Latin America. Numerous institutes have been conducted under the auspices of various universities, at which scholars gathered to discuss their common problems, and Regional Councils of Latin-American Studies hold annual meetings for the exchange of information and views. The Hispanic Foundation of the Library of Congress and the Committee on Latin-American Studies of the American Council of Learned Societies have actively promoted this extraordinary development of research and instruction in Latin-American history, including the sponsoring of the annual *Handbook of Latin-American Studies*. The results of this enormous volume of historical studies are gradually being reflected in the teaching of history in American high schools, thereby reaching a much larger number of persons than is possible through higher institutions of learning. Until recently, high-school history courses in this country almost entirely ignored the history of Latin America, and while the average graduate was familiar with Nebuchadnezzar and the worthies of Plutarch, he had seldom heard of Bolívar or Juárez.

Similarly fruitful has been the work of American anthropologists and archaeologists in the Latin-American field. Extensive research has been carried on by a large company of distinguished scholars, which includes Morley, Spinden, and others, of the Carnegie Institution of Washington, in the Mayan areas of Mexico and Central America; Redfield, of Chicago; the late Krober, of California; Wagley, of Columbia; the late George Vaillant, of Pennsylvania; and Steward, Metraux, and Stirling, of the Smithsonian Institution's Bureau of Ethnology. The culmination of the rich literature which has resulted from their field and historical researches is the monumental *Handbook of South-American Indians*, a symposium prepared by American and Latin-American scholars and published by the Smithsonian Institution as a project of the United States Congress.

In addition to the work of the historians, geographers, and anthropologists, much research and writing of a high and objective order has been done in the United States on other areas in Latin-American studies. There has also been much useful popularization of information about the Latin-American countries in the books of the more responsible travel writers, and in the publications of the Foreign Policy Association and similar organizations.

The regular American news services have long been established in Latin America, where they supply a large number of local newspapers with news from the United States and provide a cable service for papers in this country. Coverage of Latin-American news in the American press is fitful and generally tends to play up sensational incidents and developments, such as political disturbances. A few newspapers, like *The New York Times* and the *Christian Science Monitor*, maintain regular correspondents in Latin America and accordingly provide their readers with a much better balanced and more consistent coverage of Latin-American events. On the other hand, the traveling correspondents who have frequently been sent on tours of Latin America by important dailies and newspaper chains have often lacked the background of knowledge, the familiarity with the languages of the countries, and the time necessary for accurate and dependable reporting. The leading news weeklies generally comment on the more important developments in Latin America, and even issue special airmail editions for distribution in Latin America.

In spite of postal, customs, and censorship difficulties the circulation of American magazines in Latin America is increasing. The more popular magazines are widely offered for sale at newsstands, and American technical and professional periodicals have a growing popularity among engineers, architects, physicians, and businessmen. Two long-established magazines published in Spanish in this country are *Ingeniería Internacional*, an engineering monthly, and *La Hacienda*, a high-class magazine devoted to agriculture. The most successful magazine publishing venture of this kind is represented by the Spanish and Portuguese editions of *Reader's Digest*.

During the past ten years there has been a large increase in the sale of American books in Latin America. Part of this development is due to a new curiosity among Latin Americans about the United States. The growing number of Latin Americans who read English has contributed to the sale of American books. So has the publicity given to them by traveling book exhibits and by the new American libraries in Latin America. Inability to obtain books from France and other European countries during World War II promoted a greater interest in American books. At the same time American publishers became aware of the possibilities of the Latin-American market, particularly after a group of five of them had made an extended personal survey of the field in 1942. The export trade in books was better organized and many new retail outlets were opened by new American bookstores in Latin-

American cities. The principal obstacle to the further development of the business is the high original cost of American books, to which must be added fees for consular invoices, transportation charges, import duties, expenses for customs clearance, an allowance for currency fluctuation, and sometimes an exaggerated markup by the retail bookseller. Meanwhile, the increase of paperback editions has done much to promote the sale of American books.

Even more than the sale of American books in the original, their translation into Spanish and Portuguese has increased. These translations include works of fiction, technology, science, economics, history, and nearly every other category of literature. Up to 1944 almost 400 American books had been translated into Portuguese in Brazil, and many more have been translated in the publishing centers of Spanish America. Among favorite contemporary authors of the United States whose works have been translated, are John Dos Passos, Ernest Hemingway, Sinclair Lewis, Archibald MacLeish, and John Steinbeck.

For all practical purposes, Latin-American books in their original languages are unobtainable in all but two or three cities of the United States. On the other hand, the works of Latin-American authors are extensively used in the teaching of Spanish or Portuguese, usually in anthologies or collections of short stories published by American textbook companies. Also, a growing number of works of both fiction and non-fiction have been translated into English and published in the United States. Among the more serious Latin-American writers whose works are now available in English translation are Machado de Assis (1830-1909), considered by many to be the foremost novelist of Brazil, two highly successful contemporary Brazilian novelists, Erico Verissimo and Jorge Amado, Germán Arciniegas, the Colombian historian, Euclydes da Cunha, author of the Brazilian classic *Os Sertões*, Gilberto Freyre, the Brazilian sociologist, Fernando Ortiz, Cuban social historian, and Domingo Faustino Sarmiento, Argentine statesman and educator of the last century. There remain many books which might well find a receptive reading public in this country and which would raise the imaginative and intellectual product of Latin-American culture in the esteem of the American people.

During the First World War, the teaching of Spanish in American high schools and colleges made considerable headway at the expense of the teaching of German. Since then, the movement has made great progress, as our interest in Latin America has been intensified, until today instruction in the Spanish language is provided in practically all large high schools and in virtually every university and college. Much of this teaching is in the hands of Puerto Ricans or native Spanish Americans. At the same time, the regular foreign-language schools have enormously increased the enrollment in their Spanish classes. Though much of this study of Spanish is not carried very far, great numbers of Americans now have a fair speaking knowledge of Spanish. In fact, some speak it more fluently and correctly than many American businessmen who have spent years in Spanish America.

On the other hand, little attention has been paid in this country to the study of Portuguese, the language of Brazil and so of nearly 40 percent of all Latin Americans. A surprising number of otherwise well-informed Americans are ignorant of the fact that Portuguese, and not Spanish, is spoken in Brazil.[5] And while Brazilians have little difficulty in understanding Spanish, they tend to resent the excessive emphasis placed on the study of that language in the United States as against their own tongue.

Until recently, the volume of travel between the United States and South America has been small. In 1961, it was estimated that American tourists spent only about $45,000,000 in South American travel, or about 2 percent of all tourist expenditures for that year. The only South American government which made a serious effort to attract American tourists was that of Colombia, with the result that in that year tourism was the third dollar earner for the country after coffee and petroleum. The low level of tourist travel in South America has largely been due to the more familiar counterattractions of European travel and to the greater cost and time involved in a South American tour.

The first of these factors has influenced even more the travel habits of South Americans, many of whom were accustomed to make frequent voyages to Europe. Though sailing time between New York or New Orleans and the leading ports of South America has been shortened somewhat, it is still two or three times that of the faster ships

[5] The president of one of the largest American universities once remarked to the writer that Spanish was the language of Brazil. He has also heard a former United States senator address a group in Rio de Janeiro, which included several Brazilians, on the beauty of the Spanish language.

between the Atlantic seaboard and the ports of western Europe. As a rule passage rates have been relatively high. During the Second World War, ships in the Latin-American trade were taken over by the government and many of them used as transports. Due to sinkings by enemy submarines, the time required for reconditioning, and the high cost of replacement of lost tonnage, it was long after the war before shipping accommodations again reached the level of 1938. In the meantime New Orleans had become an increasingly important terminal of inter-American shipping, and the West Coast ports of the United States had lost much ground in that area.

The airlines have absorbed an ever larger amount of passenger business between the United States and South America, as they have extended their services and reduced their flying time and fares. All transportation media have endeavored to take advantage of the widespread urge to travel that followed the war. A few of the Latin-American countries publicize their tourist attractions in the United States through their national tourist offices. Also, hotel and other facilities for the accommodation and entertainment of travelers in the larger cities of South America compare favorably with those in any part of the world.

In the Caribbean area, conditions have been much more favorable to inter-American travel. Distances are short, and the time and money required for travel are correspondingly smaller. Official requirements for the entry of tourists have been greatly simplified. For many years, there has been a heavy current of American travel to Mexico, and the opening of through highways between the border and Mexico City has resulted in a large increase of American tourist travel.

The American public has long been familiar with the popular music of Latin America. Sentimental Mexican songs like *La Paloma*, *La Golondrina*, *Estrellita*, and *Allá en el Rancho Grande* have had a wide popularity. Equally familiar are the heavy tango measures of Argentina, the lively sambas of Brazil, and the half-African *sones* of Cuba. Latin-American concert musicians like the Brazilian pianist Guiomar Novaes, and soprano, Bidú Sayão, have made tours of the United States.

Il Guarany, the best-known opera of Brazil's classical composer, Carlos Gomes, has been produced in this country, and the works of some of the leading contemporary composers of Latin America, such as Ernesto Lecuona of Cuba, Carlos Chávez of Mexico, and Heitor Villa-Lobos of Brazil, have been featured by concert orchestras in the United States.

Latin Americans have had little familiarity with or interest in the music of the United States, and that largely with such special forms as Negro spirituals, military marches, local ballads, the compositions of Gershwin, and our less violent and cacophonous dance rhythms. American symphony orchestras, whose work is widely known through the short-wave radio and long-playing records, are greatly admired in Latin America, and orchestras under the direction of Leopold Stokowski, Arturo Toscanini, and Leonard Bernstein have made successful concert tours of South America. Much has been done to bring about a wider mutual appreciation of each other's music by the leading musicologists of the hemisphere, like the Americans, Carleton Sprague Smith, Charles Seeger, Gilbert Chase, and Vanett Lawlor (in the field of school music); the Uruguayan, Francisco Curt Lange; and the Chilean, Domingo Santa Cruz.

Until the present generation, Latin-American art was virtually unknown in the United States, and Latin America still knows as little about the art of the United States as it does of the art of Australia or South Africa. The Hispanic Society of America had sponsored an exhibit of the paintings of Cesáreo Bernaldo de Quirós, the Argentine painter who re-created on his flaming canvases the life of the pampas during the last century, but this and other efforts of the Society aroused little interest in the American public in the larger phases of Latin-American art.

Widespread popular interest in the art of the southern republics was first awakened by the work of the great Mexican muralists, Diego Rivera and José Clemente Orozco, and was largely confined to the remarkable development of popular art in that country. No other foreign painter of this age is probably so well known in the United States as is Rivera, some of whose murals are found in the Detroit Institute of Arts and the San Francisco Stock Exchange. Also, thousands of Americans have seen Rivera's enormous murals of the Revolution in the Ministry of Education in Mexico City and at other places in his native country. Examples of Orozco's more somber frescoes are seen in the Rand School for Social Research, in New York City, and in the library of Dartmouth College. Another Mexican artist, of a different genre, who has had a wide reputation in the United States, is the illustrator, Miguel Covarrubias. In May, 1940, the Museum of Modern Art, of New York, held "the largest exhibition of Mexican art ever held anywhere (including Mexico itself)." A collection of nearly 6,000 items, representing every period of Mexico's art from pre-Conquest days to the present, was displayed for several months. The exhibition received wide publicity and did much to increase still further the familiarity of the American public with Mexico's extraordinary artistic life.

Although American motion pictures have long been a major factor in the entertainment of Latin Americans, they have not always been a force for inter-American good will nor have they always placed American ways in a favorable light before the peoples of Latin America. The Mexican government protested several times against the representation of Mexican characters in certain Hollywood productions. However, there has been a great improvement in this respect and care is now taken to avoid offending the racial sensibilities of Mexicans and other Latin Americans. No American pictures have enjoyed greater popularity in Latin America than the animated cartoons of Walt Disney, particularly those for which local characters were created and in which the phantasy was laid in local scenes. A few movies made in Brazil, like *Os Cangaceiros* and *Black Orpheus*, have attracted attention in the United States.

In our dealings with the Latin Americans, we are too prone to minimize the wide psychological barriers that divide our peoples.[6]

---

[6] James Bryce, an unusually well-informed and sympathetic critic of the United States, commented thus: "There is little intellectual affinity, and still less temperamental sympathy. The South Americans do not feel that the name 'American' involves any closer community or cooperation with the great Teutonic republic of the north than it does with any other people or peoples. They are just as much a race or group of peoples standing by themselves as if the lands they occupy had been that entirely detached continent out in the southern seas, supposed to lie far away from other continents, to which the name of Amerigo Vespucci was first applied." *South America: Observations and Impressions* (New York: The Macmillan Co., 1914). T. R. Ybarra, in his breezy book, *America Faces South* (New York: Dodd, Mead, 1939), after reiterating "You can't court a continent," says: "North is North and South is South, and never the twain shall meet. Latin Americans are essentially different from North Americans. They just don't have the same mentality" (p. 118). Ybarra was a well-known American newspaper correspondent and author, the son of a Venezuelan father of distinguished family and a New England mother.

At a gathering of intelligent and well-disposed Americans and Latin Americans, both sides are certain to be on their good behavior. Since conversation is liable to be confined to pleasant generalities, the temptation is to ignore those differences which each displays among his own kind and when freed from the demands of universal good manners. Conditioned by their separate pasts and environments, these differences involve basic habits of thought and action, as well as of language. For example, the very rules of ordinary social intercourse are sometimes far apart.

There are certain "sore spots" in our permanent points of contact with the Latin-American peoples. One is the Canal Zone. Except for the higher officers, who have well-defined social responsibilities, members of the armed services generally maintained an attitude of aloofness and ill-concealed disapproval toward Panamanians and other Latin Americans, whatever their social rank. This feeling is particularly strong among officers from the southern states, whose color prejudices are liable to assert themselves whenever they are stationed among the mixed populations which predominate around the shores of the Caribbean. Texas has been another "sore spot" in our Latin-American relations. While the civic and cultural leaders of that state are genuinely cooperative with the government's plans for improving our relations with Latin America, the rank and file of Texans have occasionally been slow to follow their example. A long background of friction between Texans and Mexicans, the Texan's aggressive superiority complex where Mexicans are concerned, and his discriminations against the latter in many fields, have colored the relations between the two peoples and affected the attitude of the Mexican government toward this country. Nor has the average American business community in Latin America fully availed itself of its great opportunity to strengthen the esteem in which their fellow-countrymen are held. Its members arrive too often with little or no knowledge of the language and customs of the country where they are to reside. Frequently they exert themselves too little to remedy either deficiency beyond that barely necessary to carry on the business of their employers. Outside business hours they may shut themselves off from the life of the people about them, of whose ways they are too often audibly critical. The highest compliment they can pay a native is that "He speaks our language," or "He is like one of us," and the ultimate tribute they can bestow on a whole people is to call them "the Yankees of South America." To them the measure of government has too often been the extent to which it "sits on the lid" and keeps the people "in their place." As a rule, American wives in Latin America are even less interested in the country where their husbands' work has brought them and tend to remain strangers to the deeper currents of its national life.[7] The exceptions are some of the "old timers," who have lived long in the country, formed close and satisfying ties with many of its inhabitants, and accepted with graciousness and tolerance the peculiar demands of its way of life. These men are the backbone of the average American community, the mainstay of long-range American business, and its liaison of good will with the native population and its leaders.

By their conduct American travelers in Latin America bear a considerable responsibility for inter-American cooperation. Their public manners have improved greatly since the alcoholized tourist junkets of prohibition days scandalized native onlookers in those hospitable oases. In general, they make a much better impression on the nationals of the various countries than did our tourists of the 1920s. They are less boisterous and more serious of purpose, less given to bragging of the things they left behind them, and less critical of the inevitable inconveniences of foreign travel. And even when the Latin American is prone to be critical of the United States as a nation, he is disposed to consider the individual American on his personal merits.

A factor generaly ignored until recently in inter-American relationships was our failure to utilize Puerto Rico as a natural bond with the Latin-American peoples, since as a psychological bridge between the Americas, it might have done much to interpret the one to the other. Latin Americans tended to consider its status as "colonial" and our early efforts to superimpose American cultural elements on its Spanish intellectual heritage were not lost on their Spanish-speaking cousins in the southern republics. However, the remarkable progress made by the island during the Muñóz Marin regime has raised it greatly in the esteem of other Latin Americans.

Withal, the chances for the progressive strengthening of the

[7] A few years ago, a group of American wives residing in Lima, Peru, prepared a helpful booklet for the guidance of other American women who might be faced with the problem of adjustment to life in Peru. See Mrs. Ples Harper and others, *The Peruvian Way* (Lima, 1943).

inter-American system are very favorable. The peoples of the Americas contrast the customary peace of their continent with the Old World's millennial hates and recurrent descents into savagery, and they find it good. If the Latin Americans still guard some mental reservations as to the permanence of the new inter-American dispensation, it is only a natural skepticism. Like the reconciliation of long-estranged friends or the tardy coming-together of neighbors who have held aloof from each other, only time and an open mind can bring full confidence.

Economic Relations. The outbreak of the Second World War quickly produced a crisis in the economic affairs of the Latin-American republics. The first result was the closing of the important German market for their exports. As the war was intensified and the sphere of German conquest and military alliances was extended over the continent of Europe, the commercial situation of Latin America was progressively aggravated. By the middle of 1940, of the major European customers for its export products, only Great Britain remained. And even the normal character of British trade was materially changed under the pressure of war. Meanwhile, France, Italy, the Scandinavian and Balkan countries, Belgium, and the Netherlands were eliminated from the calculations of the Latin-American nations, both as sources of supply of manufactured goods and as outlets for their raw materials. Spain was crippled beyond early repair by the ravages of her long civil war and dragged into the political orbit of the axis powers by the government of Franco. As surpluses piled up in its warehouses, the impact on the economies of Latin America threatened to be catastrophic. The immediate prospects included a dislocation of normal industrial life, radical retrenchment of government expeditures and a corresponding curtailment of its ordinary activities, and widespread unemployment and social unrest. If continued, these conditions might menace the existing political order and create an atmosphere favorable to the infiltration of totalitarian propaganda.

The ultimate alternative, in the event of a German victory, would have been the enforced subjection of the Latin-American economy to the needs of a new and ruthless world order. It was only as the extreme political implications of a German triumph became apparent that the full measure of their precarious situation dawned upon the Latin

Americans. In the meantime, for one motive or another, many had been disposed to a conciliatory attitude toward the approaches made by Germany. However, the growing revulsion toward the methods used by Germany in the conquered lands, her former ties with Communist Russia, and the strength of British resistance resulted in a change of sentiment and strengthened the desire of the peoples for a self-contained continental economy that would free them from the dangerous dependence on their trade with Europe. The problems of adjustment to new conditions were tremendous, and it was obvious that no satisfactory settlement of their difficulties would be possible without the cooperation of the United States.

This country had viewed with grave concern the possibilities in the Latin-American situation. It was evident that if events were allowed to take their course, the bulk of Latin America might gravitate by default into the economic—and political—sphere of Germany, with disastrous consequences to our economic interests and military security. Fortunately for the success of any joint action to meet the problem, the Latin-American nations were favorably disposed in advance toward the United States by the results of the "good neighbor" policy. But it was also apparent that the financial burden of any plan for dealing with the situation would fall on the United States. And the United States would probably have to write off much of the cost of such a program to political expediency.

The most urgent phase of the problem, and, in fact, the crux of the whole dilemma of the Latin republics was the disposal of their mounting surpluses of agricultural and mineral products. The first move on the part of the United States government was a proposal for an inter-American marketing cartel, which would handle the sale of the exportable surpluses of Latin America. An international corporation, in which all the countries of the Americas were to be partners, would become responsible for buying up and marketing the unsold reserves of coffee, cotton, sugar, cacao, wheat, and other staples which normally found buyers in Europe. For obvious reasons, it would be incumbent on the United States to underwrite this gigantic project. However, this plan for the adoption of the totalitarian device of controlled trade found few supporters and the suggestion was soon dropped. In line with the Pan American convention which provided for consultation of the governments on matters affecting their vital interests, a series of special conferences were held during the second half of 1940. These included the Inter-American Conference of Foreign Ministers, at Havana in July; the Pan American Neutrality Conference, at Panama in September; the Pan American Conference of Treasury Officials, at Guatemala City in November; and the meeting of the Inter-American Financial and Economic Advisory Committee, held in Washington during the same month. These conferences considered policies and measures for common action on hemisphere defense and the preservation of neutrality and laid down some general principles for commercial and financial cooperation; but their specific accomplishments in the latter field were meager. The formalities having been complied with and the gestures made, the initiative still remained with the United States.

The program which was eventually followed by the United States involved (1) the extension of dollar credits to the Latin-American countries, (2) the increase of American purchases of Latin-American goods, and (3) aid and advice to the Latin-American republics in modernizing their economies and developing new sources of wealth. In view of the large volume of defaulted American loans to the governments of Latin America, there was considerable opposition to permitting those countries to contract further obligations whose repayment might be problematical. However, in the transactions which followed, strictly financial considerations were waived in favor of the larger exigencies of continental solidarity and defense precipitated by the world emergency. Up to September, 1940, the Export-Import Bank had authorized loans to Latin-American governments to a total of $143,000,000. A special $2,000,000,000 currency stabilization fund was also drawn on for the relief of the southern republics with depressed or fluctuating exchanges. With the authorization of Congress, the Reconstruction Finance Corporation then placed an additional $500,000,000 at the disposal of the Export-Import Bank for similar purposes. Among the objectives for which it was anticipated the credits might be utilized were the stabilization of national currencies and the loosening of government exchange controls, which had so hampered American export trade, the purchase of military equipment and other materials, such as railroad supplies, and the establishment of new industries. Wherever possible, it was designed that American industry should also profit from the use of these credits.

Of the earlier credits, Argentina had received an advance of $20,000,000 from the stabilization fund. This amount was liquidated by a $60,000,000 credit in December, 1940. At the same time, Uruguay received a credit of $7,500,000, which wiped out a previous short-term advance of $4,000,000. In 1939, a credit of $19,200,000 was extended to Brazil, largely for the purpose of putting her exchange situation in order. During 1940, Brazil received a further credit of $20,000,000, which was earmarked for use in the construction of a steel plant. The Export-Import Bank also made a loan of $2,300,000 to help the Brazilian government finance the purchase of fourteen ships from the Moore-McCormack Lines for the Lóide Brasileiro Steamship Company. Early in 1941, an additional credit of $25,000,000 was placed at the disposal of Brazil. In November, 1939, the United States loaned Paraguay $4,000,000, of which $3,500,000 was to be used for road construction and the balance for stimulating trade between the two countries. A credit of $4,600,000 was advanced to Costa Rica for the construction of the local section of the Pan American Highway. In December, 1940, Peru was authorized to draw $10,000,000 through its Central Reserve Bank. By a deal with Simón Patiño and other Bolivian tin interests, the United States government agreed to finance the construction of a tin smelter in this country, which would demand an increase in the output of tin ores in Bolivia. As the program of financial "cooperation" progressed, negotiations for the allocation of credits to other countries proceeded between the Export-Import Bank and the interested governments.

The creation of a number of special corporations for the purchase of essential materials as a phase of the defense program facilitated the acquisition of large stores of Latin-American products. For example, through the Metals Reserve Company, one of the subsidiaries of the Reconstruction Finance Corporation, contracts were made during the latter part of 1940 for the purchase of 300,000 tons of Chilean nitrate and 100,000 tons of copper from Chile, Cuba, and Mexico.

Through the medium of its Bureau of Foreign Agricultural Relations, the Department of Agriculture assumed an important role in the government's Inter-American program. It was particularly interested in encouraging the establishment of new agricultural industries or in furthering the development of existing industries to which the United States could assure a larger market. To this end, it sent survey parties to Latin America and loaned members of its technical staff to Latin-American governments for special purposes. Its Soil Conservation Service advised the Venezuelan government on methods of preventing soil erosion and on the diversification of its agriculture and another special mission studied the possibilities of growing the cork oak in Colombia. One of the largest projects undertaken by the Department of Agriculture was the despatch of four survey parties to investigate the suitability of the American tropics for the development of rubber plantations, a field which had been thoroughly covered by similar surveys in 1923–24.

American geologists, representing the Geological Survey and the Bureau of Mines, aided some of the countries in the investigation of their mineral resources. Experts from the Bureau of Public Roads advised several governments on the development of their highway programs, and furnished special technical aid in connection with plans for the completion of the Pan American Highway. Specialists loaned by the United States Tariff Commission served as advisers to the Paraguayan government in the improvement of its customs service. In the meantime, earlier arrangements for American naval and military missions to instruct the armed forces of some of the republics, such as Brazil and Peru, were expanded to include other countries and also the aviation arm of their services.

But all of these wartime emergency measures were not sufficient to stave off the ever-growing and ever-worsening economic problems and social evils which continued in the postwar era to plague the whole of the southern hemisphere: rampant inflation, food and housing shortages, military takeovers of governments, growing illiteracy, poverty, and disease, a very high rate of population growth, lower per capita production and earnings, much corruption in high places, widespread tax evasion—all aided and abetted by the usual Communist tactics of infiltration and subversion.

There arose, too, after the close of the war, a period of discontent and disillusionment when the Marshall Plan for the recovery of Europe was put into effect, and Latin America was seemingly forgotten by the United States. Latin Americans noted that the Roosevelt-Truman "good neighbor" policy was allowed to lapse after 1952 and that economic aid to Latin America became a mere trickle in comparison to the billions in military and economic aid which flowed to Europe

and Asia. Latin Americans found it hard to understand how Communist countries such as Yugoslavia, recent enemy countries such as
Germany and Italy, and certain Asian countries of dubious neutrality,
could claim so large a share of American foreign aid, while they—
next-door neighbors and wartime allies—were treated and neglected
(in their view) as unwanted stepchildren.

An almost about-face in the American attitude took place shortly
after the Democrats regained control of the federal government in
1961, and President Kennedy launched his proposal for an Alliance
for Progress, a plan which calls for joint expenditures in Latin America of $20,000,000,000 over a ten-year period and which it was hoped
—and still is hoped—will enable the Latin Americans to do for themselves what the Europeans did under the Marshall Plan.

Under the agreements reached at the meeting of the Organization of American States at Punta del Este early in 1962, each of the
19 Latin-American signatories—Cuba was left out—agreed to formulate
an over-all development plan for its participation in the program of
the Alliance, including in such plan its own proposal for basic
measures to be taken such as land reform and effective taxation.

Concrete results to the end of 1962 have proven disappointing.
Most of the countries have not even formalized their plans, and the
funds so far allocated by the United States under the Alliance for
Progress have amounted to very little.

It is generally recognized now that this time lag is due primarily
to the fact that the Alianza para el Progresso, or, in Portuguese, Ali-
ança para o Progresso, has not caught the popular imagination. Latin
Americans, the people at large, think it is "just another aid program."
They are not yet aware that it is reform and revolution—their own
revolution—not a United States-imposed one.

At the October, 1962 meeting of the O.A.S. much of the discussion was devoted to concrete plans for firing the imagination of the
masses and getting them involved in the national reform efforts. National "Tell the People" committees have been organized in every
country, for it is now belatedly discovered that until the man on the
street understands its true meaning and purpose, the Alliance for
Progress cannot progress.

In the meantime, some Latin-American surpluses (such as coffee
in Brazil) continue to pile up, and some exportables (such as iron ore,

again in Brazil) remain in the ground. The recent advent of the European Common Market and rising competition in the production of raw materials, particularly in Africa, are intensifying Latin America's already critical economic problems.

The possibilities of increasing American imports from Latin America, while capable of considerable expansion, are definitely limited. With the exception of coffee, bananas, cacao, rubber, quebracho extract, tin, and manganese, the principal Latin-American staples are competitive with similar products of the United States. And while the United States regularly imports large quantities of sugar, tobacco, hides and skins, wool, linseed and other vegetable-oil materials, copper, iron ore, and petroleum, the influence of American producers would quickly make itself felt through Congress, if efforts were made by the government to stimulate any marked increase in imports from Latin America. The total potentialities from augmented imports of such lines as fibers, Argentine and Chilean wines, off-season fruits, hardwoods, alpaca wool, yerba maté, carnauba wax, special processed foodstuffs, and manufactured specialties and novelties for the department-store trade, are not to be ignored in any plan to increase our Latin-American purchases. However, this field does not promise a considerable volume of trade, and is limited not only by the capacity of the American market, but by production difficulties in certain lines. Meanwhile, the great agricultural staples, corn, cotton, wheat, and meats, can have little, if any, place in any program for the expansion of our import trade with Latin America.

Part VII

THE WAY OF LIFE

Cultural Characteristics

WHEN THEY meet, Latin Americans, like the rest of us, talk of
the weather and the state of their health and of their families.
They do not talk about cars and golf scores and the price of Scotch and
a good many other things about which Americans make conversation.
When American and Latin American meet, even with the best of
good will on both sides, they are liable to feel ill at ease after the exchange of the customary greetings that "break the ice" between
strangers all over the world. For this ice is very thick. It is made of the
results of many centuries of divergent history.

Down the road of time behind one is a tough yeomanry that forced
the medieval nobles to respect its rights; the expansion of the human
spirit in the time of Elizabeth; a strong merchant class that came to
set the practical tone of England; a government that, good or bad in
itself, interfered but little with the individual's freedom of thought
or action; Puritanism and a medley of evangelical sects, from which
the citizen could choose his religion as freely as he chose his occupation or his politics; the town meeting and the public school; the
boisterous equality of the frontier and the enforced cooperation of

the pioneers; and the spreading over the wide, rich land of a resourceful breed of small independent farmers. Behind the other is the memory
of a hard and niggardly homeland, that forced men within themselves
for the spiritual comfort and satisfactions which their physical world
denied them; centuries of Arab domination, that left deep marks on
custom; ages of warfare against Carthage and Rome, Islam and one
another, the rest of Europe and the native peoples of the Indies; a
Church all powerful over men's minds; an absolute and arrogant
monarchy, that crushed the movement of the Castilian cities for self-
government and thereafter ruled with sublime indifference to the
governed, whether in the peninsula or the Americas; wide distances between communities and classes; the violence of civil wars and dictator-
presidents ruling in the name of democracy; then the new promise
and freedom of pampa and highland and forest struggling for expression against all this heritage of denial and repression. It is no wonder
that Americans and Latin Americans, when thrown together, do not
gravitate naturally into one another's company, but seek out their own
kind.

The common Hispanic background permeates the way of life of
all the Latin-American peoples, even in countries which, like Mexico
and Peru, are ethnically more Indian than Spanish.[1] The only exception is Haiti. The basic pattern itself may vary according to the predominance of Castilian or Gallego, Basque or Andalusian, Estrema-
duran or Portuguese in the original population, but its unity is never
lost. The Latin Americans have borrowed from France, to give clarity
and lightness and plan to their own brooding and disordered genius.
They have borrowed from the United States, to implement their
dreams of democracy and the development of their natural resources.
Italians have influenced the life of Argentina. But these influences have

[1] On the Spanish character and viewpoint on life, see Salvador de Madariaga,
Englishmen, Frenchmen, Spaniards: an Essay in Comparative Psychology (Ox-
ford: Oxford University Press, 1931); Miguel de Unamuno, *The Tragic Sense
of Life* (New York: The Macmillan Co., 1921), and *Essays and Soliloquies* (New
York: Alfred A. Knopf, 1925); José Ortega y Gasset, *The Modern Theme* (New
York: W. W. Norton, 1933), and *The Revolt of the Masses* (New York: W. W.
Norton, 1932); and Angel Ganivet, *Idearium Español* (2d ed., Madrid, 1905).
There are acute observations on the Spanish character in Havelock Ellis, *The Soul
of Spain* (Boston: Houghton, Mifflin, 1926); and W. Somerset Maugham, *Don
Fernando: or Variations on Some Spanish Themes* (New York: Doubleday,
Doran, 1935).

been superficial. They have affected only the externals of Latin-American civilization—the outward appearance and forms and techniques. The substance remains stubbornly Hispanic, tempered in some of the republics by the blood or the proximity of Indian or Negro, as slaves influenced the speech and habits of the whites in our own South.

Above all, the Latin American is an individualist. Though gregarious, he is averse to merging his personality in any group or to sacrificing its claims to any mass demands. Unlike the American, who is the world's greatest joiner and liable to feel lonely and ineffectual when unorganized, he is not a good organization man, and his conferences and committees would probably be the despair of an American chairman. He does not take kindly to the restraints of teamwork and resents the discipline of the group. Among his interests, his family comes first—and the family is only a prolongation of the individual. The state, an impersonal and collective concept, comes last. He is seldom civic-minded and is little concerned with the public welfare, except as himself and his family are affected or as the public interest is dramatized.

This individualism accounts for many of the peculiarities of politics in Latin America. It explains much of the personalism in government—the persistence of one-man rule in spite of democratic forms. To have meaning to the average Latin American, the state should be embodied in the person of a man, who is resolute and self-confident, virile and intelligent—one who is *muy hombre* or "very much man." If he has a fine personal appearance, his hold on his people is all the stronger. Real issues may arise and divide the citizenry, but, except in a few of the republics, they tend to become personified in the strong man who champions them.

The ceremoniousness and formality with which the Latin American wraps much of his life are an expression of his individualism. It magnifies his ego and protects it from the ravages of familiarity and from rough handling by more free-and-easy peoples like ourselves. His language, so sonorous and lordly, lends itself to ceremony, and his natural fluency of speech falls almost effortlessly into oratorical eloquence or improvised lyricism. He is a master of hyperbole, of the ornate super-word, of the florid tribute. In comparison, we are a tongue-tied race.

The Latin American is at ease in an atmosphere of pomp and

circumstance. His public receptions and processions are lavish and impressive—and very serious. The private citizen is as punctilious and observant of the amenities in his exercise of personal etiquette and hospitality. Though the gracious attentions which a Latin-American host showers upon him may embarrass an American, accustomed to the casualness with which his own people do such things, they are the natural expression of a tradition which has its roots deep in Hispanic custom. The hospitality that characterizes high and low alike is as warm as that of the medieval Arab. As a regular ceremonial, a Latin American raises his hat to a friend or acquaintance, or, if some time has elapsed since their last meeting, they indulge in the familiar *abrazo* or embrace. A slap on the back or a knuckle-cracking "shake-hand" would decidedly not be in form on such an occasion or at an introduction.

In few respects are Americans and Latin Americans so far apart as in the latter's superior sense of personal dignity. At its best, it explains some of the finest aspects of Latin-American society. It also accounts for the common social prejudice among well-bred Latin Americans against working with one's hands. For example, young engineering students take readily enough to the textbook part of their education, but are liable to balk at putting on overalls and getting down among the machines. They would not wish to have their friends see them dressed like peons and smeared with grease, for class pride also enters into this aversion to manual labor. *Gente decente*, or "decent people," refuse to carry packages in public, and toting a tray in a cafeteria would put a *caballero* outside the social pale, as well as detract from his own self-respect. Husbands do not "help around the house" or perform any of the tasks which ordinarily fall to menials or to their womenfolk. One could not imagine a Latin American above the worker class pushing a perambulator or holding a baby within sight of his equals. The Latin-American gentleman would not remove his coat or loosen his collar in a public place, even if he were sweltering and no women were about. He dislikes practical jokes, clowning and slapstick humor, and seldom indulges in belly-shaking laughter. It is not that he has no sense of humor, for he has, though it often has a sardonic tinge, but he reserves its display for his family, or for an inner circle of friends in whose company he does not have to be on his guard. He seldom unbends at his amusements. He dances gravely, drinks decorously and moderately, and takes part in no sports where he might get "mussed up." He would never consent to put on the silly hats given out as "favors" at American night clubs or otherwise "cut up" in public places. At his first "crossing of the Line," the rowdy Neptune ceremony on shipboard is liable to be a torture to him. He would be lost at a Shriners' convention, a college class reunion, or any of the other forms of sophomoric saturnalia common to the American male in his moments of release.

The Latin American in public life is seldom guilty of the lapses from dignity to which his northern confrere sometimes resorts in order to show the voters that he is only one of them. If he indulged in such vaudeville tricks, his audience would laugh *at* him, not *with* him, and his political career would be brought to a sudden and ignominious close.

American and Latin American differ widely in their attitude toward business. At least until the depression, Americans were taught that business and hard work were ends in themselves, regardless of their material rewards. We considered our time so valuable that we displayed signs on our desks warning callers to "be brief." It was important that we appear busy and aggressive, even when it did not matter a great deal. We made fetishes of "efficiency" and "service." We created "sciences" of management and salesmanship that had the scientific standing of astrology or legerdemain. The Latin American has never experienced this exaltation of business or work for its own sake. In lieu of any other way, business is only a means of making a living, of providing the wherewithal for the enjoyment of leisure, which is the real purpose of existence. *El negocio* is not a thing to make a cult of, like *la patria* or *el amor*. Whole peoples think so little of it that they will knock off at midday for a three-hour siesta. To an American businessman, a nap at high noon would be the crowning indignity to the capitalistic system. The Latin-American businessman will leave his office in the middle of the morning, to spend an hour over coffee in a near-by café. He may take back with him a good piece of business, won more pleasantly than if it had been transacted at his desk. And if a friend comes to town, he must be entertained, for hospitality comes before business. Some of the business habits of the Latin American are liable to be highly exasperating to the American new-comer who tries to sell him something. High-power salesmanship makes little impression on him. He may prefer to string out his negotiations for days before he is ready to come to the point. In the face of this passive resistance, which is so disconcerting to the novice, the old-timer in the country realizes that it is useless to fret and adapts himself to the custom of the land. He finds it better for the nerves—and the order book. Of course, business habits have changed in places like Buenos Aires and São Paulo, where the tempo of affairs is much faster than in the cities where the native element dominates the business communities.

While bluntness and frankness are considered desirable qualities among us, the Latin American prefers to gloss over unpleasant facts which are liable to offend or hurt others. He is a master of the *beau geste*, the apt phrase, the fine courtesy, and urbanity, that smoothes the way of social intercourse. He is generally sincere, but when he is not, his intent may be not to hurt rather than wilfully to deceive. Sometimes he promises more than he can deliver; occasionally it is more than he may have a mind to yield. When occasion arises, he is expert at concealing his real thoughts. A realist at heart, he is honest with his inner self; he is skilled at deceiving others with grace and finesse. His capitals are no places for amateur diplomats.

Latin America is man's country. At least to all outward appearances, the male is still head of the family, and family solidarity is much stronger than it is with us. Family life is surrounded with a reserve that is unheard of in this country, where Americans are in the habit of keeping open house for a wide circle of acquaintances and the neighbors may run in without as much as knocking at the door. The Latin American admits only a few intimates to his home, and a foreigner who has done business with a native for many years may never have met his wife or seen the inside of his home. The Latin-American man is not favorably impressed with the freedom and restlessness of American women and is confident that his own women are much happier. He would be horrified at the thought of his women folk drinking in public places, being seen at a night club, wearing slacks outside the home, or telling an off-color story in mixed company. He heartily disapproves of the liberties which Americans permit their daughters. Latin Americans make much of young children, who often appear spoiled, but family discipline asserts itself early and sons and daughters seldom show disrespect to their parents.

The Latin American is disposed to be cynical about politics and objects to his wife or daughters participating in public affairs, except in the field of social welfare, in which women are everywhere exerting an increasing influence. He is aware that his women may wield a great deal of influence over him and that his own political views are liable to be a consensus of family opinions, of which he is the spokesman. Moreover, he probably consults his wife's advice on business matters more frequently and freely than does the American husband.

The customary relationships between the sexes is one of the most difficult phases of Latin-American life for Americans to understand. There is a tendency to sympathize with the lot of the Latin-American wife and, conversely, to criticize the attitude of the Latin-American man toward women. In respect to the normal satisfactions of life, the Latin-American wife is certainly not a proper subject for disparaging comparisons. After all, one observes remarkably few unhappy faces or indications of neurotic complexes among Latin-American women. In the more progressive republics, the range of their outside interests is increasing, but so far without visible effects on the traditional status of marriage. Like the Mohammedan whose position is measured by the number of his wives, the much-publicized philanderings of Latin-American men are largely an expression of their natural urge for the wider assertion of their individuality. Their propriety is scarcely the subject of local controversy, and even Latin-American statesmen do not suffer in the public esteem from the revelations of their far-flung intimacies. In fact, the result may be just the opposite.

Social Organization

Latin-American society is still essentially aristocratic. Wherever the aristocratic system is well entrenched, it rests on the familiar combination of tradition, land ownership, political control, white blood, and the support of the Church. Its natural base is a large dependent class of landless and illiterate peasants, whose instincts and habits from colonial times have led them to look to a chief—or *patrón*—for direction and the means of subsistence. This feudal order has been seen in its most typical form in Chile, and it is still fairly intact in Peru. The wealthy *estancieros* held the balance in Argentine politics until recently. In Brazil, aristocracy is a local phenomenon. The Paulista *fazendeiros,* a group of Mineiro proprietors, and some old families in the northern coastal states exert great influence in regional affairs. But Brazilian aristocracy lacks many of the characteristics of its counterparts in the west-coast countries, whose large Indian and mestizo populations constitute a logical source of retainers for a baronial system of society. The old Brazilian aristocracy's position was largely founded on slavery, and with the emancipation of the slaves its natural economic basis was removed. The principal differences between the various national manifestations of the aristocratic principle are in the degree of the control which the members of this class exercise over the economic and social life of their countries. Otherwise, whether they have their town houses on the Avenida Alvear in Buenos Aires, the Avenida Paulista in São Paulo, or in the Vedado at Havana, their life is marked by the same features of their class anywhere—the same luxurious and cosmopolitan tastes, the same gracious manners and lavish hospitality within their own world, and the same conservative class consciousness, tempered often by genuine paternalism toward their dependents.

A number of factors have operated to break down the traditional position of the Latin-American aristocracies, which were largely based on agriculture. The progress of industrialization has raised up a new aristocracy founded on wealth and sometimes predominantly foreign in its composition. As in Buenos Aires and São Paulo, its members are liable to include Italians, Germans, Syrians, and Jews, besides a sprinkling of other peoples. The same process has created a large class of factory and transport workers, who form a natural nucleus of democratic, and sometimes radical, leanings. Other forces working against the perpetuation of the old aristocratic order are the spread of popular education; the rise of a middle class whose ties are closer with the new industrial regime than with the landed aristocracy; the infiltration of liberalizing influences from abroad; and the failure of the aristocrats to maintain their leadership, either because of the slackening of their own moral fiber, the economic backwardness of the system they represent, or the prevalence of absenteeism, which separates them from their natural followers. Also, occasional dictators have worked to ruin the power and prestige of the national aristocracy. The Paraguayan aristocrats never recovered from the blows dealt them by Francia. The leading families of Argentina suffered much from the despotism of Rosas. The long dictatorship of Gómez, by depriving them of political

influence, by systematically harassing those whose loyalty was doubtful, and by overshadowing them as the first landlord of the country,
reduced the Venezuelan aristocrats to virtual impotence. In Mexico
and Chile important social movements have vitally affected the status
of the old landed aristocracies. The Mexican upper class has been
stripped of its lands and of its social and political leadership. While it
has been on the defensive at times, the politically astute Chilean
aristocracy still maintains a strong position in state and society.

The lower classes of Latin America are naturally made up of
many elements, whose only common social denominator may be their
relative poverty. For this purpose, the bulk of the forest Indians can
be considered outside the economic and social order; on the other hand,
in spite of their inclinations to the contrary, the sedentary Indians of
the west-coast countries from Mexico to Chile are an important factor
in the local economies. These Indians may be divided into those who
have maintained a communal status and those who are wage earners
or tenants on the properties of the dominant class of the country.
Throughout most of Latin America, the latter group is preponderantly
made up of mixed breeds whose status as agricultural and mining laborers may range from outright peonage to complete freedom of movement. The lower category of small independent farmers also belong to
this group of society. Typical of this class are the Cuban *guajiro*, the
Chilean *roto*, and the Brazilian *caboclo*.

The buying power of its members is very small, as is that of the
town laborers in the more backward districts. In some parts of Latin
America, a single aspirin tablet may be sold, and a box of matches or
package of cigarettes broken by the storekeeper. Purchases of manufactures consist largely of cotton piece goods, such as unbleached
muslin, blue overalls in Mexico, the sandals known as *alpargatas* or
huaraches, machetes and hoes, and kerosene. In certain localities, a
small portable Singer sewing machine may frequently be found in the
native huts. When one of these people has a windfall of a few pesos or
sells some produce, he may buy a bottle of cheap perfume, a bar of
scented soap, a can of talcum powder, or a piece of rayon cloth for
his woman, or a cheap watch for himself. Failure to consider these
conditions is responsible for the tendency of foreigners to overestimate
the present market of those countries for imported merchandise.

As a rule, this population of agricultural laborers and of workers in the mines and forests is illiterate and suffers from defective nourishment and unhygienic living habits. Hookworm is common and takes a heavy toll of vitality. They generally lack a knowledge of the relation between cause and effect in disease, as between mosquitoes and malaria, bare feet and hookworm, and dirt and blood infections.[2] Though the birth rate is high, so also is that of infant mortality. While the staple foods vary greatly from one country to another, the mainstays of diet among this class are beans, rice, corn, manioc, potatoes, yams, jerked beef, and the fruits of the locality. Diet generally lacks needed variety, even where soil and climate are favorable and land is available. Habit is a strong factor here, as in the universal addiction of the Mexican peasantry to the often leathery and indigestible *tortilla*. Though the housing of agricultural laborers is generally lacking in elementary comforts and conveniences, it is often remarkably well adapted to climatic conditions and skillfully utilizes local materials, such as palm thatch, split-palm trunks, beaten earth, and sun-dried blocks or adobe.

In spite of their uniform poverty, the members of this class are usually generous with their small wherewithal. They share the courtesy and hospitality common to their social superiors, and are kindly and responsive to considerate treatment. When affronted or under the influence of strong liquor, they are sometimes given to brawls or to individual acts of violence. In these matters local customs and na- a Paraguayan and a Guatemalan countryman to similar provocation or tional characteristics vary a great deal. For example, the reaction of the same set of circumstances may be very different, and a typical mob is liable to behave very differently in various countries.

In the countries with a numerous Indian population or in which, like Chile and Paraguay, the Indians have been largely absorbed by long and widespread miscegenation, the body of urban workers largely consists of mestizos. In countries where the Negro element is important, as in Cuba, Venezuela, and Brazil, mulatto workers hold a similar position. However, in places like São Paulo, Pôrto Alegre, Montevideo,

[2] Once, while traveling across a fine valley in Bolivia, which had been largely abandoned because of the prevalence of malaria, the writer asked one of the remaining inhabitants why the people of the valley were all suffering from an advanced stage of the disease. The answer was: "Because they sleep with their windows open."

and the Argentine cities, the bulk of this class is composed of white workers, either native or foreign. In Havana, the Spaniard is also an important labor element.

Living and general social conditions vary as widely among urban workers as their racial composition and their geographical location. If they are generally backward according to American standards, after all, industrialization is comparatively recent and much naturally remains to be done toward a more equitable adjustment of the position of labor, as also for the improvement of industrial and management methods. In the larger metropolitan centers, like Buenos Aires and Rio de Janeiro, the range of occupations is very wide and specialized skills are correspondingly common among factory workers and in many other fields of activity, such as electrical utilities, machine shops, and printing establishments. Though there is a normal spread between wages for skilled and unskilled labor, the level is still low, and the ratio of direct labor costs to total costs of production, even in Argentine manufacturing, still averages considerably lower than in the United States. However, wages paid in local currencies have little meaning when translated into dollars, especially when applied to the purchase of locally produced foodstuffs and certain lines of consumer goods manufactured in the country. Due to high import duties and to a faulty system of distribution that clings to antiquated pricing policies, most imported manufactures are beyond the reach of this class. The introduction of American "five-and-dime" stores in Havana, where they are known as "*el tencén*," has done something to meet the problem of the low-paid urban worker, as has the establishment in Brazil of a chain of American stores, which feature low-priced articles. Housing is frequently an acute problem for the members of this class. Facilities for financing low-rent housing are lacking outside the governments, the construction industry is overcautious and conservative in its methods, except where large well-financed projects are involved, and any building venture has to be preceded by costly legal and other requirements. As a result, there is a chronic housing shortage in this field. Some of the large industrial companies, like the principal mining and plantation companies in Latin America, also provide housing facilities for their employees, which are usually superior to the homes from which most of them come. In most respects, whatever the disadvantages of their present situation, the urban workers are in a much better position to improve their lot than are the more isolated and inert rural workers. In certain occupations, their organization has proceeded far, and they are also the special objects of a growing mass of social legislation. Schools are usually available to their children in the more progressive countries, and public medical services are often provided for their health needs.

One of the most significant social trends in Latin America is the rising influence of the mestizo class. This large group, which is variously known by such local names as *cholos* in the Andean countries and *ladinos* in Central America, formerly had an economic status only superior to that of the Indian, whose blood flowed in its veins. However, the mestizo usually lacks the Indian's inertia and fatalism, and is, moreover, unimpeded by the class prejudices which often hinder members of the upper classes from taking advantage of opportunities for material advancement. He is often enterprising and resourceful and is generally ambitious to improve his economic situation. The Bolivian tin magnate, Simón Patiño, was an example of the possibilities of this class in the industrial field. The mestizos dominate the political life of Mexico, and have given several presidents to the republic, including Porfirio Díaz and Lázaro Cárdenas. Throughout the west-coast countries, this assertive element will have to be increasingly reckoned with in both politics and business.

Though it has been steadily growing in both numbers and influence, the middle class in Latin America still holds no such place in national life as it does in the United States. The more advanced economically the country is, the stronger is the position of this intermediate group. It is important in Argentina, Chile, Uruguay, and southern Brazil; it is unimportant in Bolivia, Paraguay, and most of Central America. In these latter countries, aristocracy is largely relative, and is based on economic and political *power*, rather than on wealth. In respect to means, the average Paraguayan "aristocrat" would rate with the middle class of Buenos Aires or Montevideo. The middle class is made up of professional men, white-collar employees of the government, merchants, except the small shopkeepers, higher employees of the large business houses, and the medium group of independent farmers. While incomes of the salaried members of the group are comparatively low according to American standards, this class represents a very considerable volume of buying power. Its cultural level is generally high and its living standards have attained a fair degree of comfort, if not of luxury.

Social Movements and Legislation. Up to the time of the First World War, the traditional relationship of employer and employee had changed little. Agriculture and mining still dominated the national economies, and particularly in the former the relationship was a personal one. In their essentials, labor conditions had progressed remarkably little since colonial times. The native labor elements had given little thought to the organized improvement of their status. For the most part, governments were opposed to the organization of labor and public opinion was apathetic or hostile. Incipient labor movements in some of the South American republics had so far made little headway against the inertia of the mass of laborers and official suspicion. However, in Mexico, the train of events which followed the overthrow of the Díaz regime had prepared the ground for an aggressive and thoroughgoing campaign on behalf of the interests of national labor.

The progressive industrialization of much of Latin America during the past twenty-five years has given a strong impetus to the labor movement. It has been responsible for the creation of a large body of urban workers, who are subject to impersonal management, and are, therefore, free from the old personal tie between *patrón* and employee. Many of these workers are foreign immigrants, already familiar with the techniques of trade-union organization. Not only were there now large concentrations of increasingly class-conscious workers in the new industrial centers, but in the survival of old working conditions they had a ready-made set of grievances at hand. More specifically, the movement was favored by the rising—or uncertain—cost of living, which resulted from a combination of high protective tariffs, exchange fluctuations, housing shortages, and the violent ups and downs of export markets, with their repercussions on national prosperity.

In spite of these favoring conditions, the growth of the organized-labor movement was slow and uneven. In the River Plate countries, it was at first in the hands of anarchist and syndicalist groups from Italy and the east-coast cities of Spain. The foreign origin of this phase of the movement and its direct action methods further discredited the whole movement in the eyes of the governing classes and retarded its sound development. Later, Communism was to exert a still wider influence. Efforts of these foreign elements to organize the agricultural workers of South America in order to strike at the power of the landed aristocracy had little result. Again, it was only in Mexico that any success was had in organizing rural labor, and there the movement was frankly national in its origin and direction. In general, throughout Latin America the groups which responded most readily to attempts at organization were the dock and transport laborers, electrical utility employees, and mine workers.

Though there was much talk of solidarity among all the workers of the continent, the labor movement has generally followed national lines. Even the effort of foreign organizations to give unity to the movement has had few results. Efforts of the American Federation of Labor and the C.I.O. to form alliances with large segments of organized labor in Latin America have had little practical effect. Under the leadership of the famous Vicente Lombardo Toledano, Mexican labor unions have endeavored to bring about concerted action on important issues by labor organizations of all the republics. While the prestige of the Mexican leader is strong in international labor circles, the principal force for the unity of at least the radical elements in Latin-American labor has been Communism.

A number of special factors have impeded the progress of the labor movement in Latin America. It has suffered from a confusion of doctrines and objectives. Its leaders have often spoken a jargon beyond the comprehension of their followers, who have been interested rather in more pay and shorter hours than in the dogmas of Marx and Lenin and the special refinements of the other proletarian philosophers. The leadership of the movement has generally been mediocre. In default of a national leader among their own ranks, labor groups have often accepted an outsider, perhaps a foreigner, as their leader, with the result that the local movement lost much of its spontaneity and strength. For the vitality and effectiveness of these movements depends on the degree to which they identify themselves with the life of the community and adapt their programs of action to its peculiar conditions. Otherwise, they arouse against themselves all the latent localisms and nationalisms that are so potent a force in Latin America. The strength of the Mexican labor movement has largely lain in the fact that, in spite of the theories of some of its doctrinaries, it has drawn its real inspiration from the national scene. It is the active support of the dominant National Revolutionary Party and of the government, rather than the quality of its leadership, that has accounted for whatever success the Mexican movement has had. Luís Morones, the opportunistic chief of the CROM, or *Confederación Regional de Obreros Mexicanos*, was discredited by some of his activities, and the organization which he led has since lost its primacy to the newer body known as the CTM, or *Confederación de Trabajadores Mexicanos*.

In spite of its long delay in getting under way, the labor movement has made considerable progress in Latin America. Its leaders have organized and directed it with increasing skill and the growing political power of organized labor has won important concessions and support from several governments, such as that of Chile. Among groups which are now well unionized are miners and oil workers, transport and dock workers, the skilled crafts of the building trades, and electrical utility employees. Unionization is also spreading among the service trades and in manufacturing industry. Some unions, like the longshoremen and miners, are radical in their policies and port and mining operations have often been interrupted by prolonged strikes.

Wherever there is a strong government with dictatorial leanings, the tendency has been toward strict state control of the organized labor movement, with restrictions on the right to strike and other union activities which might threaten the public order. President Machado thus neutralized the Cuban unions in the same way that he dominated the national organization of sugar producers. While President Vargas of Brazil courted the laboring elements in that country, he never permitted them to get out of hand during his dictatorship. The conservative rulers of Argentina discouraged the full development of the organized labor movement and were quick to take repressive measures whenever workers resorted to violence. The country's highly developed economy has a heavy stake in the maintenance of industrial peace and the government has generally been vigilant in holding organized labor within bounds. Though the Perón regime espoused the cause of labor and in return for its vote made substantial concessions to the urban workers, it maintained a strong control over the unions.

The Catholic Church has taken an active part in the labor movement in certain countries, particularly in those in which the Indian or mixed element is prominent. Though the Indians are impervious to the appeals of foreign organizers, they are generally responsive to the influence of the clergy and disposed to follow it in any effort to improve their working conditions. While bitterly opposed to those radical phases of the movement which derive their ideology and direction from Communism and other revolutionary parties of international scope, the Church has based its activities on the liberal policy of the Papacy, particularly as enunciated in the encyclicals *Rerum Novarum*, of Leo XIII, issued in 1891, and *Quadrigesimo Anno*, of Pius XI, issued in 1931.

Labor Legislation. The Latin-American republics have to their credit an unusual amount of advanced social and labor legislation. In certain respects, they have anticipated similar action in the United States. Sometimes, following the precept of Bismarck, this legislation has been designed to take the initiative in social reform from the hands of organized labor and to forestall inevitable pressure on the government for concessions that might embarrass its position in the state. Often, it has represented a genuine spirit of liberalism and a desire to give the laboring class a more equitable place in the life of the nation. In order to assure the greater permanency of its programs of social welfare, their basic principles have been incorporated in several of the national constitutions, as in the famous Mexican constitution of 1917. Though unequally as between countries, these constitutional provisions and legislative acts include such matters as the right of laborers to organize in unions, to bargain on a collective basis with employers, and to strike; the principle of the eight-hour day and of the minimum wage; the protection of women and children in employment; workmen's compensation; the compulsory rest day; dismissal wages; annual vacations; and company housing of employees. Attempts have been made in several countries to codify existing labor laws, with a view to simplifying their application.

In order to administer their systems of labor and social legislation, most of the republics have set up special departments in their governments, sometimes with the rank of independent ministries. Some of the governments have cooperated closely with the International Labor Office, and have adopted a varying number of its conventions of labor standards. The principal weakness of most of the Latin-American systems of labor legislation is with respect to the enforcement of their provisions. While official inspectorates are common, the inspectors are often political appointees, without a technical knowledge of their duties or of the operating conditions of the industries whose compliance with the labor laws it is their obligation to oversee. Though laxity and inefficiency are still widespread, the superior standards which prevail in Chile, Mexico, and Uruguay point the way to a general improvement in the other countries.

A review of the specific phases of labor legislation reveals some remarkable achievements in the field. For example, in the matter of the eight-hour day Latin America has led the world. It has been mandatory in Uruguay since 1915 and on public works in Chile since 1908. Among other countries, it has been compulsory for some time in all industrial and commercial occupations in Argentina, Brazil, Chile, Colombia, Cuba, Mexico, and Venezuela. Due to the influence of the Church, the observance of Sunday as a day of rest has long been common in Latin America, and the legal requirement of one rest day in seven has been established in most of the republics. The *sábado inglés,* or English half-holiday on Saturday, has also been officially designated as a period of rest in Argentina and a few other countries. Since 1928, the tendency in the more advanced countries has been to provide for annual vacations with pay for workers with a certain period of service. In some instances the privilege is restricted to workers in specific occupations, while in a few countries the requirement applies to all wage earners in industry and trade. Collective bargaining has been resorted to in Venezuela between the foreign oil companies and their employees. There is also a strong trend toward the legal enforcement of the principle of the dismissal wage. Mexico has pioneered in this field, and a number of other countries have followed her precedent in requiring an advance of wages to workers who are dismissed from employment. Minimum-wage legislation has not made the same advances as have been shown in other fields. It has so far been largely concerned with protecting agricultural laborers against abuses connected with the ancient practice of paying in kind or with the exploitation of laborers through plantation stores or commissaries. However, as information is gathered on living costs and on the financial capacity of industries, the tendency is to extend the application of minimum-wage laws to other occupational groups. Special progress has been made in this respect in Brazil and Chile through the organization of joint committees of employers and workers to determine the bases for fixing standards of pay in particular industries and regions. Nearly all the republics now have workmen's-compensation laws fixing the responsibility of employers for the indemnification of employees who are injured or contract industrial diseases in the course of their work. The provisions in the Chilean labor code are particularly noteworthy in this respect. Government regulations for the maintenance of safe and hygienic working conditions in factories, mines, and other industrial establishments are now the general rule. Child-labor laws are on the statute books of most of the republics, though they are often of limited effectiveness, due to a too-low age limit or to lax enforcement. One of the most serious obstacles to the efficacy of this kind of law is the widespread custom of European immigrants of profiting by the early employment of their children. The Latin-American countries have generally been more thoroughgoing in making special provisions for safeguarding the health and interests of employed women. Female labor is widely prohibited in certain occupations where unusual physical effort is required or unsanitary working conditions are inevitable. There are frequent restrictions on the employment of women at night, and there is a growing tendency to require the protection of women during periods of pregnancy and confinement. Specifically, these laws usually provide for the retention of their jobs during enforced absence connected with the bearing of children, and for the payment of a certain compensation during this period. The Argentine, Brazilian, and Mexican laws are particularly advanced in these respects.

The labor legislation of the Latin-American countries is colored by the prevailing nationalism. In order to protect home labor against the competition of foreign workers, stringent immigration restrictions have been put into effect by several countries which formerly received large currents of immigrants. Also, it is now the custom to fix a percentage quota to govern the ratio of foreign to national employees in all business concerns. This requirement sometimes includes technical and supervisory personnel, with the object of ensuring greater opportunity for advancement to the more ambitious and capable workers. Much of the legislation has borne heavily and designedly on the foreign-owned corporations, who have usually carried a disproportionate share of its cost. The operating costs and margin of profit of such concerns have often been ignored in the application of this legislation, with the result that continued operation has sometimes been made precarious and uncertain. The extreme labor laws of Mexico have made the successful operation of some lines of business almost out of the question. They made the dismissal of employees for any cause almost impossible, and provide for prolonged vacation periods beyond the practice of any other country in the world. They grant the right of employees to participate in the management of business without accepting any responsibility for losses contracted in its operation. They prohibit an employer from shutting down his plant even when operations have ceased to be profitable, with expropriation and employee operation as the alternative. They require the payment of wages to striking workers and prohibit an employer from entering his place of business during a strike of his employees. They set up special tribunals to hear labor disputes, in which a decision adverse to the employer is virtually a foregone conclusion. They authorize the making of retroactive wage decisions whose compliance might force the employer to liquidate his business to raise the necessary funds. However, since the Cárdenas administration, enforcement of the more extreme provisions of the Mexican labor code has been relaxed somewhat.

Social Insurance. Comprehensive systems of social insurance are in effect in several of the republics. In a few cases, they are more advanced than that of the United States, and antedated it by several years. Most of them have grown up piecemeal and without any concerted plan or effort to coordinate their parts. They have usually originated in legislation for the benefit of a special occupational group, as the Railroad Retirement Board serves exclusively the railway workers of this country. From time to time, provision has been made for other groups, each added program generally being placed under a separate administrative organization. There are independent systems for bank employees (Argentina, Bolivia, Brazil, Cuba, Uruguay), stevedores (Brazil), coffee warehousemen (Brazil), employees of commercial houses (Brazil), railway and streetcar employees (Bolivia, Colombia), maritime workers (Brazil, Chile, Cuba), and journalists (Argentina, Bolivia, Cuba). Chile, Ecuador, Panamá, Peru and Uruguay cover all commercial and industrial employees in a single system. Brazil covers these two large groups under separate laws. Coverage in Chile is particularly complete, and extends to domestic and agricultural workers, two groups excluded under the American systems. The Chilean social insurance program even includes small merchants.

In the beginning, the Latin-American systems placed their emphasis on the retirement features of social insurance. To this was generally coupled provision for the payment of benefits in the case of disability, whether employment-connected or not. As with the American system, the plans were later extended to include the payment of benefits for the survivors of insured persons. The next step in the evolution of the Latin-American programs has generally involved the inclusion of sickness and maternity insurance. The latter form of insurance provides for medical care and for the payment of cash benefits to employed women who are on leave from their work during pregnancy and after childbirth. The Latin-American countries have been slow to make provision for unemployment insurance, probably because in the present stage of their development the risk of prolonged unemployment is much less than it is in the more highly industrialized nations. Certainly, the incidence of unemployment in Latin America has never reached such proportions as it has in the United States and western Europe. However, changed conditions in countries like Argentina, Brazil, Chile, and Uruguay are gradually increasing the importance of this problem. Meanwhile, Uruguay is the only country which makes provision for the payment of benefits to unemployed workers.

There is great diversity in the plans followed in the old-age insurance systems, and in the related programs for survivors' and disability insurance. This applies to such matters as coverage, methods of financing and contribution rates, retirement age, benefit schedules, and administrative organization. Though a number of close parallels to the American system occur, the divergences are even more numerous. In practically all the systems, contributions are based on a percentage of the insured worker's income. As in our old-age and survivors' insurance program, there is usually a maximum income beyond which contributions are not assessed. In most of the systems, the rate of contribution varies from 3 to 5 percent, which is considerably higher than in the corresponding American program. For individual groups, such as bank employees, the rate ranges from one percent in

Bolivia to 8 percent in Brazil. In the special retirement system for officers of the Chilean merchant marine, the rate is 10 percent. In about half of the systems in force, employers match the contributions of their employees; in most of the other systems the employers' contributions depend on such variable factors as sales and profits. The government makes contributions in varying ratios to several of the systems. The retirement age prescribed is generally lower than in the American social security system. About half of the systems permit retirement at between 50 and 55 years; in two of the special programs retirement is optional at 45 after 25 years' service, and several provide for retirement at 60. It is to be noted that these programs are not referred to as *old-age* insurance systems, but as *retirement* systems. The Brazilian system for industrial workers does not provide for retirement at a specified age, but only for disability, that is, when the insured employee is no longer able to continue in employment for reasons of physical incapacity. The period of service required to qualify for retirement benefits varies from 15 to 30 years. In the Latin-American systems, there is nothing comparable to the liberal provision in the American law for the retirement of aged workers with only a very short period of covered employment. However, some of the systems make provision for the repayment of accumulated contributions to wage earners who leave covered employment before they have completed the necessary qualifying period.

As in the amended American law, retirement benefits are generally based on the average wage for a specified period of years. The most common base used is the average for the five years preceding retirement; in others it is the previous three years, and in only one case is the benefit computed on the average income for the entire period of employment. The scale of benefits paid usually varies from 60 percent of the average wage to the full wage at time of retirement; in other systems, the amount of benefits is determined by a variety of formulae, which take into consideration age at retirement, whether retirement is compulsory or voluntary, length of employment, and average wage.

Most of the Latin-American social insurance systems include provisions for the payment of disability benefits, though some of them limit their application to cases of disability incurred in the performance of the wage earner's regular duties. The rates of disability payments are calculated on a variety of bases, including percentage of the individual's retirement benefit or pension, average wage, and period of employment, or on a varying combination of these factors.

Survivors' benefits paid to the dependents of wage earners are directly related to the benefit rate of the insured person, as in the American system. Widows of deceased workers usually receive one-half of the base rate, and sometimes the other eligible survivors jointly receive an equal amount. Survivors entitled to receive benefits generally include the widow (or widower), sons under 18 years of age, unmarried daughters, and in some cases minor unmarried sisters and dependent parents.

A special feature of some of the systems is the provision for the payment of funeral expenses of insured persons. This is somewhat similar to the provision in the American system for the payment of lump-sum death benefits. In some instances, a flat sum is paid, and in others the amount of the payment is a multiple of the deceased person's monthly wage.

Sickness insurance is included in the social insurance systems of Brazil, Chile, Ecuador, and Peru. The plans are usually limited to the payment of cash benefits, but three of the special Brazilian programs provide for medical care and hospitalization. There is a considerable diversity as to the required period of service and the amount of contributions paid in order to qualify for the receipt of benefits or medical treatment. Chile has the most far-reaching plan of state medicine in the western hemisphere. Beneficiaries of her social insurance system may receive medical and hospital care for 26 weeks, which period may be extended to a year for those whose insured status under the system is fully established. Cash benefits are also paid during sickness, the amount depending on whether or not the insured person has dependents. For an additional contribution of 5 percent of wages, the privilege of medical and pharmaceutical care is extended to the members of the worker's family. In 1938, an elaborate program of preventive medicine was initiated in Chile for all persons covered by the social insurance system. By special arrangements, this service is made available to persons covered by a large number of provident associations.

Eight separate systems in five different countries make provision for the payment of maternity benefits. In these five countries, coverage includes all wives in the general category of commercial and industrial employees. Details of the plans vary widely, but, as a rule, the service provides for cash benefits or medical and hospital treatment, or both, for a specified time before and after childbirth.

The machinery set up to administer the various Latin-American social insurance systems differs greatly from the pattern followed in the United States. In the latter, the administration is exclusively in the hands of government agencies, either federal or state; in the former, the systems are generally administered by independent boards, composed of employees and employers. The government is usually represented in varying degrees in these special administrative bodies, and the appropriate government department exercises supervision over the work of the boards. In Chile, this department is the Ministry of Health, Welfare, and Social Assistance. Ecuador has a National Institute of Social Welfare, which supervises the two national systems of social insurance. In Peru, a similar function is fulfilled by the National Social Insurance Fund, which has an administrative council of nine members, representing the various interests concerned in the operation of the program. Uruguay's advanced social insurance system is administered by the official Retirement and Pension Institute.

Social services, some of them long established, supplement the work of the regular systems of social insurance. However, except in a very few of the republics, welfare work is backward in its methods and inadequate in its accomplishments. For example, there is almost nothing comparable to the public assistance features of the American social security program, with their provision for the needy aged and blind and dependent children, who are outside the scope of social insurance. There generally is lacking any such programs for child welfare as are administered by the Children's Bureau of the Federal Security Agency in cooperation with state governments. Yet, real progress is being made in the social welfare field. The creation of a school of social work in Santiago, Chile, in 1926, was a recognition of the need for greater attention to this phase of welfare activities. In 1933, a National Child Welfare Conference was held at Rio de Janeiro. Work relief on lines similar to those followed by the Works Progress Administration has been resorted to in a few countries in order to provide work for the unemployed on the construction of public works. Direct relief for the indigent is largely dependent on the initiative of private charities. Of these, church organizations have a long tradition of such service and perform a highly useful function in many localities. Associations of women are increasingly active in this field, and, particularly in Argentina, are an important factor in the relief of need. Government housing projects for workers in Buenos Aires, Lima, Mexico City, and other places have done much to relieve distress due to overcrowding and unsanitary living conditions in city slums.

Latin America has an unusually large number of mutual aid or beneficent societies. Sometimes, these are organized by groups of persons engaged in the same occupation, such as newspaper or bank employees; often they are established by racial or regional groups to provide certain social services for their members. Examples of the latter were the Spanish regional societies in Cuba. These organizations maintained large clubhouses, which served as social centers for their members. They also operated hospitals with regular staffs of physicians, which attended to the health needs of members. These services were supported by small monthly contributions, gifts, and the income from certain endowments. The fine institutions of the *Beneficência Portuguêsa* perform similar services for the large Portuguese communities in Brazil.

Public Health Services. The public health services of the Latin-American countries have shown remarkable improvement in this century. Much valuable aid in the form of funds or of professional advice has been given by the Pan American Sanitary Bureau, the United States Public Health Service, the Institute of Inter-American Affairs, and the International Health Board of the Rockefeller Foundation. The latter has, moreover, carried on several extensive campaigns for the extirpation of certain diseases, such as hookworm, malaria, and yellow fever. In these undertakings, it has cooperated closely with the public health departments of the countries where it has worked, as with the efficient *Saúde Pública* of Brazil. It has also done much to promote the training of physicians and nurses, bringing doctors to this country for specialized study and affording opportunity to promising medical students to complete their training in American schools and hospitals. The Brazilian public health service, or *Saúde Pública*, has an excellent record in dealing with the special problems of malaria and yellow fever. Its achievement in freeing Rio de Janeiro and Santos from the anopheles and stegomyia mosquitoes, which are the carriers of these diseases, ranks with the work of the Americans at Panama and with that of the Americans and Cubans at Havana. A special branch of its work is the *Profilaxia Rural,* or Rural Sanitary Service, which aims to improve health conditions in the thinly settled interior of Brazil. Most of the public health services of Latin America maintain general hospitals and dispensaries in the principal cities. Some of these hospitals are excellently equipped and staffed with competent physicians and surgeons. Among the foremost institutions of this kind are the group of Uruguayan national hospitals at Montevideo. This country has one of the lowest death rates of any nation in the world, due, not only to its unusually healthful climate, but also to the high quality of medical service available to its citizens. Among other examples of well-conducted public hospitals are those of the Mexican *Beneficiencia Pública,* the large Calixto García Hospital in Havana, and the similar institutions in Buenos Aires. Other factors in the public health situation are the numerous private clinics and sanatoria, church—and mission—supported hospitals, like that of Santa Catarina, in Rio de Janeiro, and the Seventh-Day Adventist hospital at La Paz, Bolivia; and the excellent hospitals of some of the large mining and plantation companies, such as those of the United Fruit Company, and those at Cerro de Pasco and Chuquicamata in South America.

Among the outstanding public health problems of Latin America are the impure water supply and inadequate sewage disposal facilities of most cities. Many public markets, including the vast San Juan de Letrán Market in Mexico City, are sources of widespread infection. Another defect in the public health services of Latin America is the general failure to provide for the needs of the rural population. Until recently few countries had made more than perfunctory efforts to deal with this important problem. However, the cooperative sanitary services set up by the Institute of Inter-American Affairs in combination with several of the national governments have been particularly concerned with raising the standards of rural health.

Revolutionary Movements. Communism made few gains in Latin America before the Second World War. Russia had diplomatic relations with very few of the republics, and sometimes bungled these, as

when the famous Mme. Kollontaý was expelled from Mexico for in-
terfering too flagrantly in Mexican affairs. In 1935, the Uruguayan
government claimed to have discovered evidence that the Soviet
Legation was being used as an agency of the Third International for
disseminating Communist propaganda in South America and particularly for carrying on agitation in Brazil. As a result, Uruguay severed
diplomatic relations for a time with the U.S.S.R. Meanwhile, except
in Chile, Communist propaganda had little to show for its efforts.

With the war, Russia initiated an active campaign to win the
favor of Latin America. Her efforts became increasingly effective
after the Soviet armies checked the Germans at Stalingrad and began
their recovery of the national territory. Latin Americans were impressed by the military power of Russia as they had previously admired the military might of Germany before the failure of Rommel's
North African campaign. Latin-American countries which had withheld recognition of Soviet Russia now welcomed her diplomatic
overtures. Under the skillful direction of Constantin Oumansky, who
was transferred from Washington to Mexico City for the purpose,
Russian diplomacy was widely successful in the northern republics of
Latin America. A strong initial position in Chile was further secured
and for several years the Communists remained an important factor in
Chilean politics. Wherever Russia made diplomatic advances, the
local Communist party showed corresponding gains in membership
and political influence. Gains were particularly large in Brazil and
Cuba, where the party's national leadership was especially able.

The general pattern of Communist activity was uniform throughout Latin America. The party's organizers capitalized on the obvious
inequities in Latin-American life and on the frequent social callousness of the conservative classes. Communist newspapers sprang up in
important cities to serve as organs of propaganda, in which they were
aided by the large mass of printed material distributed by the Soviet
diplomatic missions. Though local Communist parties claimed to be
free from outside influence and the Soviet diplomats avoided the appearance of cooperation with them, their reactions everywhere to
international events were suspiciously similar. Thus, as relations became increasingly strained between the United States and the
U.S.S.R., Latin-American Communists intensified their violent campaigns against this country and its interests in Latin America.

At the same time, Russia's obstructive tactics in the organization of the United Nations, her attempts to delay a peace settlement in Europe, and the insidious methods used to dominate the states of eastern Europe lost her—and the Communists—much of the ground which they had won in Latin America. The reaction against Russia came first in Brazil, when the Brazilian government outlawed the local Communist party and severed its diplomatic relations with the U.S.S.R. in 1948. Relations were re-established, however, in 1961 by President Jânio Quadros. Chile, under the leadership of President González Videla, followed suit by expelling the Communists from the government, breaking its relations with Russia, and boldly denouncing the Communist coup in Czechoslovakia in the Assembly of the United Nations. After the Pan American Conference in Bogotá had been interrupted by a political revolt, which Communists were accused of inciting, it passed a resolution condemning the interference of Communists in the political life of the republics. In the 1960s, the spread of *Fidelismo*, or support of the pro-Communist policies of Fidel Castro in Cuba, led to further charges of Communist interference in Latin America's internal affairs.

Two social revolutionary movements of a definite character have arisen in Latin America, but both are indigenous growths. One is the Peruvian movement known as *Aprismo*, from the initials of the *Alianza Popular Revolucionaria Americana*. APRA was founded by Raul Haya de la Torre, who has ever since remained its leader. *Aprismo* has borrowed some of the conventional precepts of Marxism, especially its emphasis on economic factors in history, but it differs from Marxism in certain fundamental respects. It accepts religion as a necessary element in any plan for the reconstruction of society, and, denying the Marxist contempt for the bourgeoisie, it declares the cooperation of the middle class to be essential to the success of its aims. However, its evident intent to reconstitute the whole social and economic order of Peru along new lines early aroused the bitter opposition of all the conservative interests in the country. In spite of long, and sometimes violent, repression by the government, its undercover strength remained strong. However, when it was admitted to full participation in the political life of the country in 1945, its leaders lacked the practical experience required to make the most of their opportunity.

The series of developments in Mexico since the fall of Porfirio

Díaz as truly constitute a social revolution as did their French and Russian counterparts. However, the Mexican Revolution lacks the clear-cut character of those movements, though its basic objectives are as well defined. In their simplest and most extreme form, these include the emancipation of an agrarian proletariat that was in a state of peonage, the redistribution of the large estates, the gradual reconstruction of the national economy on collectivist principles, the extirpation of organized religion, and a general leveling of social classes. But the Mexican Revolution defies any effort at simplification. Its progress has been too halting and confused; it has had to compromise with too many of its fundamental aims; it has had to take into consideration the basic weakness of the national economy and its dependence on outside markets; it has been unable to ignore the opinion of foreign countries, especially that of the United States; and it has suffered from the opportunism and greed of many of its leaders. In view of these circumstances, it is to be marveled at that it has achieved so much of its original purpose. With time, its methods have become more orthodox and of late the Mexican government's objectives have been primarily the economic development of the country along more conventional lines.

Education

In the past two decades, the Latin-American republics have made remarkable progress in the field of public education. The official and public consciousness of the nations has been thoroughly awakened to the heavy burden of illiteracy,[3] and to the need for better equipping their youth for the tasks of a new era in national life. Much yet re-

[3] Dependable estimates of illiteracy rates do not exist. It varies greatly from one country to another, between different sections of the same country, and between the urban and the rural population. Excluding the large cities, where educational opportunities are fairly ample, it is relatively low in Uruguay, the State of São Paulo, and the Province of Buenos Aires. The rate for all Argentina is probably at least 20 percent. It is very high in Bolivia, the Peruvian *Sierra*, Paraguay, Guatemala, Nicaragua, Honduras, Venezuela, Haiti, and parts of northern Brazil. It is possible that for Brazil as a whole the rate is over 50 percent. It probably reaches between 80 and 95 percent in large areas of some of these countries. In spite of the remarkable educational accomplishments of the present regime in Mexico, there is still a large amount of illiteracy among its population.

mains to be done, for the time has been short, the resources limited, and the point of departure so remote from the goal. But the essential steps forward have been taken, and it is unlikely that there will be backsliding from the pursuit of an objective so vital to the welfare of these peoples.

Achievement has been especially noteworthy in the field of rural education, in liberalizing the secondary-school system, and in making provision for adult education. Teachers are better trained, and, if still inadequately recompensed, somewhat better paid; budgets have been increased; the quality of textbooks and other instruction materials has been improved; large numbers of new school buildings have been built; and advisory councils of public-spirited leaders have been set up to guide the educational programs along sound and progressive lines.

There is also a strong tendency to use the public schools as instruments of the new nationalism or of the prevailing ideology of the state. This policy has been carried to great lengths in Mexico, where the public-school teachers have been widely employed to indoctrinate their communities with the principles of the Mexican Revolution and the course of study closely adapted to the official philosophy. While less extreme in its application, this trend toward the nationalization of the content of instruction is general. It is apparent in the growing emphasis placed on the teaching of national history and in efforts to acquaint the youth with the contemporary life of their country and with its social and economic possibilities. Much of the new vocational education is deliberately—and wisely—aimed at the development of the nation's special resources. In the federal republics, the central government tends to assume an increasing control over public education, not only with the idea of improving its quality, but in order to strengthen its own authority over the outlying parts of the federation. Federal subsidies, or grants-in-aid, to the states or provinces inevitably carry with them certain implications of increased power over their political life.

In line with the nationalistic policies in education are the restrictions on foreign-language schools, which sometimes resulted in their suppression. The large German colonies, in particular, abused the earlier tolerance of the republics in this respect, and tended to use their schools to preserve the language and loyalties of the younger generation against the nationalizing attraction of the native culture about them.

The Japanese in Brazil also endeavored to strengthen the natural resistance of their colonists to absorption in the Brazilian population by a system of racial schools. It is the persistent defiance of the political and cultural integrity of the nation by these institutions which led the Brazilian government to take measures for their strict control or their closing. World War II accentuated the earlier tendency of Latin-American governments to control the activities of foreign schools within their countries. These control measures might concern the language of instruction, the ratio of foreign to national teachers, instruction in the history of the country, and conformity to the official course of study and prescribed teaching standards. These restrictive regulations not only vary greatly in their content, but in the rigor with which they are enforced.

Among the large number of American schools in Latin America, some are supported by the local American community, some by mission organizations, and others by industrial concerns. Their primary purpose is to provide elementary schooling for the children of Americans resident in the country, but in many schools the enrollment of native children exceeds that of Americans. In Mexico City, American school facilities exist through the college level of instruction.

The Latin-American republics have lately begun to give much attention to the improvement of rural education. Wide areas where illiteracy was almost total now have at least rudimentary school facilities. Much has been done in this field by the cooperative educational service of the ICA or AID (Point 4). This movement not only involves the construction of school buildings in country districts but the special training of teachers and the enlistment of the necessary cooperation among parents and local officials and landowners. Following the model of Mexico, which has made special progress in this respect, the tendency is to make these schools community centers. They not only provide the local children, and perhaps their elders, with elementary instruction, but often serve to inculcate more hygienic living habits and better farming and housekeeping methods in the local population. In this connection, their opportunities for the vitalizing of rural life are very great.

Elementary education in the cities is generally much better developed than in the rural districts, and in a few cities, like Buenos Aires, it is conducted on a high plane of efficiency. In some places, the effectiveness of the urban schools suffers from a lack of suitable quarters, many schools being held in private homes, army barracks, and other buildings unadapted to the purpose. Much of this condition is due to the fact that the popular interest in public-school education has been so great that existing facilities have not been able to keep up with the rapidly growing demand for schooling.

Secondary or high-school education has hitherto been largely the privilege of the children of the better-to-do families, and has, moreover, usually been available only in the larger centers of population. It has been regarded primarily as a preparation for entrance into the university, and its plan of study and methods of instruction have been planned to that end. Private *liceos* or *colegios* have played an unusually important part in this field of education. Foreign influence, such as that of the French system of *lycées*, has been strong, and emphasis has been placed on the classical and humanistic studies. The natural facility of the Latin American for memorizing and for the acquisition of generalized knowledge has been developed in the teaching of the languages and of the theoretical side of the sciences. In recent years, as a phase of the movement for the greater democratization of the national cultures, there has been considerable pressure from organizations of workers and businessmen for a revision of the traditional curriculum along more practical lines. In spite of the opposition of the conservative elements in the educational field, the customary rigidity of the course of study has been relaxed, the system of electives has been introduced, and commercial and other vocational subjects have been included in the curriculum. Less stress is gradually being placed on the high schools as stepping stones to the university and more on their function of preparation for the immediate task of citizenship.

Much is being done to provide adults with night-school facilities, in order to enable them to overcome the handicaps of early lack of education. Argentina, Chile, Mexico, and Uruguay have been particularly active along these lines. One of the most interesting experiments in adult education was represented by the Mexican government's "Campaign Against Illiteracy" initiated in 1944, whereby children who had had the advantages of a public school education were used to teach their parents the rudiments of reading and writing.

The principal problem in connection with the public educational movement is a financial one. The taxation and budget systems are generally rudimentary and antiquated, the opposition of the moneyed classes to new levies very strong, and the taxable resources of many countries definitely limited. Moreover, the ratio of children of school age to taxpayers is excessively high. Financing of public enterprises by means of internal loans is not developed to the same degree as in the United States. The result has been that the ambitious programs adopted have sometimes proven beyond the capacity of governments to carry them out on schedule, so that readjustments in the timing of the plans have had to be made.

Costa Rica devotes a larger share of its national budget to education than any other country. Mexico spends about twice as much for its schools as for the defense establishment, and expenditures by state and local governments increase the proportion. Brazil's federal government spends only half as much for education and public welfare combined as it does for the military, while state and municipal governments generally do too little to meet the costs of public education. On the other hand, Chile's outlay for schools is higher than for defense, but in other west-coast countries the reverse is true. In backward Ecuador military expenditures are half again those of its schools, and in Peru, where elementary education levels outside Lima are low, the army and airforce receive 30 percent more of the national budget than do the country's schools. Haiti, with one of the two smallest budgets in Latin America, allocates over 40 percent more of public funds to the armed forces than it does to much-needed schools. Military and public works expenditures have generally had precedence over the needs of other branches of government, so that, when retrenchment is necessary, school budgets are liable to be curtailed.

Another obstacle to the educational programs is the opposition of certain conservative or reactionary elements to anything more than a minimum of primary schooling for the mass of the population. Some even consider the popular ability to read as an impediment to the maintenance of a sound economic and social system.

Higher education in Latin America has its roots deep in the past. The University of Mexico was founded in 1551 and the University of San Marcos, at Lima, in the same year. Other old university centers are Córdoba in Argentina, Bogotá, Santo Domingo, Salvador, Brazil, and Santiago, Chile. Among the most modern institutions of higher learning are the University of Buenos Aires, one of the world's largest institutions of higher learning, with nearly 100,000 students, the National University of Chile, and the Universities of Montevideo and São Paulo. There are also Catholic universities in several of the more important cities. The universities were formerly under control of the Church and their course of study was largely confined to such subjects as canon and civil law, logic and philosophy, and mathematics. Law is still the dominant subject in most Latin-American universities, though, like medicine, its teaching is now usually confined to a special *facultad* or department. In the new university curricula, the sciences and social studies occupy an increasingly important place, while curricula are being constantly widened and modernized by the inclusion of new subjects.

Student life in Latin-American universities is very different from that in the United States. University buildings are usually located in the older and crowded part of the city. However, as in Mexico City, Brasília, and Caracas, new "university cities" are being built in some of the Latin-American capitals. Another feature of Latin-American universities is that students and faculty representatives generally sit on their governing councils.

The scope and quality of specialized higher education have shown very considerable progress in recent years. This applies not only to instruction in the traditional subjects of the law and medicine, but in a wide variety of fields, such as engineering, dentistry, pharmacy, business management, music, the fine arts, library methods, biological research, and agriculture. Some of this instruction is given in special departments or schools of the regular universities, and much of it in independent schools devoted to a particular subject, like the large Santa Maria technical school at Valparaiso and Mackenzie University, a technical institution at São Paulo.

Religion

Political independence did not break the thread of Catholic supremacy in the religious life of Spanish and Portuguese America. However, the refusal of the Papacy to recognize the new states left the Latin-American churches without a metropolitan organization for many years, during which the influence of the Church suffered from a lack of superior guidance and discipline. The issue at stake between the Vatican and the young republics largely concerned the succession of the *real patronato*, or royal patronage, of colonial times. This was the arrangement whereby the king held the prerogative of nominating all members of the episcopal hierarchy within his dominions. The republican governments contended that the right passed to them automatically along with political sovereignty over the lands of the American Indies, a claim which the Papacy disputed.

Though matters of religious doctrine have seldom been involved, the struggle between the lay and ecclesiastical powers has occupied much of the history of the republics and has bedeviled their political life at one period or another. The principal questions which have divided Church and state have been the original issue of ecclesiastical patronage, the control of education, authority over the ceremony of marriage, the disposition of Church property, and the tolerance of dissenting sects. Sometimes, under a strongly pro-clerical regime, the state has been allied with the Church or has been its virtual servant. At other times, it has been the slave of the state, as it was under the Paraguayan dictatorships or when Rosas forcibly used it as an instrument of his tyranny over the Argentines. In the classical division between Conservatives and Liberals in early Latin-American politics the Church espoused the cause of the former party and threw the weight of its influence on its side. It feared the tendency of the Liberals to secularize national thought and the basic institutions of national life, while it counted on the Conservatives to support the traditional order of society. Whenever a Liberal president was in office, the Church might expect a program of disestablishment, state education, suppression of the regular orders, expropriation of Church property, or even more extreme measures. Among Liberal rulers who enforced anticlerical policies were Morazán of Central America, Mosquera of Colombia, Guzmán Blanco of Venezuela, and Alfaro of Ecuador. On the accession of the Conservatives to power, the anticlerical activities of their enemies were undone, and the Church restored to its privileged position in the nation. Of Conservative presidents who carried out pro-clerical programs of this kind, especially famous for their zeal were Nuñez of Colombia, Carrera of Central America, and García Moreno of Ecuador. The latter was particularly extreme in his support of the Church and turned his country into a virtual theocracy. By a concordat with the

Papacy, García Moreno renounced the right of the government to the exercise of ecclesiastical patronage, and, among other concessions to the Church, he restored its ancient monopoly of education and its control over the expression of thought by the censorship of all publications. Finally, in 1873, at his dictation, the Ecuadorean congress formally consecrated the republic to the "Sacred Heart of Jesus."

In their settlement of the religious question, the different countries have not followed a uniform pattern. In Peru, the position of the Church has remained very strong and has never been seriously challenged by an aggressive anticlerical movement. Although the Aprista party, while not hostile to the principle of religion, has been opposed to a state church, the Church enjoys the active support and cooperation of the state, which has confirmed it in the possession of its large properties, and enforced its privileged position in the field of education. The toleration of other faiths has not detracted from its favored situation in the nation, but has only spurred it to a stronger realization of its peculiar responsibilities for the spiritual welfare of the nation.

By a turn of the wheel in the long and bitter struggle between the clerical and anticlerical influences in Ecuador, the national Church finds itself in a much less favorable position than in Peru. Though disestablished, the Church has the status of a pensionary of the state. It is without political influence, its properties have been nationalized and held in trust by the government for the performance of its religious services, and it has lost its once absolute control over education.

In Colombia, the Church, which had wielded great authority over the life of the nation during the long Conservative regime, lost much of its influence outside the religious sphere since the return of the Liberals to power in 1930. The constitution of 1936 disestablished the Church and declared the secularization of public education. In the neighboring republic of Venezuela, the government has preserved its right of patronage, with its corresponding responsibility of financial support for the state Church. The practice of other cults is permitted, but instruction in the Catholic creed is mandatory in public schools.

After a long period of acrimonious controversy, Church and state in Chile established an eminently sound relationship, which has brought religious peace to the nation. A law of separation was passed in 1925 with the full approval of the Chilean hierarchy. The Church retained its properties and full control over its own schools. It became an independent entity within the state, which abandoned the important prerogative of patronage, with its implied right to interfere in the internal administration of the Church. The reasonable attitude taken by both parties to the settlement is a tribute to the basic good sense of this remarkable people. Under the disestablishment, the Church has gained in prestige and influence and nowhere else in Latin America is its position more satisfactory.

The status of the Church in Argentina is still largely defined by the constitution of 1853. Under these constitutional provisions, it occupies a somewhat anomalous middle ground between the position of a full-fledged state church and separation, such as exists in Chile. The government grants it an annual subsidy, but, beyond the rather indifferent exercise of the right of patronage, interferes little in its activities. It has lately permitted religious instruction in the public schools. The state reserves control over public education and would resent any attempt of the Church to encroach on its political sphere. The success of the practical working relationship developed under the terms of the Constitution has depended on the continued good will and moderation of both sides which was seriously disturbed by the policies of the Perón regime.

The religious settlement in Uruguay contains most of the features of the Chilean disestablishment. The Uruguayan Church is completely independent of the state and is unhampered in its educational activities, though restricted in the public celebration of its religious festivals. Church and state were also separated in Brazil without attendant bitterness or friction and to the mutual advantage of both. Like the Cubans, the Brazilians are Laodicean in their faith and little inclined to religious controversy. The Church has profited in harmony, if not in zeal, from this circumstance.

In Mexico, a conventional quarrel between Church and state ultimately came to assume a character of intransigence and violence unknown in the rest of Latin America, and to poison the social life of the nation with its uncompromising bitterness. The quarrel first reached serious proportions in the 1850s, when a combination of laws struck at the power and wealth of the Church. The Jesuit order was banned from the country, and by the Lerdo Law the vast ecclesiastical properties were freed from mortmain and declared alienable. The constitution of 1857 enunciated the principle of state supremacy over the Church and of complete religious toleration. The so-called "Laws of the Reform," which followed three years of civil war between Conservatives and Liberals, disestablished the Mexican Church, and ordered the suppression of the monastic orders and the nationalization of all remaining properties of the Church. Under the long rule of Porfirio Díaz, the Church regained much of the ground it had lost under Benito Juárez, but under the Revolution which began in 1911 it was to reap the whirlwind.

Granting the inferior order of Mexican leadership during much of the nineteenth century, the Church had also been deficient in statesmanship. It had been too much concerned with the maintenance of its strong temporal position; its enormous accumulations of property hindered the development of a sound economic life in the nation; it had consistently placed itself on the side of reaction and had neglected its great opportunity to lead in raising the Mexican masses from their condition of peonage and general backwardness; and it had permitted the quality of its ministers to deteriorate. The Mexican Church had much to answer for.

After 1911, it had to face, not the customary anticlerical policies of Liberal governments, but a deliberate and systematic anti-religious movement which was bent on its destruction. As the Revolution progressed and more extremist elements came into power, the lot of the Mexican Church became more difficult. Under a more conciliatory regime in the capital, the Church had an occasional respite, but this might be counterbalanced by unusually severe treatment at the hands of one of the more radical state governments, like that of Vera Cruz. Meanwhile, the dominant Revolutionary party worked to deprive the Mexican people of the ordinary ministrations of the Catholic faith by closing the churches or limiting their services to those performed by lay readers. Persecution of the Church and its priesthood was met by fanaticism and by outbreaks of guerrilla warfare like that waged by the *Cristeros* in the hill country of Jalisco. The opposition of much of the peasantry to the extreme measures of the government threatened the peace of the country and the national unity necessary to carry out the other features of the revolutionary program. Since the Cárdenas administration, Mexico has come a long way toward religious peace. Progress was especially notable during the presidency of Manuel Avila

Camacho (1940–1946) and has been furthered by the general desire
among Mexicans for social harmony within the nation.

The Church has occasionally been concerned that the contagion
of the Mexican example might spread to other countries where there
are strong radical elements. It views with alarm the occasional manifestations of statism in Latin America, as during the Vargas dictatorship in Brazil. The Church is naturally jealous of its spiritual leadership.
Wherever it is permitted to carry on its work under an intelligent and
reasonable political regime, as in Chile, the Church has risen to its opportunity. It has done much to modernize its educational system, taken
the initiative in social work, and otherwise improved the level of its
public services. It has demonstrated that its moral power under free
conditions can be very great. The large Indian population in certain
countries presents a special problem to the Church. While grateful
for the loyalty of the Indians, it has few illusions as to the depth of the
Indian's faith. It is fearful of what the slow pressure of an all-powerful
state might eventually do to its own tenuous moral dominion over
this element in the population. The work of the lay organizations
known as *Acción Católica* is doing much to strengthen the hold of the
Church on the male population of Latin America. For Latin-American
men, while generally recognizing the value of the Church as a bul-
wark of traditional social values, have too often been inclined to leave
actual participation in its observances to their womenfolk. Better preparation of the clergy for their more exacting responsibilities in this age
will do much to heighten the prestige of the Church in Latin-American
society. Improvement in the standards of Roman Catholicism in Latin
America was given recognition in 1946 by the creation of six new
cardinals. There are now eleven cardinals in the Latin-American
Church, including three in Brazil. In Mexico, the Archbishop of
Guadalajara is a cardinal. The Church is greatly concerned, however,
with the severe shortage of priests throughout the continent. An
article in a Rio de Janeiro newspaper in 1959 pointed out that Brazil
had little more than 10,000 priests when it should have at least 60,000.
It noted, moreover, that half were "foreigners without roots in the
country."

In point of numbers, Protestant missionary effort has made relatively little headway in Latin America. Its largest gains have probably
been in Brazil, whose people are unusually receptive to new religious

ideas. In Mexico in 1950, only 1.3 percent of the adult population declared themselves to be of the Protestant faith. In the Brazilian census of the same year, only 34 of every 1,000 citizens registered as Protestants. Much of Protestantism is unsuited to the genius of the Latin-American peoples, and, as aliens, its American and British missionaries labor under a disadvantage in the face of cultural differences and growing nationalism. The Protestants have done much to familiarize the natives of certain countries with the Bible, and their schools have made a highly valuable contribution to both general and specialized education. Especially active in the educational field have been the Presbyterians, Episcopalians, Methodists, and Seventh-Day Adventists.

The Positivist philosophy of Auguste Comte has had an influential following in Brazil. Positivists like Benjamin Constant took a prominent part in the movement which led to the establishment of the republic. The cult's high principles of humanity have affected Brazilian life and official policy in many fields. Among such fields has been the special service for the protection of the Indians in Mato Grosso, headed by the late Marshal Rondon, who was one of the leaders of the Positivist group.

Literature

The literature of colonial Latin America was largely religious or historical in its content and clerical in its execution. The clergy were the only lettered class, the Jesuits controlled virtually all the non-official printing presses in the colonies, until their expulsion in 1767, and the Inquisition censored all writings in the interests of orthodoxy. Later, the literary life of the young republics was as restricted as had been that of the colonial period. A small aristocracy of lay scholars took the place of the priests. As, outside their small and select circles, illiteracy was almost universal, its members literally wrote for the edification of one another. They indulged in political polemics, often on a high plane, and some of them, as the Ecuadorean Olmedo did, composed heroic poems of the wars of independence. In default of a national literary consciousness, their style was largely influenced by the stately classical models of Spain.

As the cultural level of the peoples was slowly raised and the political confusion of the times subsided somewhat, the scope of literary activity widened and became more closely identified with the life of the nations. Leaders like the Argentine presidents, Mitre and Sarmiento, gave encouragement and prestige to the profession by their able historical and political writings. The long career of the cosmopolitan Alberdi, the outstanding political philosopher of the time, reached down into the mid-century years, to influence the form of Argentina's government. Beginnings were made in the writing of fiction.

It was not until the latter part of the century that literature began to reach its full stature. Though French influence on style supplanted the early Spanish in the field of poetry, especially among the poets of the Modernista movement, as a rule the new writers kept close to the Latin-American soil for their inspiration. The heritage of colonialism had largely worked itself out, and in spite of the attraction which Montparnasse still exercised over the new generation of writers, they gradually lost their diffidence as spokesmen of a new culture, and took a defiant pride in their "Americanism."

Poetry has remained the favorite form of literary expression in Latin America, though certain peoples, like the Colombians, are more given to the writing of poetry than are others, like the Mexicans and the Argentines. Probably the greatest of all Latin-American poets is the Nicaraguan, Rubén Darío (1867–1916), who was also a writer of exquisite prose. The leader of the Modernistas, Darío reflected the influence of contemporary French poets like Verlaine and Hugo, and of Poe and Whitman. Among the best known of his lyric poems are *Canción de Otoño en Primavera* and *Letanía de Nuestro Señor Don Quijote*. Other pre-eminent poets of the same school are the violent Peruvian, José Santo Chocano (1875–1934), and the austere Colombian Guillermo Valencia (b. 1874).

Latin Americans have also excelled in the essay, which they have widely used both as a medium of pure letters and criticism, and for conveying political ideas. Most famous of the essayists of this century is José Enrique Rodó (1872–1916). The brilliant Uruguayan formulated the ideals of a whole generation of youth. His best-known work, *Ariel*, is a statement of the racial spirit of Latin America, as contrasted with the "materialism" of the "Caliban" of the north. Among other outstanding essayists have been the Peruvians, Francisco García Calderón and González Prada, and the Argentine, José Ingenieros.

It was only late that fiction became a major phase of Latin-American literature. Most of the classic novels have been written in the past seventy years. To mention only a few, these include *María*, Jorge Isaacs' sentimental story of a Colombian plantation, *Doña Barbara*, Rómulo Gallegos' novel of the Venezuelan plains, and *La Vorágine*, José Eustasio Rivera's grim tale of the Colombian Amazonia. Some of the best Brazilian fiction had been produced before 1890, notably that of Machado de Assis. *Sertão*, Coelho Netto's collection of short stories of the hinterland of the north, appeared in 1896. Six years later Euclydes da Cunha wrote *Os Sertões*, his famous chronicle of the war against the fanatical followers of Antonio Maciel, and Graça Aranha's *Canaan*, a novel of the new Brazilian melting pot, was published.

Many Latin-American novelists have drawn their motifs from the Indian life of their countries. The earliest of these "Indianist" novels, like the Ecuadorean Juan León Mera's *Cumandá* and the Brazilian José de Alencar's *Iracema*, romanticized the aborigine after the style of Cooper. Later novelists of the same genre have gone to the opposite extreme and in a series of morbid and violent novels have treated the Indian as the victim of social oppression. Among the bitterest of such novels is *Huasipongo*, by the Ecuadorean, Jorge Icaza. The Mexicans have developed a cycle of novels about the events of the Revolution, the best known of which is Mariano Azuela's *Los de Abajo*, which has been translated into English as *The Under Dogs*. The realistic school has had a large following among Latin-American writers of fiction, among the best-known examples of which are Aluízio Azevedo of Brazil, author of *O Mulato* and *O Cortiço*, and Eduardo Barrios of Chile, author of *Un Perdido*. Much Latin-American fiction is characterized by a deep sense of catastrophe—of helplessness before the physical and social environment. Its characters are generally defeated by the forces arrayed against them, whether embodied in urban economics or the impersonal ruthlessness of the jungle.

The reading public anywhere in Latin America is still small, in relation to the population, but is growing rapidly. The publishing business is well organized, particularly in Argentina and Mexico. In fact, Buenos Aires has become one of the leading publishing centers of the

Latin world and its books are sold wherever Spanish is read. Large annual book fairs in the principal cities give wide publicity to the literary
output of the year and well-stocked bookstores everywhere cater to
the needs of an ever-growing body of readers. The growth of large
and modern public libraries in cities like Bogotá, Santiago, and São
Paulo has greatly stimulated the sale and use of books.

The economic position of the writing class remains difficult in
most Latin-American countries, and it is only in two or three of the
larger cities that an author, even of fiction, can live by the proceeds
from his books. Most writers depend on another source of income—
teaching, the law, public service, or journalism. Governments have
frequently subsidized their national writers by providing sinecures
for them in the consular or diplomatic service. Rubén Darío roamed
from capital to capital as Nicaraguan consul, and the brilliant poet,
Amado Nervo, died as Mexican Minister in Uruguay. Gabriela Mis-
tral, the famous Chilean poetess and winner of the Nobel Prize, was
appointed as consul of her country in California. Though the material
rewards of literature are generally meager, a successful writer has considerable prestige in his community. Even generals and businessmen
hold the local poets in respect, and the newspapers of their home city
are always generous with space for their melodious and melancholy
verses. When Guillermo Valencia, "The Master" of Colombian letters,
died in 1944, a day of national mourning was declared.

In probably no respect is Latin-American culture so well equipped
as in the matter of newspapers. Even the smaller cities have a surprising number of daily papers and the press of the larger centers com-
pares favorably with that of any country. This development is all the
more remarkable when one considers the difficulties under which
newspapers are published. These include the high illiteracy of the
population, the low buying power of the masses, the general lack of
large advertising revenues, the high cost of newsprint, and often the
censorship of a capricious government. Yet, in spite of all these obstacles, newspapers in small provincial capitals make a brave effort
for survival. Though their physical appearance may leave much to
be desired, they are liable to contain much good writing. Only the
more prosperous papers can afford the regular news services, and
may depend for their news columns on what they pick off the radio
or on tardy digests of the news from the metropolitan press of their

countries. As a result, they give an unusual proportion of their space to local happenings and to literary and editorial comment.

In contrast to these struggling journals are the leading newspapers of a few large cities. In their news coverage, makeup, and quality of their writing, *La Prensa* and *La Nación* of Buenos Aires rank with the world's great newspapers. Backed by wealthy and influential families, with high traditions of journalism and public service, these dailies are national institutions. Moreover, their position is so strong that they can generally defy a hostile administration with impunity, and their independence is a strong force for better government throughout the republic. *La Prensa* even survived its long captivity under the Perón government, when it was published by the printers' union.

The *Estado de São Paulo* is Brazil's first newspaper and one of the four or five best dailies in Latin America. In Rio de Janeiro, the *Correio da Manhã* and *O Jornal*, of the Chateaubriand chain, are papers of superior quality.

Among other outstanding dailies of Latin America are the excellently written *El Tiempo* of Bogotá, the various Chilean editions of *El Mercurio*, the property of the famous Edwards family, and *Excelsior*, *Universal*, and *Novedades*, of Mexico City.

GLOSSARY

READING LIST

INDEX

Glossary

adelantado	administrator of a frontier district in colonial times.
altiplano	Andean plateau.
APRA	*Alianza Popular Revolucionaria Americana*, a socio-political movement in Peru.
Aprismo	body of policies and doctrines of APRA.
Aprista	follower of the APRA movement.
audiencia	high administrative and judicial court in the Spanish colonial system.
ayllu	tribal unit or community of the former Inca dominions.
Banda Oriental	eastern march of the River Plate lands, Uruguay.
Bandeirantes	members of a *bandeira*, or band of early Portuguese gold- or slave-hunters in the interior of Brazil.
bárbaros	uncivilized Indians.
Blancos	members of an Uruguayan political party.
caatinga	semi-arid part of northeastern Brazil; also, the vegetation peculiar to that region.
caboclo	Brazilian countryman.
cachuela	rapids or waterfall.
cachoeira (Port.)	
caciquismo	rule of a *cacique* or Indian chief; rule of local political bosses.

343

campos	open grasslands in the interior of Brazil.
capitania	land grant made to original settlers of Brazil.
carretera	highway, road passable for wheeled vehicles.
caudillismo	rule of *caudillos*, dictatorship.
caudillo	military or political leader, dictator.
chapada, chapadão	bench land or plain of the interior plateau of Brazil.
charqui *xarque* (Port.)	jerked beef.
cholo	mestizo, or mixture of Indian and white, in the central Andean countries.
Colorados	members of an Uruguayan political party.
Conquista	the Spanish Conquest in the New World.
conquistador	one of the early Spanish conquerors.
creole *criollo* (Sp.)	native-born, specifically, white person born in the New World.
donatário	holder of an original land grant in early Brazil.
ejidatario	member of an *ejido*, or Indian commune in Mexico.
encomienda	tract of land granted by the Spanish crown to one of the original conquerors.
engenho	mill for grinding sugar cane in Brazil.
estancia	farm (Argentina).
estanciero	owner of an *estancia*.
fazenda	plantation (Brazil).
fazendeiro	owner of a *fazenda*.
fortín	small military outpost.
frigorífico	meat-packing plant.
gaucho	cowboy of River Plate countries; colloquially, a native of the Brazilian State of Rio Grande do Sul.
golondrina	seasonal immigrants into Argentina from southern Europe.
guajiro	Cuban countryman.
hacendado	large landed proprietor.
hacienda	farm, estate, ranch, landed property.
Independencia	the Spanish-American wars of independence.
indiada	Indians collectively.

Indianismo	policy of stimulating native Indian culture.
interventor	State or provincial governor appointed by the federal government of Argentina or Brazil to supplant the regular local authority.
jefe político	"political chief," local political boss.
ladino	mestizo, or mixture of Indian and white, in Central America.
latifundia	large estate or landed property.
latifundismo	system of large landholdings.
llaneros	natives of the *llanos*.
llanos	tropical grasslands of the Orinoco basin and of El Beni in Bolivia.
mameluco	mixture of Indian and Portuguese in early Brazil.
meseta	tableland.
mestizo	mixture of Indian and white.
Mineiro	native of the Brazilian State of Minas Gerais.
montaña	semi-tropical zone on eastern slope of the Andes.
nevado	snow-capped peak.
nucleo	immigrant colony.
oficina	nitrate plant in northern Chile.
pampa	open plain.
páramo	higher regions of the Colombian Andes.
patrón	employer, master, chief.
patronato	patronage, specifically, right of the lay authority to control high ecclesiastical appointments.
paulista	native of the Brazilian State of São Paulo.
peon	unskilled laborer, commonly bound to his employer by debt.
peonada	peons collectively.
planalto	plateau.
Porteño	citizen of Buenos Aires.
ranchero	small farmer.
rancho	small farm, as opposed to *hacienda* or *estancia*.
residencia	investigation of the official conduct of a colonial administrator.

roto	unskilled, usually mestizo, Chilean laborer.
sabana	open plain.
saladero	plant for the production of jerked beef.
seringueiro	Brazilian rubber-gatherer.
serranía	range of low mountains.
sertão	hinterland of northeastern Brazil.
sierra	mountain range, a mountainous region as dis-
serra (Port.)	tinguished from lowlands.
tierra caliente	hot country (Mexico).
tierra fria	cold country (Mexico).
tierra templada	temperate country (Mexico).
valorization	Brazilian government device for control of the coffee market.
vaquero	cowboy
vaqueiro (Port.)	
várzea	marginal floodlands in the Amazon valley.
vega	cultivated plain.
yungas	temperate zone on eastern side of the Bolivian Andes.
zambo	mixture of Indian and Negro.

Reading List

This bibliography is designed for the use of those who wish to do further reading in the Latin-American field. With one exception, only materials in English are included. The items listed are offered as representative or typical, and many worthwhile works are necessarily omitted. For those interested in a wider or more specialized range of titles, there is recommended R. A. Humphreys' *Latin America: a Selective Guide to Publications in English* (New York: Oxford University Press, 1942). For yearly additions to the writings on Latin America, *The Handbook of Latin American Studies,* published by the University of Florida Press at Gainesville, is the standard source. There are many short reading lists in the books listed below. A particularly extensive and useful list is in Hubert Herring's *A History of Latin America from the Beginnings to the Present* (New York: Alfred A. Knopf, 1961). Unless current statistics are a major factor or radical changes have recently occurred in the area under consideration, the publication date of a work may not be an important determinant in the selection of a book. There are books, like George McCutcheon McBride's *Chile, Land and Society* (New York: American Geographical Society, 1936) and Ernest Gruening's *Mexico and Its Heritage* (New York: Appleton-Century, 1928), that remain indispensable.

GENERAL

This category embraces reading materials of a general or nonspecialized nature. It includes studies of analysis or evaluation, descriptive works, and country or regional books devoted largely or exclusively to Latin-American subjects.

ARCINIEGAS, GERMÁN (ed.). *The Green Continent: a Comprehensive View of Latin America by Its Leading Writers.* New York: Alfred A. Knopf, 1944.

———. *The State of Latin America.* New York: Alfred A. Knopf, 1952.

BRYCE, JAMES. *South America: Observations and Impressions.* New York: The Macmillan Co., 1914.

HANKE, LEWIS. *Modern Latin America: Continent in Ferment.* 2 vols. Princeton, N.J.: Van Nostrand, 1959.

SCHURZ, WILLIAM LYTLE. *This New World: the Civilization of Latin America.* New York: E. P. Dutton, 1954.

COUNTRY AND REGIONAL BOOKS

The offerings in this field are very unequal. There are no first-rate books on Argentina and Peru. On the other hand, Americans have written more books about Mexico than about any other country. Some of them are of excellent quality. These include Charles McComb Flandrau, *Viva Mexico!* (New York: Harper & Bros., 1908); Lesley B. Simpson, *Many Mexicos* (Berkeley, Calif.: University of California Press, 1959); the writings of Frank Tannenbaum, especially *Mexico: the Struggle for Peace and Bread* (New York: Alfred A. Knopf, 1950); and the sociological studies of Oscar Lewis (see p. 355). Among other localized works are:

ARCINIEGAS, GERMÁN. *Caribbean: Sea of the New World.* New York: Alfred A. Knopf, 1946.

BIESANZ, JOHN AND MAVIS. *Costa Rican Life.* New York: Columbia University Press, 1944.

———. *The People of Panama.* New York: Columbia University Press, 1955.

BUTLAND, GILBERT J. *Chile, an Outline of Its Geography, Economics and Politics.* New York: Oxford University Press, 1956.

FERGUSSON, ERNA. *Venezuela.* New York: Alfred A. Knopf, 1939.

FITZGIBBON, RUSSELL H. *Uruguay, Portrait of a Democracy.* New Brunswick, N. J.: Rutgers University Press, 1954.

FRANKLIN, ALBERT. *Ecuador.* New York: Doubleday, 1943.

FREYRE, GILBERTO. *New World in the Tropics*. New York: Alfred A. Knopf, 1959.

GALBRAITH, W. O. *Colombia: a General Survey*. London: Oxford University Press, 1953.

GRUENING, ERNEST. *Mexico and Its Heritage*. New York: Appleton-Century, 1928.

HILL, LAWRENCE F. (ed.). *Brazil*. Berkeley, Calif: University of California Press, 1947.

JONES, CHESTER LLOYD. *The Caribbean since 1900*. New York: Prentice-Hall, 1936.

——. *Guatemala, Past and Present*. Minneapolis: University of Minnesota Press, 1940.

LEYBURN, J. G. *The Haitian People*. New Haven: Yale University Press, 1941.

MARTZ, JOHN D. *Central America, the Crisis and the Challenge*. Chapel Hill, N.C.: University of North Carolina Press, 1959.

OSBORNE, HAROLD. *Bolivia, a Land Divided*. London: Oxford University Press, 1955.

PENDLE, GEORGE. *Argentina*. London: Oxford University Press, 1955.

——. *Paraguay, a Riverside Nation*. London: Oxford University Press, 1956.

——. *Uruguay, South America's First Welfare State*. London: Oxford University Press, 1957.

RAINE, PHILIP. *Paraguay*. New York: Scarecrow Press, 1956.

ROMOLI, KATHLEEN. *Colombia, Gateway to South America*. New York: Doubleday, 1941.

SCHURZ, WILLIAM LYTLE. *Brazil, the Infinite Country*. New York: E. P. Dutton, 1961.

WILGUS, A. CURTIS (ed.). *The Caribbean*. A series of annual symposia. Gainesville, Fla.: University of Florida Press, 1951–.

WILSON, CHARLES M. *Middle America*. New York: W. W. Norton, 1944.

GEOGRAPHY

BOWMAN, ISAIAH. *The Andes of Southern Peru*. New York: American Geographical Society, 1916.

——. *Desert Trails of Atacama*. New York: American Geographical Society, 1924.

BUTLAND, GILBERT J. *Latin America: a Regional Geography*. New York: Longmans, Green, 1960.

CARLSON, FREDERICK A. *Geography of Latin America*. New York: Prentice-Hall, 1951.

JAMES, PRESTON E. *Latin America*. New York: Odyssey Press, 1959.

RICH, J. L. *The Face of South America: an Aerial Traverse*. New York: American Geographical Society, 1942.

WHITBECK, R. H., and others. *The Economic Geography of South America*. New York: McGraw-Hill, 1941.

MAPS AND ATLASES

For the average reader, the most useful maps of Latin America are those of the National Geographic Society, of Washington, D.C. For wall display purposes, the best map is a large three-section map prepared by the American Geographical Society of New York. Some good country maps are distributed by oil companies, particularly for Mexico. All the standard commercial atlases contain satisfactory maps of Latin America. Especially valuable is the *Times Atlas of the World*, vol. V, *The Americas* (Boston: Houghton-Mifflin, 1955). Preston E. James, *Latin America* (New York: Odyssey Press, 1959) contains a fine collection of detail maps. Of official country atlases, particularly noteworthy is the *Atlas do Brasil*, by the cartographical department of the Brazilian Institute of Geography and Statistics.

HISTORY

There is a large number of general histories of Latin America or Spanish America. Most of them are one-volume college texts.

BAILEY, HELEN MILLER, AND ABRAHAM NASATIR. *Latin America: the Development of Its Civilization*. New York: Prentice-Hall, 1960.

BANNON, JOHN FRANCIS. *History of the Americas*. 2 vols. New York: McGraw-Hill, 1952.

———, and P. M. Dunne. *Latin America: an Historical Survey*. Milwaukee: Bruce Publishing Co., 1958.

BERNSTEIN, HARRY. *Modern and Contemporary Latin America*. Philadelphia: J. B. Lippincott, 1952.

CHAPMAN, CHARLES E. *Colonial and Republican: Hispanic America*. New York: The Macmillan Co., 1947.

DAVIS, HAROLD E. *The Americas in History*. New York: Ronald Press, 1953.

HARING, C. H. *The Spanish Empire in America*. New York: Oxford University Press, 1947.

HERRING, HUBERT C. *A History of Latin America from the Beginnings to the Present*. New York: Alfred A. Knopf, 1961.

HUMPHREYS, ROBIN A. *The Evolution of Modern Latin America*. New York: Oxford University Press, 1946.

JONES, TOM B., AND W. DONALD BEATTY. *An Introduction to Hispanic American History*. New York: Harper & Bros., 1950.

KIRKPATRICK, F. A. *Latin America, a Brief History*. New York: The Macmillan Co., 1939.

MADARIAGA, SALVADOR DE. *The Fall of the Spanish-American Empire*. New York: The Macmillan Co., 1948.

————. *The Rise of the Spanish-American Empire*. New York: The Macmillan Co., 1947.

MUNRO, DANA G. *The Latin American Republics: a History*. New York: Appleton-Century, 1950.

PATTEE, RICHARD. *Introducción a la Civilización Hispanoamericana*. Boston: D. C. Heath, 1945.

RIPPY, J. FREDERICK. *Latin America: a Modern History*. Ann Arbor, Mich.: University of Michigan Press, 1958.

ROBERTSON, WILLIAM SPENCE. *History of the Latin American Nations*. New York: Appleton-Century, 1943.

THOMAS, ALFRED BARNABY. *Latin America: a History*. New York: The Macmillan Co., 1956.

WILLIAMS, MARY WILHELMINE. *The People and Politics of Latin America*. Revised by R. J. Bartlett and Russell E. Miller. Boston: Ginn & Co., 1955.

WORCESTER, DONALD E., AND W. G. SCHAEFFER. *The Growth and Culture of Latin America*. New York: Oxford University Press, 1956.

REGIONAL HISTORIES

There are very few first-rate histories of the individual republics. Generally sound, but dull, examples are the works, in translation, published by the University of North Carolina Press. Among these are Calogeras, *Brazil* (1939); Galdames, *Chile* (1941); Hènao and Arrubla, *History of Colombia* (1938); and Levene. *Argentina* (1937).

ANGELL, HILDEGARDE. *Simón Bolívar, South American Liberator.* New York: W. W. Norton, 1930.

ALTAMIRA Y CREVEA, RAFAEL. *A History of Spain.* Translated by Muna Lee. New York: Van Nostrand, 1949.

CASTRO, AMERICO. *The Structure of Spanish History.* Princeton, N.J.: Princeton University Press, 1954.

CHAPMAN, CHARLES EDWARD. *History of the Cuban Republic.* New York: The Macmillan Co., 1927.

DIAZ DEL CASTILLO, BERNAL. *The Discovery and Conquest of Mexico, 1517-1521.* Translated by A. P. Maudslay. New York: Farrar, Straus, 1956. The greatest soldier's story in the history of war.

FREYRE, GILBERTO. *The Masters and the Slaves.* New York: Alfred A. Knopf, 1956. An account of colonial society in northeastern Brazil.

HANKE, LEWIS. *The Spanish Struggle for Justice in the Conquest of America.* Philadelphia: University of Pennsylvania Press, 1959.

HARING, C. H. *Empire in Brazil: a New World Experiment with Monarchy.* Cambridge: Harvard University Press, 1958.

HUMPHREYS, R. A. *Latin American History: a Guide to the Literature in English.* New York: Oxford University Press, 1958.

KEEN, BENJAMIN. *Readings in Latin American Civilization, 1492 to the Present.* Boston: Houghton-Mifflin, 1955.

KIRKPATRICK, F. A. *A History of the Argentine Republic.* Cambridge: Cambridge University Press, 1931.

LIVERMORE, H. V. *Portugal and Brazil, an Introduction.* London: Oxford University Press, 1953.

MERRIMAN, ROGER B. *The Rise of the Spanish Empire in the Old World and the New.* 4 vols. New York: Cooper Square Publishers, 1918–34.

MORISON, SAMUEL ELIOT. *Admiral of the Ocean Sea: a Life of Christopher Columbus.* Boston: Little, Brown, 1942.

NOWELL, CHARLES E. *A History of Portugal.* New York: Van Nostrand, 1952.

PARKES, HENRY B. *A History of Mexico.* Boston: Houghton-Mifflin, 1960.

PRESCOTT, WILLIAM HICKLING. *The Conquest of Mexico* and *The Conquest of Peru.* Written in the 1840s, these classic works have been reprinted in many editions, including Everyman's (nos. 301, 397, 398) and Modern Library (no. G29).

RENNIE, YSABEL FISK. *The Argentine Republic*. New York: The Macmillan Co., 1945.

ROBERTSON, WILLIAM SPENCE. *The Rise of the Spanish American Republics as Told in the Lives of Their Liberators*. New York: Appleton-Century, 1918.

TREND, J. B. *Bolívar and the Independence of South America*. London: The Macmillan Co., 1948.

VAZQUEZ DE ESPINOSA, ANTONIO. *Compendium and Description of the West Indies*. Washington, D.C.: Smithsonian Inst., 1942. An account of much of the Spanish colonial empire in the early 1600s by a wandering and observant Carmelite friar.

WARREN, H. G. *Paraguay, an Informal History*. Norman, Okla.: University of Oklahoma Press, 1949.

GOVERNMENT AND POLITICS

ADAMS, RICHARD N., and others. *Social Change in Latin America Today: Its Implications for United States Policy*. New York: Harper & Bros., 1960.

ALEXANDER, ROBERT J. *Communism in Latin America*. New Brunswick, N.J.: Rutgers University Press, 1957.

BLANKSTEN, G. I. *Ecuador, Constitutions and Caudillos*. Berkeley, Calif.: University of California Press, 1951.

———. *Perón's Argentina*. Chicago: University of Chicago Press, 1953.

CHRISTENSEN, ASHER N. (ed.). *The Evolution of Latin American Government: a Book of Readings*. New York: Henry Holt, 1951.

DAVIS, HAROLD E. (ed.). *Government and Politics in Latin America*. New York: Ronald Press, 1958.

FITZGIBBON, RUSSELL H. "Measurement of Latin American Political Change," in *The American Political Science Review* (June, 1951; September, 1956; September, 1960).

GOMEZ, ROSENDO. *Government and Politics in Latin America*. New York: Random House, 1960.

HIRSCHMAN, A. O. (ed.). *Latin American Issues: Essays and Comments*. New York: Twentieth Century Fund, 1961.

JOHNSON, JOHN J. *Political Change in Latin America: the Emergence of the Middle Sectors.* Stanford, Calif.: Stanford University Press, 1958.

JORRÍN, MIGUEL. *Governments of Latin America.* New York: Van Nostrand, 1953.

LIEUWEN, EDWIN. *Arms and Politics in Latin America.* New York: Frederick Praeger, 1961.

MACDONALD, AUSTIN F. *Latin American Politics and Government.* New York: T. Y. Crowell, 1954.

PIERSON, WILLIAM W. (ed.). "Pathology of Democracy in Latin America: a Symposium," in *The American Political Science Review* (March, 1950).

———, AND FEDERICO G. GIL. *Governments of Latin America.* New York: McGraw-Hill, 1957.

PIKE, FREDERICK B. (ed.). *Freedom and Reform in Latin America.* Notre Dame, Ind.: University of Notre Dame Press, 1959.

PORTER, CHARLES O., AND ROBERT J. ALEXANDER. *The Struggle for Democracy in Latin America.* New York: The Macmillan Co., 1961.

SILVERT, K. H. *A Study in Government: Guatemala.* New Orleans: Tulane University Press, 1954.

STOKES, WILLIAM S. *Honduras: an Area Study in Government.* Madison, Wisc.: University of Wisconsin Press, 1950.

———. *Latin American Politics.* New York: T. Y. Crowell, 1959.

SZULC, TAD. *Twilight of the Tyrants.* New York: Henry Holt, 1959.

———. *The Winds of Revolution: Latin America Today—and Tomorrow.* New York: Frederick Praeger, 1962.

TUCKER, W. P. *Mexican Government Today.* Minneapolis: University of Minnesota Press, 1957.

WHITAKER, ARTHUR P. *Argentine Upheaval.* New York: Frederick Praeger, 1956.

WILGUS, A. CURTIS (ed.). *South American Dictators During the First Century of Independence.* Washington, D.C.: George Washington University Press, 1937.

ECONOMIC AND SOCIAL

GENERAL TREATISES

ADAMS, RICHARD N., and others. *Social Change in Latin America*

Today: Its Implications for United States Policy. New York: Harper & Bros., 1961.

BENHAM, F., AND H. A. HOLLEY. *A Short Introduction to the Economy of Latin America.* London: Oxford University Press, 1960.

GORDON, WENDELL C. *The Economy of Latin America.* New York: Columbia University Press, 1950.

HANSON, SIMON G. *Economic Development in Latin America.* Washington, D.C.: Inter-American Affairs Press, 1951.

STARK, HARRY. *Social and Economic Frontiers in Latin America.* Dubuque, Iowa: William C. Brown, 1961.

COUNTRY STUDIES

ELLSWORTH, P. T. *Chile, an Economy in Transition.* New York: The Macmillan Co., 1945.

HANSON, SIMON G. *Utopia in Uruguay: Chapters in the Economic History of Uruguay.* New York: Oxford University Press, 1938.

MAY, STACY, and others. *Costa Rica, a Study in Economic Development.* New York: Twentieth Century Fund, 1952.

MOSK, SANFORD A. *Industrial Revolution in Mexico.* Berkeley, Calif.: University of California Press, 1950.

SPIEGEL, HENRY W. *The Brazilian Economy.* Philadelphia: Richard D. Irwin, 1949.

WEIL, F. J. *The Argentine Riddle.* New York: John Day, 1944.

WYTHE, GEORGE, and others. *Brazil, an Expanding Economy.* New York: Twentieth Century Fund, 1949.

LAND AND RURAL SOCIETY

FORD, THOMAS R. *Man and Land in Peru.* Gainesville, Fla.: University of Florida Press, 1955.

GILL, TOM. *Land Hunger in Mexico.* Washington, D.C.: C. L. Pack Forestry Foundation, 1951.

HERSKOVITS, M. J. *Life in a Haitian Valley.* New York: Alfred A. Knopf, 1937.

HUTCHINSON, H. W. *Village and Plantation Life in Northeastern Brazil.* Seattle: University of Washington Press, 1957.

LEWIS, OSCAR. *Life in a Mexican Village: Tepoztlán Restudied.* Urbana, Ill.: University of Illinois Press, 1951. The novel, *Children of Sanchez* (New York: Random House, 1961), also by Oscar

Lewis, is a fictional treatment of a related sociological problem.

McBride, George McCutcheon. *Chile, Land and Society*. New York: American Geographical Society, 1936.

Redfield, Robert. *Tepoztlán, a Mexican Village*. Chicago: University of Chicago Press, 1930.

Senior, Clarence. *Land Reform and Democracy*. Gainesville, Fla.: University of Florida Press, 1958.

Simpson, Eyler N. *The Ejido: Mexico's Way Out*. Chapel Hill, N.C.: University of North Carolina Press, 1938.

Simpson, Lesley B. *The Encomienda in New Spain*. Berkeley, Calif.: University of California Press, 1950.

Taylor, Carl C. *Rural Life in Argentina*. Baton Rouge, La.: Louisiana State University Press, 1948.

Wagley, Charles. *Amazon Town: a Study of Man in the Tropics*. New York: The Macmillan Co., 1953.

INTERNATIONAL RELATIONS

Allen, Robert Loring. *Soviet Influence in Latin America: the Role of Economic Relations*. Washington, D.C.: Public Affairs Press, 1959.

American Assembly of Columbia University. *The United States and Latin America*. Edited by Herbert L. Matthews. New York: American Assembly, 1959.

Cline, Howard F. *The United States and Mexico*. Cambridge: Harvard University Press, 1953.

Dozer, Donald Marquand. *Are We Good Neighbors? Three Decades of Inter-American Relations, 1930–1960*. Gainesville, Fla.: University of Florida Press, 1959.

Duggan, Lawrence. *The Americas: the Search for Hemispheric Security*. New York: Henry Holt, 1949.

Gantenbein, James W. (ed.). *The Evolution of Our Latin American Policy: a Documentary Record*. New York: Columbia University Press, 1950.

Guerrant, Edward O. *Roosevelt's Good Neighbor Policy*. Albuquerque, N.M.: University of New Mexico Press, 1950.

Haring, C. H. *Argentina and the United States*. Boston: World Peace Foundation, 1941.

HOUSTON, JOHN A. *Latin America in the UN.* New York: Carnegie Endowment, 1956.

IRELAND, G. *Boundaries, Possessions, and Conflicts in Central and North America.* Cambridge: Harvard University Press, 1941.

——. *Boundaries, Possessions, and Conflicts in South America.* Cambridge: Harvard University Press, 1938.

MARTZ, JOHN D. *Central America: the Crisis and the Challenge.* Chapel Hill, N.C.: University of North Carolina Press, 1959.

McGANN, THOMAS F. *Argentina, the United States, and the Inter-American System, 1880–1914.* Cambridge: Harvard University Press, 1958.

MECHAM, J. LLOYD. *The United States and Inter-American Security, 1889–1960.* Austin, Tex.: University of Texas Press, 1961.

PALMER, THOMAS W., JR.: *Search for a Latin American Policy.* Gainesville, Fla.: University of Florida Press, 1957.

PERKINS, DEXTER. *Hands Off: a History of the Monroe Doctrine.* Boston: Little, Brown, 1941.

——. *The United States and Latin America.* Baton Rouge, La.: Louisiana State University Press, 1961.

——. *The United States and the Caribbean.* Cambridge: Harvard University Press, 1947.

RIPPY, J. FREDERICK. *Globe and Hemisphere: Latin America's Place in the Post-War Foreign Relations of the United States.* Chicago: Henry Regnery, 1958.

STUART, GRAHAM H. *Latin America and the United States.* New York: Appleton-Century, 1955.

UNITED STATES SENATE. *United States–Latin American Relations: Studies for Committee on Foreign Relations.* 7 vols. Washington, D.C., 1959–60.

WHITAKER, ARTHUR P. *The United States and Argentina.* Cambridge: Harvard University Press, 1954.

——. *The United States and South America: the Northern Republics.* Cambridge: Harvard University Press, 1948.

——. *The Western Hemisphere Idea: Its Rise and Decline.* Ithaca, N.Y.: Cornell University Press, 1954.

WOOD, BRYCE. *The Making of the Good Neighbor Policy.* New York: Columbia University Press, 1961.

CULTURE

(INTELLECTUAL, SPIRITUAL, AND ARTISTIC LIFE)

AZEVEDO, FERNANDO. *Brazilian Culture*. New York: The Macmillan Co., 1950.

CONSIDINE, JOHN T. *New Horizons in Latin America*. New York: Dodd, Mead, 1958.

COVARRUBIAS, MIGUEL. *Indian Art of Mexico and Central America*. New York: Alfred A. Knopf, 1957.

———. *Mexico South*. New York: Alfred A. Knopf, 1946.

CRAWFORD, W. REX. *A Century of Latin American Thought*. Cambridge: Harvard University Press, 1944.

FEUCHTWANGER, FRANZ (ed.). *The Art of Ancient Mexico*. New York: Thames Publishing Co., 1954.

FITTS, DUDLEY. *An Anthology of Contemporary Latin American Poetry*. Norfolk, Conn.: New Directions, 1942.

FLORES, ANGEL, AND DUDLEY POORE (eds.). *Fiesta in November: Stories from Latin America*. Boston: Houghton-Mifflin, 1942.

GRIFFIN, CHARLES C. (ed.). *Concerning Latin American Culture*. New York: Columbia University Press, 1940.

HELM, MACKINLEY. *Modern Mexican Painters*. New York: Harper & Bros., 1941.

HENRIQUEZ UREÑA, PEDRO. *Literary Currents in Hispanic America*. Cambridge: Harvard University Press, 1946.

HESPELT, E. HERMAN (ed.). *An Outline History of Spanish American Literature*. New York: Appleton-Century, 1941.

KNELLER, G. F. *The Education of the Mexican Nation*. New York: Columbia University Press, 1951.

LANNING, JOHN TATE. *Academic Culture in the Spanish Colonies*. New York: Oxford University Press, 1940.

LEONARD, IRVING. *Books of the Brave*. Cambridge: Harvard University Press, 1949.

MECHAM, J. LLOYD. *Church and State in Latin America*. Chapel Hill, N.C.: University of North Carolina Press, 1934.

NORTHROP, F. S. C. *The Meeting of East and West*. New York: The Macmillan Co., 1946.

ONÍS, HARRIET DE (ed.). *Golden Land: an Anthology of Latin American Folklore in Literature*. New York: Alfred A. Knopf, 1948.

PUTNAM, SAMUEL. *Marvelous Journey: a Survey of Four Centuries of Brazilian Writing.* New York: Alfred A. Knopf, 1948.

ROMANELL, PATRICK. *Making of the Mexican Mind.* Lincoln, Nebr.: University of Nebraska Press, 1952.

SPELL, J. R. *Contemporary Spanish American Fiction.* Chapel Hill, N.C.: University of North Carolina Press, 1944.

TAVARES DE SÁ, HERNANE. *The Brazilians, People of Tomorrow:* New York: John Day, 1947.

TOOR, FRANCES. *A Treasury of Mexican Folkways.* New York: Crown Publishers, 1947.

TORRES-RÍOSECO, ARTURO. *The Epic of Latin American Literature.* Berkeley, Calif.: University of California Press, 1959.

VERISSIMO, ERICO. *Brazilian Literature: an Outline.* New York: The Macmillan Co., 1945.

WILGUS, A. CURTIS (ed.). *Readings in Latin American Civilization.* New York: Barnes & Noble, 1946.

WOLFE, BERTRAM. *Diego Rivera: His Life and Times.* New York: Alfred A. Knopf, 1939.

ANTHROPOLOGY

CASO, ALFONSO. *The Aztecs, People of the Sun.* Norman, Okla.: University of Oklahoma Press, 1958.

COLLIER, JOHN, JR., AND ANIBAL BUITRÓN. *The Awakening Valley.* Chicago: University of Chicago Press, 1949.

LINTON, RALPH (ed.). *Most of the World.* New York: Columbia University Press, 1949.

MACGOWAN, KENNETH. *Early Man in the New World.* New York: The Macmillan Co., 1950.

MEANS, PHILIP AINSWORTH. *Ancient Civilizations of the Andes.* New York: Charles Scribner's Sons, 1931.

MORLEY, SYLVANUS G. *The Ancient Maya.* Stanford, Calif.: Stanford University Press, 1956.

PIERSON, DONALD. *Negroes in Brazil.* Chicago: University of Chicago Press, 1942.

RAMOS, ARTHUR. *The Negro in Brazil.* Washington, D.C.: Associated Publishers, 1939.

RYCROFT, W. STANLEY (ed.). *Indians of the High Andes.* New York: Committee on Cooperation in Latin America, 1946.

SPINDEN, HERBERT J. *Ancient Civilizations of Mexico and Central America*. New York: American Museum of Natural History, 1928.

TANNENBAUM, FRANK. *Slave and Citizen: the Negro in the Americas*. New York: Alfred A. Knopf, 1947.

THOMPSON, J. ERIC. *The Rise and Fall of the Maya Civilization*. Norman, Okla.: University of Oklahoma Press, 1954.

VAILLANT, GEORGE. *Aztecs of Mexico*. New York: Penguin Books, 1950.

Index